LATIN AMERICAN LIBERATION THEOLOGY

RELIGION IN THE AMERICAS SERIES

General Editor
HECTOR AVALOS

VOLUME I

LATIN AMERICAN LIBERATION THEOLOGY

BY

DAVID TOMBS

BRILL ACADEMIC PUBLISHERS, INC.
BOSTON • LEIDEN
2002

Library of Congress Cataloging-in-Publication Data

Tombs, David, 1965–
    Latin American liberation theology / by David Tombs.
        p. cm. — (Religion in the Americas; v. 1)
    Includes bibliographical references and index.
    ISBN 0–391–04148–7
        1. Liberation theology. 2. Theology, Doctrinal—Latin America—History.
    I. Title. II. Series

BT83.57.T65 2002
230'.0464'098—dc21

                                                    2002011568

ISSN 1542–1279
ISBN 0–391–04148–7
Paperback 0–391–04181–9

PRINTED IN THE UNITED STATES OF AMERICA

Contents

Acknowledgments

I wish to thank the many people who have contributed in different ways to this book and especially to my students at the University of Surrey Roehampton, who shared my enthusiasm for the subject during the years that I taught there. My own teachers of theology have influenced the book in different ways, and I am grateful to Ian Walker, Trevor Williams, James Cone, Joseph Laishley SJ, and James Hanvey SJ for the ways that they have challenged my thinking over the years. Each of them has been vital to the process, although no doubt they would all make different criticisms of the final product! The Society of the Sacred Heart supported my research on liberation theology, and I am grateful to the Arts and Humanities Research Board for funding a semester's sabbatical in 1999. Many colleagues gave valued encouragement along the way, and I am particularly grateful to Andrew Bradstock, Danny Caroll, and the Hector Avalos for their support in bringing my work through to publication. The biggest personal influence on my thinking from outside academia has been my partner, Rebecca Dudley of Christian Aid. She has consistently pushed me to engage with the challenges that liberation theology poses for Christian faith and communicate their importance as best I can.

I am very grateful to Patrick Alexander at Brill for his interest in this field, and his help in bringing this work to fruition. Meg Davies of the Society of Indexers provided the Index with speed and care. Special thanks also to Sheffield Academic Press for permission to rework some of the material in Chapter 12 that I initially published with them as "Machismo and Marianismo: Sexuality and Liberation Theology," in M. A. Hayes, W. Porter, and D. Tombs (eds.), *Religion and Sexuality* (RILP 4; STS 2; Sheffield: Sheffield Academic Press, 1998), pp. 248–271. Thanks also to SCM Press and Orbis Books for permission to use the extracts from Gustavo Gutiérrez, *A Theology of Liberation*, Orbis Books and SCM Press, 2nd edition, 1988 (original ET 1973).

Abbreviations

AAA	Argentinean Anti-Communist Alliance
AACC	All Africa Conference of Churches
AP	Popular Action, *Ação Popular*
CCA	Christian Conference of Asia
CDF	Congregation for the Doctrine of the Faith
CELAM	Latin American Bishops Conference, *Consejo Episcopal Latino-americano*
CEPAL	Economic Commission for Latin America, *Comisión Económico para América Latina*
CLAR	Conference of Latin American Religious
CNBB	Brazilian Bishops National Conference, *Conferência Nacional dos Bispos do Brasil*
CPT	Pastoral Land Commission, *Comissão Pastoral da Terra* or
CTC	Commission on Theological Concerns
EAAT	Ecumenical Association of African Theologians
IDOC	International Documentation Service
ISAL	Church and Society in Latin America, *Iglesia y Sociedad en América Latina*
JEC	Young Catholic School Students, *Juventude Estudantil Católica*
JUC	Young Catholic Students, *Juventude Universitária Católica*
JOC	Young Catholic Workers, *Juventude Operária Católica*
LADOC	Latin America Documentation Service
LARR	*Latin American Research Review*
MEB	Base Education Movement, *Movimento de Educaçao de Base*
NAFTA	North American Free Trade Association
OAS	Organisation of American States
ONIS	National Office of Social Information, *Oficina Nacional de Información Social*
SODEPAX	Committee on Society, Development, and Peace
UNCTAD	United Nations Congress on Trade and Development
WCC	World Council of Churches

Introduction

The figure of Christ the Redeemer on top of the Corcovado mountain over-looking Rio de Janeiro is one of the most well-known images in the world. The outstretched arms of the statue offer a welcome to all and seem to promise safe protection against any threat. The scene represents how the Catholic church in Brazil and throughout Latin America has understood its mission. However, it is easy to get only a partial impression of the scene. The statue looks down over the affluent areas of the city, the famous beachfronts of Copacabana and Ipanema, and out to the sea. It has traditionally welcomed trade and passenger ships from Europe and watched over the rich. Behind the statue, on the other side of the mountain, the fragile houses and shacks of the poor stretch into the distance seemingly ignored. This scene portrays another history of the church's presence in Latin America.

Since its arrival in the early sixteenth century, the institutional church has been marked by its wealth, power, and privilege. As centuries passed, the church did little to change the daily hardships faced by the poor and powerless. During the conquest, millions of indigenous inhabitants suffered untold misery from war, disease, and slave-like conditions under Spanish conquistadors who claimed the name of Christ. In the colonial period, the church supported the crown and the landowners as a bulwark of the traditional *status quo*. Independence in the nineteenth century brought political and commercial gain to Latin America's local elites but did little for the poor and oppressed. Likewise, the grand hopes for economic development in the twentieth century have failed to close the enormous social divide between the rich and poor. Five hundred years after the church's arrival in Latin America, poverty and social injustice are as much a part of Latin American reality as they have ever been.

It is against this backdrop that the changes associated with Latin American liberation theology need to be understood.[1] The dramatic rise of liberation theology, and the commitment of many in the church to make an option for the poor, might best be symbolised as the Christ on Corcovado metaphorically turning around 180 degrees. In the late 1960s, prophetic figures within the Latin American church tried to shift their focus away from the middle and upper class environment in which they felt most comfortable to stand in solidarity with the poor clinging to life on the slippery slopes of Latin American society.

---

[1] Contextual theologies that address liberation include Latin American, Black, Feminist, Asian, and African theologies. However, since the focus of this book is on Latin American liberation theology, it will only address other liberation theologies in relation to Latin America.

Not surprisingly, this movement has been the subject of heated controversies. Opinions about the value and permanence of its contribution are often sharply divided. Some argued that liberation theology incarnated the gospel in modern society and revitalized the life of the church. Others attacked it for confusing faith with politics and reducing Christian theology to determinist Marxism. However, many observers—both critics and advocates—saw the 1990s as marking an end of an era for liberation theology. Reports of liberation theology's death were premature and ignored its continuing influence. However, by the 1990s liberation theology was a much different movement than it was in previous decades.

Daniel Levine, a long-term observer of the church in Latin America, identified a common problem with many of the obituaries of liberation theology. They ignored the very significant internal developments in the movement during the 1970s and 1980s. Levine argued:

> Such obituaries are premature. They misread the current situation, and reflect a basic misunderstanding of what liberation theology was and is all about. Liberation theology is pictured in static terms. . . . But liberation theology is anything but static: both the ideas and their expression in groups and movements have evolved substantially over the years.[2]

This book examines how liberation theology developed from its earliest formulations in the late 1960s to its decade of crisis in the 1990s. It is an analytic history of liberation theology as a theological movement and an assessment of its contribution to theology in each decade of its existence. As a contextual theology, liberation theology in Latin America must be contextualised in time as well as place. The broadly chronological structure of the book is intended to show how and why these contextual transformations took place. The central thesis in the book is that Latin American liberation theology is best understood in terms of an initial political option for the poor that was followed by a subsequent epistemological option for the poor, which was added after the mid-1970s. During the 1980s, it deepened and broadened its understanding of oppression and refined its methodology further. Many of the best publications belong to this period, but in retrospect, many of the issues that would provoke the crisis in the 1990s first arose in the 1980s. Primary among these were the rapidly changing economic situation and the hostile reaction of conservative church authorities. As a result, liberation theology as a movement started to lose momentum after the 1980s. The language of liberation became problematic in the new economic order and did not sit well with postmodern concerns. However, although it is quite reasonable to see the 1990s as an end of an era in terms of a cohesive theological movement at the cutting edge of political theology, it would be quite wrong to think that many of its ideas and method-

---

[2] See D. Levine, "On the Premature Reports of the Death of Liberation Theology," *The Review of Politics* 57.1 (Winter 1995), p. 105.

ological innovations will not remain highly relevant to new challenges in the future. To appreciate how the movement's theological legacy might long out-last the movement itself, it is necessary to separate out the different strands of emphasis and methodology that were once part of the movement, and see how these are related to each other.[3]

In writing this book, two particular concerns have influenced both the structure and style. First, it is meant to be an accessible introduction to the theological challenges raised by Latin American liberation. It is intended to let readers explore the literature of liberation theology in a more informed way. It is not offered as an alternative to the primary works that are cited here, but simply as a gateway to what they offer.

This first purpose arises out of my experiences as a lecturer in theology, first inspired by liberation theology while a student of theology. Despite the inevitable limits of my vantage point as a Protestant First-World observer of a primarily Catholic and Third-World phenomena, I have tried to communicate the challenges of Latin American liberation theology for a number of years to my students. I have wanted to write the sort of book that my students—and hopefully others as well—will find useful to engage the extensive literature, which is now available in English, and indicate the challenges that they raise. For this reason, I have tried to summarise—perhaps at times over-summarise—substantial debates and critical discussions. I hope, however, that the bibliography and appropriate notes will encourage the reader's own further investigations and reflections.

My second purpose is to make a modest, but I hope, helpful analytic contribution to studies of theology by organising material from the four decades when liberation theology was active as a movement in a broadly chronological way. In doing so, I hope that it will not only facilitate my first purpose—of providing an accessible gateway to the literature—but also provide a useful guide for the journey of exploration itself. By surveying the changes in liberation theology from the late 1960s to the 1990s, it is possible to trace the central unity and the evolving emphases that the movement has shown and to assess the long-term legacies of the movement in a more informed way. Gustavo Gutiérrez once observed

> From the beginning, the theology of liberation had two fundamental insights. Not only did they come first chronologically, but they have continued to form the very backbone of this theology. I am referring to its theological method and its perspective of the poor.[4]

---

[3] A summary of these strands linked to the decade in which they became prominent is offered in Appendix 1.

[4] Gutiérrez, *The Power of the Poor in History* (trans. R. R. Barr; Maryknoll, N.Y.: Orbis Books; London: SCM Press, 1983 [Spanish orig. 1979]), p. 200.

The purpose of this book is to elaborate how these these two fundamental insights were understood and what they entailed at different stages. To achieve this aim, and to make the vast literature manageable, I have given relatively less attention to the geographical contextuality of liberation theology between different countries. I have also had to be selective in choosing to focus on representative figures in the movement, especially Gustavo Gutiérrez, Leonardo Boff, and Jon Sobrino. The book is meant to give an understanding of Latin American liberation theology movement as a whole, but many of the illustrations are drawn from their work. Each, in his own way, is associated with crucial developments in the movement and/or contributed seminal literature to it. Furthermore, in their countries of writing (Peru, Brazil, and El Salvador respectively) they are immersed in national contexts that have been of particular importance for the development of liberation theology.

Part 1 explores the role of the church on the side of the privileged between the arrival of Columbus in 1492 to the Cuban revolution of 1959. Within this, Chapter 1 describes the period of conquest and colonial era up to the early nineteenth century. Chapter 2 looks at the Independence movement of 1808–1825 and the post-Independence century to 1929. Chapter 3 examines the slow move from economic depression to development in the decades from 1930 to 1959.

Part 2 presents the 1960s as a decade of reform and renewal during which the church began to engage with wider society in a new way. Chapter 4 (1960–1965) assesses the spirit of renewal in the Catholic church (especially the Second Vatican Council, 1962–1965) and reforms in Latin American economies (such as the Alliance for Progress). Chapter 5 examines the disillusion with development theories and the emergence of the earliest liberation writings in solidarity with the poor between 1965 and 1969.

Part 3 traces the development of liberation theology in the 1970s as it lived out its political option for the poor and added a further epistemological option as the decade progressed. Chapter 6 on the early works of the decade identifies the key principles behind the new theological movement and its political option for the poor. Chapter 7 explores liberation theology's understanding of revolution and its early relationship to Marxist analysis and socialist movements. Chapter 8 turns to the development of base communities as a popular church that expressed the ecclesial vision of liberation theology. It shows how the everyday experiences of the poor and the political repression that the church suffered, challenged liberation theologians to deepen their methodology and their understanding of the political option for the poor with a new epistemological option for the poor. Chapter 9 focuses on the bible in liberation theology and shows how by the second half of the 1970s, the work of leading theologians started to develop a new tone and style to the their work as they began to work the political and epistemological options in their reading of the bible.

Part 4 explores the revision and redirection of liberation theology in the 1980s as liberation theologians continued their reflection on the God of Life in societies that were characterised by early and unjust death. In retrospect, this was the decade in which many of the most profound works of liberation theology were written; yet it was also the decade that laid the foundation for the crisis that was to come in the 1990s. During these years, liberation theology developed new areas of focus beyond its original political-economic concern for the poor. This was a necessary development if liberation theology was to address oppression in a more integral way. However, for a variety of reasons liberation theologians found it hard to maintain the power of their work in these new areas or to preserve their cohesion as an organised theological movement. Chapter 10 looks at the deepening understanding of oppression generated within the movement, and the attempts by theologians to do greater justice to issues of culture, race, and ethnicity. It also notes the new aspects of liberation theology's methodology in terms of spirituality, contemplation, and silence. Chapter 11 reviews the history of conflict with the Vatican, including the tension with the radical church in Nicaragua, the Vatican's two *Instructions* on liberation theology, and the high profile conflicts with Leonardo Boff and Gustavo Gutiérrez. Chapter 12, turns to what may be the greatest failure of many male liberation theologians on issues of gender. Despite imaginative and insightful work by women liberation theologians during these years, most male theologians failed to engage issues of gender and patriarchy beyond superficial lip service.

Against these different strands in the development of liberation theology, Part 5 explores the 1990s as a time of crisis. The 1990s marked an end of an era in at least two important ways. First, it was an end to liberation theology as a cohesive group that met and worked closely together. Although individual liberation theologians continued to offer insightful new ideas, they were no longer operating as an organised movement or likely to reconstitute themselves as such. Second, changes in the global order meant the language and terminology of liberation faced a new crisis of relevance. Many of the problems for liberation theology that began in the 1980s became critical and unavoidable after 1990. On top of this, the appointment of conservative bishops to key posts in Latin America had steadily weakened liberation theology's advocates within the progressive church and the base communities were in decline and facing strong completion from Pentecostal churches.

The final chapter, Chapter 14, is devoted to an assessment of liberation theology in terms of its historical and theological importance especially for Christians in the First World. Although the language of liberation may no longer be useful, liberation theology's commitments to the poor and its pioneering methodology have made a profound contribution to church and academia in the past thirty years and offer a way forward for any socially engaged theology of the future.

In situating this basic argument in the field of other literature, it is useful to briefly compare it with various other influential works on the subject that have been written in English or are available in translation. Over the years a number of overviews of liberation theology have emerged. Some, such as Philip

Berryman's *Liberation Theology* (1987), have examined it primarily in terms of a religious movement.[5] Others, such as Leonardo and Clodovis Boff's work *An Introduction to Liberation Theology* (1987), have focussed on its key ideas and distinctive methodology.[6] Both books discuss liberation theology in the 1970s and early 1980s but have less to say on shifts that took place during the 1980s and offer little glimpse of what was to come in the 1990s.

Christian Smith's excellent work on *The Emergence of Liberation Theology* (1991) provides a sophisticated and detailed study of liberation theology's development as a social movement.[7] More than any other work, Smith's book shows that liberation theology was a movement in at least three senses. First, the pioneering figures shared a basically common agenda and were in close touch with each other. Second, liberation theology was not just an academic matter, but also a social movement that found expression within the progressive church. Third, there was movement within liberation theology. This is to say that it changed and evolved in a number of distinct ways. Smith therefore, distinguishes between the period from Vatican II to Medellin (1965–1968), the groundbreaking work at Medellin (1968), the developments from Medellin to Sucre (1968–1972) and then from Sucre to Puebla (1972–1979), and then finally Puebla itself (1979). Although he has a chapter on theology after Puebla, it is not treated with the detail of the earlier periods, and his work is basically a treatment of liberation theology in the 1960s and 1970s. Furthermore, Smith's work is an exercise in sociology informed by political science and especially models of political process. While he has a great deal of illuminating commentary on the theological writings of leading figures in liberation theology, he is understandably more concerned with the social processes involved and less with the theological ideas as such.

Alongside Smith's work, other helpful works on the Latin American church during this period include Penny Lernoux's *Cry of the Poor* and *People of God*. Both books provide a wealth of detail on the struggles of the progressive church (focussing on the 1960s–1970s and the 1980s respectively). Jeffrey Klaiber's invaluable recent work *The Church, Dictatorships, and Democracy in Latin America* covers the 1960s to the 1990s in a single work with chapters devoted to twelve different countries during this period.

Alfred Hennely's *Liberation Theology: A Documentary History* is an invaluable collection of primary documents relevant to liberation theology, which I refer to extensively in what follows. *The Church in Latin America: 1492–1992* (edited

---

[5] Philip Berryman, *Liberation Theology: The Essential Facts about Revolutionary Movements in Latin America and Beyond* (New York: Pantheon; London: Taurus; 1987).

[6] Leonardo Boff and Clodovis Boff, *Introducing Liberation Theology* (trans. P. Burns; Maryknoll, N.Y.: Orbis Books; Tunbridge Wells, Kent: Burns and Oates; 1987 [Portuguese orig. 1986]).

[7] Christian Smith, *The Emergence of Liberation Theology: Radical Religion and Social Movement Theory* (Chicago and London: University of Chicago Press, 1991).

by Enrique Dussel) provides a fascinating collection of scholarly perspectives on the wider history of the church in Latin America and includes particularly interesting chapters on the era of liberation theology.

In terms of the development of liberation theology during the 1970s and the 1980s, Paul Sigmund's work *Liberation Theology at the Crossroads: Democracy or Revolution?* (1990) is a useful starting point.[8] Sigmund is especially helpful in stressing that the liberation theology developed a significantly different emphasis as time passed. In particular, he points to the move away from its early Marxist phase and toward democratic grass roots participation as a basic shift in axis. In his final assessment he concluded:

> Liberation theology does seem to have reached a new stage. It has abandoned most of the revolutionary rhetoric of the earlier period, concentrating on biblical and participatory themes, and appealing to what is now a mainstream element in official social teaching of the church—the preferential love for the poor. Even in the area of ecclesiology, the liberation theologians continue to insist on the importance of remaining in communion with the church hierarchy, although they criticize its pretensions to total control.[9]

However, as a political scientist, Sigmund orientated his work toward political issues rather than the theological. He highlighted the central issue but left much work to be done on how much liberation theology had shifted from its emergence in the late 1960s, through its development in the 1970s, and its period of maturity in the 1980s. Nor was he able to anticipate how dramatically things would change with the 1990s.

A recent collection that goes some way to correcting these weaknesses is *Liberation Theologies on Shifting Grounds* (1998)[10] by Georges De Schrijver based on a conference at Louvain in 1996. De Schrijver's own extended introductory essay discusses what he calls "the paradigm shift" in liberation theologies in the 1980s and 1990s. According to Schrijver:

> The fact of a paradigm shift in Third-World theologies of liberation from socio-economic analysis to cultural analysis can be gleaned from their different publications where socio-economic and cultural analyses stand in tension with one another.[11]

However, it is important to recognise that this shift has been in two stages that De Schrijver does not clearly distinguish. First, there was dialogue with other Third World theologies in the 1980s, which encouraged the Latin Americans

---

[8] Paul Sigmund, *Liberation Theology at the Crossroads: Democracy or Revolution?* (Oxford: Oxford University Press, 1990).

[9] Sigmund, *Liberation Theology at the Crossroads*, p. 175.

[10] Georges De Schrijver, "Paradigm Shift in Third World Theologies of Liberation: From Socio-Economic Analysis to Cultural Analysis" in idem (ed.), *Liberation Theologies on Shifting Grounds: A Clash of Socio-Economic and Cultural Paradigms* (Leuven: Leuven University Press, 1998), pp. 3–83.

[11] De Schrijver, "Paradigm Shift in Third World Theologies of Liberation," p. 3.

to add more analysis of ethnicity and culture to their economic analysis but did not in any way replace economics with culture. Second, there were the difficulties for any programme of economic analysis created by globalisation and the free market international economy in the 1990s. Thus, while De Schrijver's work addresses the theological shift in liberation theology it does not go on to separate out the different strands of the theological shifts. In what follows, I suggest that this separation is crucial to an understanding of liberation theology and assessment of its legacies.

Beyond these works the wider range of work available in English on Latin American liberation theology and the recent history of the church in Latin America is far too long to list. However, as will be clear in the footnotes and bibliography, the work of knowledgeable commentators such as Edward Cleary, Daniel Levine, Scott Mainwaring, Arthur McGovern, Harvey Cox, Robert McAfee Brown and many others has been invaluable at different points in attempting my task.

Part I

Power and Privilege
1492–1959

CHAPTER ONE

Conquest and Colonialism, 1492–1808

> Your Highnesses, as good Christian and Catholic princes, devout and propagators of the Christian faith, as well as enemies of the sect of Mahomet and of all idolatries and heresies, conceived the plan of sending me, Christopher Columbus, to this country of the Indies . . . to convert these regions to our holy faith.
>
> Christopher Columbus, *Diary*[1]

INTRODUCTION

Latin American liberation theology must be understood against the history of greed and violence, suffering and oppression, and death and destruction that have characterised Latin America for five centuries since the arrival of Christianity.[2] The so-called discovery of the Indies by Christopher Columbus was to have a cataclysmic effect on a vast continent, and its historical consequences have been etched deeply into today's societies.

The driving force behind Columbus's voyage was the quest for fame and financial profit. The fall of Constantinople in 1453 and the dominance of the Moors

---

[1] "The Diary of Columbus" cited in M. H. Goodpasture (ed.), *Cross and Sword: An Eyewitness History of Christianity in Latin America* (Maryknoll, N.Y.: Orbis Books, 1989), p. 7.

[2] This is not to ignore the violence that existed before the Spanish and Portuguese arrived in 1492. The Aztec and Inca empires were as bloodthirsty as any other imperial system. On the major pre-Columban civilisations, see I. Clendinnen, *Aztecs: An Interpretation* (Cambridge: Cambridge University Press, 1991); N. Davies, *The Ancient Kingdoms of Mexico* (London: Allen Lane, 1982); N. Hammond, *Ancient Maya Civilization* (Cambridge: Cambridge University Press, 1982); A. Métraux, *The History of the Incas* (New York: Pantheon Books, 1969). On the role of violence in pre-Columban societies, see especially: D. Carrasco, *City of Sacrifice: The Aztec Empire and the Role of Violence in Civilization* (Boston: Beacon Press, 1999); R. C. Trexler, *Sex and Conquest: Gendered Violence, Political Order, and the European Conquest of the Americas* (Cambridge: Polity Press, 1995).

in the eastern Mediterranean made the spice and silk trade with the East much more expensive and hazardous. Most of the traders in the great Italian trading cities had no alternative but to continue to trade with the Moors and pay the increased prices. However, the Portuguese were more adventurous and led the search for an alternative sea route to Asia by going south and trying to sail around Africa. In 1434, Portuguese ships had rounded Cape Bojador which allowed them to trade directly for gold and slaves with what was then known as the kingdom of Sudan in the western and central regions of sub-Saharan Africa. When the need for a new route to India became pressing the Portuguese were already well situated to press south.

In 1480, the Genoese sailor Columbus was living in the Portuguese colony of Madeira—far out from the mainland into the Atlantic—and he was convinced that he could find a lucrative new trade route to Asia by sailing due west across the Atlantic.[3] Columbus approached the Portuguese monarch John II to ask support for his bold enterprise, but the commission that studied Columbus's plan rejected it. Educated people knew that the world was round, not flat. A western route was therefore recognised as possible in principle, but it was thought to be impossible in practice. Ships were limited in the journeys they could undertake without fresh supplies. Columbus mistakenly believed his route to Asia was possible, because he dramatically underestimated the distance to Cipango (Japan). The Portuguese pointed this out, and because nobody—especially not Columbus—was expecting a whole new continent to lie between the Canary Islands and Asia, they rejected his proposal. Columbus, however, was not to be deterred and turned instead to Spain. He spent six years persuading the monarchs Ferdinand and Isabella to support him and promising plentiful gold waiting to be discovered in Asia. During this time, he was given a modest stipend by the Spanish crown, but this did not stop him from trying again to interest the Portuguese in his plan. His second attempt with the Portuguese was more successful at first but ended when Bartholomew Diaz rounded the Cape of Storms (promptly renamed the Cape of Good Hope) in 1488.[4] This forced Columbus to return to the Spanish court while his brother Bartolomé attempted to interest the French and English monarchs in the enterprise.

Eventually, with the help of Genoese bankers, he signed an agreement with Ferdinand and Isabella at Santa Fe in April 1492. The plan still seemed to be based on miscalculation, but the Spanish monarchs had now completed the

---

[3] A long-standing classic on Columbus and his voyages is S. E. Morison, *Admiral of the Ocean Sea: A Life of the Admiral Christopher Columbus* (2 vols; Boston: Little Brown, 1942). Regrettably Morison's work is largely uncritical of the European imperialism that Columbus served. A much briefer (and less flattering) interpretation is offered in H. Koning, *Columbus: His Enterprise* (London: Latin America Bureau, 2nd ed., 1991 [1976]).

[4] Ten years later Portuguese explorations to the south finally yielded the prize they sought when Vasco de Gama reached India (1497–1498). In the sixteenth century the Portuguese developed a highly lucrative trade with the Far East via bases at Colombo (on the coast of modern day Sri Lanka, founded 1517) and Macao (on the coast of China, founded 1557). They enjoyed a European monopoly on this route until the seventeenth century when the Dutch (who rounded the Cape in 1590) started to displace them.

reconquest of Spain and were eager to compete with Portugal in the quest for the Indies. Therefore, Queen Isabella was willing to take a chance on Columbus. With her support for his venture, Columbus finally set out from the Andalusian port of Palos with three ships on 3 August 1492. After repairs and restocking in the Canary Islands, they sailed west on 9 September into the uncharted Atlantic horizon.

THE "NEW" WORLD

On 12 October, Columbus landed at a small island in the Caribbean (in what is now known as Barbados).[5] Unaware of his mistake, he believed that he had at last found a new trading passage to India. Columbus claimed the land for Isabella and Ferdinand, gave thanks to God, and named the island *San Salvador* (the Saviour). His arrival was to have a momentous impact on the islands of the Caribbean and the huge landmass that came to be known as America.[6] The discovery of the new lands came at a critical point in Spanish history. On 2 January 1492, Spain finally completed a nearly 800 year process of reconquest against the Moors in Spain. The Spanish monarchs were ready to extend their recently consolidated power out into new areas of the world and begin a new imperialist age.[7] Sadly, this imperial glory would be built on the suffering of its victims.

---

[5] Columbus's arrival in the Caribbean was a result of the north-easterly winds that prevail below the Tropic of Cancer. Columbus picked up these winds largely by chance when he sailed south from the Canaries, and they ensured that he arrived across the Atlantic at this latitude. His return to Spain was possible because when he sailed north, he picked up the westerly winds that prevail north of the Tropic of Cancer. During the colonial period, the Spanish trans-Atlantic shipping convoys (the *carrera de las Indias*) would follow more or less the same route

[6] Even after encountering the mainland on his third voyage Columbus clung to his mistaken belief until his death. Columbus always referred to them as "the Indies" and to their inhabitants as the "Indians." The term New World is credited to the Florentine explorer Amerigo Vespucci who made three well-publicised journeys to the new territories a short time after Columbus. The continent came to be known as "America" in recognition of Vespucci's travels.

[7] Moors invaded Spain in 711 and conquered the peninsula within seven years. The Spanish reconquest took over seven centuries. The final phase of reconquest became possible after Prince Ferdinand of Aragon and Princess Isabella of Castille married in 1469. When their respective fathers died (Henry IV of Castile in 1474 and John II of Aragon in 1479) their marriage resulted in the unification of Catholic Spain. Their united forces finally triumphed over the kingdom of Granada and took the Alhambra citadel in 1492. During this process the political importance of Spain's Catholic identity came to the fore and was reflected in the institution of the Inquisition in Spain 1480. On the Spanish imperial period which was to follow under the Habsburg dynasty, see J. H. Elliott, *Imperial Spain: 1469–1716* (Harmondsworth: Penguin, 2nd ed., 1972 [1963]); J. Lynch *Spain under the Habsburgs* (2 vols; London: Oxford University Press, 1964 and 1969); on the period under the Bourbon dynasty (which replaced the Habsburgs in 1700, introduced some notable reforms into Latin America in the later part of the eighteenth century and endured until Latin American independence in the early nineteenth century), see J. Lynch, *Spanish Colonial Administration, 1782–1810: The Intendant System in the Vice-royalty of Río de la Plata* (London: Athlone, 1958).

Discovery and Destruction (1492–1519)

From San Salvador, Columbus explored the nearby small islands before going south. He sailed along the north coast of Cuba and then east along the north coast of the island of Hispaniola (*La Isla Espanola*, which today is Haiti and the Dominican Republic) where he founded an initial settlement *La Navidad* (Christmas).[8] He then returned home in January 1493 to be greeted with all honours by the Spanish court.[9] Allocation of newly discovered lands was under papal jurisdiction and Pope Alexander VI happened to be a Spanish Borgias. In 1493, he issued a papal bull that gave his support for further exploration to extend the Catholic faith to new peoples. He granted dominion over the isles that Columbus had already discovered and everything that was discovered west of them to the Spanish crown.[10] To prevent clashes between the Spanish claims to the Indies in the west and Portuguese claims to new lands in the south, a demarcation line was drawn on maps of the Atlantic at a longitude one hundred leagues to the west of the Azores and Cape Verde Islands, off the west African coast. Spain would have dominion to the west of these and Portugal to the east.[11] A year later, at the treaty of Tordesillas (1494), the western extent of the Portuguese rights were extended a further two hundred and seventy leagues (about 1,400 miles). An unexpected result of this became clear a few years later. In 1500, Pedro Álvares Cabral tried to lead a Portuguese expedition to India around Africa. He was very badly off course, and then blown even further away from his proposed direction by a storm. Eventually, he landed on undiscovered territory that the amended treaty of Tordesillas unwittingly designated as Portuguese. It was Brazil.[12]

---

[8] The settlement was known as *La Navidad*, because when Columbus lost a ship on Christmas day 1492, he took it as sign from God that he should establish a settlement at the point. In all probability, his belief that the island was the source for the gold that he had seen elsewhere also influenced his decision. The cruelty of the settlers when their greed for gold was frustrated, led to the destruction of the settlement by the Indians before Columbus could return on his second voyage.

[9] The terms of the *Capitulaciones de Santa Fe* signed before the voyage were extremely generous for Columbus. He was given the title Viceroy of the Indies and the hereditary title of Admiral of the Ocean. He was promised the governorship of all lands discovered on his voyage and one tenth of all the riches resulting from his discoveries.

[10] Before his second voyage, the Pope mandated Columbus to take the Catholic faith to all the residents and inhabitants of his discoveries and Queen Isabella also emphasised that she was concerned for the conversion of those that he encountered on his travels (see Goodpasture, *Cross and Sword*, p. 5).

[11] On Portuguese explorations, see J. H. Parry, *The Age of Reconnaissance: The Age of Discovery, Exploration and Settlement, 1450–1650* (London: Weidenfeld and Nicolson, 1963); C. R. Boxer, *The Portuguese Seaborne Empire* (Harmondsworth, Penguin Books: 1973).

[12] Although the land was claimed for Portugal as "the land of the true cross" on 26 April 1500, the first group of settlers did not arrive until the 1530s. The Portuguese were later able to extend their boundaries into the sparsely populated interior well beyond what had been agreed. Modern Brazil is about half of the landmass and half of the population of the South American continent as a whole. The name "Brazil" is derived from

Columbus was eager to return to the Caribbean. His second expedition (1493–1496) involved many more men and seventeen ships (which included a different *Santa Maria* as his flagship). He followed a similar trans-Atlantic course and reached the Leeward Islands of the Caribbean and Puerto Rico before coming to Hispaniola from the East. Since the fort he established at La Navidad had been destroyed, he founded a new coastal settlement—Isabella— to the west of it on 2 January 1494. From here, the Spanish started to search Hispaniola and the other nearby islands in the misguided belief that the gold jewellery of the inhabitants showed that great quantities of gold were available for the taking.[13]

The quest for gold in Hispaniola was a disaster for the island's indigenous people and subsequently, for the inhabitants of the whole continent.[14] When the goldfields failed to materialise, the Spanish turned on the local inhabitants and forced them to supply a quota of gold every three months. Every man, woman, and child was liable for this quota; the Spanish cut a hand off those who failed and hanged or burned any who resisted. After only two years, an estimated half of the population had died or been killed—an estimated 125,000 to 500,000 people. Those who survived Spanish cruelty were vulnerable to European diseases for which they had no immunity. When it was clear that the little gold available was exhausted, the *conquistadores* forced the inhabitants to work the land for them instead.

The history of Hispaniola was the testing ground for the colonial patterns that would spread throughout the continent. In 1503, Queen Isabella decreed that the Indians were not to be enslaved, but—in order for them to be con-verted to Catholicism—should be forced to work as paid labourers on the estates of Spanish settlers, known as *encomiendas*.[15] In theory, in exchange for

---

the dyewood of that name that was its primary trade export in the sixteenth century until the Portuguese introduced sugar plantations from Madeira. For a helpful histori-cal overview on Brazil, see E. B. Burns, *A History of Brazil* (New York: Columbia University Press, 1970).

[13] It was not until the third voyage (1498–1500) that Columbus came to the main-land coast of what is now Venezuela just south of Trinidad. During his fourth and final voyage (1502–1504) he discovered the Caribbean coast of Central America. Even so, it appears that when he died two years later, he still believed that he had found the western sea passage to Asia that he had always hoped for.

[14] Columbus went inland in search of the goldfields and established an inland colony called San Tomas under the control of his younger brother, Diego. However, the small quantities of gold that may have first drawn Columbus to settle in Hispaniola were from alluvial rivers rather than the bountiful gold fields that the Spanish believed must exist. Undeterred, in April Columbus sailed west to Cuba (which he believed was China), then south to Jamaica and back around the southern coast of Hispaniola. The whole voyage took about six months. Having failed to find gold, he rounded-up a large num-ber of inhabitants and sent 500 of the best specimens back to Spain as tribute to the Spanish monarchs.

[15] Abuse of the *encomienda* system was widespread and persistent despite a further attempt by Ferdinand in 1512 to regulate them more strictly under the Laws of the

this labour, the settlers were required to treat the Indians well, pay them daily wages, protect them from dangers, and provide for their religious instruction. In practice, the laws were widely ignored and did little to prevent appalling conditions of abuse and virtual slavery on the *encomiendas*. War, disease, and the inhuman conditions of work took a terrible toll on the Indians.

The church failed to protect the people from the violence. Most of the church authorities colluded with the genocide of the native people. The social privileges enjoyed by the church, the close connection between crown and church, and firmly held beliefs in the moral and spiritual superiority of the conquistadores over the natives, prevented the church from criticising or acting against the genocidal destruction. When protests were made, they came from courageous individuals within the church rather than the church as a whole. In 1515 probably no more than 10,000 native inhabitants were left in Hispaniola, and by 1540 they were almost wiped out. The virtual disappearance of the indigenous peoples in Hispaniola started the practice of enslavement and transportation of African workers to replace them. A practice that was to add the iniquities of a slave trade to the horrors of the conquest without provoking the church to concerted protest.

Coercive and cruel labour practices laid the foundations for a colonial period, which would last over three centuries. The Spanish consolidated their settlement of Hispaniola and then moved out from the Caribbean to conquer and colonise the mainland.[16] The fate of Latin America was determined by the wills of the Iberian monarchs and the missionary zeal of the Pope. The Spanish and Portuguese pioneered the European ideology in which the world was theirs to conquer and rule for the social and religious good of other peoples. For the indigenous people, there was little to distinguish between church and state power in their violent destruction.

Burgos. Continuing abuse led to the attempted abolition of the system, and New Laws of the Indies were introduced in 1542. However, faced by a revolt from Spanish settlers, the crown was forced to compromise and did not enforce the new laws. By the 1560s, traditional *encomiendas* were in decline and during the seventeenth century the *hacienda* (ranch estate) system emerged out of and replaced the sixteenth-century *encomiendas*. Although in the beginning, the *haciendas* were supported by a *repartimiento* system that forced Indians to undertake a certain amount of temporary labour, they gradually came to be based on a permanent resident labour force—often employed at such miserable wages they were little more than serfs; see E. Williamson, *The Penguin History of Latin America* (Harmondsworth: Penguin Books, 1992), pp. 108–112; L. S. Simpson, *The Encomienda in New Spain* (Berkeley: University of California Press, 1950).

[16] In the sixteenth century Spain's colonial centre of gravity shifted to the mainland, but maintained its presence on the Caribbean islands of Hispaniola, Cuba, and Puerto Rico. In the case of Cuba and Puerto Rico, Spanish rule continued until the end of the nineteenth century. Elsewhere in the Caribbean during the seventeenth century, other European nations—especially England, France, and the Netherlands—established themselves with bases on other islands, which allowed them initially to harass Spanish shipping and later to develop their own lucrative plantation export economies from the seventeenth century onwards. Britain wrested Jamaica from Spanish control in 1655 (recog-

Conquest and Colonialism (1519–1808)

Spanish America

The first expeditions to the mainland focussed on the Caribbean coast of Colombia and Venezuela and the Central American coastline adjacent to them.[17] In 1513, Vasco Núñez de Balboa crossed the Panamanian Isthmus and sighted the South Sea. He waded into the water and claimed the Pacific Ocean and all kingdoms for Spain. There were rumours of a powerful province with great riches beyond the sea, but before Núñez de Balboa could undertake his planned expedition, he fell out with the crown representative and was beheaded. In the meantime, Spanish attentions turned to Mexico. In 1519, Hernán Cortés set out from Cuba with about 600 men to conquer the Aztec kingdom of Mexico.[18] He landed on the Mexican coast on Good Friday 1519 and founded the city of Veracruz (City of the True Cross). The Aztec Emperor Montezuma feared that Cortés might be the god Quetzalcoatl (who in some accounts had been prophesied as returning from the east) and feared to strike against him. Instead, he sent lavish gifts which only fed Cortés's desire for further riches.

Cortés took advantage of the situation and proceeded to the Aztec centre Tenochitlán where he and his men were courteously welcomed. After a week as an honoured guest, Cortés suddenly turned against his host and took Montezuma hostage. However, shortly after this grab for power—while Spanish success was still very much in the balance—Cortés had to leave his lieutenant Pedro Alvarado in charge so he could return to the coast temporarily.[19] While

---

nised by a treaty in 1670) and French presence in the western half of Hispaniola was formally recognised by a treaty in 1697. Under its new name "Saint Domingue," it remained a French colony during the eighteenth century, until a slave revolt in 1793 established it as a free republic (Haiti) in 1804. On the eastern half of the island, Santo Domingo, there were periods of rule by both France and Haiti in the early nineteenth-century and the colony finally gained independence in 1844 as the Dominican Republic. On the history of the Caribbean, see E. Williams, *From Columbus to Castro: The History of the Caribbean, 1492–1969* (London: Andre Deutsch, 1970).

[17] On the conquistadors and their conquests, see F. A. Kirkpatrick, *The Spanish Conquistadores* (London: A & C Black, 3rd ed., 1963 [1934]).

[18] For a highly readable narrative account, see H. Thomas, *The Conquest of Mexico* (London: Pimlico, 1994 [1973]). The self-serving letters that Cortés sent back to court make fascinating reading of the Spanish political intrigues that accompanied the conquest, as well as his account of the conquest itself, see H. Cortés, *Letters from Mexico* (trans. and ed. A. Pagden; New Haven, Conn.: Yale University Press, 2nd ed., 1987 [ET 1972, Spanish orig. 1519–1526]). A further primary account is offered by the soldier Bernal Díaz who was part of the group, see B. Díaz del Castillo, *The Conquest of New Spain* (trans. J. M. Cohen; Harmondsworth: Penguin Books, 1963). An interesting collection of sources giving the perspective from the indigenous peoples is offered in M. León-Portilla (ed.), *The Broken Spears: The Aztec Account of the Conquest* (trans. L. Kemp; Boston: Beacon Press, rev. ed., 1992 [1961]).

[19] Cortés set out without waiting for the necessary royal permission, and in deliberate defiance of the Cuban governor Diego Velázquez, who was planning his own expedition. Velázquez had previously sent two scouting expeditions (in 1517 and 1518) and

he was away, the situation deteriorated rapidly. Shortly after Cortés returned, Montezuma was killed and Cortés on 30 June 1520 was forced to withdraw from the city. The Spaniards suffered heavy casualties in their withdrawal, and it is remembered in Spanish tradition as the *noche triste* (sorrowful night).

After six months, Cortés returned in December and began to prepare for a stronger offensive. On 13 August 1521, the new Aztec emperor Cuauhtemoc surrendered the city after a brutal struggle in which most of the city was destroyed. The conquistadors replaced the Aztec rulers at the top of the social pyramid and inherited their subjects. Cortés renamed the kingdom "New Spain," and in return, Charles V appointed him as governor and rewarded him lavishly with huge grants of land.[20] The conquest of Mexico in the early 1520s was the first great prize of the Spanish conquest and inaugurated Spanish colonialism on the main land. In contrast to the Caribbean islands where the inhabitants had basic subsistence economies, in Mexico the Spanish took over a sophisticated, wealthy, and organised society with a developed religious system.[21] They suddenly had control over a huge empire from which they could extract considerable riches. Furthermore, the amazing success of Cortés's adventure fuelled the drive of other *conquistadores* to explore and conquer similar prizes. From Mexico, Pedro de Alvarado launched the conquest of Guatemala and El Salvador (1524–1534), and Francisco Hernández de Córdoba extended Spanish presence south to Nicaragua in 1524 where it connected with explorations north from the early settlements in the Isthmus which had begun in 1522.

Within ten years, the Spanish had a second success—the conquest of the Inca kingdom of Peru. In December 1530, Francisco Pizarro set out from Panama's pacific coast and landed in modern day Ecuador.[22] At the time, the

---

was waiting for permission for his expedition when Cortés set out. Cortés's departure from Tenochitlán was prompted by news that Velázquez had sent a force under Pánfilo de Narváez to Veracruz to force Cortés to return to Cuba. Cortés needed to continually protect himself from Velázquez, and at the same time he sought to go over Velázquez's head with a direct appeal to the crown. In fact, it was not until October 1522 that Charles V finally judged in Cortés's favour and made him safe from retribution.

[20] Cortés served as governor until 1527, but faced a steady loss of power after 1526. In 1528, he left Mexico to defend his interests in Spain. He was well received, his landholdings confirmed, and his title elevated to Marqués del Valle de Oaxaca, but he was not re-appointed as governor. After 1527, formal authority in New Spain lay with an *audiencia* (royal court) until an official Viceroyalty was created in 1535. Cortés returned to live on his estates in Mexico in 1530 without an official appointment and retired back to Spain in 1540. As with Columbus before him, Cortés died a bitter man feeling that he had been cheated out of the proper rewards for his achievements.

[21] For an analysis of the role that religion may have played in Aztec imperial society, see G. W. Conrad and A. M. Demarest, *Religion and Empire: The Dynamics of Aztec and Inca Expansion* (Cambridge: Cambridge University Press, 1984).

[22] In 1513, Pizarro accompanied Vasco Núñez de Balboa in the discovery of the Pacific and made a disappointing first trip to Peru 1524. In 1527, a second trip was much more encouraging and convinced him that a serious attempt at conquest was worthwhile. A vivid account is offered by J. Hemming, *The Conquest of the Incas* (London:

Inca leader Atahuallpa had just established his power after a civil war, but had not been able to adequately consolidate his authority. The political wounds of the civil war were still fresh and had not had time to heal. Like Cortés, Pizzaro was able to take advantage of the situation, and following Cortés example, Pizzaro managed to take Atahuallpa hostage at Cajamara in November 1532. Atahuallpa's subjects paid a huge ransom of gold, but nevertheless, the Spanish killed him. Pizzaro took advantage of the political turmoil that ensued to march on the capital of the Inca empire at Cuzco. After winning a number of battles on the way, he managed to enter Cuzco in November 1533.

From Cuzco the Spanish consolidated control over the central areas of the Inca kingdom (modern day Peru and Bolivia) and moved out to strike at the north (modern Ecuador) and south areas (Chile). Ecuador proved the more straightforward conquest. Quito was captured in 1534 and used to launch expeditions into Colombia and Venezuela (the area the Spanish referred to as New Granada). By contrast, Chile was more obdurate and resisted a first invasion in 1535, and then put up fierce resistance to the eventually successful Spanish campaign of 1540–1553. By this time, only forty years after their first incursions on the mainland, a Spanish empire had been established over a vast area.[23] It ran from Middle America (Mexico and Central America) along the Caribbean coast (Venezuela) and south for thousands of miles west of the Andes (Colombia, Ecuador, Peru, Bolivia, and Chile).[24] At this time, despite this vast stretch of territory, the Spaniards had made very little impact in South America to the east of the great Andes mountains. The new Spanish empire basically remained centered on the existing empires of the Aztecs and Incas and was organised as the viceroyalties of New Spain and Peru that extended out from Mexico City and Lima. Settlement of the New World was therefore

---

Macmillan, 1970). For personal accounts, see Agustín de Zárate, *The Discovery and Conquest of Peru* (trans. J. M. Cohen; Harmondsworth: Penguin Books, 1968).

[23] The Spanish did not completely extinguish organised resistance until much later. It was not until 1572 that they finally overcame and executed Tupac Amaru (the last free Inca Ruler). Even then, his legacy remained potent and was taken up again in the eighteenth century in a major rebellion led by José Gabriel Condorcanqui who assumed the name of Tupac Amaru II, see L. E. Fisher, *The Last Inca Revolt, 1780–83* (Norman: University of Oklahoma Press, 1966).

[24] Venezuela and the Caribbean came under the Viceroyalty of New Spain (Mexico) while the rest of South America was under the Viceroyalty of Peru, which was organised into *audiencias* (royal courts). These *audiencias* included: Panama (1538); Lima (1542); Santa Fé at Bogotá for what is now Colombia (1549); Charcas (1559) which stretched from Bolivia to Buenos Aires (although very little east of the Andes was actually settled); and Chile (1565). These divisions later determined the basis for the emergence of nation states in the nineteenth century. Before that, in the eighteenth century the vast Viceroyalty of Peru was divided to create new Viceroyalties in the north at New Granada (1717) covering modern day Colombia and Ecuador, and in the southeast at La Plata (1776) covering modern-day Bolivia, Argentina, Uruguay, and Paraguay. For a selection of helpful maps, see E. Williamson, *The Penguin History of Latin America* (Harmondsworth: Penguin Books, 1992), pp. 605–616.

very uneven. Many areas of South America east of the Andes were untouched by Spanish influence for years.[25]

Spanish success was due partly to their ruthless and single-minded determination which sustained their reckless courage and ambitious greed. It would, however, have been impossible without their superior weapons of war. The swords, canons, horses, and ferocious dogs of the *conquistadores* were a crucial military advantage in their drive for glory and gold. A further, and crucial factor, was their luck. Both Cortés and Pizzaro enjoyed remarkable strokes of fortune—or as they interpreted it, benefited from a favourable divine providence—which prevented the Aztec and Inca kings from taking effective action against their initial expeditions.[26]

Perhaps the most important factor of all was the ready support of local inhabitants against their existing overlords. The *conquistadores* played astute politics of divide and rule and recruited and then betrayed local allies. They took advantage of hostitilty amongst subject peoples toward the harsh rule of the Aztec and Inca kings. They used this to overthrow the Aztecs and Incas and then quickly established themselves as the new lords over the same empires and the local peoples that had helped them. Finally, great waves of disease such as smallpox in Mexico swept through the Indian population during the sixteenth century as a result of European contact.[27] These epidemics consolidated the initial military and political defeats of Aztec and Inca power.

Thus, against all likelihood and in a very short time, the tiny forces of *conquistadores* in Mexico and Peru overcame forces that vastly outnumbered them and ushered in a period of colonial rule that lasted about three centuries. Cortés had about c. 600 men, 16 horses, 14 cannons, and 13 muskets on his first attempt at conquest in 1520 (though he had received some reinforcements before his second attempt in 1521). Pizzaro had only about 60 horsemen and 100 footsoldiers when he defeated the Incan army of more than 6000 and

---

[25] It was only in the 1560s that explorers crossed the Andes from Chile into what is now the interior of Argentina. The Spaniards largely neglected the Atlantic coast of the continent, and although Buenos Aires was first founded in 1535, it was destroyed in 1541 and not re-founded until 1580 and would only start to rise to real significance two hundred years after this. When it was designated the capital of the new Viceroyalty of the River Plate (1776), it was still a relatively small seaport, but its potential as a channel for Atlantic trade was enormous. The reorientation of trade from the interior to Buenos Aires rather than Lima in the late eighteenth century, started to shift the economic axis of Latin America from the west to the east of the Andes.

[26] It seems that Cortés landed in Mexico in the aftermath of a succession of demoralizing omens amongst the Aztecs and some feared that he might be a vengeful representative of Quetzalcóatl (the God of Priestly Wisdom). Likewise, the civil war within the Incan ruling dynasty that was just ending when Pizzaro arrived, presented the tiny Spanish forces with a fortuitous opportunity for success.

[27] The spread of smallpox in Mexico in 1520 prepared the way for Cortés's successful second assault on Tenochitlán. The Aztec emperor Cuitlahuac (who succeeded Montezuma) was one of its victims.

seized Atahuallpa at Cajamarca.[28] In both cases they faced experienced troops who had subdued vast territories on previous campaigns.

The promise of gold, which drove the Spanish conquest proved to be largely illusory. Atahuallpa's ransom was a fabulous treasure, but Spanish hopes for *El Dorado*—a mythical gold city—proved illusory. The most lucrative area for gold proved to be in the northwestern part of New Granada (modern day Colombia). However, the vast Aztec and Incan civilisations offered significant alternative rewards, especially in the form of silver. The *conquistadores* of the sixteenth century forced the local people to extract this mineral wealth and made fortunes. Silver mines at Zacatecas (north of Mexico City) and in Potosí (in Upper Peru, to the distant south-east of Lima, which is now Bolivia) yielded riches that were transported to Mexico City and Lima. The silver was taken from Mexico City to the Caribbean port of Veracruz or from Lima to the harbour at Callao and then to Panama and transferred to the Caribbean overland. In both cases it then made the transatlantic voyage to Seville.[29] The extraction and transport of Latin America's mineral wealth—accompanied by cruel and exploitative labour practices—led the twentieth century Uruguayan historian Eduardo Galeano to describe the whole continent as a person whose blood was being slowly drained away.[30] Galeano's image of the "Open Veins of Latin America" captures both the pillage of the continent's resources and the cost in blood and sweat of the indigenous people who were forced to participate in their own impoverishment.

The manner of conquest and history of colonialism left a number of legacies that remain powerful on Latin American societies to this day.[31] Spanish adventurers disdained physical work and sought to make their personal fortunes with a minimum of their own labour. The legacy of this contrast between those who have to work, and those who are able to force others to work for them, remains to this day. The conquest established a pattern whereby personal industry was rejected for the exploitation of the native people and natural resources. The conquest also established a European attitude to Latin America as a continent to serve the needs of distant lands and enrich a small local elite at the

[handwritten margin note: Colonialism Legacies]

---

[28] Williamson, *The Penguin History of Latin America*, pp. 17 and 24.

[29] After the Spanish conquest of the Philippines (as they were named in honour of King Philip II of Spain) in the 1560s, a transpacific cargo trade was established from Manila to Acapulco on the Pacific side of Mexico, overland via Mexico City to Veracruz, and across the Atlantic. This trade went unmolested until the Dutch arrived in the Pacific in 1615.

[30] E. Galeano, *Open Veins of Latin America: Five Centuries of the Pillage of a Continent* (trans. C. Belfrage; New York: Monthly Review Press, 1973 [Spanish orig. 1971]).

[31] For more on the Spanish colonial era, see especially C. Gibson, *Spain in America* (New York: Harper & Row, 1966); idem, *The Aztecs under Spanish Rule: A History of the Indians of the Valley of Mexico, 1519–1810* (Stanford, Calif.: Stanford University Press, 1964); C. H. Haring, *The Spanish Empire in America* (Oxford: Oxford University Press, 1947).

expense of the majority of the population.[32] The way the new lands were conquered also contributed to the grossly unequal distribution of land that has
remained ever since. The leader of the expedition divided up the conquered
land amongst the chief *conquistadores*.[33] This pattern of land distribution laid
the foundation for the dominance of *latifundios* (large holdings) and *haciendas*
(ranches) that continues and is a major factor in today's imbalance between
rich and poor.

Brazil

The course of colonial history for the Portuguese in Brazil was initially rather
different from that of Spanish America.[34] In Brazil no parallels to the advanced
kingdoms of the Aztecs or Incas existed, and the Portuguese focussed more on
trade. Portugese settlement was much slower and primarily centered on the northeast part of the country. From its very beginning until the twentieth century,
Brazil was based on an agro-export economy. Initially, this was wood from the
Brazil (used to make dyes) from which the country got its name. As the sixteenth century progressed, sugar plantations based on slave labour were introduced to the northeast from Madeira.[35] Later, coffee became the principle crop
and the basis of the economy in the nineteenth century. Coffee ruled the economy until industrialisation made serious headway after the 1930s. Even in the
seventeenth century, much of the Brazilian interior was untouched. However,
as time passed, without the Andes as a natural barrier to expansion into the
interior the Portuguese gradually extended their areas of interest westward
beyond the line of demarcation. Portugal eventually laid claim to a vast territory,
which virtually matched the Spanish territories in South America, and helped it
become Latin America's superpower by the second half of the twentieth century.

---

[32] The legal division of the population further reinforced this social polarisation. For
most of the colonial period two republics existed side by side. The Spanish Republic
existed for the elite, while the Indian Republic covered the overwhelming majority.

[33] See Williamson, *The Penguin History of Latin America*, p. 81. A clear precedent for
the unequal distribution lay in the land distribution of the Iberian peninsula that the
conquistadors had left behind. This had been exacerbated by the vast grants of land as
rewards to the powerful during the reconquest in Spain. It should, however, be noted
that although all the conquistadors could expect a share of land, they were not all entitled to free labour. The crown determined the granting of labour under the *encomienda*
system of labour grants, which were reserved for Spaniards of appropriate social status.

[34] Some of the differences between the Portuguese and Spanish colonial experiences
are drawn out in J. Lockhart and S. B. Schwartz, *Early Latin America: A History of Spanish
America and Brazil* (Cambridge: Cambridge University Press, 1983).

[35] Unfortunately for the Portuguese, in the seventeenth century the Dutch managed
to occupy some of the sugar areas and disrupted Portuguese production, see C. R. Boxer,
The Dutch in Brazil (1624–54) (Oxford: Clarendon Press, 1957). When the Dutch were
finally driven away in 1654, they took the techniques they learned to start sugar plantations in the Caribbean and created new competition for Brazil's sugar industry.

THE CROSS AND SWORD

The church wholeheartedly supported the tumultuous and violent conquest of the Americas. Missionaries arrived in Latin America with the *conquistadores* and the cross and sword supported each other's power throughout the colonial period. The state protected and promoted the church, and in return, the church sanctioned the Spanish and Portuguese authorities as embodiments of the will of God. This close political collaboration between church and state authorities—commonly referred to as Christendom—has been a major factor in Latin American societies ever since.[36]

Missionary Zeal (1492–1519)

Columbus himself was a fervent Catholic, and missionary zeal was an important motivation in his enterprise.[37] The ship that took Columbus to the Caribbean was named the Santa Maria, a fitting name in view of his devotion to the Virgin and his desire to carry Christ with him to new territories.[38] The name San Salvador or Holy Saviour (the name of the first island discovered on his first voyage) reflected his wish to impose Christian culture wherever he went. He expressed the hope that the "heathens" he encountered would be converted to Christianity and that the gold he would bring back might be used to start a new crusade for the Holy Land.

Columbus was not alone in his sense of Christian destiny in his arrival in the Caribbean. Spanish conquest and domination in the Americas was supported by an ardent belief in the divine character of their task. The Spaniards interpreted the victory over the Moors (which had been completed in 1492) as a sign of God's blessing for a righteous crusade. They carried this conviction to the New World. The language and emotion closely echoed the religious fervour of the old Crusades against enemies of the Christian faith. In the same year that Columbus started to claim the inhabitants of the Indies for the Spanish throne and the Christian faith, the Jews were expelled from Spain.

---

[36] See E. Dussel, *A History of the Church in Latin America: Colonialism to Liberation (1492–1979)* (trans. and rev. A. Neely; Grand Rapids, Mich.: Eerdmans, 1981 [Spanish orig. 1974]). An extensive collection of chapters by different authors and an excellent bibliography are offered in idem (ed.), *The Church in Latin America: 1492–1992* (Maryknoll, N.Y.: Orbis Books; Tunbridge Wells, Kent: Burns and Oates, 1987).

[37] On the spiritual influences on Columbus' enterprise, see P. M. Watts, "Prophecy and Discovery: On the Spiritual Origins of Christopher Columbus' 'Enterprise of the Indies,'" *American Historical Review* 90 (1985), pp. 73–102. On Columbus as an interpreter of scripture, see H. Avalos, "Columbus as Biblical Exegete: A Study of the *Libro de las profecías*" in B. F. Le Beau and M. Mor (eds.), *Religion in the Age of Exploration: The Case of Spain and New Spain* (Omaha, Neb.: Creighton University Press, 1996), pp. 59–80.

[38] Cristoforo Colombo (known in English as Christopher Columbus, or in Spanish as Cristobal Colon) means "Christ Carrying Dove." For a helpful collection of primary sources on the relation of cross and sword in the colonial period, see Goodpasture (ed.), *Cross and Sword*, pp. 5–103.

The monarchs Isabella and Ferdinand saw Christianity as a civilising force, and evangelisation was an essential part of the colonisation process. No priests accompanied Columbus on his first voyage, but on the second voyage, Friar Bernal Boyl led a small group of friars. However, Boyl returned to Spain in 1494 and serious efforts at evangelisation of Hispaniola did not start until 1500 when a Franciscan mission arrived and was reinforced with a second contingent in 1502. The Franciscans formally established the Mission of the West Indies in 1505, and in 1510 they were joined by a group of Dominicans under Pedro de Córdoba. In 1511, three dioceses were created for the Caribbean at Santo Domingo (for northern Hispaniola), Concepción de la Vega (for southern Hispaniola—which was later abolished in 1528) and San Juan (for Puerto Rico).[39] Their bishops—who were to be suffragans to Seville—were consecrated the following year, and the first to arrive was Alonso Manso as Bishop of San Juan.[40]

With hindsight, it is easy to see how the Christian expression of the *conquistadores* mission excused, and even extended, violence against the people. When the *conquistadores* desire for gold conflicted with the church's work with the Indians, the *conquistadores* had little time for their obligations to the church. At times the church even encouraged the harshness of the *conquistadores*.[41] Although some church clerics took pity on the suffering Indians and even questioned the moral rights of the Spanish to treat them so harshly, these were usually seen as separate from the theological issues that should concern the church. Because the church sought to claim the souls of the inhabitants for the glory of God, their concern for the Indians was often exclusively for the state of their disembodied souls, rather than the conditions of their life under colonial rule. God's glory was seen in terms of the number of conversions, rather than the survival of the converts. Some may have felt that a concern for social welfare was an appropriate addition to this, but there was no precedent in their tradition to encourage them to take the suffering of the Indians as a theological starting point for reflection on Christian faith.

Colonial Christendom (1520–1808)

Church and State

In colonial Christendom the Catholic church and Spanish monarchy made an alliance of temporal and spiritual power for the glory of God and the Spanish

---

[39] See M. A. Rodríguez León, "Invasion and Evangelization in the Sixteenth Century" in Dussel (ed.), *The Church in Latin America*, pp. 43–54.

[40] Bishop Alonso only stayed in Puerto Rico for two and a half years before returning to Spain for four years. When he returned to the Caribbean, it was with the title of Inquisitor General of the Indies, and he set to work building a new cathedral through Indian slave labour.

[41] For example, Friar Bernal Boyl urged Columbus to deal harshly with the Indians on Hispaniola who had destroyed the settlement at La Navidad.

crown. It was a political arrangement in which the church and state worked hand-in-hand for the governance of a Christian kingdom. In theory the Church was the senior partner. It represented the permanent realm of the divine and spiritual. By contrast, the state was a temporary partner to take care of the temporal world of the secular and mundane.[42] In practice, the power of the civil authorities (and the temptations of civil privileges and wealth) frequently ensured that the state had the upper hand on the church in most matters of governance.

The first diocese on the mainland was founded at Santa María la Antigua of Darien in 1521, after the early exploration of Panama.[43] In Mexico, a Mercedarian friar (Bartolomé de Olmedo) accompanied Cortés as chaplain in 1519 and Cortés built the first church at Tlaxcala in 1522, but evangelisation did not really begin until a group of twelve Franciscans arrived five years later.[44] The so-called twelve apostles landed at Veracruz in 1524 to begin the evangelisation of mainland Latin America. A small group of Dominicans followed them in 1526 and seven Augustinians arrived in 1533. During the next thirty years, the three orders grew rapidly and were at the forefront of evangelisation and church life. The first bishop of Tlaxcala was the Dominican Juan Garcés, and the first bishop of Mexico was the Franciscan bishop Juan de Zumáragga.[45]

A major step forward in the church's attempts at evangelisation took place in 1531 when Juan Diego received an apparition of the Virgin of Guadalupe at Mount Tepeyac, to the northwest of Mexico City.[46] It is widely believed that Mary appeared to Juan Diego, a poor Indian, and told him to tell the local bishop that a church was to be built for her. The bishop dismissed Juan Diego's story and ignored his message until a miracle forced him to concede the authority of what he said. The appearance of the Virgin on Latin American soil, speaking the language of the colonized rather than the colonizer, addressing Juan Diego as son and taking the side of the peasant against the bishop, has been an icon of popular religion ever since. The poor of Latin America have

---

[42] The Church's sense of seniority is seen in the Bull of Pope Boniface VIII, *Unam Sanctam* (1302): "... there are two swords, namely the spiritual and the temporal.... It is necessary that one sword should be beneath the other, and that the temporal authority should be subjected to the spiritual power.... Clearly we must acknowledge that the spiritual power excels any earthly power both in dignity and in nobility, in as much as spiritual things excel temporal" (cited in B. McSweeney, *Roman Catholicism: The Search for Relevance* (Oxford: Basil Blackwell, 1980), p. 14.

[43] Panama City was founded in 1519, but the Spaniards had first visited the Isthmus in 1501.

[44] Pope Clement VII elevated Tlaxcala to a diocese in 1525, but the Episcopal see was subsequently moved to Puebla de los Angeles in 1539.

[45] The diocese of Mexico was established in 1530 and elevated to an Archdiocese along with Lima and Santo Domingo in 1546.

[46] See the special issue of the *Journal of Hispanic/Latino Theology* 5 (1997) which is dedicated to the Virgin of Guadalupe. I am grateful to M. D. Carroll R. for drawing this journal to my attention.

understood this appearance of Our Lady of Guadalupe as a sign of Mary's adoption of the native peoples and her solidarity with the oppressed. Devotion to the Virgin also facilitated the spread of the church through the integration of Catholicism with the worship of indigenous mother-goddesses. Mount Tepeyac where the events occurred was previously a place of pilgrimage to the indigenous mother-goddess Tontantzin-Cihuacóatl.[47]

The *Patronato Real* of Pope Julius II set the legal framework in which the church's work took place in 1508. This granted authority to the Spanish crown to appoint the bishops and other church personnel for its recently established settlements. In exchange, the crown would pay all the church's expenses. Under this arrangement, twenty Dominicans arrived in Cuzco in 1538 with the new bishop Vicente de Valverde, a Dominican who had accompanied Pizarro on the original conquest, and systematic organisation of the church began with First Provincial Council of Lima (1551–1552).

In Brazil, a similar *Padroado Real* was granted to the Portuguese monarchs temporarily in 1515 and confirmed permanently in 1551. The Jesuits arrived in Bahía in 1549 led by the Society's first Captain-General to serve in Latin America (dispatched from Lisbon to start an official government for the country). The diocese of Bahía was created in 1551.

The royal patronage brought great benefits to both the monarchy and the institutional church, but it severely limited the church's potential to oppose the state's power. It meant that Rome would not have direct contact with the Latin American church, but would have to go through the mediation of the Spanish and Portuguese monarchs. Latin American church historian Enrique Dussel describes this arrangement as a unique form of "colonial or dependent Christendom." It was "Christendom" in as much as the political and ecclesial powers were closely integrated, just as they were in the Roman and Byzantine empires. However, it was "colonial" or "dependent" because Latin American Christendom was always at the periphery and dependent on Spain's power.[48]

The close connection between church and state in the colonial period is revealed in the number of clerics appointed to political positions. For example, after the death of Ferdinand in 1516, the temporary regent was Cardinal Jiménez de Cisneros who had previously been spiritual adviser to Isabella.[49] When Charles V replaced Cisneros it meant a return to favour for the Bishop of Burgos, Juan Rodríguez de Fonseca. Fonseca had been the principle adviser to

---

[47] There is debate over the extent to which the church knew about and encouraged such syncretism. For the parallel process of the integration of Catholic religiosity with indigenous religion in Peru, see J. Szeminski, "From Inca Gods to Spanish Saints and Demons" in S. Kaplan (ed.), *Indigenous Responses to Western Christianity* (New York: New York University Press, 1995), pp. 56–74.

[48] E. Dussel, *History and the Theology of Liberation* (trans. J. Drury; Maryknoll, N.Y.: Orbis Books, 1976 [Spanish orig. 1973]), pp. 75–109 (esp. 75).

[49] At one point Cisneros appointed Jeronymite friars to serve as the crown's official representatives on Hispaniola.

Ferdinand and Isabella on the affairs of the Indies, and his niece was married to the governor of Cuba, Diego Velázquez. Previously, as archdeacon in Seville he had supervised preparations for Columbus' second trip and he remained a key figure in the affairs of the Indies. Under Charles he helped influence the setting up of the Council of Indies. The Council had responsibility for everything in the Indies (including the church), until it was replaced with government by vice-regents. Its first chair was the king's confessor, Bishop Barcía de Loaisa.[50]

State sponsorship of the church ensured that churches were built at the heart of each Spanish settlement of any significance according to a consistent pattern. The central plaza had a church (or for important cities, a cathedral) on its eastern side and the key buildings of civil government (such as the governor's house and the jail) on the other sides of the square or rectangle.[51] The historical pattern whereby the church would stand in the social order alongside the rich landowners and the agencies of the state found visible expression in this layout. The church, landowners, and institutions of civil government formed an alliance as the three pillars of colonial society.

The church was a powerful landholder (second only to the crown in the colonial period) and benefited from Indian labour (under both the *encomienda* and *repartimiento* system) as well as a system of tithes and gifts. Some of the wealth it acquired went into adorning the magnificent churches and other buildings that it sponsored for elaborate worship services.

At a charitable level it supported education and medical facilities (albeit very unevenly) and was the main source of charity for the poor. Priests might be poor but bishops could be fantastically wealthy, and most enjoyed the full trappings of wealth and power. These attractions—combined with its traditional theology and Euro-centric confidence in the truth of its message—usually meant that the church as an institution was a willing collaborator in colonialist assertions of power. From the centres of Spanish settlement, itinerant missionaries went out to celebrate Catholic rites in the Indian settlements. However, efforts to evangelize the indigenous peoples met with mixed success. Often the rites of Catholicism did not displace the Indian's traditional religious cultures but were added to them. The results were new forms of religious beliefs and behaviour. This folk religion defies easy classification to this day. This new amalgam of faith often showed a markedly Catholic appearance (with Latin rituals and the veneration of Christian saints), but the underlying religious outlook did not necessarily change.[52]

---

[50] See Dussel, *The Church in Latin America*, p. 58. The Council of the Indies began in 1519 as part of the Council of Castille and was confirmed in 1524 when it became the fourth central council of Spanish government alongside Castille, Aragon, and Navarre.

[51] The rest of the settlement usually extended out from this central square on a square grid of streets. The most important citizens would have residences either close to or actually on the central plaza, and a person's social standing was reflected in the distance from the plaza.

[52] The absence of a native priesthood also contributed to the problems that the

Despite the many obvious failings of the church during the colonial period, there were some courageous exceptions to the general trend of its alliance with Spanish oppression. From the early years of the church's presence in Latin America, a minority of priests and church workers preserved a prophetic alternative to the collusion with exploitation that marked the institutional church. Two particularly important strands can be picked out: the Dominicans in the sixteenth century and the Jesuits in the seventeenth and eighteenth centuries.

The Dominican Protests: The Indians as Human Beings

"I am the voice of one out in the desert" (Jn 1.23 cp., Mt. 3.3, Mk 1.2, Lk 3.4). On 21 December 1511, the Dominican Antonio de Montesinos preached on the words of Isaiah 40.3 echoed by John the Baptist. The Spaniards, he said, were guilty of mortal sin in their treatment of the Indians, and he refused to give them absolution. Indignant Spaniards complained to Spain and made representations to the king. However, Montesinos and his colleague Pedro de Córdoba defended themselves successfully before the Spanish court. In 1512, their protests led to Laws of the Burgos, the first legislation dealing with the Indies and intended to afford some protection to the Indians.

For Montesinos, the key issue in the dispute with the Spanish colonisers was whether the Indians were human beings like themselves. If so, they deserved to be treated as such. Montesinos pressed for more humane forms of evangelisation and treatment of the Indians. The debate on the status of the Indians and how they should be treated became a source of conflict between the Dominicans and the colonists for decades to come. The colonists appealed to Aristotle and other ancient authorities to justify their claims that the Indians were naturally slaves, and that it was therefore entirely permissible to treat them differently from other people. From the Dominican side, the champion against such claims was a former *encomedor* who had heard Montesinos's challenge and taken his message especially to heart. His name was Bartolomé de las Casas.[53]

Las Casas was born in Seville in 1484 and witnessed Columbus's return from his first voyage to the Caribbean in April 1493. His father and two uncles sailed with Columbus on the second voyage and in 1502, Las Casas himself set out for Hispaniola. He spent the next four years as a colonist. During this time, he trained for the priesthood while living on the labour of the Indians. In 1506, he travelled to Rome, and the following year he was ordained as a dioce-

---

mission orders faced. Despite papal attempts to promote a local secular clergy in the 1520s, the mission orders resisted such efforts, and throughout almost the whole of the colonial period, the clergy remained of European origin (see Williamson, *The Penguin History of Latin America*, p. 102).

[53] On Las Casas and his significance for liberation theology, see especially G. Gutiérrez, *Las Casas: In Search of the Poor of Jesus Christ* (Maryknoll N.Y.: Orbis Books, 1993 [Spanish orig. 1992]). For an account of Las Casas's life through his own writings at different points in his life, see G. Sanderlin (ed.), *Witness: Writings of Bartolomé de Las Casas* (Maryknoll, N.Y.: Orbis Books, 2nd ed., 1992 [1971]).

san priest. He then returned to the Caribbean in 1509 and began his life as a priest while maintaining his *encomienda*.

When the Dominicans first came to Hispaniola in 1510 under Pedro de Córdoba, Las Casas seems to have been unmoved by their criticism of the treatment of the Indians. Las Casas accompanied Pánfilo de Narváez as a chaplain on the Spanish conquest of Cuba (1512–1513) and was granted a further *encomienda* in Cuba by the governor, Diego Velázquez. However, as the Indian population collapsed from disease, overwork, and cruelty, Las Casas became increasingly troubled. He had watched the genocide in Hispaniola and was distressed to see it repeated with such zeal in Cuba. In 1514, as he prepared his sermon for Pentecost, the words of Ecclesiasticus 34.18–22 struck him with full force. The judgement on those who make sacrifices and other religious rituals before God and yet oppress their fellow human beings, spoke directly to his feelings about the ill-treatment of the Indians. He set free his Indian workers and prepared a special sermon for the Feast of Assumption on 15 August 1514.

From then on, he sought to challenge the laws that governed the treatment of Indians throughout the new lands. He sent his own protests back to Spain to persuade the King to strengthen the Laws of Burgos. At the end of 1515, he travelled back to the Spanish court to present his protest in person. Unfortunately, King Ferdinand died a short time later. Las Casas then saw Bishop Juan Rodríguez de Fonseca but found him unmoved by his concerns. When the Bishop's secretary tried to bribe him to drop his protests, it was clear that he could expect little help from him. However, shortly afterward, a further change in fortune led to his official appointment as "Protector of the Indies," and a return to the Indies in an unsuccessful attempt to end the *encomienda* system 1516–1517. In 1515, he had developed an elaborate settlement plan which he hoped would offer peaceful co-existence between Indians and Spaniards. In 1520, Charles V granted him land in Venezuela where he could try it out. He attempted to set up the settlement in 1521, but the outcome was disastrous because he was unable to stop slave raids by other colonists.[54]

In 1522, he joined the Dominicans in order to advocate the Indian cause more effectively. He started a new Dominican monastery on the north of Hispaniola and started his great work *History of the Indies* to counterbalance the accounts recorded by conquistadors. His arguments that evangelisation should only be carried out peacefully influenced Pope Paul III who issued a papal Bull in 1537 that affirmed the rationality of the Indians and the importance of their evangelisation. These were important affirmations in a time when apologists for conquest denied both.

That same year Las Casas started work as a missionary in northern Guatemala. He returned to Spain in 1540 to recruit further missionaries and stayed for awhile to impress on the King the mistreatment of the Indians. For this purpose, he wrote the graphic *Short Account of the Destruction of the Indies* (c. 1540), a fierce

---

[54] See Sanderlin, *Witness*, pp. 6–8.

attack on the suffering caused by the Spanish.[55] The passage of the New Laws
(1542–1543), which strengthened some of the Laws of Burgos, was partially in
response to these efforts. Las Casas was named bishop of Chiapas in 1543,
where he worked diligently to improve the lot of Indians in his area until he
returned permanently to Spain in 1547.

Back in Spain he wrote his *Defence of the Indians* in preparation for a debate in
Valladolid with theologians from Salamanca including Juan Ginés de Sepúlveda
(1550–1551).[56] A critical element in this dispute was whether the Indians had
souls. Their human identity—and therefore their shared human nature with
the Spaniards—was seen to rest on the answer to this question. This, in turn,
was seen as critical for whether it was legitimate for the Spanish to rule over
them without their consent. The opponents of Las Casas argued that the
Indians did not have souls, and therefore were not fully human, and might
justifiably be compelled to serve the Spanish for their own good. Las Casas argued
that they were equal in nature, and the Spanish could only legitimately rule
over them if they consented. The Pope agreed with Las Casas, it was an important victory. It did not bring an end to colonialism or the suffering of the
Indians, but it did at least affirm the principle of universal human solidarity.[57]

Las Casas died in 1566. In retrospect he was the first colonialist to distinguish between being Spanish and being Christian. The church and the State
had merged this identity for their own reasons, but Las Casas repeatedly emphasised that Christianity should not be identified with the colonial culture of
oppression. He was not the only activist who kept the spirit of Montesinos alive.
During his brief period as bishop of Chiapas one of his close colleagues was
Antonio de Valdivieso, bishop of Nicaragua (1544–1550).[58] Valdivieso's period
in Nicaragua was marked by an intense conflict with the governor Rodrigo de
Contreras over the mistreatment of Indians. Like Las Casas, Valdivieso was
active in sending reports back to Spain and pressing for changes. His attempts
to ensure that the New Laws were respected eventually provoked his martyrdom. A soldier who supported the governor stabbed him to death in León on
26 February 1550. Other important mid-sixteenth-century figures that strug-

---

[55] B. de Las Casas, *A Short Account of the Destruction of the Indies* (trans. N. Griffin;
Harmondsworth: Penguin Books, 1992 [Spanish orig. 1542]).

[56] B. de Las Casas, *In Defence of the Indians* (DeKalb: Northern Illinois Press, 2nd
ed., 1992 [ET 1974, Spanish orig. c. 1549]).

[57] Tragically Las Casas's concern for the Indians had led him to briefly ignore this
principle and support the importation of slaves from Africa to replace Indians in their
hard labours on *encomiendas*. This had been legal since 1501 and Las Casas and many
of his contemporaries signed a petition to support it in 1516. However, it is clear that
Las Casas came to bitterly regret this decision and was one of the first to denounce the
slave trade.

[58] Close collaboration between Las Casas and Valdivieso was not easy. When Las Casas,
Valdivieso, and Marroquín (Bishop of Guatemala) met in Guatemala in 1545 for a
Commission of Thanksgiving to God, the colonists in Guatemala were so outraged that
they tried to apprehend Las Casas.

gled on behalf of the Indians included: Cristóbal de Pedraza (Bishop of Honduras, 1545–1583); Pablo de Torres (Bishop of Panama, 1547–54); Juan del Valle (Bishop of Popayán, New Granada, 1548–1560); and his successor Agustín de Coruña (1565–1590). Enrique Dussel describes them as the Latin American "Fathers of the Church."[59]

The Jesuits: Evangelization through Civilization

Jesuit missionaries arrived in Bahía, northeast Brazil, in 1549. Friction with the first bishop of Brazil quickly forced them to travel south to the captaincy of São Vicente where they helped to establish a new colony at São Paulo in 1554.[60] Their work in Spanish America began in the following decade with missions in Mexico and Paraguay starting in 1568.[61] In many places (including Mexico, Paraguay, and Brazil), the Jesuits gathered the Indians into special mission settlements, known as *reducciónes*. The *reducciónes* were intended to facilitate the evangelisation and civilisation of the Indians. By the end of the seventeenth century, there were at least thirty major reductions amongst the Guarani Indians (on the Paraguay and Paraná rivers) with a total population of more than 100,000. Unfortunately, the settlements were vulnerable to Portuguese raiders from Brazil (*bandeirantes*) who were in search of Indian slaves. These raids increased markedly in the seventeenth century when the Dutch seized control of Angola (1641–1649) and cutoff the supply of African slaves. The Jesuits vigorously resisted these raids. After open warfare in 1641, they even armed the Indians for self-protection.

Enslavement of the Indians was a longstanding cause of conflict between the Jesuits and colonists in Brazil. Enslavement of Indians had been outlawed in Spanish America but was practised in Brazil despite vigorous opposition from the Jesuits. In 1570, the Portuguese king decreed that Indians were not to be enslaved unless they were cannibals. Unfortunately, this was repealed under pressure from the colonists in 1574. In 1655, the Jesuits of the Amazon region persuaded the king to issue a new decree that outlawed the enslavement of Indians but it proved hard to enforce and led to new conflict with settlers. Settlers expelled the Jesuits by force from the Amazon in 1661 and 1684.

---

[59] Dussel, *A History of the Church in Latin America*, p. 50. Dussel comments: "A study of the lives of these heroic bishops reveals that they risked everything, committing themselves without reservation, suffering expulsion from their dioceses, imprisonment, deportation, and even death on behalf of the Indians who were being violently oppressed and exploited by the Spanish colonists. The lives of these pastors should serve as an example for bishops of our era where the majority of violence is inflicted—as in the time of the *conquistadores*—by 'men of arms'" (p. 51).

[60] São Vicente—near modern-day Santos—was established in 1530 as a royal colony in the south to prevent French interest in the area. In 1567, the Portuguese settled at Rio de Janeiro to oust a French presence established in the 1550s.

[61] Jesuit missions to Florida started even before this, and their work in California began in 1607.

The ethos of the *reducciónes* was extremely paternalistic. They reflected the same unquestioned racist confidence of Europeans that had marked relations with the local people since Columbus. The Jesuits, like all other settlers, took for granted that they should naturally be in a position of authority over the Indians, and that their own civilisation was superior. The settlements provided some level of protection to immediate dangers, but over the long-term they deprived the Indians of opportunities to organise and govern themselves. This left the Indians more vulnerable than ever when they were finally abolished. However, despite their limitations, the *reducciónes* were a genuine attempt by the Jesuits to care for what they saw as their charges and to replace evangelisation through threat and force with a more positive ethos that treated the Indians as real people. Their commitment to the work was to cost them dear. In 1750, a treaty assigned these areas to Brazil, but the Jesuit missions refused to accept Portuguese authority. Jesuit relations with the powerful Portuguese first minister, the Marquis Pombal, were extremely difficult and open conflict broke out in 1754–1756. The Jesuits, as a missionary order in contrast to the secular clergy, were more independent of the local bishops, and therefore harder to control under the terms of the Portuguese *Padroado Real*. They were willing and able to appeal directly to the Pope when they felt obliged to do so, and this independence increased the crown's suspicion and hostility toward them. In the Amazonian region, the Jesuits of Para resisted the state's attempts to press Indians into labour service for the proposed plantations during the 1750s. In 1759, Pombal expelled the order from all Portuguese territories. In 1767, Charles III banned them from Spain and all its territories and ordered the confiscation of their property. This was a serious blow to the Jesuit order and also a huge loss for the Latin American church.[62]

The institutional church was severely weakened by this blow. The Jesuits had been in the forefront of education and mission work, and their skills and expertise were hard to replace. The church hardly recovered before the Independence movement prompted an even greater crisis that loomed in the first decades of the nineteenth century.

CONCLUSION

For nearly three centuries, Latin America was part of the Iberian empires and served the needs of Spanish and Portuguese colonial masters. During this period, a privileged elite governed a rigidly hierarchical society. The suffering of the majority was in stark contrast with the affluence of the few. The indigenous people paid a particularly high price for the greed of their conquerors and this set the pattern for centuries to come. The majority of indigenous Latin Americans—joined by millions of enslaved Africans—worked in cruel and brutal servitude.

---

[62] See M. Mörner, *The Expulsion of the Jesuits from Latin America* (New York: Alfred Knopf, 1965).

Cross and sword arrived together, and the church offered divine sanction for colonial society. The colonial church was a highly conservative force, which stood firmly on the side of the powerful. Despite the celebrated prophetic exceptions, such as Montesinos and Las Casas, the church usually served as an uncritical chaplain to colonial power and encouraged its exploitative practices. It preached that life was a vale of tears, that God ordained social positions, and that obedience to God, to the church, and to the colonial order were inseparable. The ordinary people were left to find solace in their prayers for charity and their hopes for a better life in another world.

CHAPTER TWO

Independence and
Neo-colonialism, 1808–1929

> Workers have been given over, isolated and defence-
> less, to the callousness of employers and the greed of
> unrestrained competition . . . so that a small number of
> the very rich have been able to lay upon the masses
> of the poor a yoke little better than slavery itself.
>
> Leo XXIII, *Rerum Novarum*, § 2.

INTRODUCTION

As the eighteenth century drew to a close, it became clearer that the balance
of power between Spain and its colonies in Latin America had reached a critical point. Spain's power had steadily dwindled as the vast wealth it had gained
from its colonies in the New World had been used for short-term glory and
expensive wars against the Protestants of northern Europe. Spain had done little to develop an industrial base, and much of the silver and gold from Latin
America was spent in importing manufactured goods from England and other
nations that were starting to expand their manufacturing base. Indirectly, the
real beneficiary of this pattern was England. Its exports stimulated the economy to long-term growth while the Spanish economy stagnated. By the nineteenth century, English merchants were seeking direct trade with Latin America,
and the social elites in the colonies were eager to reciprocate since Spain could
not satisfy their desire for manufactured goods.

After three centuries, Spanish colonialism in Latin America was under threat.
The creole elites of Latin America were ready to assume political leadership,
and the British were poised to be the new economic power in the region. The
transition took place with surprising speed in the first three decades of the nineteenth century and Latin America began a new era of history: post-Independence.
However, despite these major political changes, the colonial legacy of dependency on Europe was hard to escape. The new era was based on a new form
of colonialism referred to as *neo-colonialism*. The neo-colonialism of the nineteenth

century permitted—even encouraged—political independence, but continued the continent's economic dependence. The new creole governments that replaced the Spanish did little to redistribute wealth. The traditional imbalance of power between the powerful social elites and the vast majority of people remained unchanged. Therefore, for the day-to-day lives of the Latin American poor, very little changed with independence. Even in the early twentieth century when the U.S. started to replace Britain as the main neo-colonial power, the same pattern of foreign economic control continued. The dominant centre shifted westward from Europe to North America, but the deep inequalities in Latin American societies remained. In most countries, the peasants were still treated as little better than slaves, and the rights that workers might have had in theory were widely ignored in practise.

For liberation theology, the failure of the Independence movement in the nineteenth century was a valuable historical lesson. The nineteenth century showed that fine words and brave hopes in progress did not necessarily benefit the majority. The rhetoric of freedom and confidence in the modern age might disguise deep divisions in society. Only some groups benefited from the modern age and the freedom it offered. True political freedom was more than the right to replace one elite group with another. For the poor, any reforms were largely worthless without a real change in the distribution of power. It also showed that major economic reforms were needed for political changes to lead to social development in which the poor could share.

FROM INDEPENDENCE TO DEPRESSION (1808–1929)

The power vacuum created by the French Revolution (1789) encouraged a slave revolt against the French in the Caribbean at Saint-Domingue in August 1791 (the western half of Hispaniola).[1] After a bitter struggle in which Napoleon attempted reconquest, the French finally conceded defeat, and the former slaves declared themselves the Republic of Haiti on 1 January 1804.[2] Within a few years, the Napoleonic wars in Europe also created the political conditions in which Independence became both a more serious possibility and a more attractive option for the Spanish colonies.[3] The defeat of the Spanish navy at Trafalgar (1805) ended Spain's ability to regulate trade with Latin America. Napoleon's invasions of Portugal (1807) and Spain (1808) opened up the question of Latin America's political allegiances. In Brazil, the outcome was fairly

---

[1] The British colonies in North America had already pointed the way in their own successful struggle for independence fifteen years earlier (1776–1783).

[2] The French eventually accepted Haiti's freedom in 1825, after imposing punitive damages to compensate the planters who had previously benefited from the islands slavelabour. On the Haitian revolution, see: C. L. R. James, *The Black Jacobins* (New York: Vintage Books; 2nd ed., 1963); T. O. Ott, *The Haitian Revolution* (Knoxville, Tenn.: University of Tennessee, 1973).

[3] See R. A. Humphreys and J. Lynch (eds.), *The Origins of the Latin American Revolutions, 1808–1826* (New York: Alfred A. Knopf, 1965).

straightforward. The Portuguese court was evacuated from Lisbon to Rio de Janeiro under British escort (November 1807–January 1808), and this served to strengthen the links between Brazil and Portugal in the period 1808–1821. In Spanish Latin America, the story was different.[4]

The Struggle for Independence

When Napoleon invaded Spain in 1808, Charles IV abdicated in favour of his son, Ferdinand VII. However, Napoleon moved quickly to force both Charles and Ferdinand to renounce their claims and then imprisoned Ferdinand in France.[5] The way was then clear for Napoleon to appoint his own brother Joseph to the Spanish throne, but this did not end Spanish resistance. A rebellion in Madrid quickly spread to other cities, and the rebels set up their own opposition councils (*juntas*) linked to a supreme *junta* in Seville, which was loyal to Ferdinand. Meanwhile, in Latin America, these competing claims to authority precipitated a constitutional crisis in the colonies. Few members of the Spanish American colonial elite felt loyalty to the French, and so, the colonies pledged themselves instead to the *junta* in Seville and still loyal to Spain.

However, when Napoleon's forces captured Seville, the power of the Spanish *junta* was severely undermined. The centre of authority for Spanish resistance passed to a Council of Regency in Cadiz in January 1810. This time, independence leaders in Latin America saw an opportunity for full independence.

Venezuela, Colombia, and Ecuador

The drive for independence surfaced first in the captaincy-general of Venezuela, under the influence of radical voices such as Simón Bolívar.[6] In 1810, Caracas— which was one of the first cities to hear the news on the new situation in Europe—rejected allegiance to the Council of Regency and set up their own *junta* with direct allegiance to Ferdinand VII. The following year, they declared full independence as a Republic.[7] The movement spread to other areas in the vice-royalty of New Granada (modern day Colombia and Ecuador). The drawn out process of independence was under way. This first Republican authority was short-lived. Spanish forces re-asserted their control in Venezuela with reason-

---

[4] For general overviews on Independence, see L. Bethell (ed.), *The Independence of Latin America* (Cambridge History of Latin America 3; Cambridge: Cambridge University Press, 1987 [1985]); J. Lynch, *The Spanish American Revolutions 1808–1826* (New York and London: W. W. Norton, 2nd ed., 1986 [1973]); J. I. Domínguez, *Insurrection or Loyalty: The Breakdown of the Spanish American Empire* (Cambridge, Mass.: Harvard University Press, 1980).

[5] Ferdinand remained in prison until French rule in Spain eventually collapsed in March 1814. He became King shortly afterwards.

[6] Bolívar came from one of most influential families in the aristocracy of planter families. On his background and life, see G. Masur, *Simón Bolívar* (Albuquerque: University of New Mexico, 1969).

[7] Venezuela had been the site of some of the earliest independence initiatives; however, the 1806 revolt led by Francisco de Miranda received little support, and a creole proposal to set up a governing council in 1808 was quashed by a spate of arrests.

able ease the following year. However, the Spanish authorities made a serious mistake in permitting Simón Bolívar—who had been a military leader for the defence of the Republic—to leave the colony.

Bolívar returned in 1813 and reentered Caracas in August to set up a Second Republic. Like its predecessor, it was short-lived. The defeat of Napoleon's forces in Spain and the restoration of the monarchy under Ferdinand VII in 1814 swung the advantage back toward Spain. Royalist forces quickly re-established Spanish control throughout New Granada. Even before this, Bolívar's forces had run into other problems. A rebellion against the Republic by José Tomás Boves forced Bolívar to move from Caracas to Bogotá in 1814, and then leave for the Caribbean in 1815. His fortune turned when he found shelter on Jamaica and was given assistance by Haiti. This allowed him to return to Venezuela in 1816, and in 1817, he set up a new Republican stronghold on the River Orinoco at the port of Angostura. On this third attempt, the tide of events finally flowed in his direction. In 1819, Bolívar won a decisive battle for control of Bogotá and central New Granada. After further campaigns, he finally established control over Venezuela in 1821 and Quito in 1822 and consolidated the territory into Gran Colombia.

Argentina, Chile, Peru, and Bolivia

Elsewhere in Latin America, the Viceroyalty of Peru had remained staunchly loyal to Spain but in May 1810 Buenos Aires followed the example of Venezuela in declaring the Viceroyalty of Río de la Plata as loyal to Ferdinand, but not to the Spanish Council of Regency.[8] The captaincy-general of Chile followed this lead in September. This decision had much stronger support in the areas of the Viceroyalty that today make up Argentina, than in the other countries. In general, Paraguay, Bolivia and Montevideo did not support moves to independence.[9] Even in the parts of the Viceroyalty where independence from Spain

---

[8] For a concise account of the progress toward independence in the Viceroyalty of the River Plate, see D. Rock, *Argentina: 1516–1987: From Spanish Colonisation to Alfonsín* (Berkeley: University of California Press, rev. ed., 1987 [1985]), pp. 79–96.

[9] In 1809, a bid for independence in La Paz had been quashed and this experience may explain Bolivia's reluctance to follow Buenos Aires. For Paraguay and Uruguay, the sense of rivalry with Buenos Aires may also have influenced the course of events. In fact, Montevideo set up its independent *junta* in opposition to Buenos Aires in 1808, but then reversed its attitude and declared allegiance to the Council of Regency. The attempts by Buenos Aires to enforce its authority on Paraguay and Montevideo resulted in their independence from Spain without allegiance to Buenos Aires, and they were both able to assert independence in their own right. Paraguay successfully defended itself against invasions from Buenos Aires in 1811, and set up its own *junta* shortly afterward. Buenos Aires finally took Montevideo in 1814, but was unable to hold it. It withdrew in 1815 and Montevideo came under Portuguese control in 1816, until finally achieving independence after the war between Brazil and Argentina, 1825–1828. Likewise, forces from Buenos Aires failed to liberate Bolivia in the campaigns of 1810 and 1813. When independence finally came to Bolivia in 1825 (through the intervention of an army from independent Peru), it was firmly separated from Buenos Aires.

had support, there were different views on what type of political structure should replace it.[10]

As in Venezuela and elsewhere, the Río de la Plata declaration was therefore a crucial first step, but well short of full independence.[11] It was not until 1816 that what is now Argentina declared full independence. In 1817, the military commander José de San Martín crossed from Argentina to Chile to assist the independence movement there.[12] On arrival, he led his "Army of the Andes" against the royalist forces sent from Peru which had re-established control over Chile in 1814. The Chilean leader Bernardo O'Higgins came to San Martín's aid, and their successes led to the capture of Santiago. O'Higgins took over the government and declared independence in February 1818, even though the final defeat of the royalists took until 1820.

After Bolívar's success at Bogotá in the north and San Martín's at Santiago in the south, the two great independence leaders started a pincer movement on Peru, Ecuador, and Bolivia. In 1820, the situation in Spain had changed yet again. The army rebelled against the king, a liberal group held power, and the king was now in opposition. The new *junta* in Spain moved to reaffirm its more liberal measures of 1812, including a noticeable anti-clericalism. The conservatives of Latin America now saw independence from Spain as a way of preserving traditional values rather than abandoning them. This ensured that when the liberators finally got to Peru, their task was much easier than it would have been previously.

When San Martín finally secured Chile in 1820, he left O'Higgins in charge and set sail with his army for Peru. He entered Lima in July 1821 and declared Peruvian independence, but much of the country remained under Spanish control for another three years. In the meantime, Bolívar was moving down into Ecuador, and San Martín helped him in the liberation of Quito in 1822. What happened next between the two great independence leaders is disputed, but the upshot was that San Martín left Latin America for Europe in September and never returned.[13] Bolívar landed at Callao (Lima's port) the following year. From here, he overcame loyalist resistance in Peru (1824) and in Bolivia (1825), which completed the liberation of Spanish territories in South America.[14]

---

[10] There was some support for creating an independent Latin American monarch, perhaps inviting a new monarch from Inca ancestry or from the royal family of another European country (see Williamson, *The Penguin History of Latin America*, p. 221).

[11] At first, the new *junta* in Buenos Aires was at least nominally loyal to Ferdinand and independence for the United Provinces of the Río de la Plata was not declared until 9 July 1816. Shortly after this, the military commander José San Martín set out across the Andes from Mendoza to Chile in 1817.

[12] On Martín's life and his role in the Independence movement, see J. C. Metford, *San Martín the Liberator* (London: Longman, 1950).

[13] Both men brought their considerable military reputations to the meeting but Bolívar came fresh from his success in Gran Colombia, whereas San Martín's progress in Peru was quite slow. This may have given Bolívar the crucial edge in their meeting.

[14] See T. E. Anna, *The Fall of Royal Government in Peru* (Lincoln: University of Nebraska Press, 1979).

Mexico and Central America

Meanwhile, a third major strand in the independence process was taking place in Mexico and Central America.[15] At the start of the nineteenth century, the Viceroyalty of New Spain was the richest of the colonies. Its vast territory stretched from Oaxaca and the Yucatan at the south of modern day Mexico, up to a line across from Northern California to Texas. Its sphere of influence extended to what are now Cuba and Costa Rica and included the Captaincies General of Cuba and Guatemala.[16] The constitutional crisis caused by Napoleon generated considerable social unrest and peasant uprisings in Mexico after 1810, but the Spanish authorities resisted moves toward independence.

After the restoration of Ferdinand in 1814, it looked as if Spanish power might survive. However, when the army in Spain mutinied at Cadiz in 1820, the aura surrounding the authority of the Spanish crown evaporated and conditions arose for independence initiatives from the Mexican creole elite. In February 1821, the former royalist commander Iturbide put forward the Plan of Iguala based on "religion, independence, and union." This made independence attractive or at least tolerable to all the key political forces in Mexico and Central America. Strong public support followed. On 13 September 1821, Spanish royalist forces finally surrendered, three hundred years after Aztec Emperor Cuauhtemoc surrendered to Cortés. The original compromise plan had been to invite a member of the Spanish ruling dynasty to assume the title of Emperor for independent Mexico. When none would accept, Iturbide—with backing from the army—was made Emperor in May 1822. His brief reign was not a success; he was forced to abdicate and go into exile in March 1823. When he attempted to return in 1824 he was executed. But there was no going back on the independence he had brought.

The progress of independence in Central America closely followed Mexico. Guatemala declared independence on 15 September, to be followed by El Salvador, Nicaragua, and Honduras.[17] After regional jostling on the post-independence political order, the Central American provinces created their own provisional *junta* independent of Mexico on 1 July 1823. In 1824, they

---

[15] See T. E. Anna, *The Fall of Royal Government in Mexico City* (Lincoln: University of Nebraska Press, 1978).

[16] The Captaincy General of Cuba covered the Spanish Caribbean (Cuba and Puerto Rico) as well as Florida. The Captaincy General of Guatemala covered Chiapas (in modern Mexico), Guatemala, El Salvador, Honduras, and Nicaragua (which included Costa Rica). Modern day Panama was part of New Granada.

[17] Chiapas had already committed itself to the Plan of Iguala in August 1821. This meant that after independence, it would be linked to Mexico rather than Central America. Despite the declarations of independence in Guatemala and El Salvador, a serious division quickly emerged between Guatemalan and Salvadoran leaders. The Guatemalans wished to be incorporated into the Mexican Empire but the Salvadorans were opposed to this. Initially Guatemala got its way, and the entire kingdom was united with Mexico on 9 January 1822. A Mexican force was despatched to El Salvador to enforce this but when Iturbide's abdicated in 1823 only Chiapas stayed loyal to Mexico.

became the Federal Republic of Central America. However, the Federal Republic was short-lived, and in July 1838, Central America divided into nation states.

Cuba

The one exception to the general course of events in Spanish America was Cuba. Spanish colonialism had arrived in the Caribbean first and would remain there the longest, despite the interruption imposed by the British capture of Havana in 1762 during the Seven Years war.[18] After the 1793, revolution in Saint Domingue, colonial Cuba had received many of sugar plantation owners and Cuba's own sugar had developed rapidly. It soon had a prosperous export economy based on the backbreaking work of its slave labour force. This sudden prosperity—and the reports of violence in Haiti—was one reason that Cuba's creole elite did not join the independence movement that swept the rest of Spanish America in the first quarter of the nineteenth century. As Spain's largest possession in the Caribbean and the base for Spanish administration there, Cuba remained loyal, and Puerto Rico followed its example. It was not until 1868 that a serious Cuban independence movement initiated an unsuccessful ten-year war with Spain.[19] Some years later, the same urge resurfaced for nationhood and the poet José Marti gave it voice and led a second uprising in 1895. However, Marti died early in the struggle and progress was slow until 1898 when the USS Maine blew up in mysterious circumstances in Havana harbour and the U.S. government was quick to blame Spain. Public outcry in the United States, the legacy of the Monroe Doctrine, influential business interests, and the opportunity for strategic gains for the military, all combined together to demand direct intervention by the U.S. against Spain and resulted in the Spanish-American War of 1895–1898. Spain's defeat meant the loss of Cuba, Puerto Rico, and the Philippines. Cuba's hope of real independence was frustrated. The United States replaced Spain as the power overseeing each country. This was a critical turning point in the neo-colonial designs of the U.S. on the Caribbean and Latin America. It heralded a new era of expansionist U.S. intervention and control in the region as the newly dominant foreign power for the new twentieth century.

Brazil

Brazil followed a slightly different course.[20] The Portuguese court moved to Brazil under João VI during the Napoleonic wars and this prevented any major independence movement during the period 1808–1821. João VI gained further

---

[18] The British returned Cuba to the Spanish at the conclusion of the war.

[19] In the 1840s, some plantation owners recommended annexation to the U.S. but nothing came of it.

[20] For a number of views on the gradual process of transition see, A. J. R. Russell-Wood (ed.), *From Colony to Nation: Essays on the Independence of Brazil* (Baltimore, Md.: Johns Hopkins University Press, 1975).

Brazilian loyalty when he announced the equality between Brazil and Portugal and relaxed restrictions on its trade. When Napoleon was defeated in 1814, the king stayed in Brazil. Portugal was governed by a Regency Council until 1820 when influential liberals set up a new constitutional government and demanded the king's return. João was reluctant to return, but he feared that he would lose his authority in Portugal if he did not and eventually set off for Lisbon. To protect his interests in Brazil, he left his son as Regent in charge of Brazil in his absence. The following year the government in Lisbon tried to exert its authority over the Regent by recalling him. With the encouragement of many Brazilians, Dom Pedro ignored their calls. On 7 September 1822, a formal declaration of Brazilian independence was proclaimed. Dom Pedro was crowned as emperor and ruled until 1831 when he abdicated in favour of his young son. Portugal formally accepted Brazil's independence under pressure from the British in 1825. At the same time, the British negotiated a favourable trade agreement for themselves with Brazil and forced Brazil to end the slave trade.[21]

Neo-colonialism

The independence movement took a heavy toll on the Latin American economy. Civil conflicts stalled agricultural and mining production, and widespread unemployment followed. In many places, the economy did not start to recover until the after the 1850s.

In their respective countries, the creole elite had been the main driving force for political independence, and they were the main beneficiaries in the era that followed. They wanted most of all to trade with Britain and other European nations. After independence, their privileged social positions made them reluctant to change much else and address the social gulf that separated the privileged

---

[21] Britain—and especially the ports of Bristol and Liverpool—gained much from the slave trade in the seventeenth and eighteenth centuries. However, by the beginning of the nineteenth century, slave-based economies no longer served Britain's long-term economic interests. Under pressure from moral reformers in parliament, such as William Wilberforce, Britain abolished its involvement in the trade in 1807 and slavery as an institution was abolished in the British Caribbean dominions in 1833. Furthermore, after 1814, Britain started to use its political influence with other countries to prevent their involvement in the trade as well. In most of Spanish-speaking Latin America, slavery was abolished at Independence but it survived for much longer in Brazil. It was not till the 1840s that Britain and France took effective measures against slave traders operating from the West African coast and finally began to bring the trade to a stop. Slavery was formally abolished in Brazil at the end of the Empire in 1888. On the extent of the slave trade, see P. Curtin, *The Atlantic Slave Trade: A Census* (Madison: University of Wisconsin Press, 1969); on the role of slavery in colonial Brazil, see G. Freyre, *The Masters and the Slaves: A Study in the Development of Brazilian Civilisation* (trans. S. Putnam; New York: Alfred Knopf; 1963); on its abolition in Brazil, see L. Bethell, *The Abolition of the Brazilian Slave Trade: Britain, Brazil and the Slave Trade Question, 1807–1869* (Cambridge: Cambridge University Press, 1970); R. Conrad, *The Destruction of Brazilian Slavery, 1850–1888* (Berkeley: University of California Press, 1973).

from the impoverished. Colonial rule was replaced by creole regimes committed to maintaining the law and order necessary to allow business to flourish. Economic and social inequalities continued, but now the creoles were at the head of the social pyramid. For the vast majority of people, one set of masters simply replaced another. Political colonialism had ended, but economic neo-colonialism continued to extract vast wealth from the continent to the benefit of a few. Europe—especially Britain—and the United States continued to dominate the economic life of Latin America. But British and North American political involvement was more subtle.

In 1823—when the turmoil of the Independence movement seemed to invite interference from other European powers into the area—the President of the United States, James Monroe, declared what became known as the "Monroe Declaration." This proclaimed that America should be for the Americans and warned European powers not to interfere in its affairs. On the surface, this was an anti-colonialist statement of the hemisphere's hopes for autonomy from colonial powers.

In the early nineteenth century it would have been hard for the U.S. to enforce its policy if seriously challenged, but luckily, British policy on Latin America largely coincided with the Monroe Doctrine. The British maintained direct rule over their colonies in the Caribbean, which included Jamaica (1655–1962), Trinidad (1797–1966), and a host of smaller islands.[22] However, despite some half-hearted attempts, the British did not need to establish new direct governments on the mainland to serve their economic interests.[23]

One exception to this general rule was the Caribbean coast of Central America and what is now Guyana, where there was a longstanding British influence dating back to the seventeenth century.[24] Apart from this, the finan-

---

[22] Smaller British colonial Caribbean territories included: the Bahamas, Barbados, Dominica, Grenada, St. Lucia, St. Vincent, the Grenadines, Antigua, St. Kitts, Nevis, and the thirty-six British Virgin Islands.

[23] During the Napoleonic wars, the British made two attempts (June 1806 and February 1807) to seize Buenos Aires with the desire to replace Spain as the colonial power, but were repulsed on both occasions. In both cases, it was the local inhabitants rather than the Spanish colonial authorities that defended the city. The self-reliance of the citizens (and the obvious inadequacies of the authorities) contributed to the growing current that favoured independence.

[24] This was especially true of the area from Nicaragua through Honduras and up to modern-day Belize. After a decisive naval victory in the Caribbean against the Spanish in 1798, Britain was able to increase its influence on the area (largely unimpeded) and proclaimed it a British protectorate. In the nineteenth century, the British established Belize as a formal British colony known as "British Honduras." The Spanish had taken little interest in the area, and in the seventeenth century the long coral reef along Belize's coast made it attractive to pirates who wished to evade the authorities. In 1670, the Spanish struck a deal with the British to prevent piracy, and the pirates began to settle on the coast as traders instead. In 1862 (when the U.S. was occupied with its Civil War and unable to even attempt to enforce the Monroe Doctrine) the British seized the opportunity to formalise their presence. British Honduras became a formal British

cial and political interests of the British and the creole elites were of sufficient mutual benefit to encourage economic trade without direct political rule.[25] This characterised Latin American economies throughout the nineteenth century. To begin with, the British were content to concentrate on trade.

After 1870, direct investment into the economy started to increase. From 1870 until 1913, British investment went from 85 million pounds to 757 million.[26] Neo-colonial investment in Latin America and the repatriation of profits back to Britain was a new stage in the exploitation of the continent. However, although British influence in Latin America grew steadily in the nineteenth century, what was of even greater significance for the future of Latin America was the expansion of the United States. In the nineteenth century, the English-speaking colonies on the eastern seaboard of North America managed an astonishing growth westward to occupy most of the vast territory that constitutes the United States today.[27] In the early eighteenth century the French started to settle the huge province of Louisiana (east of the Mississippi and west of the Rockies), which had previously been claimed by the Spanish along with Florida under the Captaincy General of Cuba.[28] During the Napoleonic Wars,

---

colony attached to Jamaica and in 1884 the country became a crown colony in its own right. It was renamed Belize in 1973 and finally gained independence in 1981 although a British protection force remained because it was not until 1992 that Guatemala finally withdrew its claims to the territory and recognised Belize's right to exist.

British settlers started to arrive along the coast of what is now Guyana in the seventeenth century when the Dutch already controlled the area. In 1667 Britain formally ceded its claim over the area to the Dutch in exchange for New Amsterdam in North America (which they renamed New York). However, during the Napoleonic wars Britain seized the area from the Dutch and a boundary was later agreed between British Guiana in the west and Dutch Guiana in the east. British Guiana did not gain independence until 1965 and Dutch Guiana (now Suriname) unitl 1975. To the west of Dutch Guiana, French Guiana was one of France's oldest possessions overseas. French settlement dated back to the early seventeenth century. Today it is the only Latin American country to remain without independence. It was captured by the British in 1809 but restored to France a few years later.

[25] The turmoil that Bolívar witnessed in New Granada seems to have shaken his Republican confidence in the viability of democracy in Latin America. He felt that a less democratic British style constitution (which might include a constitutional monarchy) might be more realistic for Latin America and that Latin American might benefit from British protection when finally free from Spain.

[26] See T. E. Skidmore and P. H. Smith, *Modern Latin America* (Oxford: Oxford University Press, 4th edn, 1997 [1984]), p. 43. For detailed treatments on different countries, see also R. Graham, *Britain and the Onset of Modernization in Brazil, 1850–1914* (Cambridge: Cambridge University Press, 1968); H. S. Ferns, *Britain and Argentina in the Nineteenth Century* (Oxford: Clarendon Press, 1960); H. Blakemore, *British Nitrates and Chilean Politics, 1886–1896: Balmaceda and Lord North* (London: Athlone Press, 1974).

[27] Hawaii and Alaska were later additions.

[28] Colonial influence over North America at this time was divided between the British (on the eastern seaboard of present-day United States), the French in the north (based around Montreal in present-day eastern Canada, and stretching south in a vast arc to

Thomas Jefferson purchased the French controlled area west of Mississippi in 1803 for $15 million. This included the city of New Orleans and all the land between the Mississippi River and the Rocky Mountains. A few years later, the War of 1812 prompted the U.S. to invade Florida, and Spain surrendered it to the U.S. in 1819. In the eighteenth century, Texas and the modern south-western United States (which were then known as New California and New Mexico) were formally Spanish, but there was little to stop U.S. settlers from moving into them. After independence they were part of Mexico, but Texas rebelled and seceded in 1837. U.S. belief in its Manifest Destiny to expand its territory westward led to the admission of Texas as a U.S. state in 1845. After the Mexican-American War 1846–1848 the United States acquired California and the rest of its current Southwest Territory in 1848 (Arizona, New Mexico, Colorado, Nevada, Utah, and Wyoming) under the Treaty of Guadalupe Hidalgo.[29] Thus by the mid-nineteenth century the United States had become a territorial giant that stretched from the Atlantic to the Pacific. Furthermore, the U.S. invasion of northern Mexico and occupation of Mexico City in 1847 confirmed the feeling in the United States that they could (and should) inter-vene directly into the affairs of their southern neighbours when it served their interests.

By the beginning of the twentieth century, U.S. politicians were ready and willing to displace Britain as the neo-colonial power and main economic influence throughout Latin America. They were also much more willing than Britain—or perhaps simply more able—to back up this influence with military force. The

---

the west of British colonies down through Louisiana to New Orleans and the Gulf of Mexico), and the Spanish in the Southwest and Florida. The Caribbean was divided between the British, French, Spanish, and Dutch. From the end of the seventeenth cen-tury and for much of the eighteenth century, Britain and France fought a sequence of wars as they competed to extend control over North America and the Caribbean. These culminated in 1756–1763 with the Seven Years War that also spread to Europe and India. During the war, the British captured Havana from the Spanish (1762) and their eventual victory over France was recognised in the Treaty of Paris (1763) which ceded French land east of the Mississippi to Britain. In addition, the British had captured both Canada and the Caribbean island of Guadeloupe during the war and were only willing to return one. The French were more concerned for their valuable plantations than the sparsely populated and snowy Canada, and so this vast territory became British. The French had secretly granted their territory west of the Mississippi (and the city of New Orleans itself) to Spain by an agreement the previous year, so the treaty also enacted Britain's return of Cuba to Spain in exchange for Florida. However, Spain managed to reclaim Florida in 1783 when the English-speaking colonialists on the eastern seaboard won independence from Britain (1776–1783). This also led to the effective return of land west of the Mississippi to France, and in 1800, Napoleon forced the Spanish to return the territory east of the Mississippi to France as well. When further war between Britain and France became inevitable and left French territory vulnerable once more—and after French reverses in the Caribbean—Napoleon sold it to the U.S. as the Louisiana Purchase in 1803.

[29] This effectively halved the size of Mexico in return for just $15 million.

Monroe Doctrine (that had perhaps first been issued as an anti-colonialism declaration when the U.S. was vulnerable to aggression) became the mainstay of the neo-imperialist belief that the United States had a special right to interfere in Latin America.[30] This was especially true in the Caribbean and Central America, which were close enough to the U.S. to be regarded by North Americans as their backyard. In the last decades of the nineteenth century, U.S. corporations developed strong economic interests in Cuba (sugar) and Central America (especially United Fruit companies in Nicaragua and Honduras). Economic penetration of Latin America increased in the twentieth century.

At the close of the nineteenth century, President Theodore Roosevelt typified newly assertive attitudes of the U.S. with his "big stick" policy. The gunboat diplomacy of the U.S. helped Panama secede from Colombia in 1903 and this prepared the way for U.S. control over the Panama Canal that opened in 1914. United States Marines invaded Nicaragua in 1912, and although they withdrew temporarily in 1925, they re-invaded the following year and remained until 1933, when they finally withdrew under Franklin Roosevelt's new "Good Neighbour Policy."[31] Likewise, U.S. troops invaded Haiti in 1915 and remained stationed there until 1934. Elsewhere in Latin America, outside the Caribbean area, the U.S. was less directly interventionist in the first half of the twentieth century. However, its greater proximity and gradual rise to superpower status gave it a much closer and more active interest in the security of the continent that Britain had shown in the nineteenth century.

While these major changes were happening on the international scene in the nineteenth century, at the level of national politics, most Latin American countries witnessed a bitter struggle between conservatives and liberals. Conservatives were usually drawn from the landholding oligarchy, who saw little reason to change the traditional pattern of society. They regretted the demise of the monarchy and the values for which it stood. They were closely allied to the institutional church and the old order. The liberals, by contrast, admired the values of the European enlightenment and the example of the North American revolution.[32] They championed individual rights to property and freedom

---

[30] On the development of the Monroe Doctrine, see D. Perkins, *A History of the Monroe Doctrine* (Boston: Little Brown, 1955).

[31] In the nineteenth century, Nicaragua also suffered from the particular attention of U.S. expansionists. In 1855, the U.S. adventurer William Walker managed a successful incursion with a small group of followers and had himself elected as President for two years. During this time, he tried to enforce English as the official language and attempted to reverse the 1822 law that had outlawed slavery. The other Central American republics eventually drove him out in 1857, after he attempted to expand his control into them. However, in the next three years, he made two further unsuccessful attempts to return to power until he was captured by the British Navy and handed over to the Hondurans who executed him. For his autobiographical account of his time in Nicaragua, see W. Walker, *The War in Nicaragua* (Phoenix: University of Arizona Press, 1985 [1860]).

[32] See A. P. Whitaker (ed.), *Latin America and the Enlightenment* (Ithaca, N.Y.: Cornell University Press, 1961).

of commerce. Many also believed in individual social freedoms—of speech and thought—which led to serious tensions with the church and often erupted into full-blown anti-clericalism.

Liberal concern for freedom and individual rights should have been a positive foundation for democratic and constitutional government. However, these hopes proved hard to establish in the turbulent nineteenth century and many liberals were prepared to prioritise economic freedoms over social rights. They often settled for authoritarian government if it offered stable law and order for free commerce. Many countries were dominated by powerful *caudillo* figures who won political support through patronage and charismatic authority, rather than political manifestos. Despite many of the liberal ideals, often their policies resulted in further exploitation of Indian labour. For example, as liberals gained increasing dominance after 1850, they pushed through legislation on private property that converted Indian community lands into individual plots. This was extremely disruptive to traditional farming practices, and Indian families struggled to adapt to their new individual plots. Hacienda and plantation owners then bought many of these plots at reduced prices (or simply seized them), and put them to use growing crops for the expanding export economy. The newly landless Indians were forced to accept pitifully low wages to continue work on the new plantations, growing export crops like coffee. This further concentration in land distribution contributed to the entrenched poverty and social polarisation that marked the twentieth century.

In terms of the national economies, Latin American exports started to grow steadily (especially after the 1870s), and the increased trade drove a marked process of social development in the areas concerned. Cities and ports grew, and transport infrastructure, especially railways, facilitated the import-export trade. The British encouraged these developments, particularly through the financing and building of the railways.

However, although the economic development of export industry was significant in the areas concerned, it only had a very limited effect on Latin America's wider social problems and did little to address the situation of the rural poor. Development plans focussed on promoting the extraction of Latin America's rich resources and their export to Europe (and later the United States). In return, Latin America received imports of finished products from European and North American industries. Wealthy landowners and the commercial elite were the key beneficiaries. They maintained a close control over national politics. Furthermore, on the whole, the new nations were more concerned with their external trading links to Europe than their links with each other and this kept the continent as a whole in a weak position. Latin America's trading partners were able to dictate the terms of trade to their own advantage.[33] As a result, little was

---

[33] The trans-national sentiment that contributed to independence in many countries ebbed away and Bolívar's hopes of continental cooperation in the new era did not take hold. He particularly hoped to link Greater Colombia (Colombia, Ecuador, and Venezuela)

done to develop Latin American industry with its potential for greater economic returns in the long-term. The same basic Latin American export-economy survived into the twentieth century until the Wall Street crash of October 1929.[34]

Toward the end of the nineteenth century, the population of some countries—notably Argentina and Brazil—started to diversify as new immigrants from Europe arrived. Immigrants came particularly from Italy and Spain but also from England and Germany. The economies of both countries expanded as new skills and expertise boosted their production. This consolidated the shift of the continent's economic centre of gravity away from the Pacific Coast toward the Atlantic. This shift, which had begun in the eighteenth century, was to be particularly noticeable in the twentieth century. By the early twentieth century, Argentina had emerged as an economic world power and leader of Latin American development.

A side effect of the wave of immigration was the growth in labour organisation as the urban working class increased and workers from Europe brought socialist and anarchist ideas with them. The frequency of strikes increased, but because the immigrants were not able to vote unless they were naturalised citizens, the corporate bosses could rely on the politicians to protect their interests with few repercussions.

As in earlier periods, Brazil's political progress during the nineteenth century was separate from the other countries. The empire that had been established as politically independent from Portugal in 1822 lasted until 1889.[35] It ended when the army stepped in and deposed the Prime Minister and Emperor and established a Republic with the motto "Order and Progress."[36] During this period, Brazil's economic growth was based on coffee exports which boomed in the 1850s and 1860s. The coffee growing São Paulo region replaced the sugar growing areas of the northeast as the economic engine of the country and the political muscle that came with it.

For most Latin American countries, the nineteenth century gave way to the twentieth without major change. The First World War in Europe provided a boost to the export economies of many Latin American economies as the demand for food and minerals increased. The drain of the war on the British economy speeded the inevitable replacement of Britain by the U.S. as the regional power. On the whole, the first decades of the twentieth century saw fairly high levels of economic growth in the export economies. Europe's need to rebuild after the war and the prosperous 1920s in the United States

---

with Peru and Bolivia in a Confederation of the Andes. However, his plan never attracted support. He organised a First Assembly of American States in Panama in 1826 but little came from it. Even his hopes for a looser league of Spanish American states failed.

[34] See B. Albert, *South America and the World Economy from Independence to 1930* (London: Macmillan, 1983).

[35] See C. H. Haring, *Empire in Brazil: A New World Experiment with Monarchy* (Cambridge, Mass.: Harvard University Press, 1958).

[36] See G. Freyre, *Brazil from Monarchy to Republic* (New York: Alfred Knopf, 1970).

contributed to this further. However, as always before, the benefits were unevenly distributed. A minority got rich, but majority remained impoverished and many remained destitute. Despite the richness of its resources, Latin American economies remained dependent on foreign markets. This left them vulnerable when the boom in exports proved to be short-lived. In October 1929, the Wall Street Stock Market plummeted, and soon the world plunged into a depression that had a devastating effect on Latin American exports. A new period in the economic and social history of Latin America was about to begin.

THE CHURCH IN THE NINETEENTH CENTURY

The Church and the Independence Struggle

By the nineteenth century, the church was the largest landowner in Latin America apart from the crown. During the independence movements, the church hierarchy sided with Spain. The crown appointed all the bishops under the *patronato*, and the vast majority were *peninsulares*.[37] Their opposition to independence was firmly backed by the Vatican. Both Pius VII and Leo XII condemned independence in the clearest terms.[38] In many countries, the clergy, who were usually creole, were split on independence and reflected whatever the prevailing sentiment might be. In areas such as Peru that were generally opposed to independence, the clergy also opposed it—especially clergy from religious orders which tended to be mainly *peninsulares*.

However, even in the eighteenth century, some priests had shown sympathy for independence.[39] In Mexico and Central America, some of the most prominent leaders of independence were clergy, and independence found wider clerical support. For example, Father Delgado and thirteen other priests added their names to Guatemala's declaration of independence.

In Mexico in 1810, the Creole priest Miguel Hidalgo led an uprising of Indians and *mestizos*. He proclaimed independence in the name of Ferdinand VII and the Virgin of Guadalupe on 16 September 1810 and attracted an eager following. Hidalgo enjoyed early success and soon captured the city of Guanajuato. However, the massacre of the city's defenders presented a propaganda victory to his opponents and the tide of opinion was against him. In October, he marched on Mexico City with up to 80,000 men but after an initial setback many deserted, and he was defeated in early November. During the retreat, Hidalgo's control over his followers degenerated and chaos ensued. Despite his

---

[37] Spaniards born on the Iberian peninsular rather than *creoles* who were born (to Spanish parents) in Latin America.

[38] See Pius VII's encyclical *Etsi longissimo* (30 January 1816) and Leo XII's encyclical *Etsi iam diu* (28 September 1823).

[39] In the eighteenth-century Bourbon period, some priests were the first to call for independence. These included Peruvian Jesuit Juan Pablo Viscardo and the Mexican Friar Servando Teresa de Mier (see Williamson, *The Penguin History of Latin America*, p. 202).

attempt to regroup his forces in Guadalajara, he was again defeated in January 1811 and captured and executed in July of that year.[40]

With Hidalgo's death, leadership of the revolt then passed to another priest, José Maria Morelos. Morelos was also devoted to the Virgin but in contrast to Hidalgo, his proclamation of independence in 1813 was in explicit opposition to Ferdinand VII. Morelos kept the revolt going for a further five years but eventually he was captured in November 1815. By this time, over one hundred priests in Mexico had been killed or executed and many more excommunicated.

The independence struggles took a heavy toll on the church. A substantial amount of church property was requisitioned, and a significant number of priests who supported independence were killed. The wars left many missions in ruins, and the credibility of bishops and clergy who opposed independence was dramatically weakened. Many bishops chose to return to Spain, leaving a gap in the leadership, which was not filled for decades in some areas.

The Alliance with Conservatism and Conflict with Liberalism

After independence, the church failed to establish a viable new relationship with the state for over a century.[41] During the nineteenth century, the church remained dominated by the Christendom mentality of the bygone era in which it had taken its colonial "option for power." To maintain this after independence, it allied itself closely to conservative parties in a bid to maintain its position in society and continue to exercise the power over society it had enjoyed since the conquest. Not surprisingly, the fortunes of the institutional church rose when the conservatives were in power but often came under attack when liberals were in control. As the century progressed and liberalism gradually gained ascendancy, the church's attachment to the Christendom model meant its position got weaker and weaker.

Even when it found itself favoured, the church's institutional fate made little difference to the Latin American poor during this period. The church's priority was usually to protect its institutional interests rather than present a prophetic voice on the suffering of the disadvantaged. Although the old Christendom ideal had broken down, it continued to remain the ideal to which the vast majority within the church clung to and hoped to see restored. This failure of imagination prevented the church from finding a better way forward to confront the future.

Most of the new republics initially recognised the Catholic church as the state religion, but they abolished the Inquisition and protected some level of freedom for worship. The new republics were eager to claim for themselves the rights of the *patronato* to name the replacements of bishops, but Spain

---

[40] The date 16 September continues to be recognised and celebrated as the start of the independence movement in Mexico, despite the failures of Hidalgo's own revolt.

[41] The new relationship known as neo-Christendom that finally emerged after 1930 is discussed in Chapter 3.

pressured the Vatican not to cooperate with such appointments. As a result, many of the empty dioceses were left unfilled. It was not until Pope Gregory XVI (1831–1846), that the Vatican finally gave formal recognition to independence. This restored official relations with the new republics and the many vacancies started to be filled. By then, however, it was hard for the church to recover its previous position.

Some of the new political elite influenced by European rationalism and liberalism were inclined to anti-clericalism as a result.[42] Separation of church and state gathered speed as more liberal republics passed new constitutions in the 1850s.[43] Under pressure from the British, the new republics also passed legislation granting freedom for Protestantism, and Protestant churches sprang up in the ports and major trading areas. Although they mainly served ex-patriate British residents and attracted very few local converts, they signalled the end of Catholicism's monopoly over Christian faith in Latin America.

In Mexico, the church and liberals fought a particularly protracted conflict with longstanding consequences. Despite the role that Mexican priests played in the independence struggle, the church in Mexico remained a conservative institution that commanded enormous wealth, while so many people struggled in poverty.[44] In 1917, the new government passed the Queretaro Constitution. Alongside important social reforms this included a number of harsh anti-clerical provisions. These included prohibition of the Jesuits, expulsion of Spanish priests, confiscation of church property, and restrictions on worship. In the face of popular opposition, for nearly ten years little was done to enforce these provisions. However, when the socialist Plutarcho Calles came to power (1924–1928), the situation started to change. From 1926, anti-clerical laws were enforced with vigilance and sparked open civil conflict. *Cristeros* (followers of Christ the King), who opposed the secular government, rose in revolt. Both sides inflicted damaging attacks on each other until full-scale religious persecution ended with a mediated peace in 1929.[45] The legacy from these battles was a history of ten-

---

[42] Confiscation of church property and expulsions of mission orders took place in many countries during and after the wars of independence. This often had very disruptive social consequences. For example, the Franciscans, who had replaced the Jesuits on the Guaraní reductions, were expelled from Paraguay in 1810 and this allowed the colonists to loot the missions and disperse the Guaraní. During the post-Independence turmoil in Mexico, the Franciscans were also expelled from Texas, New Mexico, and California. This encouraged further U.S. settlement in these areas and speeded their eventual seizure by the United States.

[43] The liberal government of Colombia in 1849 took the lead in this and was followed by Argentina in 1853, and other countries during the 1850s. For a recent study of church-state relations in Argentina during this time, see A. Ivereigh, *Catholicism and Politics in Argentina* (New York: St. Martin's Press; London: Macmillan, 1995).

[44] In 1870, the Catholic church in Mexico still owned a quarter of Mexican territory. See A. Rhodes, *The Vatican in the Age of Dictators, 1922–1945* (London: Hodder & Stoughton, 1973), p. 95.

[45] The peace left the laws unchanged, but reached an agreement over less vigorous

sion between an anti-clerical government and anti-socialist church that remains a powerful division in Mexican society. In Mexico, after the *Cristero* movement, the first president to renew the invitation to church dignitaries to his inauguration was Carlos Salinas de Gortari in 1988.

The problems facing the church in Latin America during the nineteenth century were reinforced by difficulties of the church in Europe. In the aftermath of the French Revolution, Catholicism in Europe had struggled unsuccessfully to oppose the onset of modernity and progress just as it had previously opposed the Protestant Reformation.[46] Science and new ideas were deeply distrusted during the nineteenth century. Even the idea of democracy received condemnation. During this time, the influence of the Catholic church in Europe was politically conservative and heavily favoured the values of the old regime.[47] The rise of Italian nationalism and the loss of the Papal States in the nineteenth century marked the end of old-style Christendom as a political force in Europe.[48] However, it lived on as an ideal to which the church clung, and the church retreated into an increasingly defensive mentality. Pius IX (1846–1878) issued the Syllabus of Errors in 1864 that condemned progress, liberalism, and the modern world—along with socialism—as vigorously as possible. Vatican I in 1870 reiterated this hostility.

The Start of a Social Tradition

On social issues, the nineteenth-century church hierarchy invariably supported the *status quo* against potential uprisings or even modest reforms.[49] It was not

---

enforcement. Most *Cristeros* reluctantly agreed to this, but some continued the struggle for a further decade.

[46] For Catholicism's hostile response to modernity and progress in the nineteenth century, and the persistence of its animosity up to Vatican II (1962–1965), see B. McSweeney, *Roman Catholicism*, pp. 22–134.

[47] Pius IX had initially appeared more liberal, but the upheaval in Europe of 1848 and its anti-clerical character transformed him into an archconservative.

[48] The Papal States in central Italy (an area approximately twice the size of Wales) was first granted to Pope Stephen II in 754 CE by the king of the Franks, and later additions enlarged it further. The loss of the states to the Italian King, Victor Emmanuel II (1861–1878), began in the 1860s and completed with the occupation of Rome in September 1870. See A. Rhodes, *The Vatican in the Age of Liberal Democracies, 1870–1922* (London: Sidgwick & Jackson 1983), pp. 15–26.

[49] Despite the conservative nature of the established church, religious faith could still provide inspiration to individuals for dramatic social protests. The Canudos uprising in Bahía (1893–1897) was a particularly violent and tragic instance of this. A Catholic visionary, known as Antônio the Counsellor, led over 30,000 people against the Brazilian Republic. The movement held out for four years until the army suppressed it with a series of savage onslaughts—see R. M. Levine, *Vale of Tears: Revisiting the Canudos Massacre in Northeastern Brazil, 1893–1897* (Berkeley: University of California Press, 1992); E. Da Cunha, *Rebellion in the Backlands* (trans. S. Putnam; London: Picador, 1992 [1957]). Likewise, in 1911, a visionary known as José Maria led a movement in the south of Brazil to restore the monarchy. It lasted until 1915 when the Republican army finally quashed it (see Williamson, *The Penguin History of Latin America*, p. 412).

until Leo XIII (1878–1903) that important new developments in the church's attitude to wider society began.[50] One of the most important features in this was that progress toward a Catholic tradition on social matters started to be made. This was extremely important, because any new development in Catholicism would have to be based on an authoritative tradition of past declarations. Although the start of social tradition in the nineteenth century was a very modest beginning, it was an essential first step toward the strong stand for justice taken by progressives in the Latin American church in the 1960s.

Leo's social encyclical *Rerum Novarum* (Of New Matters), issued in 1891, set an important new precedent in speaking directly to social issues.[51] The encyclical's title *On the Condition of Labour* indicated its social and economic orientation, and it is recognised as the start of formal Catholic social teaching.[52] Prior to this point, the church had commented on social issues and judged them by moral standards, but it had not attempted to systematise its teaching in a serious way. In *Rerum Novarum* Leo broke new ground in addressing social and economic issues that related to work and labour. The encyclical expressed concern for "the misery and wretchedness which press so heavily at this moment on the large majority of the very poor" (§ 2).

Leo's primary concern was Europe and the social conditions of European workers. He had little awareness of Latin America and the exploitative conditions under which its peasants laboured. However, the condemnation of various industrial work patterns as little better than slavery was significant for Latin America.[53] In many Latin American countries the near feudal agricultural patterns inherited from the time of conquest resulted in labour practices as coercive and brutal as slavery.

The encyclical was motivated by the rise of socialism and maintained a consistent line of condemnation for what it saw as socialist teachings.[54] At the same

---

[50] On the policies of Pius IX's successors, Leo XIII (1878–1903), Pius X (1903–1914), and Benedict XV (1914–1922), see A. Rhodes, *The Vatican in the Age of Liberal Democracies*.

[51] *Rerum Novarum: On the Condition of Labour* (15 May 1891). Catholic encyclicals are usually known by the first two or three words of the Latin in which they are written.

[52] The major documents of this teaching are gathered together in D. J. O'Brien and T. A. Shannon (eds.), *Catholic Social Thought: The Documentary Heritage* (Maryknoll, N.Y.: Orbis Books, 1998). For analysis and interpretation of this tradition, see J. A. Coleman (ed.), *One Hundred Years of Catholic Social Thought: Celebration and Challenge* (Maryknoll, N.Y.: Orbis Books, 1991); D. Dorr, *Option for the Poor* (Dublin: Gill & Macmillan, rev. ed., 1992); P. Vallely (ed.), *The New Politics: Catholic Social Teaching for the Twenty-First Century* (London: SCM Press, 1998).

[53] ". . . workers have been given over, isolated and defenceless, to the callousness of employers and the greed of unrestrained competition . . . so that a small number of the very rich have been able to lay upon the masses of the poor a yoke little better than slavery itself" (*Rerum Novarum*, § 2).

[54] Criticisms of socialism are spread throughout the document, but there is little detailed engagement with socialist thought or reference to textual sources. The driving force behind socialism is presented simplistically as sedition (§ 1) or envy (§ 2). A the-

time it criticised the unfettered free-market and the abuses of capitalism. The encyclical sought a path between unbridled free-market and authoritarian social-ism that was guided by the "common good." It was not a balanced critique; socialism was attacked on the basis of its allegedly real objectives, while the criticism of the free-market was limited to obvious abuses. Nonetheless, the crit-icisms of the free-market were still very powerful. It argued that private prop-erty was a natural right and the first thing that must be safeguarded (§§ 5, 19, and 30). However, it also confirmed the justice of a living wage, that is, enough to support the wage earner in "reasonable and frugal comfort" (§ 34). When wages were below this level, it condemned the situation as an injustice based on violence.[55]

In addition to the just wage, *Rerum Novarum* set out other responsibilities that an employer has to an employee (§§ 15–17, 31–34). The encyclical recog-nised the existence of class differences but rejected the idea that class struggle is a natural consequence (§ 15). Leo called for cooperation rather than conflict to settle disputes and praised the role of Christianity in preventing strife. He gave special emphasis to the dignity of labour and the moral values that it should be founded upon (§ 20). Leo's vision was that Catholics would engage with the modern world, not on its own terms, but from a distinctly Catholic standpoint. This was typified in his recommendation that that the workers' association of previous times (such as trade guilds) should be revitalised to play a valuable role in the new environment (§§ 36–43). He hoped that these would be polit-ically centrist (§ 40) and follow the Church's teaching obediently (§ 42).

Previously, the church had provided charitable services and encouraged indi-vidual charity, but it had done little more to address social justice. *Rerum Novarum* provided the first clear principles for the church to move beyond this and address social justice. It established the importance of the common good and introduced distributive justice into Catholic social teaching. These princi-ples become central to the Catholic social tradition and have influenced lib-eration theology. An equally important contribution, though one that seems to have hardly been recognised, is that *Rerum Novarum* provided the first clear Catholic endorsement of an "option for the poor"—the principle on which

---

ological objection to its utopian vision is stated in terms of sin and the Fall: "hardships of life will have no end or cessation on this earth; for the consequences of sin are bit-ter and hard to bear, and they must be with man as long as life lasts. To suffer and to endure, therefore, is the lot of humanity, let men try as they may, no strength and no artifice will ever succeed in banishing from human life the troubles which beset it. If any there are who pretend differently—who hold out to a hard-pressed people freedom from pain and trouble, undisturbed repose, and constant enjoyment—they cheat the peo-ple and impose upon them, and their lying promises will only make the evil worse than before. There is nothing more useful than to look at the world as it really is—and at the same look elsewhere for a remedy to its troubles" (§ 14).

[55] "If through necessity or fear of a worse evil, the workman accepts harder condi-tions because an employer or contractor will give him no better, he is a victim of force and injustice" (§ 34).

liberation theology rests—even though it is not explicitly named as such. Leo expressed it as follows:

> . . . the poor and helpless, have a claim to special consideration. The richer population have many ways of protecting themselves, and stand less in need of help from the State; those who are badly off have no resources of their own to fall back upon, and must chiefly rely upon the assistance of the State . . . [and] should be specially cared for and protected by the commonwealth (§ 29).

This "option for the poor" was not so much an option *taken* by the church as an option *advocated* by the church and to be taken by the civil authorities. Nonetheless, it pointed to the principle of preferential treatment for the poor on which liberation theology successfully built a new political understanding in the late 1960s, and a new epistemological understanding in the late 1970s.

The novelty of Leo's approach was significant but limited. *Rerum Novarum* allowed for greater social involvement, but it placed strict limits on what was permissible. It encouraged Catholics to engage with the wider world but only on the terms set by the church. In terms of the church's relations with the modern world it allowed the church to move from defence to counterattack but it left the fundamental assumptions of hostility unchanged. The basic assumption that the church and the modern world were enemies remained dominant until the 1960s and Vatican II. Nonetheless, the encyclical began to lay the foundations that contributed toward a new relationship between church and state.

The emergence of this relationship took time. The Vatican did not come to terms with the end of the old Christendom until after the first decades of the twentieth century. In fact, Leo had followed his predecessor into self-imposed exile in the Vatican. In 1871, when the Italian government seized the Papal States, Pius IX retired to the Vatican as a self-imposed prisoner. His successors followed his example until 1929, when the Lateran Treaty finally ended this hostile stand-off after nearly sixty years. Under the treaty, the Italian state gave up its claims to Vatican territory in Rome, and the Vatican City became a sovereign state. In return the Vatican gave up its claims to the Papal States and received financial compensation for them. In addition, a concordat was agreed that recognised Catholicism as the state religion of Italy.[56] The Pope remained a sovereign and retained notional temporal power within the tiny city-state of the Vatican but beyond the city walls, it was the end of old style Christendom. On the positive side, the church in Europe and elsewhere could now engage with the wider world on a new basis.

---

[56] See A. Rhodes, *The Vatican in the Age of the Dictators*, pp. 37–53 (esp. p. 45).

CONCLUSION

The failure to generate a more equitable social structure, a political democracy and a diversified economy in the nineteenth century was the great missed opportunity for Latin America. The creole elite benefited from the successes of the Independence movement—and replaced the *peninsulares* at the top of the social pyramid—but class divisions went unhealed, and national economies remained weak and dependant. Latin America's historical patterns of agro-export production continued largely undisturbed until the Depression in 1929 exposed the fatal dependency of Latin America on foreign powers. In the nineteenth century, Britain displaced Spain as the dominant economic power and in turn was displaced from this role in the twentieth century by the United States. The neo-colonial pattern of investment and trade that Britain and the U.S. promoted brought technological gains and financial benefits to the new elites. However, it betrayed the majority of Latin Americans to underdevelopment and poverty while the church offered little by way of protection and nothing by way of protest. For most of this era, the Catholic Church in Latin America was struggling to hold on to a bygone era of political power and committed itself to alliances with conservative political parties. It was not until toward the end of the nineteenth century, that a new self-understanding in the church started to gain ground. The Lateran Treaty of 1929 signalled the Vatican's reluctant acceptance of the passing of old Christendom. Like the Wall Street crash the same year, the Lateran Treaty marked the transition from one era to another. The way was clear for a new vision of the relationship between church and society—neo-Christendom—to rise to prominence in the 1930s.

CHAPTER THREE

From Depression to Development, 1930–1959

> It is the duty of rulers to protect the community and its various parts, but in protecting the rights of individuals they must have special regard for the infirm and needy.
>
> Pius XI, *Quadragesimo Anno*, § 25.

INTRODUCTION

The Wall Street stock market crash of October 1929 and the Great Depression that followed, marked a decisive turning point in the history of Latin America. During the middle decades of the twentieth century, Latin American countries faced the transition from pre-modern to modern economies. In the period 1930–1959 the more advanced Latin American economies underwent major political and economic modernization. The most powerful regional economies such as Argentina and especially Brazil were relatively successful and consolidated their continental leadership. Poorer economies such as Peru, Bolivia, and most of Central America showed less progress. However, even though this period marked the start of significant industrialization and economic growth in Latin America, the social disparities between rich and poor remained as wide as ever. Furthermore, the growth of urbanization and internal migration from countryside to city loosened the church's authority and contributed new social problems that the church was slow to address.

As Latin American societies shifted from pre-modern to modern, the Catholic church shifted from a Christendom to a neo-Christendom vision of its place in society. After the Lateran Treaty of 1929, church leaders abandoned hopes of direct influence over political matters and readjusted to a new social role in which they exerted political authority indirectly through the secular activities of the laity guided by the church's social principles and moral guidance. To make this more effective, greater emphasis had to be given to developing and applying the Catholic social tradition through "Catholic Action." Furthermore, far-sighted church leaders also began to explore pastoral changes and institutional reforms that would strengthen the church's voice in society. This would prove an important foundation for liberation theology but at the time the needs of the poor were not of paramount concern. The church's primary interest was in protecting its institutional privileges now that it was in a situation where it no longer had direct political power. It was not until the end of the period that the Cuban Revolution jolted the church out of its complacency on social issues and more radical pastoral options started to develop.

MODERNIZATION AND SOCIAL CHANGES

The Great Depression in the 1930s dealt a severe blow to world trade and particularly affected Latin America's export of primary goods which had sustained its Latin American economies since colonial times. Because Latin American countries were so dependent on what happened in richer countries, they had little control on what happened to their own economies. The demand for Brazil's coffee and sugar, Bolivia and Chile's metals, and Argentina's beef fell abruptly. In turn, this restricted the imports of finished goods from industrialised countries. In the short-term, the economic hardships had to be borne as best as national economies were able. For the long-term, however, there was potentially a more positive side. The depression highlighted the continuing vulnerability of Latin America's import-export model on world events and suggested that it needed to be rethought.

Steps toward Industrialisation

Some of the more advanced Latin American countries had already developed a light industrial base in the late nineteenth century (especially Argentina, Brazil, and Mexico) and they took the lead in nationalist drives to modify the traditional import-export model. Typically, this involved replacing imported foreign goods with home produced commodities, and thereby boosting industrial manufacturing. Brazil was in particular need of a new economic strategy. In most Latin American countries, exports had been healthy during and after the First World War. Brazil's coffee exports had faced increasing competition since the First World War and could no longer be relied on to support the economy. The Depression compounded the already difficult situation.

The Second World War pushed this shift forward as matter of urgency and necessity. The war encouraged demand for Latin America's exports but severely disrupted its imports. Other Latin American countries had to follow the lead of the leading regional economies and develop import substitution policies (ISI). For political reasons the United States was willing to provide assistance in return for Latin American support for the Allied war effort. In exchange for support to the Allied cause, the U.S. offered technical and financial assistance for the new ISI industries. What began as nationalist policies, became closely identified with growing U.S. involvement in the region. Brazil was able to take particular advantage of this and its economy benefited accordingly.[1] The ISI initiative in Brazil coincided with the industrialisation drive of the *Estado Nôvo* (New State) announced by President Vargas in 1938. By the late 1950s, Brazil had the strongest economic base in the region and was poised to establish a new sense of continental leadership in the 1960s.

The first stage of ISI also seemed reasonably successful in other countries. The buoyant demand for exports during the war and post-war reconstruction provided the necessary influx of money for investment and industrialisation. The manufacturing industry then provided jobs and generated economic growth. The overall effect on the economy was still relatively modest, but nonetheless in the 1940s and 1950s, many Latin American countries showed significant growth in their manufacturing industries. The underlying political and economic problems with the ISI would not come to a head until the 1960s.

Migration, Urbanization, and Populism

In the meantime, the expansion of industry was changing the social landscape. The economic opportunities in the urban centres of industry stimulated large-scale migration and urbanization of industrial areas. Modern Latin American cities started to grow at rapid rates. Urban migration disrupted many long-standing rural patterns of social cohesion and control. The newly arrived city dwellers were much freer from traditional authorities than they had been in the countryside. Overall, many would doubtless have welcomed this as a positive change and showed little inclination to reinvent the more conservative aspects of church or patronal authority from the countryside. However, one of the prices of city life was the more impersonal social climate. Uprooted from the past and living in rapidly evolving cities, many migrants faced questions of identity and meaning in new ways.

The growing urban worker force also had political consequences. The industrialised working classes constituted a new political constituency that had much better opportunities to influence national politics than the rural peasants ever had. Their political support was a crucial factor in the populist political movements of the period. Strong leadership by charismatic personalities—rooted in the *caudillo* tradition of the previous century and the heritage of the conquistador before that—often found a strong support base amongst the urban workers. This allowed populist leaders to harness the workers' votes to their political causes and hold together political coalitions across class lines. For example, Getúlio Vargas, who dominated politics in Brazil during the period (as president in 1930–1945 and again in 1950–1954), headed a movement characterised by cross-class populism.[2]

---

[1] Argentina's sympathy for the Axis powers cost it U.S. support and it lost a vital competitive edge against Brazil. This was to prove a critical point in Argentina's evolution from having one of the leading world economies in the early twentieth century to the economic difficulties of later decades (Rock, *Argentina 1516–1987*, pp. 214–261).

[2] See T. Skidmore, *Politics in Brazil, 1930–1964: An Experiment in Democracy* (New

Vargas's first period of power began in 1930. Brazil's March 1930 elections had been bitterly contested. Eventually the Brazilian military invited Vargas to assume the presidency despite the fact that he had been defeated in the election itself. Vargas then transformed his provisional appointment into a sustained period of power. He suspended the presidential election of 1938 and announced the start of an authoritarian *Estado Nôvo* (New State). The New State was committed to industrialisation and Vargas's nationalism played an important role in this. The substantial aid from the United States gave an immense boost to the industrialisation programme and drew the military into a close alliance with their northern counterparts in the U.S.[3]

Vargas promised an election for 1943, but because of the war, he suspended it until December 1945. By this time Vargas was losing his grip on power. The United States indicated that the election must take place, and since it seemed that Vargas might try to avoid it again—and thereby jeopardise the close relationship with the U.S.—the Brazilian military forced him to resign in October 1945. The elections were then duly held and General Eurico Gaspar Dutra was elected to power (1946–1950). However, Vargas was able to bide his time and came back to win the 1950 election and govern again from January 1951 to August 1954. During this period, the economy grew significantly, but was marked by rising inflation and debt as Vargas struggled to pay for the industrialisation programme. By 1954, Vargas was again under pressure from the military to resign, and he committed suicide on 24 August 1954.

Despite the rising economic difficulties, Juscelino Kubitschek—who won the October 1955 election and governed from 1956 to 1960—continued with many of Vargas's policies and pressed on with a very ambitious development programme. As a centrepiece for this work, he built the futuristic new capital Brasília in the previously sparsely inhabited state of Goiás to stimulate the development of the interior. Brasília was an extraordinary international symbol of Latin America's development and captured the ambiguities of Latin America's development process. The ultra-modern city contrasted with areas of Brazil that remained so backward, they had hardly progressed from the colonial period. Furthermore, the cost of Brasília and other projects only worsened the underlying economic problems that Brazil faced. These problems were exacerbated by a fall in the world price for coffee in the late 1950s.

Class divisions always meant that coalitions around populist figures were fragile.[4] When such regimes faced economic adversity, they usually fell back on

---

York: Oxford University Press, 1967). For a biography of Vargas, see R. Bourne, *Getúlio Vargas: Sphinx of the Pampas* (London: Charles Knight, 1974).

[3] Despite the fascist aspects of his movement Vargas managed to develop a close military and economic alliance with the U.S. during the 1940s. A small force of Brazilian troops served in Italy alongside the Allies, and the Brazilian navy helped to patrol the south Atlantic.

[4] Juan Perón built a similar mass base amongst the workers of Buenos Aires in the 1940s known as Peronism.

extreme authoritarian measures to ensure their own survival. Because movements relied on personality rather than unified ideology, when the leadership needed to be replaced—or if it could not enforce its authority—the coalition could degenerate very rapidly, because it had always rested on personality rather than a unified ideology. This could provoke the military to step into the power vacuum to control the social unrest. The populist movements in both Argentina and Brazil eventually led to the imposition of authoritarian military regimes in the 1960s and 1970s.

From Good Neighbour to Cold War and the Cuban Revolution

For the most part, under Franklin Roosevelt's Good Neighbour Policy the United States adopted a less belligerent attitude to its southern neighbours in the 1930s and 1940s. Direct military intervention declined and even in Central America and the Caribbean—which the U.S. saw as special cases for protecting its legitimate interests—there was a switch from direct to indirect military involvement. U.S. Marines withdrew from Nicaragua in 1933 but only after training a repressive National Guard with Anastasio Somoza at its head.[5] Client dictators, such as Somoza, offered a less costly way for the United States to control events in Central America without risking U.S. troops.[6] However, as the Cold War developed in the 1950s the U.S. became more aggressive in defending what it saw as its hemispheric sphere of influence under the Monroe Doctrine.

When a new reformist government came to power in Guatemala under Jacobo Arbenz the United States was quick to protect the commercial interests of its business. Arbenz was elected President in 1950 and governed from

---

[5] Somoza's great-uncle Bernabé Somoza had been a much-feared nineteenth-century bandit who made a short-lived bid for political power in 1848.

[6] Augusto César Sandino began a nationalist movement of guerrilla resistance against the Marines in 1929 and the United States was eager to disentangle itself from the conflict. In February 1934 Somoza had Sandino killed after luring him into truce talks with the figurehead president, Juan Sacasa. Two years later, Somoza overthrew Sacasa and in January 1937, he gained the Presidency on the basis of fraudulent elections. With U.S. support Somoza was then able to establish his own dynasty in Nicaragua. Somoza's control over Nicaraguan politics and the economy allowed him to build a vast family fortune until he was assassinated in 1956. His son, Luis Somoza Debayle, immediately succeeded him in the Presidency, and then (after a brief interval when close Somocista associates had formal power) another son, Anastasio Somoza Debayle, was elected in 1967. The next twelve years of Nicaraguan history were particularly corrupt and repressive. During this time, armed opposition from the Sandino National Liberation Front (FSLN) grew and spread. The FSLN was formed in 1962 in memory of the assassinated Sandino. In 1979 they finally triumphed against Somoza's National Guard and forced Somoza to flee into exile. The socialist orientation of the Sandinista regime was an important factor in the dramatic increase in U.S. intervention in Central America in the 1980s. For a history of Nicaragua with particular reference to the Somoza dynasty (that ends just before the final offensive in 1979), see E. Crawley, *Dictators Never Die: A Portrait of Nicaragua and the Somozas* (London: C. Hurst, 1979); on the Sandinista revolution and Nicaragua in the 1980s, see J. Dunkerley, *Power in the Isthmus* (London: Verso, 1988), esp. pp. 221–333.

1951 to 1954. He had previously been a minister in the reformist government of Juan José Arévalo (1945–1950) and initially continued Arévalo's moderate reformist programme. In 1952, the administration became more radical in its proposals and started to upset the big business interests of the U.S. based company United Fruit. United Fruit had a tight grip on the Guatemalan economy and very close relations with the U.S. government.[7] The United States saw Arbenz's government as a threat to its economic interests and claimed that they were stooges for Soviet communism. As a military man, President Eisenhower was quite prepared to step into the fray. The CIA trained an invasion force of exiles in Honduras and launched its attack in June 1954. While hostile planes flew over Guatemala City and terrified the population, Arbenz attempted to organise a national defence. However, the Guatemalan military command refused to fight for him and the coup was virtually unopposed.

For the United States, this marked the beginning of successive Cold War interventions in the hemisphere. For Latin American reformers it was a painful foretaste of what was to follow in the next decade.[8] Before then, however, a further major shift in regional politics took place—the Cuban Revolution of 1959.

The Spanish-American War, which ended Spain's control of Cuba, allowed the U.S. to extend its military interests into the Caribbean. The war was notionally fought for the cause of Cuban independence, but Cuba's independence treaty was negotiated between Cuba's colonial master (Spain) and neo-colonial master (the United States) with very little concern for the Cubans themselves.[9] Cubans had little influence over what happened, and U.S. troops occupied Cuba in 1901–1903 and returned to occupy Cuba four more times between 1909 and 1921.[10] An additional legacy of the period was that U.S. companies entrenched their control of the economy—a control that had begun during the 1868–1878 war with Spain that destroyed many Cuban planters. This bound the Cuban economy ever more tightly to the United States and encouraged the feeling in the U.S. that it had a legitimate right to step in to ensure that its interests were protected whenever it saw fit.

Fulgencio Batista first came to power in Cuba in a military coup in 1933. Between 1933 and 1940 he ruled indirectly via presidential appointees, and then

---

[7] Eisenhower's Secretary of State, John Foster Dulles (1953–1959), was a militant anti-Communist and his law practice represented United Fruit. His brother Allen Welsh Dulles was head of the CIA (1953–1961) and oversaw the invasion of Guatemala and the Bay of Pigs in April 1961.

[8] In the 1960s, the U.S. supported the military coup in Brazil (1964) and intervened directly in its traditional "backyard" (Central America and the Caribbean) with an invasion of the Dominican Republic (1965). For an overview of U.S. intervention in Central America and the Caribbean, see J. Pearce, *Under the Eagle: U.S. Intervention in Central America and the Caribbean* (London: Latin America Bureau, 2nd ed., 1982 [1981]).

[9] Puerto Rico (which was also liberated during the struggle) was absorbed more permanently into the political sphere of the U.S. with the status of a freely associated territory and continues as such today.

[10] See Williamson, *The Penguin History of Latin America*, p. 440.

took direct control in 1940 only to lose an election in 1944 and be out of power for eight years. He returned in 1952 and began a second period of dictatorial rule. The following year, the young lawyer Fidel Castro led a small force of young insurgents in an attack against the Moncada barracks in Santiago. The attack failed, and Castro was captured and put on trial. On 26 July, he delivered a stirring speech in his own defence, which was partly inspired by the nineteenth-century pro-Independence Cuban poet José Marti. He attacked the injustice of the Batista regime, committed himself to its overthrow, and ended with the confident declaration "History will absolve me." He was released from prison in 1955 and left for Mexico, where he started to gather a group of nationalist sympathisers (known as the "26 July Movement" after the failed attack against the Moncada barracks).[11]

The small band of 26 July Movement cadres returned to Cuba at the end of 1956 and began their guerrilla campaign based in the mountains of the Sierra Maestra. Progress was slow, but Batista's brutal repression gave Castro a vital advantage in public sympathy for his cause. At the end of 1958, Castro's forces started to close on the capital. On 1 January 1959 Batista fled, and Castro's field-commander, Che Guevara, triumphantly led his troops into Santiago. During the rest of the year, Castro consolidated his control on the country in an increasingly authoritarian way and imposed restrictions on the press and other civil institutions. Elections were scheduled for July, but never took place. Meanwhile, Castro sought to end the control of U.S. companies over the economy. In May 1959, an agrarian law was passed that legalised the formation of cooperatives on the land of foreign-owned farms and large estates. Castro still hoped to get support for Cuba from the United States but relations between the two countries rapidly deteriorated and he was soon forced to look for help elsewhere.

Neo-Christendom

Just as the Wall Street stock market crash of 1929 marked a transition to a new period in Latin American economic policy, the Lateran Treaty of 1929 was also an important milestone for the future of the church in its relations to society. The most significant area of change for the church between 1930 and 1959 was in the area of social teaching that Leo initiated in 1891 and which helped the church in Europe and Latin America develop a new relationship to society. In general, during the years 1930–1959, there was minimal change in the doctrinal theology of the church.[12] Pius XI (1922–1939) and Pius XII (1939–1958)

---

[11] A surprisingly important recruit was the asthmatic Argentinean doctor, Ernesto "Che" Guevara. Guevara was from a professional middle-class background but became passionate over the situation of injustice throughout Latin America during a trip he had taken through much of the continent. He was present in Guatemala during the U.S.-backed coup against Arbenz the previous year, and this convinced him that peaceful reforms would never be allowed to make meaningful changes.

[12] Leo XIII encouraged a slightly more adventurous spirit in the late nineteenth century, and the backlash in the early twentieth century was partly a result of this. The

followed the course set by their predecessor Pius IX (1903–1914), and the church remained firmly set against the wider culture and profoundly suspicious of theological innovation.[13] However, by the first decades of the twentieth century the church was badly bruised by the liberal republicans in the anti-clerical battles of the nineteenth century. It was institutionally weak and seemed to have little to offer the new urbanized working class, even where it had a mind to do so. At the same time, the church was starting to lose its influence over intellectual thought. As the century progressed, secular thought gained ground at Latin American universities and influenced the younger generation. Even though it showed no signs of a change in its theology, the church needed a new basis with which to engage with society. During the 1930s, theological developments in Europe started to show how this might happen.

Jacques Maritain's work on *Integral Humanism* argued for the Christianization of culture that would be the basis for "New Christendom" or "Neo-Christendom."[14] Under the old Christendom model the church sought—and was usually granted—at least some level of direct control over political matters, but Maritain argued for a clearer distinction of planes between the temporal and spiritual. He suggested that in the new era, the church should not seek direct political control but should influence the social sphere through lay action. His thoughts had a major impact on how the church understood its mission in both Europe and Latin America. In many Latin American countries, it allowed the church to separate itself from its alliance with Conservative parties dating from the nineteenth century. The Catholic laity were to be free to join political parties, but the church would not officially endorse any particular party. The idea was for the church to influence politics through moral leadership and the work of the laity in whatever political arena they found themselves.

The church sought to exercise this moral influence on society—which it distinguished from a directly political influence—through a variety of strategies. In particular these included: updating and extending Catholic social teaching; encouraging the movement known as Catholic Action; and strengthening the church as an institutional organisation.

---

clampdown began with Pius IX's condemnation of what he called "modernism" in 1908. Similar policies continued under his successors until 1958. Until the end of Vatican II (1962–1965) all priests were required to swear an anti-modernist oath (see McSweeney, *Roman Catholicism*, pp. 80–91).

[13] On the Vatican during this time, see A. Rhodes, *The Vatican in the Age of the Dictators*. The church in Latin America—which had traditionally been marked by a conservative stamp—showed no inclination to deviate from this conservative role and simply followed the Vatican line.

[14] On the term "New Christendom," see J. Maritain, *Integral Humanism* (trans. J. E. Evans; New York: Scribner's Sons, 1968 [French orig. 1936, ET 1938]). For an excellent treatment of Maritain's thought and its influence in Latin America with reference to Chile, see W. T. Cavanaugh, *Torture and Eucharist: Theology, Politics and the Body of Christ* (Oxford: Basil Blackwell, 1998). For broader background, see B. E. Doering, *Jacques Maritain and the French Catholic Intellectuals* (Notre Dame, Ind.: University of Notre Dame Press, 1983).

Social Teaching

During the period between 1930 and 1959, the church in Latin America followed Rome's lead on social and economic matters, and the most important document of the period was Pius XI's *Quadragesimo Anno* (After Forty Years) in 1931.[15] Pius used the fortieth anniversary of Leo's *Rerum Novarum* to issue a new encyclical on social issues to encourage and guide Catholic engagement with social affairs. Pius recognised that much had changed in forty years since *Rerum Novarum*. Leo defined his thought primarily against the challenge of liberalism and the threat of socialism. Leo's encyclical needed to be restated and extended to address the new context and the issues that it raised. In 1931, the confident liberal assumption that progress was unstoppable had been severely challenged by the First World War and the Wall Street stock market crash. Meanwhile, the threat from socialism had increased politically (with the 1917 revolution in Russia) and evolved ideologically (with the thought of Lenin, Trotsky, and Stalin). Another important change was that wider society was more secular than it had been in 1891.[16] Furthermore, other powerful new social movements—especially fascism and nationalism—had arisen and presented new dangers in modern society.

The first part of *Quadragesimo Anno* was a review of *Rerum Novarum* and the events that followed it.[17] Pius recalled the context of the first encyclical and referred to the working classes as "oppressed by dire poverty" and "victims of these harsh conditions."[18] He also repeated Leo's statement that it is the poor who are most in need of public protection by the civil authorities and should be given special care.[19] He thereby repeated and affirmed the foundational element for liberation theology's "preferential option for the poor" that would be taken up as a political option by liberation theologians in the late 1960s and an epistemological principle in the mid-1970s.

In the second part of the encyclical, Pius reaffirmed Leo's central principles and developed his social teaching further.[20] He started with a justification of the church's right to speak on social and economic problems, and then proceeded to elaborate the teaching itself. Like Leo, he offered a firm defence of private property, but also reaffirmed concern for the common good that avoided both individualism and collectivism.[21] He criticised abuses of capital and offered

---

[15] *Quadragesimo Anno*, (15 May 1931). Like Pius, later Popes have also used anniversaries of *Rerum Novarum* to issue new encyclicals and social teaching. These include: John XXIII, *Mater et Magistra* (1961); Paul VI, *Octogesima Adveniens* (1971); and John Paul II, *Laborem Exercens*, (1981) and *Centesimus Annuns* (1991).

[16] Pius notes with frankness, if a certain exaggeration, ". . . we are confronted with a world which in large measure has almost fallen back into paganism" (§ 140).

[17] *Quadragesimo Anno*, §§ 1–40.

[18] *Quadragesimo Anno*, § 3 and § 4.

[19] *Quadragesimo Anno*, § 25, cp. *Rerum Novarum*, § 29.

[20] *Quadragesimo Anno*, §§ 41–98.

[21] *Quadragesimo Anno*, §§ 44–46.

guidance on the just distribution of wealth and property.[22] He noted that in many developed states the situation was better than forty years before; however, as other countries became more industrialised, the number of the "dispossessed labouring masses whose cries mount to heaven increased exceedingly."[23] He echoed Leo on the importance of a living and just wage and set out principles for its determination. Pius also commended corporatism and emphasised the value of "subsidiarity" in the social order.[24] The encyclical called on all social groups to seek social justice and the common good rather than their own interests. Above all, however, Pius called for harmony between groups in society, and like Leo, he recognised the existence of classes but emphatically rejected class struggle.[25]

The third part examined the changes that had taken place since Leo's time.[26] He discussed developments in the free-market economic system and gave special attention to socialism. Pius followed Leo in plotting a course between unrestrained individualism and socialism.[27] On the one hand, he decried that because of excessive individualism, "economic life has become hard, cruel, and relentless in a ghastly measure."[28] On the other, he condemned communism because it taught a "merciless class warfare and the complete abolition of private ownership."[29] His views on more moderate versions—which he distinguished as "socialism" rather than "communism"—were a little more nuanced. He accepted the possibility that if it continued to change, its program of reforms might be no different from the program of those inspired by Christian principles. However, he ultimately rejected socialism as an erroneous theory that could not be reconciled with Christianity because of its view of human society which restricted human liberty and failed to safeguard human dignity.[30]

---

[22] *Quadragesimo Anno*, §§ 54–58.

[23] *Quadragesimo Anno*, § 59.

[24] *Quadragesimo Anno*, § 80. The principle of subsidiarity—which remains central in Catholic social teaching—is that larger groups (including the state) should not lay claim to tasks that can be carried out by smaller groups or individuals.

[25] *Quadragesimo Anno*, §§ 81–83. Leo XIII spoke of the grave inconvenience of strikes and their threat to public peace. However, he supported reform to the long working hours, insufficient wages, and hard conditions that frequently caused strikes and did not issue a blanket condemnation of strikes as such (*Rerum Novarum*, § 31). Pius takes a harsher line and condemns the use of strikes outright (§ 94).

[26] *Quadragesimo Anno*, §§ 99–148.

[27] Pius is more willing to use the term "capitalist" than Leo (see, for example, *Quadragesimo Anno*, § 103).

[28] *Quadragesimo Anno*, § 109.

[29] *Quadragesimo Anno*, § 112. Pius adds that "the antagonism and open hostility it has shown Holy Church and even God himself are, alas! well proven by facts and known to us all" (§ 112).

[30] *Quadragesimo Anno*, §§ 111–126. This section is particularly interesting. Pius concedes that "it cannot be denied that its [socialism's] programs often strikingly approach the just demands of Christian social reformers" (§ 114). He adds: "If these changes [on class war and private ownership] continue, it may well come about that gradually the

Pius argued that a renewal of the Christian spirit is the necessary condition for social reconstruction and moral renovation.[31] He blamed the social malaise on doctrines of rationalism that undermined morality and economic teaching that gave free rein to human avarice.[32] He saw the remedy as a return to the gospel and the participation of all Catholics in a Christian renewal of society.

This development of Leo's social tradition provided encouragement, leadership and a framework of moral principles for a new engagement with society. Catholic Action was at the vanguard of this new movement in Latin America and prepared the way for liberation theology in many important ways. In addition, Pius's vision of a new evangelization based on society encouraged institutional reforms to improve the church's effectiveness as the moral voice of society.

Catholic Action

Catholic Action originated in Europe and spread to Latin America in the early twentieth century, where it gained significant momentum in the 1930s and was an important influence in many countries. Early versions of Catholic Action in Latin America tended to follow the Italian model. Groups were organised according to age and sex, but not divided by occupational categories. This model attempted to embrace all social groups—irrespective of class-status—around common general goals. After 1945, there was a shift to the more specialized models that had been developed in France and Belgium under Joseph Cardijn in the 1920s.[33] These focussed on particular social groups, for example, farm-

---

tenets of mitigated socialism will no longer be different from the program of those who seek to reform human society according to Christian principles" (§ 114). However, he then says that even if this were to be the case, socialism could not be "baptized into the Church" because "it conceives human society in a way utterly alien to Christian truth" (§ 117). He also claims that socialism ignores the Christian values of liberty and human dignity in its vision of society (§§ 118–120). He therefore concludes: "If, like all errors, socialism contains a certain element of truth (and this the sovereign pontiffs have never denied), it is nevertheless founded upon a doctrine of human society peculiarly its own, which is opposed to true Christianity. 'Religious socialism' and 'Christian socialism' are expressions implying a contradiction in terms. No one can be at the same time a sincere Catholic and a true socialist" (§ 120).

[31] *Quadragesimo Anno*, §§ 127–148. Pius also sets the significance of temporal renewal in a broader context by relating it to the ruin of souls: "For most men are affected almost exclusively by temporal upheavals, disasters, and ruins. Yet if we view things with Christian eyes, and we should, what are they all in comparison with the ruin of souls? Nevertheless, it may be said with all truth that nowadays the conditions of social and economic life are such that vast multitudes of men can only with great difficulty pay attention to that one thing necessary, namely their eternal salvation" (§ 130).

[32] *Quadragesimo Anno*, § 133. Pius sees this criticism as relevant to both socialism and capitalism, but in this section he is particularly concerned with abuses under capitalism. He condemns the "abominable abuses" of certain corporations (§ 132) and notes the harmful inversion of modern manufacturing processes whereby ". . . dead matter leaves the factory ennobled and transformed, where men are corrupted and degraded" (§ 135).

[33] See M. de la Bedoyere, *The Cardijn Story: A Study of the Life of Mgr. Joseph Cardijn*

ers, workers, or students and recruited young men and women into special movements united by these share interests. These included: Catholic Youth Farmers (JAC); Catholic Youth Factory Workers (JOC); Catholic Youth University Students (JUC); Catholic Youth Secondary Students (JEC); and Catholic Youth Independent Movement (JIC). During the 1950s and 1960s, these movements were at the forefront of church attempts to respond to the new social environment created by industrialisation and urbanisation. JUC was particularly favoured in many Latin American countries, and its members rose to leadership of student movements in many universities.

To carry out this work Catholic Action developed a new methodology summarised as "see-judge-act."[34] This simple, but effective process for social engagement was an essential stepping stone to liberation theology. The movement's aim was to promote the moral values of traditional Catholicism in the wider and more secular society. Catholic Action gave the laity morally safe opportunities to live, work, and participate in society through movements with a clear Catholic identity. A major concern of the movement in the 1950s and early 1960s was to oppose communism and it usually had a conservative political bias in its views on social issues. It was not intended as a radical challenge to the injustices that society's *status quo* represented, but a way to reestablish the influence of the church in Latin American society and promote social reforms in accordance with a traditionalist moral code.

Catholic Action's attempt to win back social influence under the traditional terms of the church's moral authority expressed the neo-Christendom mentality of the time. It was a moderately progressive movement in as much as it addressed social concerns, put more responsibility on the actions of the laity, and accepted that the church should respect the rights of secular government. However, the clergy controlled the movement's activities. Its vision of social action remained traditionalist and guided by *Quadragesimo Anno* and other ecclesial pronouncements which saw the laity as passive recipients and willing servants of the church. As a movement it was concerned with specific reforms and improvements but did little to address more structural issues of social

---

and the Young Christian Workers' Movement (London: Longman's, Green and Co. 1958). Leo's encouragement of Catholic workingmen's associations in *Rerum Novarum* prepared the way for this development.

[34] Edward Cleary explains: "The goal of Catholic Action was for lay persons to influence the secular milieu in which they worked. In small cells or groups they were to *see* and describe the situation in which they worked or lived, to *judge* the situation in the light of Christian principles (such as justice and charity), and then to *act* realistically to correct or enhance their milieu. It is worth noting that this model of Catholic Action is sometimes thought to imitate communist organization and tactics. It was no accident that the organizational structure of the French model of Catholic Action resembled the interlocking cells of the Communist Party. But the methodology of see-judge-act (even if it owed something to Marxist praxis) came from Thomas Aquinas's teaching on prudence" (*Crisis and Change: The Church in Latin America Today* [Maryknoll, N.Y.: Orbis Books, 1985], p. 4).

injustice. Nonetheless, its social orientation and methodological approach were important foundations on which liberation theology could build. Furthermore, it provided training and established a system of networks for a generation of Catholic thinkers in the 1950s and 1960s.

In Peru, young students embraced the bishop's pastoral letter of 1958 on the social requirements of Catholicism with particular enthusiasm, and this made the youth eager to embrace the new directions indicated by Vatican II. However, because of Catholic Action's ambivalent character—part traditionalist and part progressive—many in the JUC experienced social and political tensions as they became more conscious of their privileged position in the society and the hardship faced by the great majority. This often led to a process of radicalization and sense of frustration at the limitations in the church's approach. In some cases, they were impatient for even faster changes and the more direct political action that seemed to be necessary to overcome Latin America's long-standing social problems.[35]

Institutional Changes

During the 1950s, the Latin American bishops became increasingly aware of the church's institutional weakness. Hélder Câmara had become national assistant to Catholic Action in Brazil (ACB) in 1947, and his role there provided the opportunity to coordinate occasional meetings of the Brazilian bishops.[36] For Câmara and other influential figures, the value of these meetings indicated the importance of establishing a more structured format for regular meetings between bishops as a national body. This led to proposals for the Brazilian bishops to organise into a national body, the National Conference of Brazilian Bishops or CNBB (Conferência Nacional dos Bispos do Brasil). Câmara's contacts with the Vatican Secretary of State, Cardinal Montini (who later became Pope Paul VI) helped to gain a sympathetic hearing for the proposal in the Vatican. The bishops drew up the structure of the CCNB in 1951, and it was officially instituted in 1952. Hélder Câmara was elected secretary general and held the post for twelve years, during which time he worked closely with the apostolic nuncio Dom Armando Lombardi for renewal of the institutional structures and a more progressive orientation for the Brazilian church.[37]

In the same year, Câmara was appointed the auxiliary bishop of Rio de Janeiro from 1952 to 1964. His status as an auxiliary bishop gave him time to

---

[35] This was especially true for the students that the young Peruvian priest Gustavo Gutiérrez worked with as a university chaplain in the 1960s. Their experiences prompted him to an analysis of the limits of the movement and what might be needed as an alternative.

[36] Câmara was ordained as a priest in 1931 and was a pivotal figure in the Brazilian church in the 1950s and the emergence of liberation theology in the 1960s.

[37] Lombardi was papal nuncio in Brazil from September 1954 until May 1964, see Bruneau, The Political Transformation of the Brazilian Catholic Church (New York: Cambridge University Press, 1974), p. 117.

devote his energy and charisma to the development of CNBB. The CNBB was a vital step forward for the church in Brazil, but not an instant solution to its institutional weaknesses. On the positive side, it gave the bishops a more powerful platform to address society and allowed them to engage with social issues more comprehensively and systematically. Its links with the Brazilian branch of Catholic Action were also particularly important. This provided valuable support for progressive tendencies in the episcopate when they started to emerge, especially amongst the bishops working in the Northeast. When individual bishops had to be very careful on what they said, the national body could speak from a position of greater strength on controversial issues. It was sometimes safer for the CNBB to act as the spokesperson rather than an individual bishop. To begin with the CNBB lacked finances and did not have an institutional headquarters. Even its official status under canon law was unclear.[38] However, with time and under Câmara's leadership, by the mid-1960s the progressive tendency in the Brazilian church increasingly took advantage of the new structure for organising its pastoral activities and disseminating its teachings through its pastoral network.

Câmara's other vision was for a similar body to unite the bishops throughout the continent. Working closely with his friend Manuel Larraín, the bishop of Talca (Chile), Câmara was largely responsible for the eventual success of the idea. The bishops from the different Latin American countries came together as a unified body—the Conference of the Latin American Episcopate or CELAM (*Consejo Episcopal Latinoamericano* in Spanish or *Conselho Episcopal Latinoamericano* in Portuguese).

The first joint meeting of the Latin American bishops conference—known as CELAM I—was in Rio de Janeiro, 24 July–4 August 1955. The primary challenge discussed at the meeting was evangelization.[39] The central question was how to present Christian faith in an increasingly secular culture. In addition, they noted that Catholic observance seemed more formal than deeply rooted. The superficiality of much Catholic devotion seemed to make it particularly vulnerable to secular influences. Matters were discussed, but very little was agreed in terms of concerted action. CELAM I was a modest start for the new body of Catholic bishops. The outlook was still largely traditional, and there was little discussion of the church's wider social mission. But that was only the beginning for CELAM, it would come into its own at its second general meeting in Medellín, Colombia 1968 and Puebla, Mexico, 1979. CELAM I was mainly significant, because these later meetings would have been impossible without the organisation of the group in the 1955. The bishops of Colombia offered

---

[38] Important recognition for national conferences was given at Vatican II (see especially *Cristus Dominus* §§ 36–38, published 28 October 1965) and in Paul VI's address at Medellín. However, national bishops councils have never had formal authority over the individual bishops who comprise them.

[39] It included attention to the competition from Protestant sects, an issue that remains a major source of concern for the church, see chapter 13 below.

to host the new organization and provided it with its institutional headquarters at Bogotá so that it might continue to work and meet annually for ordinary meetings.[40]

During the rest of 1950s, CELAM was generally conservative in its social outlook. At its fourth annual assembly in November 1959—with the Cuban Revolution in mind—it warned about the traps of communism and emphasised the incompatibility between communism and Christianity.[41] However, even within these cautious first years, important foundations for the future started to take shape. In 1958, CELAM decided to set up biblical institutes in Latin America, which made a tentative start to what would eventually be more distinctive Latin American readings of the bible. This initiative complemented the founding of new theological schools at Latin American universities. These included: Bogotá (1937); Lima (1942); Medellín (1945); and São Paulo and Rio de Janeiro (1947). Centres of Social and Religious Research were also founded in Buenos Aires, Santiago, and Bogotá. In the 1960s, when Vatican II gave a boost for national church organisations, CELAM was well placed to build on these foundations and provide vigorous leadership for a more socially engaged church in Latin America.[42]

Meanwhile, in 1958 Pius XII died. His replacement was Angelo Giuseppe Roncalli, who took the name John XXIII. Roncalli was seen as a short-term appointment who was unlikely to make major changes, but in the same month as Castro's victory, he made an announcement that would have profound long-term effects for the church. On 25 January 1959, he called for an ecumenical council to take place for the renewal of the church.[43] At the time, there was little indication of the momentous changes that lay ahead. However, when the council finally got under way (1962–1965) it led to sweeping changes in the church and had a particular impact in Latin America. Like the Cuban revolution, it was to be a major influence in the decade that was to come.

---

[40] CELAM usually refers to the organisation, whereas CELAM I, CELAM II, CELAM III, and CELAM IV refer to the four extraordinary meetings that have so far taken place at Rio (1955), Medellín (1968), Puebla (1979), and Santo Domingo (1992).

[41] Dussel, "From the Second Vatican Council to the Present Day" in Dussel (ed.), *The Church in Latin America*, pp. 153–182 (157).

[42] See Dussel, *A History of the Church in Latin America*, p. 112.

[43] Ecumenical in this sense was limited to the whole *Catholic* church although the council proved to be an ecumenical event in the wider sense that it marked a major step forward in relations with other churches. In 1960, John created a Secretariat for Christian Unity under Cardinal Augustin Bea. On 2 December 1960, the Pope received the Archbishop of Canterbury Geoffrey Fisher at the Vatican. This was the first visit from the head of the Anglican communion since the Reformation, and other distinguished ecumenical visitors followed in the next couple of years. Orthodox and Protestant official observers attended the Council itself and one of its most significant documents was the "Decree on Ecumenism," see P. Hebblethwaite, *John XXIII: Pope of the Council* (London: Fount, 1984), p. 409.

January 1959 also marked another event that was to prove significant for the direction of church reform in Latin America. A Peruvian seminarian, Gustavo Gutiérrez, born in 1928, was ordained as a priest. After studying medicine at San Marcos University (Lima) he decided to train for the priesthood instead.[44] He studied philosophy and theology in Lima and Santiago (Chile) before travelling to Europe to take his training further. He spent the 1950s at some of the great centres of Catholic education, including Louvain for philosophy and psychology (1951–1955) and the University of Lyons for theology (1955–1959). After ordination he completed a further year at the Gregorian University in Rome (1959–1960) and was then ready to return to Latin America and begin work with university students in Lima. More than any other single person, Gutiérrez's writing and work would develop the leads taken by the council convoked by John XXIII into the movement that would become known as liberation theology.

CONCLUSION

The period 1930–1959 was a crucial period of transition in Latin American society and the Latin American church. Latin American societies moved from a period in which they had been largely static for centuries, to one that from 1960 would change with ever increasing speed. Industrialisation and urbanisation started to change the Latin American economic landscape and brought with them important social changes. At a national level, the rapidly growing populations created pressure for political changes, and the new urban working classes were better organised to press for political reforms. At an international level, Latin America moved more firmly into the political orbit of the United States. The U.S. started to extend its hegemony beyond the Caribbean and Central America to the rest of the hemisphere, and the U.S. military developed a special relationship with their counterparts in Brazil.

While all this was happening, the Latin American church remained largely wedded to the past and was poorly positioned to respond. It did, however, initiate a new role for itself in society (the move from Christendom to neo-Christendom), organised itself more effectively to make its message heard and developed its social teaching. Catholic Action involved a new and important engagement with society, but its parameters were severely limited, and some of the youthful activists who tried to implement it felt frustrated by the limits of the church's political vision. When the Cuban Revolution of 1959 heralded an end to the old order, it seemed like much that the church stood for was on the wrong side of history. The increasingly radical Catholic youth felt that the church must reform or it would be increasingly irrelevant to Latin America's

---

[44] For an excellent study of Gutiérrez's life and work see R. M. Brown, *Gustavo Gutiérrez: An Introduction to Liberation Theology* (Maryknoll, N.Y.: Orbis Books, 1990). The biographical details here are taken from pp. 22–23.

pressing social issues. The church surrendered its claim on direct political power but the colonial option for power was replaced by a revised option for influence and privilege through neo-Christendom. During the 1950s, there was little sign that a major transformation might change many within the church toward an option for the poor. However, in retrospect, it is clear that the foundations on which this transformation would be based were starting to come together.

Part 2

Engaging the World
1960–1969

CHAPTER FOUR

Reform and Renewal, 1960–1965

> At all times the Church carries the responsibility of reading the signs of the times and of interpreting them in the light of the Gospel, if it is to carry out its task.
>
> Vatican II, *Gaudium et Spes*, § 4.

INTRODUCTION

The sixties was a decade of pastoral renewal in the church and attempted economic reform in Latin American societies. The Cuban Revolution showed that the United States could not take the traditional *status quo* in Latin America for granted. The fact that a nationalist popular uprising had overthrown a United States client regime sent a shock wave throughout Latin America. The new Kennedy administration (1961–1963) was determined to prevent other countries from following Cuba's example and promised to promote much-needed political and economic reforms in the region.

By now, Western Europe had largely recovered from World War II and United States aid could be channelled to development in Latin America instead.[1] The United Nations declared the 1960s a decade of development, and the United

---

[1] Beginning in 1947, the United States started to pump $13 billion of aid into Western Europe as part of the European Recovery Programme (commonly known as the Marshall Plan, after the United States Secretary of State, George Marshall). It was a policy of mutual benefit to ensure that Western Europe remained in the Free World. Stronger economies reduced the appeal of communism and a strong Western Europe was a valuable counterbalance to the influence of the Soviet Union in Eastern Europe. At the same time, to further strengthen the security of the region, the United States also committed itself to the defence of the region through the creation of a North Atlantic Treaty Organization (NATO). During the 1950s, the policy of economic development, political democracy, and military security ensured that Western Europe recovered quickly and cemented its close alliance with the U.S. In the 1960s, it seemed that Latin America might be next to benefit from a similarly pragmatic approach.

States promised its support for democracy and development throughout Latin America. An Alliance for Progress with promises of reform fitted long-term United States interests by reducing the chances of social upheaval and possible revolution. However, to cover the different possibilities the policy combined economic "carrot" with military "stick." Alongside the development aid was a less publicised military strategy. This included selling arms, training police, providing intelligence information, and advising on counter-insurgency strategies. If economic reforms did not work, the United States wanted to prepare its allies in Latin American militaries for whatever might follow.

ECONOMIC AND SOCIAL DEVELOPMENT

Castro's success in Cuba showed that the colonial and neo-colonial history that had continued unbroken since the conquistadors might finally be about to change. However, in 1959, he was not yet a committed communist and the Cuban Revolution could have led in a very different direction.

The 26 July Movement had started as a nationalist group and Castro initially hoped that the United States would support their nationalist hopes for freedom.[2] He went to the United States in April 1959 to ask for aid in rebuilding and modernising the Cuban economy. He met with Vice President Nixon, but Nixon decided that Castro could not be trusted. Castro was forced to look elsewhere for economic partners.[3]

The Soviet Union was eager to embrace Castro's revolution and on a trip to address the United Nations in New York later that year, Castro met with the Soviet Premier Nikita Khruschev. Rebuffed by the United States, Castro was happy to accept Soviet promises of assistance. In February 1960, the Soviet Union agreed a five-year deal for Cuban sugar and contracts with China and Poland followed. These agreements with the Socialist regimes increased the tension between Cuba and the United States. The CIA began covert sabotage of Cuban ports and crops. Castro responded with fiery anti-imperialist rhetoric that inflamed the situation further. Perhaps most importantly, he started a sweeping land reform and nationalized United States landholdings. In retaliation, President Eisenhower imposed a trade embargo that pushed Cuba even further into dependency on the Soviet Union.

Guevara's book *Guerrilla Warfare*, published in 1960, alarmed the United States even more. Guevara hoped to export the revolution to other long-standing dictatorial regimes in the Caribbean and Central America, especially Anastasio Somoza's Nicaragua and Rafael Trujillo's Dominican Republic.[4]

---

[2] During the guerrilla campaign some of the group developed a more far-reaching social vision, but not necessarily pro-Soviet at this stage.

[3] President Eisenhower was too suspicious to even meet Castro, and Nixon's report confirmed his concerns.

[4] The United States had particularly close ties with both dictators. Rafael Trujillo ruled the Dominican Republic from 1929 until his assassination on 30 May 1961. During this time, Trujillo and his family acquired a huge fortune through corruption and brutality.

Previously, the orthodox communist line had been that revolutionary efforts should be concentrated on the urban proletariat and that the full conditions for revolutionary change needed to be present before launching an armed struggle. Guevara argued that insurrectional *foco* (guerrilla groups operating in the countryside) could defeat regular forces and bring about revolution without waiting for the full conditions of revolution to develop.[5]

Eisenhower ordered the CIA to prepare a mission of Cuban exiles to invade Cuba and overthrow Castro.[6] However, before the invasion was ready, John F. Kennedy beat Nixon in the presidential election of 1960 and was sworn into office in January 1961. Kennedy was more cautious about the likely success of the CIA plot and more fearful about the international repercussions if the United States was seen to be behind it. Nonetheless, on 16 April 1961 (when, for the first time, Castro proclaimed that the Cuban Revolution was socialist), Kennedy agreed to let the operation proceed but without combat support or air cover (since this would make United States involvement obvious).

More than a thousand Cuban exiles landed on the south coast at the Bay of Pigs on 17 April 1961. However, Castro enjoyed widespread popular support, and Cuban nationalism ensured a willingness to help him defend the island against a foreign-backed invasion. In addition, the lack of air support fatally weakened the original CIA plan, and within three days the Cuban army overcame the invaders.

Cuba proclaimed its victory to the world, and Castro's military success was an important boost for his prestige among leftists in Latin America. He used it to denounce the neo-imperialist ambitions of the United States and fan the hopes of successful revolutions elsewhere. In the United States, the failed

---

On the moral propriety of United States support for Trujillo's dictatorship, President Franklin D. Roosevelt famously commented, "He may be an S.O.B., but he is *our* S.O.B." In 1965, the United States sent marines to restore order when a reformist coup against Trujillo's political heirs threatened meaningful social changes in the Dominican Republic. There was similarly unswerving support for Nicaragua's Somoza dynasty in Nicaragua. With the backing of the United States, the Somoza family controlled Nicaragua for nearly fifty years under Anastasio Somoza Senior (1937–1956), Luis Somoza (1956–1963), and Anastasio Somoza Junior (1967–1979). The Sandinista Revolution finally brought the Somoza dynasty to an end in 1979.

[5] At this stage, Guevara did not expect revolutions to be successful in the larger countries of South America because their sheer size would have required a different logistical approach. Furthermore, because most of South America preserved the trappings of democracy in the 1960s, the political conditions for revolution were seen to be much more difficult. It seems that it was not until after 1965, that Guevara extended his vision to the whole of Latin America with the hope that the Andean mountains would play the role of Cuba's Sierra Maestra for much of South America. He saw the United States invasion of the Dominican Republic in 1965 as clear evidence that the struggle with imperialism needed to be continent-wide.

[6] The invasion was masterminded by many of the same CIA team that had orchestrated the overthrow of Arbenz in Guatemala in 1954. They adopted a similar strategy on a number of operational details.

invasion was a major embarrassment. Despite Kennedy's refusal to commit United States' troops, the involvement of the United States was impossible to hide and this escalated the Cold War tension with the Soviet Union. The Soviet Union had previously promised military support for Cuba should it be threatened with invasion. It now started sending arms shipments. In October 1962, a United States spy plane revealed that Soviet weaponry included nuclear missile installations. Kennedy threatened to destroy the missile sites if the missiles were not removed, and a tense superpower stand-off developed. The potential nuclear war was only averted when Kennedy pledged not to invade Cuba in exchange for the withdrawal of the missiles. Under Soviet protection, the Cuban Revolution survived and Cuba became institutionalised as a communist state.

In the decades that followed, Cuba became an important symbol of anti-"Yankee imperialism" for many in Latin America. However, it paid a heavy price for its defiance. The effects of a punitive embargo undermined many of the successes of the regime. The regime could take pride in its excellent record on many public services (especially education and health), but Cuba's long-term prospects for development were seriously undermined. Furthermore, the threat from the United States strengthened the authoritarian tendencies of the regime to defend itself against both internal and external opposition. Even the dream of independence was only partially realized. Cuba had to withstand continuing hostility from the United States short of actual invasion—including numerous plots to assassinate Castro—and became as politically and economically dependent on the Soviet Union as it had been on foreign companies under Batista. Just as the independence movements of the nineteenth century only swapped one set of rulers for another, the Cuban Revolution failed in its basic objective of national freedom.[7]

After failing to reverse the Cuban Revolution, the United States was determined to at least prevent other revolutions from taking place elsewhere in Latin America. To do this, John F. Kennedy—the first ever Catholic President of the United States—initiated an Alliance for Progress with Latin America. At the launch conference in Uruguay in August 1961, the United States promised a multibillion-dollar package of aid for Latin American countries. In theory, the new initiative was intended both to aid development throughout the region and to counter further threats of social insurrection through political reforms. Unfortunately, in practice, these two goals were often in conflict.

To promote development, the United States tried to promote moderate land reform and other policies that gave the rural peasantry and urban workers an improved deal and a greater stake in the capitalist system. However, rather than welcome the long-term benefits of such reforms, the economic and political elites in Latin America responded to protect their short-term financial interests. They

---

[7] See H. Thomas, *Cuba or The Pursuit of Freedom* (London: Eyre and Spottiswoode, 1971).

opposed any meaningful redistribution of their privileges as a dangerous social-ism. Since the United States saw these elites as its key allies in the region (espe-cially because of their aggressive anti-communist stance), it invariably gave way to this forceful opposition.[8] The reforms that made it on to the statute books were either too weak to have an impact or were not actively promoted or both.

Even when reforms had some success at a local level, they tended to run up against the wider issues related to the overall control of the economy and its general direction. Small-scale reforms could not solve the larger problems of Latin America's dependant economies and polarised societies. By the end of the 1960s, the gap between rich and poor had widened, while Latin American foreign debt more than doubled to $19.3 billion (from $8.8 billion in 1961).[9] As matters got worse rather than better, an inevitable disillusionment with the Alliance for Progress set in.

The Import Substitution Initiative that provided new direction for the more advanced Latin American economies in the 1930s and spread to other coun-tries in the 1950s, reached its limit in most countries by the end of the 1950s. The easy stage (which had concentrated on light manufacturing) needed to be complemented by a new stage that focussed on heavy manufacturing. Some coun-tries, like Brazil, were eager to push on with this second stage. However, the poor paid heavy social costs for this development. For example, between 1958 and 1970 the real wages of Brazilian workers declined 64.5%.[10] Even so, inflation in many countries started to get out of hand. The double burden of rising prices and restricted wages put the working class under intense pressure. Social unrest started to increase and governments responded with increasingly repres-sive measures. The move towards authoritarian military governments began throughout the region.

The military coup in Brazil (1 April 1964) signalled the general direction that politics in Latin America would take for the rest of the sixties and sev-enties.[11] Jânio da Silva Quadros became president in January 1961 and pushed through a sweeping economic program. Many of his measures were prompted by the financial problems created by Brazil's drive for development from 1930 to 1960, under Getulio Vargas and Juscelino Kubitschek. However, Quadros resigned unexpectedly in August and was succeeded in September 1961 by João Goulart (who had been Labour minister under Vargas). The military was very wary of Goulart and suspected a leftward orientation in his politics. At the time, revolutionary sentiments inspired by the Cuban Revolution were gaining ground

---

[8] This was especially the case in the Caribbean and Central America where the anti-communism of United States client governments in the Dominican Republic, Nicaragua, El Salvador, and Guatemala ensured virtual immunity from any real pressure to change.

[9] P. Lernoux, *Cry of the People: The Struggle for Human Rights in Latin America—the Catholic Church in Conflict with U.S. Policy*, rev. ed. (New York: Penguin Books, 1982), 211.

[10] Lernoux, *Cry of the People*, 205–206.

[11] For an account of the period leading up-to the coup see T. Skidmore, *Politics in Brazil, 1930–1964* (Oxford: Oxford University Press, 1967).

at universities and in labour movements.[12] Goulart was unable to control the economy and inflation spiralled upward. His attempt at a combined land reform and economic stabilisation in 1963 (to be financed by the Alliance for Progress) promised to tackle the worst of the problems, but it antagonised both the political left (as being too modest) and the political right (as being too much).

Under pressure from both sides, Goulart tried to bolster his position with a bid for popular support. His speeches became more populist and the uneasiness of the military increased. On 31 March 1964, a military revolt began and support for Goulart crumbled. With the political support of the United States— and the blessing of the Brazilian church—the military took power on 1 April under the chief of staff, Humberto Castello Branco.[13] Thus began the new era in Latin American politics that set the political and economic context for the emergence of liberation theology.[14]

The military's involvement in politics was not new in Brazil (or anywhere else in Latin America). Ever since independence, the military in most Latin American countries had been crucial power brokers in political matters and military men had held electoral power for temporary periods. However, the Brazilian coup of 1964 was different because the military assumed direct political control of the country for a sustained period.[15] The military regime was not willing to act simply as an interim force and hold power until civilian politics returned as normal. Instead, it consolidated its grip on power and embarked on ambitious development policies to make Brazil the region's military and economic superpower.

A major priority was to control inflation. The regime passed new anti-labour laws and enforced tight wage controls on workers. New legislation also reduced civil liberties and opportunities for social protest. In the second half of the sixties these policies developed into a full-blown doctrine of the National Security State. This doctrine gained wide currency throughout Latin America in the next decade and supplied the ideological context for the reigns of terror that swept the region.

---

[12] The military only agreed to Goulart's election after they had negotiated major curtailments to the executive power of the President. A plebiscite in 1963 allowed the restoration of many of these powers, but by then the economy was in serious trouble.

[13] Many figures who later became prominent in liberation theology and opposition to the military regime—for example, Clodovis Boff—initially prayed in gratitude for the coup and supported its intentions; see M. Puleo, *The Struggle Is One: Voices and Visions of Liberation* (Albany, N.Y.: State University of New York Press, 1994), p. 145.

[14] For an excellent overview that begins with Brazil (1964–1985) and also covers the key periods in Chile (1973–1990), Argentina (1976–1983), Paraguay (1954–1989), Uruguay (1973–1990), Bolivia (1952–1989), Peru (1980–1995), El Salvador (1980–1992), Nicaragua (1979–1990), Guatemala (1954–1996), and Mexico, see J. Klaiber, *The Church, Dictatorships and Democracy in Latin America* (Maryknoll, N.Y.: Orbis Books, 1998).

[15] It was not until 1985 that civilian rule was restored.

CHURCH RENEWAL

Cuba's revolution shook the entire Latin American church. More than any other single event, the Cuban Revolution was a wake-up call to an institution, which in many areas, had become distant from people's lives. The church feared that similar revolutions would jeopardise its traditional influence and social position. In Cuba itself, relations between church and state deteriorated quickly after the revolution. The Cuban bishops spoke against the government's political orientation, and Castro responded with repressive measures against the church. Church property was seized and during the 1960s, many priests and members of religious orders were expelled or decided to leave voluntarily.[16]

The threat of revolution suggested that much more needed to be done to strengthen the church's pastoral presence in Latin America. In response to this, John XXIII called for missionaries from North America and Europe to work in Latin America, especially in areas where the number of priests was particularly low after the anticlerical measures of the nineteenth century. Many European priests heeded his call and went to work alongside their Latin American colleagues. In time, the arrival of priests who were accustomed to the economic and political situation in developed countries (which included Spain, Belgium, France, Italy, Ireland, and the United States) contributed significantly to the development of liberation theology. The influx of foreign priests encouraged a sense of renewal in the Latin American church and particularly strengthened those who believed that poverty could and should be prevented. In the many instances where progressive priests faced resistance and persecution, the foreign priests were sometimes at an advantage over local nationals.[17]

During the early 1960s, the most significant change for the future of the church in Latin America took place in Europe rather than Latin America itself. The social encyclicals of John XXIII and Paul VI placed new emphasis on the church's social ministry. Furthermore, the spirit of renewal engendered by the

---

[16] Dussel reports that: "There were 745 priests in the country in 1960; by 1969 their number had reduced to 230; the 2225 religious in 1960 were reduced to two hundred by 1970"; E. Dussel, "From the Second Vatican Council to the Present Day" in idem (ed.), *The Church in Latin America*, pp. 153–182 (157).

[17] Foreign citizenship usually meant an extra level of political protection against attacks or false imprisonment. Initially, this was weighed against the disadvantage that foreign citizens were susceptible to deportation (or more usually refusal of entry). However, as persecution grew more intense, the possibility of deportation had its advantages. The option to deport meant it was not necessary to kill a foreign priest or nun to silence them. For this reason foreigners could be bolder in developing their pastoral practice and speaking out on social issues. When foreign priests or nuns have been killed in Latin America, the international outcry has often been far louder than for Latin American nationals. For example, during El Salvador's civil conflict in the 1980s (in which an estimated 75,000 died), the rape and murder of three United States nuns and one church laywoman in December 1980, and the murder of five Spanish Jesuits and one Salvadoran Jesuit (along with their cook and her daughter) in November 1989, caused particularly high levels of international outcry.

Second Vatican Council (1962–1965) encouraged progressives within the Latin American church to apply these to Latin America with a special urgency and make it a focus of theological reflection.

The Social Encyclicals of John XXII

Catholic social teaching took an important step forward with the publication of *Mater et Magister* (*Mother and Teacher*) in 1961.[18] At the time, Europe was still recovering from the devastation of World War II, the Soviet Union had consolidated its influence in Eastern Europe and the Cold War dominated the geo-politics of the day. In Africa and Asia, a new generation of postcolonial societies were emerging more than one hundred years after Latin American independence. The encyclical offers a more open approach to the world than either of its predecessors in 1891 and 1931 had offered. *Rerum Novarum* and *Quadragesimo Anno* both offered criticism of the failures of modernity while remaining virtually silent on its strengths.[19] *Mater et Magister* marked the start of a process of dialogue and discernment, rather than exclusively hostile judgement. This was the first sign of a major transformation in the church in the 1960s.[20]

---

[18] *Mater et Magister: On Recent Developments of the Social Question in the Light of the Christian Teaching* (15 May 1961).

[19] David O'Brien notes the limitations of *Rerum Novarum* and *Quadragesimo Anno* in this area: "In some places, the Church succeeded in winning the hearts and minds of men and women damaged by modern social change. What it failed to do was to see, and to identify with, the hopes and aspirations awakened by those same social changes. The popes saw and denounced the cruel treatment of workers, but did not affirm the workers' claims to a better life. They saw and denounced the rampant inequalities of modern life, but never made their own the idea that ordinary people have the right to share responsibility for the life of their community." See D. J. O'Brien, "A Century of Catholic Social Teaching," in J. A. Coleman (ed.), *One Hundred Years of Catholic Social Thought*, pp. 13–24.

[20] The encyclical was in four parts. In the first part, it reviewed the context and teaching of *Rerum Novarum* (§§ 10–26), *Quadragesimo Anno* (§§ 27–40) and the radio broadcast at Pentecost 1941 by Pius XII (§§ 41–45). It then sketched new technological, social, and political developments that had taken place since the Second World War (§§ 47–49). In the second part (§§ 51–121), it confirmed and developed some to the details of this teaching. Then in the third part (§§ 122–211), having established its continuity with previous tradition at some length, it finally turned to new aspects of social teaching. In these sections, there was a special emphasis on human dignity. First, it commented on the problems created by industrialization and agricultural depression. Then, John turned to the economic differences between industrialised countries and those that were in the process of development. He reflected on the church's contribution in this area and offered a brief consideration of the challenges posed by the population increases alongside an optimistic view of how potential problems might be addressed. He insisted that any problems that arose must be resolved with full attention to human dignity. Then, to conclude the encyclical's third part, he outlined a global perspective on the problems faced by societies and called for greater international cooperation in meeting them. The fourth and final part (§§ 211–265) defended the value of the church's teaching and exhorted Catholics to be active in furthering its social work. Once again, it particularly emphasised the importance of human dignity as the criterion of the church's teaching (see for example, §§ 220 and 258–259).

At the level of new ideas, the encyclical made only a modest contribution. Despite bearing the title "On Recent Developments of the Social Question in the Light of the Christian Teaching," a lot of its teaching simply repeated what was said before.[21] In view of the major social upheavals of the preceding three decades, more might have been expected from such a document. However, careful reading shows that an important shift was underway.

A new emphasis on human dignity was added to the previously endorsed principles of common good and subsidiarity.[22] John also recognised that developments in travel, trade, and communications required a more global approach to economic issues. The encyclical called for greater cooperation to solve these international problems in a harmonious way—just as his predecessors had prescribed nonconflictual solutions to national problems. John called for aid and assistance to poorer countries and included the important warning that some aid policies could become another form of colonialism by seeking domination over the recipient countries.[23] Furthermore, *Mater et Magister* was the first papal encyclical to speak explicitly in favour of agricultural reforms, which made a particular impact on progressive sectors in Latin America, including the National Bishops' Conference in Brazil.[24]

Perhaps of greatest significance was the formal endorsement for the pastoral process of *see, judge, act* (adopted in Catholic Action) in the application of social teaching. This provided an important foundation for the methodology that would be at the heart of liberation theology. John wrote:

> The teachings in regard to social matters for the most part are put into effect in the following three stages: first, the actual situation is examined; then, the situation is evaluated carefully in relation to these teachings; then only is it decided what can and should be done in order that the traditional norms may be adapted to circumstances of time and place. These three steps are at times expressed by the three words: *observe, judge, act.*[25]

The encyclical was also noteworthy for what it left out. There was implicit opposition to any political or philosophical system that failed to nurture life's spiritual dimension or safeguard against the weakness of human nature; but, unlike previous encyclicals, there was little explicit criticism of socialism and communism.[26]

---

[21] For example, it stressed the importance of just wages (§§ 68–72), the need for social justice (§§ 73–81), and guidance on the ethical regulation of productive institutions (§§ 82–103). There was the usual endorsement of private property (§§ 104–112), though this was balanced with a call for just distribution (§§ 113–121).

[22] *Mater et Magister*, § 53.

[23] *Mater et Magister*, §§ 171–174.

[24] *Mater et Magister*, §§ 123–149. Although the encyclical did not call directly for land reforms, its support for family farms as an organizing principle (§§ 142–143) strengthened calls for land reform in Latin America.

[25] *Mater et Magister*, § 236 (emphasis original).

[26] *Mater et Magister*, § 213. The teaching of the previous encyclicals was summarised in the first part (especially §§ 23 and 34), but John did not stress or add to these other

Two years later, during the Second Vatican Council, John issued a second social encyclical, *Pacem in Terris* (*Peace on Earth*).[27] The immediate background to the encyclical was the new frostiness in the Cold War marked by the Berlin Wall and the Cuban Missile Crisis (which had developed as the Council opened in 1962). In addition to its stress on the importance of peace (which included a controversial plea for a cessation to the arms race), the encyclical made important advances in other social areas.[28] The concern for human dignity that is so evident in *Mater et Magister* is reemphasised and extended to a sustained consideration of human rights and duties set within a democratic framework.[29] For the first time, there is a clear endorsement of economic, social, and cultural rights as well as the right to life.[30] The encyclical advocates obedience to the legitimate authority of the state but sets moral limits on the civil powers. It demands that the civil authorities seek the common good, preserve human dignity, and ensure that human rights are safeguarded as matter of fundamental duty.[31] In this context it reemphasises the special concern for the poor that the civil authorities should observe:

---

than a brief and indirect reference that recalled the persecution of Christians in a number of countries (§ 216). John was aware of the persecution suffered by the church in communist countries and had issued harsh condemnations of communism when he was first elected Pope. However, during his pontificate, his generally preferred strategy was not to condemn the errors of the world, but simply to show the validity of the church's teaching. Furthermore, John was particularly committed to improving the church's situation in the Soviet block and the absence of fierce condemnations reflects this.

[27] *Pacem in Terris: Encyclical Letter on Establishing Universal Peace in Truth, Justice, Charity and Liberty* (11 April 1963). John wrote it during the first session of the Vatican Council and it was issued on 30 April 1963, shortly before his death in June.

[28] John began the encyclical with a consideration of the proper order that should exist in human society. This is couched in terms of human rights (§§ 11–27) and the duties that are inseparable from them (§§ 28–38). Having established this framework, John reviewed the distinctive characteristics of the time (§§ 39–45). Then, he addressed the right relation that should exist between citizens and the state's secular authorities (§§ 46–79) and the relations that should exist between one state and another (§§ 80–129). In particular, John used the encyclical to highlight the importance of peace and called for an end to the arms race (§§ 111–112) and discussed the international relations that should provide a framework for all states and individuals (§§ 130–145). He ended with an exhortation that all should work for these right relations and the peace that can be founded upon them (§§ 146–173).

[29] *Pacem in Terris*, §§ 8–38.

[30] These include: "the right to security in cases of sickness, inability to work, widowhood, old age, unemployment, or in any other case in which he is deprived of the means of subsistence through no fault of his own. By natural law every human being has the right to respect for his person, to his good reputation; the right to freedom in searching for truth and in expressing and communicating his opinions, and in the pursuit of art . . . [and] the right to be informed truthfully about public events" (§§ 11–12). Other rights mentioned are: the right to religious freedom (§ 14); the right to set up a family or follow a religious vocation (§ 15); the right to work and the right to work without coercion (§ 18); the right to assembly and association (§ 23); political rights to active participation (§ 26); and legal rights and protection (§ 27).

[31] *Pacem in Terris*, §§ 46–66.

Considerations of justice and equity, however, can at times demand that those involved in civil government give more attention to the less fortunate members of the community, since they are less able to defend their rights and to assert their legitimate claims.[32]

A new openness and optimism—perhaps over-optimism—in their appeal to wider society marked both of John's encyclicals. *Pacem in Terris* was the first encyclical that was addressed beyond the traditional "Faithful of the Catholic World" and directed to "All Men of Goodwill."[33] John's belief in the good will of all men pervades the encyclical and is typified in his hope that wealthy countries would give selfless assistance to poor countries. In a particularly hopeful passage, he wrote:

. . . since all nations have either achieved or are on their way to achieving independence, there will soon no longer exist a world divided into nations that rule others and nations that are subject to others (§ 42).

The hopes surrounding John F. Kennedy's Alliance for Progress dovetailed neatly with John XXIII's own hopes. Both Catholic leaders expressed an optimistic belief in progress and reform and contributed to the renewed efforts at development that characterised the early 1960s. This new drive for development promised to relieve the hunger, ill-health, and other problems in the so-called developing countries. It was not until later in the decade that this optimism began to evaporate and progressive thinkers started to question its basic assumptions.

The Second Vatican Council

Nobody expected John's announcement on 25 January 1959 that he would call a major ecumenical council. When the first session finally got under way on 11 October 1962, the Council participants gathered in Rome were still unsure what to expect.[34] In retrospect, *Mater et Magister*'s progressive tone and emphasis on social justice showed that he might be sympathetic to major changes. Even more prophetically, shortly before the opening of the Council, on 11 September 1962, John XXIII indicated a decisive shift in the church's social role when he said: "Where the underdeveloped countries are concerned, the

---

[32] *Pacem in Terris*, § 56. This strand of official teaching now had almost 100 years in the social tradition behind it, but the social encyclicals still placed this obligation on the civil authorities and did not yet address the church's responsibility to make a special option for the poor a central task in its own work. However, in the early 1960s, Vatican II made this crucial step possible and John's "Opening of the Council" (see below) made a major contribution to this process.

[33] His Christmas message of 23 December 1959 also focussed on peace and cited the message of the angels of Bethlehem, "Peace on earth and good will among men" (Lk. 2.14).

[34] Initially, the Council was expected to last for only one session but it quickly developed beyond this and extended to four sessions which each lasted about two months: 11 October–8 December 1962; 29 September–4 December 1963; 14 September–21 November 1964; and 14 September–8 December 1965.

Church presents herself as she is, and wishes to be regarded as the Church for all, and especially as the Church of the poor."[35] By the end of the decade, the idea of a church being especially of the poor became an effective rallying point for liberation theology. However, at the time, nobody foresaw the sweeping extent of changes that were about to take place.

To the dismay of the conservative *curia*, John called on the bishops in his opening address to make the church's unchangeable doctrine relevant to the world and adapted to the times. A few days later, the bishops rejected the *curia's* nominations for the Council Commission and the vast majority of the draft documents that had been drawn up and circulated in advance. The way was open for major revisions in the ethos and practice of the church. The scale of change was marked in one of the first documents the council issued, "The Constitution on the Sacred Liturgy" (4 December 1963).[36] It set out important reforms to the liturgy that increased lay participation in worship. Most significant was permission to depart from Latin and use the local vernacular.[37] For the first time, ordinary people could understand the words of the mass and participate more actively in the worship.

John died in June 1963 with only one session completed and the work of the council unfinished. It was his successor Paul VI (formerly Giovanni Battista Montini) who oversaw the subsequent sessions.[38] Two documents from the later sessions that particularly stand out for their impact on the worldwide church are the *Lumen Gentium* (*Light of the People*) in 1964 and *Gaudium et Spes* (*Joy and Hope*) promulgated by Paul VI on the day before the council formally ended.[39] The first addressed the need for the participation of the faithful in the faith; the second addressed the need for the engagement of the church with the world, a topic that had not been part of the original agenda of the council, but had been included at the end of the first session. Many of the concerns of French *Nouvelle Theologie* (which had previously been rejected in the Catholic church) suddenly found themselves acceptable and even setting the new consensus position. The work of theologians like Karl Rahner encouraged a new sense of history as one. That is, the traditional dichotomy of grace and

---

[35] Cited in Hebblethwaite, *John XXIII*, pp. 423–444.

[36] The documents are collected together in A. Flannery (ed.), *Vatican Council II: The Conciliar and Post Conciliar Documents* (Northport, N.Y.: Costello Publishing Company; Dublin: Dominican Publications, rev. ed., 1996), and all citations below are based on this version.

[37] The Latin liturgy had been designated as the exclusive and unchanging format of the liturgy in 1570. As late as 22 February 1962, the document *Veterum Sapientia* (*The Wisdom of the Ancients*) insisted that it be used as the teaching language for theology in seminaries.

[38] See P. Hebblethwaite, *Paul VI: The First Modern Pope* (London: Harper Collins, 1993).

[39] *Lumen Gentium: The Dogmatic Constitution on the Church* (21 November 1964); *Gaudium et Spes: The Pastoral Constitution on the Church in the Modern World* (7 December 1965).

nature that had marked the dualism of a supernatural realm, in contrast to the natural world, was replaced with a new sense of human history as graced nature. Equally important was the work of theologians like Yves Congar, who argued for the importance of the laity in the church and a new understanding of the relationship between priest and laity that put more emphasis on coresponsibility.

Lumen Gentium is famous for its presentation of the church as the "People of God."[40] The terminology—based on 1 Pet. 2.9–10—reflected the greater responsibility and respect given to the laity as actively involved in the church. An additional consequence was a new respect for the dignity of the human person in the social realm when the concept was placed alongside *Lumen Gentium* account's of the church as the body of Christ.[41] When the church is seen as both people of God and body of Christ, the link between the ordinary people and the body of Christ becomes much clearer. In this light, ordinary people may be recognised as the image of God and representatives of Christ. This, in turn, encourages new reflection on human suffering and the lives of the poor. When grinding poverty inhumanly disfigures people, it is a sin against both humanity and God. Furthermore, poverty was a condition that Jesus himself had suffered. This permitted the poor to be seen as the special representatives of Christ in the modern world. *Lumen Gentium* draws together a number of New Testament passages to make this point.

> Just as Christ carried out the work of redemption in poverty and oppression, so the Church is called to follow the same path if she is to communicate the fruits of salvation to men. Christ Jesus, 'though he was by nature God . . . emptied himself, taking the nature of a slave' (Phil. 2.6–7), and 'being rich, became poor' (2 Cor. 8.9) for our sake . . . Christ was sent by the Father 'to bring good news to the poor . . . to heal the contrite of heart' (Lk. 4.18). . . . Similarly, the Church encompasses with her love all those who are afflicted by human misery and she recognises in those who are poor and who suffer, the image of her poor and suffering founder.[42]

As noted in Chapters 2 and 3, *Rerum Novarum* and *Quadragesimo Anno* recognised that civil authorities should have special concern for the rights of the poor. *Lumen Gentium* prepared the way for the next stage in the late 1960s, in which progressives in the Latin American church embraced the option for the poor as the church's own task. The move towards this new relationship gained further impetus the following year with the publication of *Gaudium et Spes*.

Both the content and method of *Gaudium et Spes* were particularly important for liberation theology.[43] In terms of method, it followed a see-judge-act

---

[40] *Lumen Gentium*, §§ 9–17.

[41] For example, *Lumen Gentium*, § 7.

[42] *Lumen Gentium*, § 8.

[43] Some of its key ideas were anticipated in John XXIII's *Humanae Salutis*, which officially convoked the Council on 25 December 1961.

method (similar to Catholic Action and endorsed by *Mater et Magistra*) to relate its teaching to contemporary social challenges. In terms of message, it stated the church's special concern for the poor in its opening sentence: "The joy and hope, the grief and anguish of the men of our time, especially of those who are poor or afflicted in any way, are the joy and hope, the grief and anguish of the followers of Christ as well."[44] The church could not leave social justice to civil authorities, but should work for it as an integral part of its own vocation.

To carry out its social responsibilities, *Gaudium et Spes* challenged the church to read the signs of the times and respond to them.[45] The bishops recognised that many signs of the times were profoundly disturbing.

> In no other age has mankind enjoyed such an abundance of wealth, resources and economic well-being; and yet a huge proportion of the people of the world is plagued by hunger and extreme need while countless others are totally illiterate. At no time have men had such a keen sense of freedom, only to be faced by new forms of slavery in living and thinking.[46]

God desires that all people should form one family and the church is called to promote this divine plan. Yet, the world remains scarred by division and inequality rather than blessed unity and fairness. In response to this, they affirmed that the love of God cannot be separated from the love of one's neighbour.[47] This acknowledgment of social inequality (with the implication that the lives of rich and poor are inextricably linked) initiated a new era in social teaching. The bishops called on people to make themselves the neighbours of all and relieve the sufferings of others.[48] This was an inescapable Christian duty, not a matter of voluntary special merit. The urgency of the situation and the need for everyone to do more ran throughout the document.[49]

Lumen Gentium and *Gaudium et Spes* indicated a dramatic change of course for the church in its institutional identity and its relations with society. At the end of Vatican II, Paul VI summarised two key aspects of the council in his closing address. First, that the religious and theological are linked to the temporal and human; the church is called to discern the former in the latter. Second, that the church should be a humble servant, not a socially privileged institution or partner in civil power.[50]

---

[44] *Gaudium et Spes*, § 1.

[45] *Gaudium et Spes*, §§ 4 and 11.

[46] *Gaudium et Spes*, § 4.

[47] *Gaudium et Spes*, § 24. This was a crucial point in ensuring the unity of the social and doctrinal tradition. The implication is that the social tradition is not a secondary, additional, or optional tradition and should never be treated as such.

[48] *Gaudium et Spes*, § 27.

[49] See, for example, *Gaudium et Spes*, § 66: "To fulfil the requirements of justice and equity, every effort must be made to put an end as soon as possible to the immense economic inequalities which exist in the world and increase from day to day."

[50] Paul VI, Closing Address to the Council (7 December 1965).

The council documents tacitly endorsed the progressive Catholic thinkers who were seeking a new direction for the church in the world. Vatican II rejected the traditional and conservative church that had been a bastion of the *status quo* and authoritarian elites for centuries. The church was finally ready to become a committed supporter of human rights, social justice, and political democracy. Furthermore, the council gave support for local bishops to take this renewal further in their own regional contexts. Without these changes it is unlikely that the liberation theology that emerged in the late 1960s would have been possible.

THEOLOGICAL STIRRINGS IN LATIN AMERICA, 1960–1965

Even before Vatican II began, two of the most influential progressive bishops— Dom Hélder Câmara (of Brazil) and Manuel Larraín (of Chile)—took initiatives to stimulate debate in Latin America on the social challenges that faced the church. In 1961, they organised a conference to discuss a Latin American pastoral program in Rio de Janeiro.[51] This marked the start of early attempts to reflect on a distinctively Latin American pathway for the church. In August 1962, just before his departure for Rome, Bishop Larraín organised a further small theological consultation in Buenos Aires. This included the Peruvian priest Gustavo Gutiérrez and the Colombian priest Camilo Torres.[52] Later, a group of priests that included Juan Luis Segundo met in Cerro Alegre, Peru, and considered the social context of Latin America and the church's role in its future.[53]

From 1962 to 1965, Latin American bishops spent October to December in Rome.[54] They played relatively little part in most discussions, but followed events with eager interest and occasional interventions.[55] An unintended, but very important consequence of the council was that during their time in Rome,

---

[51] Both Roger Vekemans and Ivan Illich attended it. At this time Vekemans was a reformist and sympathetic to many of the initiatives behind liberation theology. However, he later became a strong critic of liberation theology and especially critical of the Christians for Socialism movement in Chile; see R. Vekemans, *Teología de la liberación y Cristianos por el Socialismo* (Bogotá: CEDIAL, 1976).

[52] Gutiérrez and Torres studied together at Louvain (Belgium) in the 1950s. In Latin America, they both combined their vocations as priests with academic work as university lecturers in Lima (Gutiérrez) and Bogotá (Torres).

[53] See "Iglesia y futuro de América Latina: Conversaciones de Cerro Alegre, en Perú sobre la realidad de Continente (1962)" in J. L. Segundo (ed.), *Iglesia Latinoamericana: ¿Profeta o Profecía?* (Avellanda, Argentina: Ediciones Busqueda, 1969).

[54] They were amongst more than 2000 bishops who took part in Vatican II. There were over five hundred bishops from Latin America at the Council, but the greatest number of participants were from Europe. These included over 400 Italians, more than 150 French, and nearly 100 Spanish. As a result, the council had been dominated by largely European questions and assumptions.

[55] The small group of theological advisers to the Latin American bishops also followed events with a keen interest. Some of the promising Latin American students who undertook graduate studies in Europe in the 1950s and early 1960s attended the council

the Latin American bishops had opportunities to meet with each other. This strengthened their sense of national and regional identity. For example, the Brazilian bishops who were already quite advanced in their national organisation developed sufficient collaboration to launch their innovative Joint Pastoral plans a few years later.

Vatican II was also important because ordinary CELAM meetings took place in Rome and were well attended. These meetings allowed the influential leadership of the progressive Brazilian bishops to support progressive bishops elsewhere and contributed to progressive leadership at the forefront of CELAM's activities. Furthermore, at the last session of the Council, the bishops took the decision to call a second extraordinary CELAM meeting (the first had been CELAM I at Rio de Janeiro, 1955) to discuss the Council together back in Latin America.

The Central European priest Ivan Illich—who had attended the meeting in Rio organised by Câmara and Larraín—went on to play a prominent role in facilitating links between the group of progressive Latin American priests that were emerging in the early 1960s.[56] As a director of two mission preparation centres (in Cuernavaca, Mexico, and Petrópolis, Brazil) Illich organised documentation services to expose new missionaries to the harsh social realities of Latin America.[57] During the 1960s, Illich's Centre for Intercultural Formation in Cuernavaca had a particularly influential role on the many Catholic missionaries that came to Latin America.[58] Illich made them aware of the social issues that the church faced in Latin America and challenged their understanding of mission work in the midst of Latin America's social tensions. Illich also started to network and organise meetings of priests who started to think along similar lines. Many missionaries who passed through his centres experienced an awakening to issues of social justice and political struggle. These initial experiences prepared them for further radicalization during their work in Latin America.[59]

---

in this capacity. These included: Gustavo Gutiérrez (from Peru), Enrique Dussel (from Argentina), and José Comblin (a Belgian who worked in Brazil). Protestant observers included the Argentinean Methodist José Míguez Bonino and the North American Presbyterian Robert McAfee Brown (who would later be a sympathetic critic of Latin American liberation theology in North American circles).

[56] Illich had moved to New York before starting work in Latin America. In educational circles, his name became well known in association with the School is Dead movement.

[57] He also established documentation centres in both places, which provided valuable information on the situation in Latin America for the missionaries and a wider church audience.

[58] Many of these came in response to John XXIII's call for European and North American priests to work in Latin America.

[59] Many of them were shocked by the social conditions and inequalities that they met in Latin America, and their experiences prompted them to take up increasingly critical positions. Since they often had greater political protection than their local colleagues, the mission priests were often in the forefront of the liberation movement at a local level.

Probably the most significant theological meeting initiated by Illich took place in the university town of Petrópolis in Brazil in March 1964.[60] A group of theologians from Latin America and Mexico met to get to know each other and exchange ideas and experiences. At this meeting, both the Uruguayan Jesuit Juan Luis Segundo and the Peruvian priest Gustavo Gutiérrez presented papers on possible new directions for the church.[61] They had both completed graduate study in Europe and were eager to engage with the challenges that the church faced in Latin America.

Segundo's paper "Theological Problems of Latin America" identified some of the key social changes that had recently taken place in Latin American societies.[62] He drew attention to urbanization and the new means of communications, as well as the growth of revolutionary sentiment amongst younger activists. He then criticised the superficiality of the demands that the church placed on believers, which allowed them to ignore the social dimension to the gospel. The church was content with the appearance of social harmony but sacrificed the integrity of its social demands and evaded the full responsibilities of its evangelical mission. Segundo had already touched on some of these issues in a talk given to students in Paris in November 1962.[63] In the same year, he published his still untranslated work *Funcion de la Iglesia en la realidad rioplatense* (*The Role of the Church in the Social Reality of the River Plate*).[64]

Gutiérrez's paper at Petrópolis indicated some of the important lines of thought that he was already developing.[65] It identified the social influences on

---

[60] See R. Oliveros, *Liberación y teología: Génesis y crecimiento de una reflexión, 1966–1976* (Lima: Centro de Estudios y Publicaciones, 1977). The section on the Petrópolis meeting is available in translation as "Meeting of Theologians at Petrópolis" in the invaluable collection of source documents provided by Alfred Hennelly, see Hennelly (ed.), *Liberation Theology: A Documentary History* (Maryknoll, N.Y.: Orbis Books, 1990), pp. 43–47.

[61] Some members of the group had first met each other as students in Europe, but found contact in Latin America more difficult. For example, Gutiérrez first met Segundo in Louvain in 1952 (Smith, *The Emergence of Liberation Theology*, p. 108).

[62] Segundo's ideas are summarised in "Meeting of Theologians at Petrópolis" in Hennelly, *Liberation Theology*, pp. 44–45. Segundo was born in 1925, studied theology at San Miguel Argentina in the early 1950s, and was ordained a Jesuit priest in 1955. He completed his licentiate in theology at Louvain in 1956 and gained his doctorate in philosophy and theology from Paris in 1963. When he returned to Uruguay, he worked at the Peter Faber Pastoral Centre in Montevideo and was its director from 1965 to 1971. During the 1960s, both Segundo and Gutiérrez contributed to courses at Illich's Centre at Cuernavaca.

[63] J. L. Segundo, "The Future of Christianity in Latin America," *Cross Currents* 13 (Summer 1963), pp. 273–281; reprinted in Hennelly, *Liberation Theology*, pp. 29–37. Hennelly sees this as the first outlining of a new and distinctively Latin American perspective (*Liberation Theology*, p. 29).

[64] J. L. Segundo, *Funcion de la Iglesia en la realidad rioplatense* (Montevideo: Barreiro y Ramos, 1962).

[65] It is summarised in "Meeting of Theologians at Petrópolis" in Hennelly, *Liberation Theology*, pp. 45–46.

life in Latin America and examined the social composition of Latin American society (which he saw in terms of a popular majority, a technocracy, an intelligentsia, and the oligarchy). In the light of this analysis, he suggested that theology should take social reality as its starting point for pastoral action and offered a theological critique of the existing pastoral work of the church. Over the next four years, Gutiérrez developed and clarified this line of thought in a series of talks to university students and in his role as the national adviser to the Peruvian student organisation.[66]

The Petrópolis meeting did not mark a formal start to liberation theology or name a new theological movement.[67] It did, however, set out in draft some of ideas that would be important for liberation theology and helped form a nucleus of socially progressive theologians working with similar convictions on the urgency of social change and the need for new direction in the church. The conference was an important event that brought them together and encouraged them to continue working on their projects and keep in touch with each other.[68] It was followed by further conferences in 1965 at Havana, Bogotá, and Cuernavaca, which gradually took their discussions further.[69]

---

[66] His work included a MIEC presentation in February 1967 in Montevideo, which was published as a book *La pastoral en la iglesia en america latina* ((Montevideo: Ediciones de Centro de Documentación MIEC–JECI, 1968) and republished as *Líneas pastorales de la Iglesia en América Latina, Análisis Teológico*, (Lima: Centro de Estudios y Publicaciones, rev. ed, 1976).

[67] There are differences of opinion on the extent to which the basic orientation of liberation theology can be discerned in Gutiérrez's paper at Petrópolis. Smith suggests that it can because "Gutiérrez's paper presented theology as 'critical reflection on praxis'" and also because in a personal interview with Gutiérrez, Gutiérrez himself said that although the idea of liberation came to him in 1968, the content was already there at Petrópolis (Smith, *The Emergence of Liberation Theology*, pp. 120 and 156). Oliveros is— I think correctly—much more tentative when he says: "Here we have in embryo what will later be called theology's critical function with regard to the praxis of Christians, and also how we discover our most profound options precisely in our praxis" (Hennelly, *Liberation Theology*, p. 46).

[68] Meanwhile, in Protestant circles a "theology of revolution" was starting to take shape. This movement was especially associated with the work of the North American missionary Richard Shaull. Shaull had arrived in Brazil in 1952 as a Presbyterian missionary and initially understood his work as part of the Cold War crusade against communism. However, within a few years he changed his position. His work *Encounter with Revolution* (New York: Associated Press, 1955) challenged Protestants to take the struggle for justice seriously. In the same year, the World Council of Churches (WCC) invited him to participate in a sequence of annual theological conferences to address social themes. The organisation ISAL (Church and Society in Latin America) developed out of these conferences in 1961 and became a focus for radical Protestant thought in Brazil and other Latin American countries. Shaull himself was a strong advocate of the theology of revolution as a more radical alternative to the reformist hopes of more conservative advocates of development. For an overview of the theology of revolution, see M. E. Marty and D. Peerman (eds.), *Theology and Revolution* (New York: Macmillan, 1969). After 1962, Shaull combined his work in Brazil with a faculty position at Princeton Theological Seminary and had close contacts with ISAL's Latin American network of

CONCLUSION

The early 1960s established the Cold War political framework in which liberation theology would emerge later in the decade. On the one hand, Cuba strengthened its links with the Soviet Union and the Socialist block after being firmly rebuffed by the United States. Cold War brinkmanship between the two superpowers reached new levels of intensity in Latin America and the Caribbean, and almost sparked a nuclear war. On the other hand, to prevent other countries from following Castro's example, the United States developed a two-pronged strategy. On the political and economic side, it sponsored reforms and development through an Alliance for Progress intended to undermine popular support for a revolution. On the military side, it consolidated its links with the region's security forces, provided them with training and equipment and encouraged a strong anti-communist line. When the Brazilian military took power in 1964, the United States could trump the USSR (and Cuba) with the most powerful and advanced country in Latin America as its own Cold War client. For the rest of the 1960s and the 1970s, the Brazil military served as a pro-U.S. police force for the whole of the southern continent. When the Alliance for Progress failed to deliver its reforms, it was Brazil, rather than Cuba that exported its revolution through the militaries of neighbouring countries.

The early 1960s also set the context for liberation theology's emergence as an ecclesial and theological movement.[70] The church, prior to the 1960s, saw the defence of human rights as the responsibility of the civil authorities and the church's role in terms of charity rather than justice. After John XXIII and Vatican II, social justice for the poor was also to be an issue for the church

---

young and socially concerned theologians, including José Míguez Bonino (Argentina) and Julio Santa Ana (Uruguay), as well as Rubem Alves (Brazil). In 1963, ISAL started to publish the journal *Cristianismo y Sociedad* (*Christianity and Society*) in Montevideo. In its early years, many of the articles promoted the theology of revolution, but in the later 1960s, attention began to shift to the idea of liberation and it became linked to the new currents of radical Catholic theology that Gutiérrez and Segundo started to develop. By the late 1960s, despite its Protestant foundations, ISAL had an ecumenical ethos and in Bolivia, Catholic membership outweighed Protestant membership (see Cleary, *Crisis and Change*, p. 36).

[69] Roberto Oliveros describes further meetings of the theologico-pastoral renewal movement that followed Petrópolis during 1965: "A conference in Havana, Cuba, July 14–16, on the topic of pastoral renewal, with talks by Segundo Galilea and Luis Maldonato among others; another meeting in Bogotá, Colombia, from June 14 to July 9, also on pastoral issues, with talks by Juan Luis Segundo and Cassiano Floristán; and finally one in Cuernavaca, Mexico from July 4 to August 14, with presentations by Ivan Illich and Segundo Galilea" (see Hennelly, *Liberation Theology*, p. 44). According to Cleary, these meetings promoted the formation of a core group of theologians committed to similar lines of development (see, *Crisis and Change*, p. 35).

[70] As will become clear, liberation theology was both an ecclesial movement and a theological one. Understanding both sides of the movement and appreciating the interaction between them and the reinforcement that they gave each other is crucial for appreciating the history and significance of the movement.

and integral to its mission. Where civil authorities failed to heed their special responsibility to the poor, the church needed to take up their cause. The Latin American bishops in Rome witnessed this major shift, and it provided the basis for the Latin America bishops to make a special commitment to the poor when they reflected on the Council's relevance for Latin America at CELAM II. Meanwhile, during the early 1960s in Latin America, a network of well-educated and socially concerned theologians started to question the adequacy of the church's pastoral strategy and argued that it needed to address Latin America's social problems more adventurously.

CHAPTER FIVE

An Atmosphere of Liberation, 1965–1969

> A deafening cry pours from the throats of millions of men and women asking their pastors for a liberation that reaches them from nowhere else.
> The Bishops of Latin America, CELAM II, 1968.[1]

INTRODUCTION

In the late 1960s, the optimism from the earlier part of the decade turned into disillusionment. Civil protests demanding change became more forceful as hopes for reforms were frustrated. In response, governments adopted repressive measures to maintain the *status quo*. United States support for the military regime in Brazil (especially after the coup in 1964) and the landing of United States marines in the Dominican Republic in 1965 showed the true priorities of the so-called Alliance for Progress. Despite the democratic rhetoric of the alliance, the prime objective of United States policy was to ensure that the region remained within the United States political orbit and served its economic interests.

The militant anti-communism of U.S. foreign policy meant that the Alliance for Progress was unable to deliver meaningful social and economic changes. Even the mildest reforms tended to provoke fears of socialism and were resisted by those in power. Since the United States remained wedded to its alliance with right-wing governments who promised to maintain stability in the face of threatened subversion, economic reforms were consistently sacrificed for Cold War concerns.

Against this political backdrop of frustrated hopes and mounting repression, the late 1960s saw the emergence of more radical voices which pressed for revolutionary changes and created a vibrant new atmosphere of liberation

---

[1] CELAM II, *Document on the Poverty of the Church*, § 2, reprinted Hennelly (ed.), *Liberation Theology*, pp. 114–119 (114).

in progressive intellectual circles.[2] The effects of this were apparent in a number of fields, including: dependency theory in economics and social sciences; the radical pedagogy of Paulo Freire in education; and the first steps towards a theology of liberation.

The first clear public use of the term "theology of liberation" came in 1968, and the first modest publications under this title started to appear soon afterwards. However, much of this work might have remained at academic level in a relatively small circle of progressive clerics, if in 1968, the Latin American bishops had not taken an unexpectedly decisive stand in solidarity with the poor at their meeting in Medellín. The church's commitment at Medellín to make concern for the poor a central task for the church, meant that the link between pastoral policy and the new theology of liberation would not just be a matter for individual innovators; it would be relevant for the whole church in Latin America.

DISILLUSION WITH DEVELOPMENT

In the 1960s, the political and economic objectives of development came under closer scrutiny. The militaristic side of the United States strategy came into sharper focus and exposed the limitations of the democratic rhetoric. Under Lyndon Johnson (1963–1968) and Richard Nixon (1969–1974), the United States committed itself to the defence of the free world wherever it felt its interests under threat.

Meanwhile, the Alliance for Progress in Latin America failed to repeat the successes of the Marshall Plan in Europe. The majority of donor country aid was tied to the purchase of goods from the donor country. The generosity of donors seemed to have little to do with benefits for Latin America and more to do with the donor's exports. Criticisms over the level and direction of Latin American development prompted a dramatic rethink of what development and progress really stood for and whose interest the alliance served.

U.S. Intervention in the Caribbean and Support for the Military in Brazil

The limits of the democratic ideals in the Alliance for Progress were brought home in 1965 when President Johnson ordered United States marines to invade the Dominican Republic. After the traumas of a dictatorship under strongman Rafael Trujillo (1930–1961), the Dominican people had elected the reformist Juan Bosch (Dominican Revolutionary Party) as President in December 1962. He was inaugurated in February 1963, but conservatives promptly accused him of being too left wing and sympathetic to Castro. In September 1963, the Dominican military overthrew him and replaced him with their own civilian junta. In April 1965, a popular uprising backed by some factions in the army

---

[2] L. Boff and C. Boff, *Salvation and Liberation: In Search of a Balance between Faith and Politics* (trans. R. Barr; Maryknoll, N.Y.: Orbis Books, 1984), pp. 14–17.

attempted to restore Bosch to power. The armed forces split into opposing camps (the army supported Bosch, while the navy and air force backed the existing *junta*), and the capital city Santo Domingo was divided into rival zones.

Worried about the destabilising effect of the crisis, the United States seized the opportunity to stamp its authority on the Caribbean and Latin America. A contingent of 22,000 United States marines invaded to restore order. They took up positions in Santo Domingo between the opposing forces while the Organisation of American States (OAS) negotiated a peaceful resolution and new elections. With United States support, Balaguer consolidated his position by defeating Bosch in the 1966, 1970, and 1974 elections.

For the political Left in Latin America, the experience in the Dominican Republic suggested that the United States would only countenance modest reforms, not dramatic change. For the most militant groups, this was seen as proof that the only meaningful way forward was Cuban style revolution.

The support of the United States for the military in Brazil gave an equally important indication of their priorities. After the military coup, the government enacted a series of measures to restore economic stability, cut the balance of payments deficit, and curb inflation. The economy went into a three-year recession and the living standard of the vast majority suffered accordingly.[3] To prevent political protests the hard-liner Marshall Artur da Costa e Silva replaced the more moderate General, Humberto Castello Branco as leader of the junta in 1966. His Institutional Act of December 1968 tightened the military's grip on the country and permitted a dramatic increase in repression against any form of political opposition. The following year witnessed urban guerrilla actions by radical groups, who took advantage of Artur da Costa e Silva's stroke in August 1969 to kidnap the U.S. ambassador to Brazil in September. However, these actions only provoked a further heightening of repression under General Garrastazu Medici who took over the Presidency in November 1969 and continued to 1974.

Under Artur da Costa e Silva and Garrastazu Medici, Brazil systematized the various elements of National Security State. This legitimated the destruction of all civil opposition, as a means to restore Brazil's traditional values of "Order and Progress" (the Brazilian motto since the Republic). With United States encouragement, the military saw its task in Cold War terms to maintain the western and Christian heritage of the country and use Brazil's position as a regional power to ensure that neighbouring countries did likewise. The adoption of similar National Security State doctrines by other countries in the years that followed prepared the way for waves of repression that swept the continent in the 1970s.

---

[3] Mainwaring notes that in São Paulo, the infant mortality rate rose 45% between 1960 and 1975 (*The Catholic Church*, p. 107). At national level, the income share of the bottom 50% of the population fell from 17.4% to 13.5% while the top 5% of the population raised their share from 28.3% to 37.9%.

Dependency Theory

Starting in the 1930s and 1940s, the United States had provided support to help Latin American countries to further develop their manufacturing base and take advantage of their home market through import substitution initiatives. It was hardly surprising that this opportunity was eagerly embraced. However, to undertake this next stage of industrialization, Latin American countries often had to import advanced machinery and equipment. The long-term intention to decrease imports was only possible by creating a new range of imports in the short-term. Furthermore, to make the policy possible, other costs (such as transport and infrastructure) increased significantly. To begin with this had been fairly straightforward. The export boom in the 1940s that came about from supplying materials during and after World War II generated significant capital in Latin America for the early stages of industrialisation. By contrast, as import substitution continued, it became more dependent on foreign loans to finance these imports. During the 1950s, this finance came as development loans and aid packages from the United States and elsewhere.[4]

By the 1960s, some progress towards industrialisation had been made but the overall impact was quite modest, and the import substitution approach ran into a number of problems. First, it only affected a relatively small sector of the overall economy. Second, it did little to address economic inequality within Latin America countries, and in many cases, it had simply increased it. Third, it had exacerbated existing social problems related to migration and urbanization and introduced new ecological problems associated with industrialization. Fourth, it left Latin America increasingly indebted and dependent on developed countries such as the U.S.

Particular problems existed over the role of multinationals. Most import substitution policies saw multinational companies as attractive sources of investment and expertise. However, by the 1960s, it was clear that they could be a serious drawback. Multinationals invested on highly favourable concessionary terms with tax breaks, transport and market links, and other benefits. The multinationals then took advantage of Latin America's cheap labour costs, but did not need to reinvest their profits back into the economy. Profits went back to the headquarters and shareholders in the United States or Europe. As a result, the multinationals usually took wealth out of Latin America instead of putting it in. This was a further variant on the historical model of colonial exploita-

---

[4] The Economic Commission for Latin America—commonly known by the Spanish CEPAL (*Comisión Económico para América Latina*)—was established in Santiago in 1948 with UN support. It became an influential centre for economists in support of these development policies. However, by the 1960s, a number of its leading thinkers were questioning its development. Raúl Prebisch was a particularly influential figure in this more radical work at CEPAL, which stressed the differences between the world's periphery (the underdeveloped nations that provided raw materials and agricultural products for export) and the centre or metropolis (the developed countries that benefited from these).

tion, which led to Latin America's deeper impoverishment. As with the Spanish colonialism of previous centuries, the economic system benefited foreign powers and a small local elite, but only entrenched the poverty of the vast majority of Latin Americans.

During the 1960s, it became clear that the Alliance for Progress was unable to solve these basic problems. Despite many initiatives on desperately needed land reforms, wealth redistribution, and basic political rights, many of the initiatives that threatened entrenched interests never made it onto the statute books. Even when they did, they were usually compromised to a level that made them worthless or were honoured in theory but not practice. As a result, attempts at reform did little to address the deeper structural problems.

At the same time, in the social sciences, Latin American dependency theory started to provide a forceful critique of the whole model of development that underlied the Alliance for Progress.

The conventional development model suggested that Latin America would follow the developed countries through set stages of development.[5] However, dependency theorists argued that trade arrangements meant that Latin America could not follow the same progressive development as Europe or North America. Therefore, the development policies of the 1950s and 1960s simply contributed to Latin America's greater dependency on rich nations. There were some gains in terms of overall economic activity and gross domestic products, but the gap between Latin America and the rich countries grew greater rather than narrower and Latin American countries were as vulnerable to exploitation as ever.

Advocates of dependency theory included the Brazilians Celso Furtado and Fernando Henrique Cardoso and the North American Andre Gunder Frank.[6] Each of these thinkers had their own individual perspective on particular problems, but there was basic agreement that the analysis needed to shift from urging development to recognising dependency and *under*development. They argued that international economic relations were unevenly matched between the centres of capital (Europe and North America) and the peripheral economies that were dependent on them (in Latin America and elsewhere). In this context of dependency, Latin America's supposed development, in fact worsened

---

[5] See esp. W. W. Rostow, *The Stages of Economic Growth: A Non-Communist Manifesto* (Cambridge: Cambridge University Press, 1960). Rostow based his work on the British economy and argued that other countries would follow the same five stages of development.

[6] See, for example, C. Furtado, *The Economic Growth of Brazil* (Berkeley: University of California Press, 1963 [Portuguese orig. 1959]); idem, *Development and Stagnation in Latin America: A Structural Approach* (New Haven, Conn.: Yale University Press, 1965); F. H. Cardoso and E. Faletto, *Dependency and Development in Latin America* (trans. M. Uruqudi; Berkeley: University of California Press, 1979 [Spanish orig. 1969]); A. G. Frank, *Capitalism and Underdevelopment in Latin America: Historical Studies of Chile and Brazil* (New York: Monthly Review Press, rev. ed. 1969 [1967]); idem, *Latin America: Underdevelopment or Revolution* (New York: Monthly Review Press, 1969). A helpful anthology on dependency writing is R. H. Chilcote and J. C. Edelstein (eds.), *Latin America: The Struggle with Dependency and Beyond* (New York: Halstead Press, 1974).

rather than improved Latin America's problems. Latin America's dependency allowed the rich countries to ensure that economic trade relations always worked to their advantage and resulted in Latin America's *continuing underdevelopment*. The loans and aid of the Alliance for Progress did not change this dependency; they only consolidated it as the gap between rich and poor countries continued to widen.

Dependency theorists said that a far more radical change was needed. This change could only come by rejecting this unfair relationship and ending the state of dependency. According to dependency theorists, what Latin America really needed was not further *development* along these lines but a *liberation* from its position in the world economy.[7] Dependency theory had a marked effect on the political framework of early works in liberation theology. Its emphasis on freedom from the old order encouraged new ways of seeing the international order and the theological use of liberation terminology.

Struggles for Liberation

As social protest movements escalated in the late 1960s, armed revolutionary groups emerged in many Latin American countries. After 1965, Che Guevara tried to export socialist revolution to other countries in Latin America and Africa. His theory of *foco* warfare was based on the belief that even small guerrilla groups operating in the countryside could eventually precipitate a popular uprising.[8] To put his words into practice he became leader of a small revolutionary band in Bolivia. However, he could not gain the support or confidence of the Bolivian peasantry (*campesinos*) and his efforts met with little success. Bolivian soldiers (trained by United States military advisers) captured and executed him in 1967.[9] Nonetheless, Guevara's idealism and adventurism inspired a generation of youth.[10]

---

[7] There have been important criticisms of both the theoretical framework and empirical data on which the early works in dependency theory drew. For an overview of the influence of dependency on liberation theology, see A. F. McGovern, *Liberation Theology and Its Critics* (Maryknoll, N.Y.: Orbis Books, 1990), pp. 135–138. For a helpful overview of different perspectives on development/underdevelopment see I. Roxborough, *Theories of Development* (London: Macmillan, 1979). For a variety of assessments on dependency theory, see especially, R. C. Bath and D. Jones, "Dependency Analysis of Latin America," *LARR* 11.3 (1976), pp. 3–54; F. H. Cardoso, "The Consumption of Dependency Theory in the United States," *LARR* 12.3 (1977), pp. 7–24; S. Jackson et al., "An Assessment on Empirical Research on *Dependencia*," *LARR* 14.3 (1979), pp. 7–28. Various contributions in the symposium published in *LARR* 17.1 (1982), pp. 115–172, show how dependency theory has responded to early criticisms.

[8] This optimism influenced a number of guerrilla movements in Latin America. However, as Guevara himself discovered, the theory of rural insurgency based on *foco* groups proved much harder to apply in South America. In the more developed countries, revolutionary efforts amongst peasants found little support and revolutionary movements tended to concentrate on urban guerrilla activities.

[9] On Guevara's life, see J. Castañeda, *Compañero: The Life and Death of Che Guevara* (London: Bloomsbury, 1997).

[10] The Bolivian soldiers only encouraged the adulation of Guevara when they pub-

Camilo Torres was one such priest. Torres was from an affluent Colombian family who felt called to a life of service and joined the priesthood.[11] Like other talented Latin American seminarians of his generation, he was sent to Europe for higher studies, which included time at Louvain studying sociology. After his return to Colombia in 1962, he became chaplain and professor of sociology at National University in Bogotá. His political outlook became increasingly revolutionary through involvement with social movements on behalf of the poor. In June 1965, he resigned from the priesthood to take more direct political action for change.[12]

Although Torres was not a communist, he advocated a Christian alliance with communists and others who sought radical change. On this basis, he attempted to set up a broadly based political movement committed to social change (the United Front of the Colombian People). Convinced that the necessary changes could only be brought through armed-struggle, he joined the National Liberation Army guerrilla group. Four months later, in February 1966, he was shot by the military at Bucaramanga in the Colombian mountains.

The example of Camilo Torres (guerrilla priest) was widely admired in left-wing circles and even inspired a small number of Christian followers to emulate his example. One of the most famous was the writer and mystic Néstor Paz, who joined the Bolivian guerrillas of Teoponte near La Paz.[13] Regrettably, in some perceptions of liberation theology, the example of Torres and others who left the priesthood to take up arms is the defining feature of the movement rather than the extreme exception.[14] In fact, very few priests went as far

---

lished a photo of him—intended to prove that he was dead—in which his prostrate corpse served as a reminder of the suffering Christ taken down from the cross. It was as if the dead Guevara exposed the hypocrisy of the moribund church and challenged Christians to respond to Christ's example of self-sacrifice and take up the cause of armed revolution as a messianic mission.

[11] For a short overview of his life and death, see J. Womack, "Priest of Revolution?" *New York Review of Books* (23 October 1969), pp. 13–16. For Torres's extensive writings on the church and society, see C. Torres, *Father Camilo Torres: Revolutionary Writings* (ed. M. Zeitlin; trans. R. Olsen and L. Day; New York: Harper & Row, rev ed., 1972); idem, *Revolutionary Priest: The Complete Writings and Messages of Camilo Torres* (ed. J. Gerassi; trans. J. de Cipriano et al.; London: Cape, 1971). For the social background to Torres's decision and the guerrilla movement that he joined, see O. F. Borda, *Subversion and Social Change in Colombia* (New York: Columbia University Press, 1969).

[12] His terse letter to the Cardinal of Bogotá on 24 June 1965 is included as "Letter Requesting Lay Status" in *Father Camilo Torres: Revolutionary Writings*, p. 263. In a press-statement published in *El Tiempo* newspaper the following day he stated: "Upon analyzing Colombian society I realized the need for a revolution that would give food to the hungry, drink to the thirsty, clothing to the naked, and bring about the well-being of the majorities in our country. I feel that the revolutionary struggle is a Christian and priestly struggle" (*Father Camilo Torres*, pp. 264–265).

[13] Paz explains his decision in N. Paz, *My Life for My Friends* (Maryknoll, N.Y.: Orbis Books, 1975).

[14] This misrepresentation usually leads to simplistic dismissals of liberation theology as idealistic but misguided, or as heroic but doomed, or as immoral and un-Christian. The idea that liberation theology was simply about priests in Che Guevara berets and

as to follow Torres's example or encourage others to do so. The vast majority of those who became involved in liberation theology rejected the use of force, but were profoundly challenged by Torres's example to develop an equally radical but nonviolent approach to social change.

Paulo Freire and Conscientization

In the field of education, the work of Paulo Freire in Brazil had a dramatic impact on educational thought throughout the continent. Freire began teaching at the University of Recife in northeast Brazil in the late 1950s. There, he developed an approach to basic adult education designed to empower marginalized people to political awareness.[15] These literacy projects provided the framework for the *Movimento de Educaçao de Base* (MEB or Base Education Movement) that was created in 1961.

The MEB was a partnership between the church and President Jânio Quadros. MEB literacy programs were transmitted on church radio stations and supported by local literacy coordinators who worked in small literacy circles with people in the Northeast and Amazon regions. These two regions suffered some of Brazil's worst poverty and the illiteracy of the peasants made them easy to exploit. Unscrupulous landowners bribed the police and judiciary to support their claims against illiterate workers, and the poor were frequently cheated out of their rightful wages and even their property rights. Excluded from political and economic power, they survived on the margins of society. In Brazil to this day, tens of thousands of such marginalized people farm the narrow strips of land at the edges of public highways—graphic illustration of the precariousness of survival for people who are on the margins.

Freire constantly stressed that people must be the agents of their own actions for liberation. He was highly critical of educational approaches that turned people into objects instead of respecting them as subjects. Freire believed that the traditional authority of the educator and the dependency of those being educated reflected and reinforced wider social processes of domination and submission.[16] The foundation of Freire's approach was the mutuality of respect between the teacher (as teacher-student) and student (as student-teacher). In this dialogue, the students and teacher would explore the world of oppression together as it was experienced in the everyday lives of the people. Freire's dialogical approach (based on two-way communication) was intended to break down rather than reinforce the usual power relationships in education and in society as a whole. This "pedagogy of the oppressed," as it came to be known, was

---

armed with AK-47 machine guns—a picture that was promoted amongst some on both the far Right and the far Left—is an example of how easily the truth about the church could be distorted in the polarised context of Latin America.

[15] It is often referred to as "popular education" because it was intended to benefit ordinary people who previously had only minimal formal education in school.

[16] P. Freire, *Pedagogy of the Oppressed* (trans. M. Ramos; New York: Continuum, 1970; London: Sheed and Ward, 1972; Portuguese orig. 1968).

therefore a way of teaching people who were oppressed and a way in which the oppressed could teach themselves and others about their experiences. This helped them to break the culture of silence and overcome the years of fatalism that their exploitation had often entrenched.

Freire's literacy lessons emphasised the early acquisition of basic words, for example the Portuguese words for house, water, or types of food. These were broken down into simple combinations of different vowel-consonants. The small group or "culture-circle" learned the make-up of the written words that were important to them by seeing how they could break them down into familiar vowels and consonants. This increased their confidence and their new skills made them eager to learn more. For example, after learning the vowels a, e, i, o, u and just three consonants t, j, l, the group could construct the vowel-consonant combinations ta-te-ti-to-tu, ja-je-ji-jo-ju, and la-le-li-lo-lu. From these, they could then construct everyday words with which they were familiar, for example *luta* (struggle), *lajota* (stone), *loja* (store), *jato* (jet), *juta* (jute), *lote* (lot), *tela* (screen) or combine them in new ways to get words like *leite* (milk).[17]

The distinctiveness and influence of Freire's approach was much more beneficial than his techniques for motivating learners who might be discouraged by more traditional methods. The learner's active involvement in the tasks contrasted with the passivity that traditional methods assumed and reinforced. Freire involved the learner in the process, not just a pragmatic ploy. The political philosophy that permeated his work meant that it extended further than the acquisition of basic reading skills.

Freire's method linked social and political literacy to basic literacy. He combined the two to help people learn more about their lives and become better able to change it. Freire described his approach as education for freedom. He aimed for both the freedom of the individual to engage with the written word, but also the political freedom of the poor to engage with the political world. Freire's approach incorporated political discussion on the social dynamics that affected their everyday life, including economic inequality, denial of rights, and repressive violence. The group's growing ability to develop identify, deconstruct, and reconstruct familiar words paralleled the development of similar skills of political literacy. Freire referred to this as *conscietazação* (conscientization or consciousness-raising).

Often, particular words from the literacy program were chosen to focus the political discussion and help the participants break the culture of silence. Words like *favela* (shantytown or slum) could generate energetic discussion within the group that the coordinator could draw upon to stimulate a more political awareness. Often, the word would be introduced with a picture. The facilitator would then invite participants to describe what they saw and discuss their own experiences of it. The inert representation would slowly come alive with the thoughts,

---

[17] See P. Freire, *Education for Critical Consciousness* (New York: Continuum, 1973 [Portuguese and Spanish origs. 1969]).

feelings, and memories that it generated for the group. The facilitator might add comments on the social dynamics hidden in the scene (for example, "Why is sanitation so poor in this area, but not others?," "Who do the people work for?" or "Why do they have no work?") and these would be discussed as well. The approach encouraged the participants to recognise that their everyday world was not something static and unchangeable, but continuously negotiated through social interactions and political processes. Their new power to name the *favela* in language and form it in writing was thereby related to a new opportunity to name the social dynamics that governed the *favela* as a social entity and to challenge and reform its oppressive elements through social action.[18]

The 1964 coup brought such innovation to an end. Freire himself was amongst the first wave to be exiled, and he moved on to Chile. The Base Education Movement survived the coup, but in a very toned down form. Nonetheless, it was very significant for having piloted Freire's dialogical approach in a major church project. Progressive church leaders who supported the project and witnessed its successes remained committed to many of its basic principles. The movement was one of the most important precursors to the base communities that developed in the 1970s. Progressive bishops who had seen the impact of MEB were more inclined to give these communities their protection and support.

THE CHURCH FINDS A VOICE

During the late 1960s, a major awakening took place within the leadership of the Latin American church. Many Latin American priests, religious, bishops, and theologians sought to ally themselves with the spirit of social change. This involved a number of factors, which were mutually reinforcing. First, a small number of socially progressive bishops such as Dom Hélder Câmara in Brazil provided dynamic leadership for institutional change and engagement with social issues. Second, Paul VI's social encyclical *Populorum Progressio* (*On the Development of Peoples*) in 1967 had a powerful impact on the worldwide church, especially in Latin America. Third, the series of preparatory conferences (1966–1968) that were part of the build-up to the second general (or extraordinary) meeting of the Latin American Bishops Council known as CELAM II encouraged the search for an alternative to development which encouraged talk of liberation. Fourth, at CELAM II in Medellín (1968) the bishops committed themselves to solidarity with the poor as a priority for the Latin American church. Fifth, the first efforts toward an explicitly identifiable and self-conscious liberation theology started to be published (1968–1969).

---

[18] For Freire's method to be successful, the coordinator had to be well versed in the social reality of the people. To help chose appropriate generative words, coordinators spent time in different communities to ensure that the words they chose would be relevant to the people concerned and would help to uncover the realities of their life.

The common factor in these different developments was the church's new social commitment to the poor. If a specific time had to be picked for the beginning of this commitment it would probably be May–August 1968. In the space of a few months, the Jesuit provincials for Latin America met in May, Gustavo Gutiérrez presented his paper on liberation theology at Chimbote in July, and the bishops met at CELAM II in August. Each of these events helped crystallise the church's new commitment to the poor. As the current of liberation swept through the continent in the late 1960s, progressives within the church were eager to give it leadership and direction and encourage Christians to play their part in it.

At this stage, there was still a strong presumption that the church should lead and direct. The church made an active commitment to liberating the poor, but there was less attention to the active participation of the poor in their own liberation. The church was *committed to the poor* but had not yet been *transformed by the poor*. It was not until the mid-1970s that this second and equally important transformation got under way through contact with the base communities.[19] However, the social commitment of the late 1960s was the necessary first stage, and it made all the later developments possible. For this reason, it is best to date the formal origins of liberation theology to this period.

Dom Hélder Câmara and the Northeastern Bishops of Brazil

Despite the social hardships that followed the 1964 coup, most of the Brazilian bishops were sympathetic to the military government and anxious to preserve the traditionally close relationship between church and state.[20] Within the CNBB, Dom José Gonçalves replaced Câmara as secretary general in October 1964 and Dom Agnelo Rossi (archbishop of São Paulo, 1964–1970) was elected President. Both were conservative and put the brakes on the generally progressive social leadership that the CNBB had previously given to the church

---

[19] It was this second transformation that generated the epistemological option for the poor (described in Chapter 8).

[20] Historically, the Brazilian hierarchy had been a highly conservative force on social issues. The church's alliance with the state was particularly close during the period of the Monarchy (1500–1889), when the church relied on the crown for its maintenance. Even when the church and state were formally separated (during the first forty years of the Republic), the church continued to see its interests in terms of the ruling class. Then, during the Vargas dictatorship (1930–1945), more formal links with the state were reestablished in the period referred to as the neo-Christendom model of the church. Between 1950 and 1964, the bishops had started to take a more reformist line especially the bishops in the Northeast. At a national level they were broadly supportive of the reforms that took place under the Goulart regime (1961–1964), particularly on land reform. However, many bishops became increasingly nervous at the uncertainty and potential social disorder that arose toward the end of the regime, and the CNBB issued a statement in support of the coup in June 1964. Even those who later became strong critics of the government, including Hélder Câmara and Paulo Arns, signalled their initial support by signing it; see Mainwaring, *The Catholic Church*, pp. 79–115.

at a local level. The CNBB remained virtually silent about military repression until the end of the 1960s.

However, despite the general timidity of the CNBB a significant minority of bishops—especially in the Amazon and Northeastern regions—became highly critical of the regime. With the intensification of repression—including the torture and imprisonment of priests and nuns in the Amazon region—relations between church and state deteriorated rapidly as these bishops became more outspoken. This drew other bishops into the conflict and prompted them to address the social problems of the country more forcefully.

In 1964, just at the time of the military coup in Brazil, Pope Paul VI appointed Dom Hélder Câmara to be Archbishop of Olinda and Recife. The Northeast was one of the poorest and least developed areas of Brazil. It suffered—and still suffers—some of the harshest poverty in the Western Hemisphere but some of the other Northeast bishops were at the forefront of the church's post-Conciliar social involvement. Câmara brought his organizational expertise with him from his work in the 1950s, and his national contacts developed through Catholic Action. In his new post, Câmara saw the failure of development policies that did little to address the basic needs of the people. Free from the watchful eye of his more conservative namesake, Cardinal Dom Jaime de Barros Câmara (his senior colleague in Rio de Janeiro), he could determine his own course more freely. As he saw the Northeast deprivation at first hand, Hélder Câmara deepened his understanding of how the system of inequality rested on repression and barely concealed violence against the poor. A campaign of intimidation and threats only made him more determined to speak frankly. Câmara's sermons and writings in the late 1960s offered an increasingly damning description of how the people in his diocese experienced poverty, violence, and exclusion. Together with the Northeast Brazilian bishops, Câmara developed a pastoral vision founded on defence of the poor.[21]

Of all his writings, perhaps his work on violence has made the most impact. At a lecture given in Paris (25 April 1968) he described the situation in Latin America as "internal colonialism" and conditions as "pre-revolutionary."[22] Emphasising the failings of both United States capitalism and Soviet socialism, he stressed the urgency of change in Latin America and a "structural revolution" throughout the whole world. In his discussion of violence, he spoke of the "order" (to which the powerful minority in Latin America appealed to repress any of the powerless majority who might oppose them) as the "orderly reign of disorder."

Câmara was determined to shift the church's discussion of violence to what he saw as its root causes. The traditional stance had been to simply condemn anyone whose defiance of state authorities led to violence. This invariably assumed that protesters, rebels, or revolutionaries were exclusively responsible for introducing violence into the system. Câmara wanted to address deeper

---

[21] See D. H. Câmara, *Church and Colonialism* (London: William Clowes, 1969).

[22] See Peruvian Bishops' Commission for Social Action, *Between Honesty and Hope* (Maryknoll, N.Y.: Orbis Books, 1970), pp. 47–54.

levels of responsibility and expose the hidden violence that already existed. Instead of just condemning those who resorted to violence, Câmara shifted attention to the triple violence that sustained the injustices in Latin America, but was rarely addressed by the church: the violence of internal colonialism; the violence of international trade; and the violence of the henchmen and private security forces working for plantation owners and factory bosses, often in close collaboration with the police and military.

Câmara repeatedly condemned the repressive violence that sustained internal colonialism and international neo-colonialism. However, while seeking to broaden discussion of violence to address the violence of all parties and to include structural and institutional violence alongside more visible violence, Câmara consistently offered his own unambiguous personal statement on violent attempts to overthrow the *status quo* rather than transform it through peaceful means.

I respect those who feel obliged in conscience to opt for violence—not the facile violence of the armchair guerrilla but that of a man who has proved his sincerity by sacrificing his life. It seems to me that the memory of Che Guevara deserves as much respect as that of Dr. Martin Luther King. I point an accusing finger at the real instigators of violence, at all those on the left and the right who wrong justice and block peace. My own personal vocation is to be a pilgrim of peace, following in the footsteps of Paul VI. Personally I would prefer a thousand times more to be killed than to kill anyone. This personal stance is grounded on the gospel. My lifetime effort to understand and live the gospel has brought me to this deep conviction: if the gospel can and should be called revolutionary, then it is so in that it demands a conversion from each one of us.[23]

Nonetheless, his work provoked the fury of the Brazilian paramilitary death squads, including organizations like the Commandos for the Hunt of Terrorists. On 26 May 1969, the twenty-eight-year-old priest, Antonio Henrique Pereia Neto, who worked as Câmara's assistant was kidnapped, tortured, and assassinated.[24] His death sent a chilling signal of the persecution that the church in Brazil and elsewhere in Latin America would face in the 1970s.[25]

---

[23] *Between Honesty and Hope*, p. 52.

[24] Gustavo Gutiérrez described the young priest as a close friend and dedicated *A Theology of Liberation* to him.

[25] There was a foretaste for this in 1969 when police arrested a number of Dominicans and kept them in an undisclosed location in São Paulo. Since most of the military bases where they were likely to have been taken were in Paulo Arns' area of the city—Arns was an auxiliary bishop at the time—Archbishop Rossi referred requests for archdiocesan intervention to Bishop Arns. The experience of tracing the missing Dominicans and witnessing the marks of torture that they and other prisoners suffered had a powerful impact on Arns. He had only been appointed as bishop three years earlier and quickly became one of the most courageous and prophetic leaders of the Brazil church. In October 1970 he was elevated to Archbishop of São Paulo and served there until 1996. Under his care the archdiocese became well known for its support of base communities in the 1970s and 1980s; see Lernoux, *Cry of the People*, pp. 321–32.

By this time, the CNBB was starting to shift its position and rediscover its prophetic voice.[26] The election of Dom Aloísio Lorscheider as CNBB secretary general earlier in 1968 restored a progressive voice in the CNBB leadership, but the political situation in the country was steadily deteriorating. In 1967, the economy had started to improve but there had been few changes for the poor. Under the Costa e Silva regime (1967–1969), social protests were met with severe repression. In December 1968, the military introduced Institutional Act V as the foundation for a National Security State.[27] Torture and other human rights abuses rose dramatically and in February 1969 the CNBB made its first public criticism of the military regime.[28]

Populorum Progressio

The publication of the encyclical *Populorum Progressio* (*The Development of Peoples*) by Paul VI on 26 March 1967 marked another important step forward in Catholic social tradition as it restated the church's concern for the poor in particularly strong terms. The opening paragraph set the tone:

> The development of peoples has the Church's close attention, particularly the development of those people who are striving to escape from hunger, misery, endemic diseases, and ignorance ... Following on the Second Vatican Ecumenical Council a renewed consciousness of the demands of the Gospel makes it her duty to put herself at the service of all, to help them grasp their serious problem in all its dimensions, and to convince them that solidarity in action at this turning point in human history is a matter of urgency.[29]

Paul reinforced the theme from *Pacem in Terris* that economic justice was necessary for world peace to be possible. In some memorable phrases, he insisted that "there are certainly situations whose injustice cries to heaven" and claimed that "the new name for peace is development."[30] Such a clear statement on social injustice and the importance of development—even if the nature of development was now under more critical discussion—had a major impact in Third World countries.

At the international level Paul advocated integral development that took account of economic and human needs.[31] He saw that existing inequalities between countries and the free trade system meant that "The poor nations remain

---

[26] The election of Dom Aloísio Lorscheider as CNBB secretary general earlier in 1968 restored a progressive voice in the CNBB leadership.

[27] It was quickly followed with further measures such as the law passed in January 1969 that authorised the expulsion of any foreigner acting against national security. This made it easier to expel foreign priests and women religious (which the military had started to do), and in 1972, these included the Belgian liberation theologian José Comblin.

[28] See Klaiber, *The Church, Dictatorships and Democracy in Latin America*, pp. 25–31.

[29] *Populorum Progressio*, § 1.

[30] *Populorum Progressio*, § 30 and § 87.

[31] *Populorum Progressio*, §§ 12–21 (esp. 14).

ever poor while the rich ones become richer still."[32] On the internal distribution of wealth, he extended the teaching of *Gaudium et Spes* that public authorities should ensure that private property is not used against the common good by stressing that the right to property and commerce must permit adequate access to created goods for everyone.[33] Most importantly of all, he gave a new sense of immediacy to the issues with a call for urgent action.[34] There was explicit praise for the example of bishops like Manuel Larraín who had given up some of the church's possessions for the sake of the poor.[35]

Paul's stance on revolutionary movements was particularly controversial. He went as far as to acknowledge that exceptional circumstances might justify revolutionary uprisings "where there is manifest, long-standing tyranny which would do great damage to fundamental personal rights and dangerous harm to the common good of the country."[36] Although these principles were in clear continuity with traditional Catholic teaching on just war, many found it shocking to hear the Pope spell out their implications in this way.

The Pope's personal friendship with Câmara may have helped him to write *Populorum Progressio* with the problems of Latin America in mind, and it was no surprise that the encyclical had a strong impact on the Latin American Church. The timing of the encyclical was opportune. *Populorum Progressio* provided an important addendum to the Conciliar documents and helped focus CELAM's preparations for the forthcoming discussions at Medellín.

Preparations for CELAM II

At the final session of Vatican II, Archbishop Manuel Larraín of Talca (Chile) who was president of CELAM encouraged the Latin American bishops to organize a second general CELAM meeting to examine the Council's teaching in the light of the Latin American situation.[37] Preparation for the meeting took

---

[32] *Populorum Progressio*, § 57.

[33] *Populorum Progressio*, §§ 22–24; cp. *Gaudium et Spes*, § 71.

[34] For example: "We must make haste. Too many people are suffering. While some make progress, others stand still or move backwards; and the gap between them is widening" (*Populorum Progressio*, § 29); "We want to be clearly understood on this point. The present state of affairs must be confronted boldly, and its concomitant injustices must be challenged and overcome. Continuing development calls for bold innovations that will work profound changes. The critical state of affairs must be corrected for the better without delay" (§ 32).

[35] *Populorum Progressio*, § 32.

[36] *Populorum Progressio*, § 31.

[37] Larraín had been elected vice president of CELAM in 1955 and president in 1964 with Câmara as his vice president. Together, they saw the opportunities that CELAM could have to make an impact on the church and pushed for them energetically. After Vatican II, they extended CELAM's work through the creation of new subdepartments and established new institutions for pastoral training, such as the Pastoral Institute for Latin America in Quito (Ecuador).

nearly three years. Sadly, Larraín died in 1966 and did not witness the dramatic events to which he had made such an important contribution. Fortunately, however, Câmara (who carried great informal influence amongst the progressive bishops) was well placed to fill the leadership gap that Larraín left.[38]

In August 1967, Dom Hélder Câmara was the driving force behind the controversial "Letter to the Peoples of the Third World" signed by eighteen bishops (nine of whom worked in Brazil) as a response and extension for *Populorum Progressio*.[39] They drew attention to historical lessons on the necessity and positive consequences of some revolutions and even endorsed socialism as a viable path in overcoming injustice.[40]

Meanwhile groups like Priests for the Third World in Argentina and the National Office for Social Information in Peru provided forums for like-minded priests to discuss their experiences with each other.[41] Many of these priests worked with poor communities and the base community movement, which was then in its early stages of growth.[42] They knew that the promises of development had done little to improve the lives of the poor majority, and they wanted the church to do more in the struggle for social justice. At this early stage, the base communities had not yet become a major factor in the church or the driving force behind new lines in liberation theology. However, the insights that many priests and women religious gained from work with the communities made them supportive of the new theological directions that were taking place.

While this was going on, the Latin American theologians who had met at Petrópolis in 1964 continued to develop their thought in the second half of the 1960s inspired by the Conciliar Documents and Papal Encyclicals.[43] Members provided important leadership to the progressive wing of the church when, after publication of *Populorum Progressio*, an openness to major changes started to grow amongst the more centrist bishops.

In preparation for the main conference in Medellín, the CELAM network sponsored a sequence of smaller preparatory conferences, which addressed important questions about the future of the church. Progressive priests and theologians provided position papers (*ponencias*) for these conferences and later revised

---

[38] Notable progressive bishops at the time included: Archbishop Marcos McGrath (Panama), Eduardo Pironio and Enrique Angelelli (Argentina), Lionidas Proaño (Ecuador), Méndez Arceo (Mexico), and Landázuri Ricketts (Peru).

[39] Third World Bishops, "A Letter to the Peoples of the Third World" (15 August 1967) in Hennelly (ed.), *Liberation Theology*, pp. 48–57. The letter emphasised the need for the poor to develop confidence in themselves, effect their own betterment and not allow themselves to be exploited (§ 18).

[40] "A Letter to the Peoples of the Third World" in *Between Honesty and Hope*, pp. 3–12; reprinted in Hennelly (ed.), *Liberation Theology*, pp. 48–57.

[41] Priests for the Third World was founded in December 1967 when a group of Argentine priests published their support for the Third World Bishops, "Letter to the Peoples of the Third World"; see Klaiber, *The Church, Dictatorships and Democracy*, p. 72.

[42] On the history and significance of Latin American base communities, see Chapter 8.

[43] The group met again in Bogotá (June 1965) and Cuernavaca (July 1965).

their ideas in light of the discussion that they stimulated.[44] Gradually, the discussion developed more and more clearly in favour of radical changes that the church needed to make. During these conferences, moves started to be made towards discussion of liberation.

At the invitation of CELAM, thirty-eight priests from throughout the continent met in Chile in November 1967 to discuss *Populorum Progressio*. The priests signed a communiqué which called for a wholehearted commitment to the church's social tasks, called for more priests to devote themselves to ministry to the poor, and stressed the need for changes to redress injustices against the poor and win their true freedom.[45] Each of these points had important political implications. Ever since the church had adopted its neo-Christendom strategy in the 1930s, it had managed to accommodate both the conservatives (who recalled the church's political power in Old Christendom) and the moderates (who saw the church's role as a moral voice on social issues but nonpolitical). Now there was a clear third position. Radical bishops and priests advocated a clear stance on behalf of the poor. They recognised that this would involve controversial political choices; they might avoid party politics, but they could not disassociate themselves from politics altogether. This relatively small group had already started to go beyond the positions found in Vatican II and *Populorum Progressio* in its political concerns. However, *Lumen Gentium*, *Gaudium et Spes*, and *Populorum Progressio* helped them defend their new direction as a genuine sign of the times.

These various developments in the period 1966–1967 meant that by the eleventh ordinary (annual) meeting of CELAM in November 1967 some of the major thinkers in CELAM had began to talk of liberation as the key term for the future.[46] Because CELAM II would only last two weeks, this emerging consensus was a critical factor in developing a coherent direction for social teaching. The progressive bishops who were in positions of influence in the CELAM (such as Câmara and the secretary Eduardo Pironio) asserted firm leadership in preparing the agenda and position papers for Medellín. The position papers were developed by a steering committee that was composed largely of moderates and progressives at Bogotá in January 1968. Hopes for a major transformation in the Latin American continued to grow in the first six months of 1968. Further CELAM sponsored conferences took place in April at Melgar, Colombia (on the church's mission) and in May at Itapuã, Brazil (on the church and social change).

---

[44] At Baños (Ecuador) they discussed collaborative pastoral ministry and social action (June 1966). At Buga (Colombia) they focussed on the role of catholic universities (February 1967); see Cleary, *Crisis and Change*, p. 34.

[45] See *Between Honesty and Hope*, pp. 70–73; reprinted Hennelly (ed.), *Liberation Theology*, pp. 58–61.

[46] See Dussel, *A History of the Church in Latin America*, p. 143. In the late 1960s, Richard Shaull and the ISAL network—which had previously worked on "theology of revolution"—turned their attention to liberation. See, for example, R. Shaull, "La liberación humana desde una perspectiva teológica," *Mensaje* 168 (1968), pp. 175–179.

Meanwhile, Pedro Arrupe SJ (the Father General of the Society of Jesus) met with all the Jesuit Provincials in Latin America in Rio de Janeiro in May 1968.[47] Arrupe was committed to the needs of the poor and an enthusiastic advocate for changes in the Society. The Jesuit provincials discussed the social problems of Latin America and pledged to make them the "absolute priority in our apostolic strategy."[48] A summarised version of their discussion was sent to every member of the Society and they called on all members of the Order to make the profound changes that were necessary for this conversion to happen.

The recognition of past failures and the need for conversion and new direction was stressed in a number of places. For example:

> We are aware of the profound transformation this presupposes. We must break with some of our attitudes in the past to re-establish ties with our humanist tradition: 'The human being fully alive is the glory of God' (Saint Ireneas). We want to avoid any attitude of isolation or domination that may have been ours in the past. We want to adopt an attitude of service to the church and to society, rejecting the overtones of power that have been attributed to us ... We are counting on you as we undertake this effort to divest ourselves of any aristocratic attitude that may have been present in our public positions, in our style of life, in the selection of our audience, in our dealings with lay coworkers, and in our relations with the wealthy classes.[49]

The letter concludes: "In this way, hopefully, the Society of Jesus in Latin America will be able to undergo the necessary conversion with God's grace."[50]

The Jesuits were careful to distance themselves from party politics or any power in civil society. Nonetheless, their talk of *oppression and liberation* (not poverty and development), reflected the shift taking place in radical sectors of the church at the time. For example, they promised that "In all our activities, our goal should be the liberation of humankind from every sort of servitude that oppresses it."[51]

Two months later, in July 1968 (just one month before Medellín) Gustavo Gutiérrez gave a talk to a meeting of priests and laity at Chimbote, Peru. His paper, entitled "Towards a Theology of Liberation," gave a clear statement of two key features that would define the methodology and focus of the movement.[52]

---

[47] Arrupe had been appointed in 1965 when he succeeded Johan Baptist Janssens. Arrupe provided clear direction for the Society in the post-Vatican II era and was fully committed to the Council's reforms. On the history of the Jesuits, see D. Mitchell, *The Jesuits: A History* (New York: Franklin Watts, 1981); M. Barthel, *The History and Legends of the Society of Jesus* (New York: William Morrow, 1984).

[48] "The Jesuits of Latin America," § 3. The document is printed in *Between Honesty and Hope* (pp. 144–150); reprinted in Hennelly (ed.), *Liberation Theology*, 77–83.

[49] "The Jesuits of Latin America," § 3.

[50] "The Jesuits of Latin America," § 11.

[51] "The Jesuits of Latin America," § 3.

[52] G. Gutiérrez, *Hacia una teología de la liberación* (Montevideo: MIEC Documentation Service, 1969), pp. 62–76; translated by Hennelly as "Toward a Theology of Liberation" in Hennelly (ed.), *Liberation Theology*, pp. 62–76. For a good overview and assessment

Firstly, Gutiérrez argued that the church should understand theology as critical reflection on prior commitment. Here, he used much more explicit terms than in his presentation at Petrópolis in 1964. At Chimbote, Gutiérrez argued that "theology is a reflection—that is, it is a second act, a turning back, a reflecting, that comes after action. Theology is not first; the commitment is first. Theology is the understanding of the commitment, and the commitment is action."[53] Gutiérrez's methodological approach was in line with *Gaudium et Spes* in as much as it took the state of the world as the starting point for reflection, rather than doctrinal presuppositions. However, Gutiérrez also went beyond this. He identified commitment and action—not just social issues—as the most important focus. Compared with earlier see-judge-act stages in the pastoral circle, this was dynamic engagement rather than detached reflection and judgement. Gutiérrez argued that theology should not stand apart from the objects of its reflections. Rather, Christians should participate in social transformation and reflect on their involvement in this active process. Theological reflection should be undertaken from within the process and contribute to the process. It should not just be an external judgement on society. The dynamic engagement transformed the pastoral circle into a more radical model for change that presupposed commitment and involved analysis, reflection, and action.

The paper's other key contribution was to develop the idea of liberation as a key theological theme. By 1968, the idea of liberation had already achieved prominence in European circles. At a political level, the Algerian independence struggle of the National Liberation Front against the French promoted serious engagement with issues of imperialism, revolution, and liberation in

---

of Gutiérrez's work, see R. M. Brown, *Gustavo Gutiérrez*; C. Cadorette, *From the Heart of the People: The Theology of Gustavo Gutiérrez* (Oak Park, Ill.: Meyer-Stone, 1988).

[53] Hennelly (ed.), *Liberation Theology*, p. 63. Reformulations of this same principle in later versions are revealing indications of the progressive development of Gutiérrez's views. For example, the next section of Gutiérrez's text at Chimbote explained that the commitment he had in mind was charity: "The central element is charity, which involves commitment, while theology arrives later on" (p. 63). The following year, at Cartigny he expressed it slightly differently, but preserved the reference to charity, "Theology is reflection, a critical attitude. First comes the commitment to charity, to service. Theology comes 'later.' It is second" (G. Gutiérrez, "Notes on a Theology of Liberation," *Theological Studies* 31.2 [1970], pp. 243–261 [244]). However, when Gutiérrez expressed the same idea in its classic form the following year, the references to charity and service were dropped. It simply read "Theology is reflection, a critical attitude. Theology *follows*; it is the second step" (Gutiérrez, *A Theology of Liberation*, p. 11). Two pages later the subject of critical reflection is identified as "Christian praxis in the light of the Word" (p. 11). However, the earlier editions of the Spanish might be better translated as "historical praxis in the light of the Word" (*La teología como reflexión crítica de la praxis histórica a la luz de la Palabra*). Gutiérrez offered an earlier version of this at Cartigny as "the Church's presence and action in the world in the light of faith" (p. 245) and at Chimbote it was "the pastoral activity of the church—that is, the presence of the church in the world. It will accompany that activity continuously, to help it be faithful to the word of God, which is the light for theology" (p. 64).

France. Franz Fanon developed this explicitly in his *Wretched of the Earth* published in 1961.[54] At a philosophical level, Herbert Marcuse addressed the issue of liberation in a number of works that drew on psychoanalytic categories.[55] Under these influences, European theologians explored new directions in theology. In Germany, Jürgen Moltmann and Johannes Metz were exploring political theologies that emphasised that God was revealed in history and challenged Christians to participate in its eschatological transformation in a spirit of hope.[56]

Others in Latin America already started to use liberation as a political alternative to development, but Gutiérrez's contribution was to show its value and validity as a theological term.[57] His analysis of liberation as a term for salvation in the framework of post Vatican II theology was a creative and bold theological statement. It made frequent references to the recently published *Populorum Progressio* and argued that what Paul VI called "integral development" might be better conceptualised in terms of liberation.[58]

At Medellín, Gutiérrez was an important advocate of liberation thought in his capacity as theological adviser.[59] The bishops did not make liberation ter-

---

[54] Gutiérrez studied psychology in Belgium and was in France during the Algerian war of independence in the 1960s. References to Fanon's works *The Wretched of the Earth* (trans. C. Farrington; New York: Grove Press, 1963) and *Studies in a Dying Colonialism* (trans. H. Chevalier; New York: Monthly Review Press, 1965) appear in Gutiérrez, *A Theology of Liberation*, p. 41 no. 35 and p. 182 no. 34.

[55] See for example, "Liberation from an Affluent Society," his contribution to the anthology of D. Cooper (ed.), *To Free a Generation: The Dialectics of Liberation* (London and New York: Collier Books, 1968), pp. 175–192; *Eros and Civilization* (Boston: Beacon Press, 1955); *One Dimensional Man* (Boston: Beacon Press; London: Routledge & Kegan Paul, 1964); *An Essay on Liberation* (Boston: Beacon Press; London: Allen Lane, 1969) which Gutiérrez refers to in *A Theology of Liberation* (see *Theology of Liberation*, pp. 31–32).

[56] Gibellini (*The Liberation Theology Debate*, p. 16) traces the start of this to the summer of 1967 when Metz gave a lecture in Toronto. Influential works include: J. B. Metz, *Theology of the World* (trans. W. Glen-Doepl; New York: Herder and Herder, 1969); J. Moltmann, *Theology of Hope* (trans. J. W. Leitch; London: SCM Press, 1967); idem, *Religion, Revolution, and the Future* (trans. M. Douglass Meeks; New York: Charles Scribner's Sons, 1969). For a survey of the similarities and differences between European political theologies and Latin American liberation theologies see R. Chopp, *The Praxis of Suffering: An Interpretation of Liberation and Political Theologies* (Maryknoll, N.Y.: Orbis Books, 1986). For Moltmann's early work, see M. Douglas Meeks, *Origins of the Theology of Hope* (Philadelphia: Fortress Press, 1974); C. Morse, *The Logic of Promise in Moltmann's Theology* (Philadelphia: Fortress Press, 1975).

[57] Gutiérrez acknowledged that talk of a theology of human liberation was already in the air, but he expressed dissatisfaction with some aspects of the previous discussion of liberation at Melgar and Itapuâ; see Hennelly (ed.), *Liberation Theology*, p. 64.

[58] Pablo Richard described this as "the explicit break, the qualitative leap, from a world vision tied to a developmentalist kind of practice to one tied to a practice of liberation"; Richard, *Death of Christendom, Birth of the Church* (Maryknoll, N.Y.: Orbis Books, 1987), p. 145.

[59] The Archbishop of Lima, Cardinal Juan Landázuri Ricketts (who was co-president of the conference), invited Gustavo Gutiérrez to act as a theological adviser. Gutiérrez was one of a group of theologians on the preparation committee, which met in Bogotá in January 1968 to write the position papers. At Medellín he was largely responsible for

minology normative for their theology in the way that Gutiérrez hoped, but references to liberation were scattered throughout the document. This helped it emerge as the organising concept for a new theological movement in the years immediately after the conference.

CELAM II at Medellín (1968)

CELAM II finally opened on 26 August 1968 at Medellín in Colombia.[60] The fortnight-long meeting (it closed on 6 September) was called "The Church in the Present-Day Transformation of Latin America in the Light of the Council."[61] By any evaluation, it was one of the most important landmarks in the first five centuries of the Latin American church. The relatively small number of progressive bishops—inspired by Paul VI's example in *Populorum Progressio*, supported by the draft documents and guided by the invited theological advisers (*peritos*)—persuaded the Conference to make the needs of the Latin American poor a critical element in their theological thinking.[62]

The conference was intended to interpret Latin America in the light of the Council.[63] Crucially, Medellín adopted the three-stage presentation of *Gaudium et Spes*: starting with a statement of facts; moving to reflections; ending with recommendations.[64] Starting with the facts of Latin America and not the texts of the Council allowed a process of mutual interpretation between them. The initial focus on facts pointed to some of the limits of the Vatican II documents in the Latin America context of acute social injustice.[65] This pushed the bishops into developing prophetic statements of their own which went beyond Vatican II in recognizing the importance of temporal history and reorienting the church's priorities.

---

the draft document on Poverty and collaborated closely with Pierre Bigo on the draft document on Peace. See Smith, *The Emergence of Liberation Theology*, p. 160.

[60] Paul VI came to open the meeting in person. He was the first Pope ever to travel to Latin America while in office. His visit spanned the end of the Eucharistic Congress in Bogotá and the opening of CELAM II. A very helpful discussion and selection of documents on the Pope's visit and the conference itself can be found in A. Gheerbrant, *The Rebel Church in Latin America* (trans. R. Sheed; Harmondsworth: Penguin, 1974 [French orig. 1969]).

[61] CELAM, *The Church in the Present-Day Transformation of Latin America in the Light of the Council* (2nd ed.; Washington, D.C.: Bishop's Conference, 1973 [Spanish orig. 1968]).

[62] Despite the relatively high status of the event compared to the ordinary annual meetings, only 146 bishops attended along with 120 advisers. Vatican II had demonstrated the value of theological advisers and the CELAM organisers, and individual bishops picked up on this with enthusiasm. Many bishops, and especially the most progressive bishops, invited advisers to assist in the deliberations and much of the practical work of writing was in the hands of these advisers.

[63] By taking this task seriously it also became an implicit interpretation of the Council in the light of Latin America.

[64] See Cleary, *Crisis and Change*, p. 22.

[65] The presence of pastoral workers and other church sectors at the conference also helped the bishops root their reflections in the lived experience of the church and not the concerns of the ecclesiastical hierarchy.

The final conclusions are quite mixed (there are sixteen documents on particular themes as well as the "Introduction" and "A Message to the Peoples of Latin America"). A number of documents are particularly worthy of note for their stress on the need to engage with the Latin American social context and their insistence that the church respond to the needs of the poor. These include the "Introduction" and the documents on Justice, Peace, and Poverty of the Church.[66]

In the "Introduction to the Final Documents" the bishops spoke of the past failings in the church and the need for action as well as words to correct this. In recognition of the rapid social transformations taking place in Latin America, they said "It appears to be a time full of zeal for emancipation, of liberation from every form of servitude . . . In these signs we perceive the first indications of the painful birth of a new civilization."[67] The bishops then drew a parallel between the new people of God in Latin America and the deliverance of the first people of God from oppression in Egypt.[68]

In the "Document on Justice" the bishops started with a bold denunciation of the situation:

> There are in existence many studies of the Latin American people. The misery that besets large masses of human beings in all our countries is described in all these studies. The misery, as a collective fact, expresses itself as injustice which cries to heaven.[69]

They rejected the temptations of Marxist systems such as Cuba's, but balanced this with a critique of the liberal capitalism that was prevalent throughout the rest of the continent. They recognised that these two systems seemed to exhaust the possibilities of transforming the economic structures of the continent, but rejected them both on the basis that "Both systems militate against the dignity of the human person."[70] The bishops drew on Freire's concern to promote the

---

[66] The rejection of dualism and emphasis on "'History as One,'" which was an important issue for Gutiérrez (see below), is found in these Medellín documents. See especially "Document on Justice," § 5: "In the search for salvation we must avoid the dualism which separates temporal tasks from the work of sanctification." See also the "Document on Catechises," § 4.

[67] CELAM II, "Introduction to the Final Documents," § 4; reprinted in Hennelly (ed.), *Liberation Theology*, pp. 94–97 (95).

[68] "Introduction to the Final Documents," § 6. Despite this mention of the Exodus story, no actual verses are cited or analysed. In general, the Medellín documents made little direct use of biblical analysis in support of its position. When the bible was referred to, references were usually to single verses taken almost exclusively from the Gospels and Epistles. Specific verse references from the Old Testament were very infrequent. There were a few references to the Prophets, but none from the book of Exodus.

[69] CELAM II, "Document on Justice," § 1; reprinted in Hennelly (ed.), *Liberation Theology*, pp. 97–105 (97).

[70] "Document on Justice," § 10.

participation of the people in their own struggles for freedom and ensure the people's active involvement in the transformation of society. In particular:

> We wish to affirm that it is indispensable to form a social conscience and a realistic perception of the problems of the community and of social structures. We must awaken the social conscience and communal customs in all strata of society and professional groups regarding such values as dialogue and community living within the same group and relations with wider social groups (workers, peasants, professionals, clergy, religious, administrators, etc.). This task of conscientization and social education ought to be integrated into joint pastoral action at various levels.[71]

The bishops praised basic communities as a practical step forward for pastoral action and committed themselves to a supporting role in the process of social transformation.[72] There were also hints at what would later become a fuller christological understanding of Jesus' role as liberator. The title liberator is not explicitly stated in the documents, but there are places where it is implied and the social component of liberation is recognised. For example:

> It is the same God who, in the fullness of time sends the Son in the flesh, so that he might come to liberate all persons from the slavery to which sin has subjected them: hunger, misery, oppression, and ignorance—in a word, that injustice and hatred which have their origin in human selfishness.[73]

The "Document on Peace" took up similar concern for the poor.[74] It condemned the underdevelopment of Latin America as an "unjust situation" which "promotes tensions that conspire against peace" and emphasised that this injustice is a "sinful situation."[75] It analysed Latin America's economic situation and place in the world economy under the heading "Neo-colonialism," drawing attention to the dependence of Latin America on other centres of economic power.[76] Amongst other indicators of the difficult economic situation they prophetically noted, "We thus run the risk of encumbering ourselves with debts whose payment absorbs the greater part of our profits."[77] They also indicated that within Latin America national tensions and excessive arms expenditure prevented urgent social needs from being properly addressed. The thought of

---

[71] "Document on Justice," § 17.

[72] "It is necessary that small basic communities be developed in order to establish a balance with minority groups, which are the groups in power. This is possible only through vitalization of these very communities by means of the natural innate elements in their environment. The church—the people of God—will lend its support to the downtrodden of every social class so that they might come to know their rights and how to make use of them" ("Document on Justice," § 20).

[73] "Document on Justice," § 3.

[74] CELAM II, "Document on Peace"; reprinted in Hennelly (ed.), *Liberation Theology*, pp. 106–114.

[75] "Document on Peace," § 1.

[76] "Document on Peace," §§ 8–10.

[77] "Document on Peace," § 9.

Hélder Câmara was particularly influential in some parts of the document, and the bishops' understanding of peace recognised an essential link with justice and rejected easy equations between peace and order:

> Peace is above all, a work of justice. It presupposes and requires the establishment of a just order. . . . Peace in Latin America, therefore, is not the simple absence of violence and bloodshed. Oppression by power groups may give the impression of maintaining peace and order, but in truth is nothing but the 'continuous and inevitable seed of rebellion and war.'[78]

The bishops made a forceful reaffirmation of Christian commitment to non-violence, but followed it immediately with a powerful statement on "a situation of injustice that can be called institutionalized violence."[79] Mass destitution, they said, was a sign of this institutional violence; enforced poverty violated fundamental human rights and required a profound transformation.[80]

The prophetic stance of the Documents on Justice and Peace certainly marked a new stage in the church's concern for the poor.[81] However, the true extent of the church's transformation is revealed most clearly in the "Document on the Poverty of the Church."[82] Running through this document is their lament for the misery of so many and their eager desire to address injustices:

> The Latin American bishops cannot remain indifferent in the face of the tremendous social injustices existent in Latin America, which keep the majority of our peoples in dismal poverty, which in many cases becomes inhuman wretchedness.[83]

Their anguish showed as they preached the need for liberation:

> A deafening cry pours from the throats of millions of men, asking their pastors for a liberation that reaches them from nowhere else.[84]

---

[78] "Document on Peace," § 14.

[79] "Document on Peace," §§ 15–16 (16).

[80] "Document on Peace," § 16. They reiterated Paul VI's encyclical *Populorum Progressio* (§ 31) on the circumstances in which revolutionary insurrection can be legitimate, but strengthened his caution that armed revolution "generates new injustices, introduces new imbalances, and causes new disasters; one cannot combat a real evil at the price of a greater evil" ("Document on Peace," § 19).

[81] There was also a commitment to a more peaceful relationship with other Christian denominations. An indication of this new spirit of partnership was that ecumenical observers were present throughout the Conference and were able to take part in its sessions. The bishops called on both Christian and non-Christian communities to collaborate in the tasks at hand ("Document of Peace," § 26).

[82] CELAM II, "Document on the Poverty of the Church"; reprinted, pp. 114–119.

[83] "Document on the Poverty of the Church," § 1.

[84] "Document on the Poverty of the Church," § 2. Various other Medellín documents also made reference to the new term liberation. In their "Introduction to the Final Documents," the bishops reflected on the "signs of the times" and said, "It appears to be a time full of zeal for full emancipation, of liberation from every form of servitude, of personal maturity and of collective integration," (§ 4); CELAM II, "Introduction to the Final Documents"; reprinted in Hennelly (ed.), *Liberation Theology*, pp. 94–97. Other

From this starting point—and aided by Gutiérrez—the bishops distinguished between three different forms of poverty.[85] First, material poverty, which is a lack of the material resources necessary to live worthily as human beings. This was described as an evil, which is contrary to the will of the Lord and usually the result of human injustice and sin. Then they addressed spiritual poverty, which they called the "disposition of one who hopes for everything from the Lord." Finally, they spoke of voluntary poverty, which they said was poverty that one accepted for oneself the situation of the poor—as Christ did—in order to "bear witness to the evil it represents and to spiritual liberty in the face of material goods." In view of these distinctions, the bishops argued that the church needed a three-fold response to poverty to address the three different aspects of poverty.[86] The bishops recalled that:

> The Lord's distinct commandment to 'evangelize the poor' ought to bring us to a distribution of resources and apostolic personnel that effectively gives preference to the poorest and most needy sectors and to those segregated for any cause whatsoever, animating and accelerating the initiatives and studies that are already being made with that goal in mind. We the bishops, wish to come closer to the poor in sincerity and fellowship, making ourselves accessible to them.[87]

---

references to liberation are made in the "Message to the Peoples of Latin America," including: "Our people seek their liberation and their growth in humanity, through the incorporation and participation of everyone in the very conduct of the personalization process," and "By its own vocation, Latin America will undertake its liberation at the cost of whatever sacrifices"; see Hennelly (ed.), *Liberation Theology*, pp. 90–94. Thus, even though Medellín did not systematically develop the idea of liberation and its theological richness, it prepared the way for liberation to become the key term of a new theological movement.

[85] "Document on the Poverty of the Church," § 4. Gutiérrez had already developed two key points in the understanding of poverty at the University of Montreal in a series of lectures in 1967, and Gutiérrez argued that the poor were a class and not just individuals. That is to say that their situation had to be understood with reference the class relations that they were caught up in and the social structures beyond their personal control. Second, that the poor are the carriers of God. These two principles had a particular influence on the Medellín's documents and later formed the basis of chapter 13 of *A Theology of Liberation*. Furthermore, in a course for students in Montevideo (1967), he developed his ideas on how the church should respond to the world—the relationship of faith to temporal realities—in terms of different Christian responses in the history of the church. In emphasising "History as One" he sought an approach that would go beyond the rigid separation of planes and critiqued both a "Christendom mentality" and "New Christendom" model. This became chapter 4, "Different Responses," in *A Theology of Liberation*, pp. 53–61.

[86] "In this context a poor church: denounces the unjust lack of this world's goods and the sin that begets it; preaches and lives in spiritual poverty, as an attitude of spiritual childhood and openness to the Lord; [and] is itself bound to material poverty" ("Document on the Poverty of the Church," § 5).

[87] "Document on the Poverty of the Church," § 9.

First Drafts of Liberation Theology (1968–1969)

The strong stance taken by the Latin American bishops attracted worldwide public attention. The Medellín documents provided support for the work of radical theologians throughout the continent and after Medellín, the loose network of like-minded thinkers started to crystallise into an organised movement.

Gutiérrez took a further step toward refining and sharing his thoughts in November 1969 when he was invited to a meeting in Cartigny (Switzerland) sponsored by the Committee on Society, Development, and Peace (SODE-PAX).[88] Other theologians were still trying to formulate a "Theology of Development" in accordance with the dominant notions of development and progress. In fact, the conference organisers had invited Gutiérrez to present on "The Meaning of Development." However, Gutiérrez wished to argue that it was liberation, not development, that offered a way forward. He therefore subtitled his talk "Notes on a Theology of Liberation."[89]

Other theologians were also working on similar themes at the same time. For example, Rubem Alves, a Protestant theologian from Brazil, presented a paper at the SODEPAX conference. His paper "Theology and the Liberation of Man" offered a complementary perspective to Gutiérrez.[90] Alves was a Brazilian Presbyterian and had completed graduate studies in the United States, where he presented his dissertation in 1968 at Princeton Theological Seminary under the title "Towards a Theology of Liberation."[91]

---

[88] Gutiérrez notes that his classic work *A Theology of Liberation* is a direct development of the Chimbote and Cartigny papers (see Gutiérrez, *A Theology of Liberation*, p. xi). SODEPAX was jointly set up by the WCC and the Pontifical Commission for Justice and Peace early in 1968 and ran for three years. The papers at Cartigny were published as SODEPAX, *In Search of a Theology of Development: Papers from a Consultation on Theology and Development held by SODEPAX in Cartigny, Switzerland, November 1969* (Geneva: WCC, 1970).

[89] G. Gutiérrez, "Notes on a Theology of Liberation" in SODEPAX, *In Search of a Theology of Development*, pp. 116–179. In the contents page of *In Search of a Theology of Development*, Gutiérrez's paper is listed simply as "The Meaning of Development," but at the start of chapter itself, a subheading alters this to "The Meaning of Development: (Notes on a Theology of Liberation)" (see *In Search of a Theology of Development*, p. 116.) In June 1970, the same paper was reprinted in a slightly different translation under the title "Notes for a Theology of Liberation" in *Theological Studies* 31.2 (1970), pp. 243–261. Gutiérrez himself uses this title when he refers to the Cartigny paper in *A Theology of Liberation*, p. xi. He also published the paper in French as "Notes pour une theologie de la libération," IDOC 30 (1970) pp. 54–78.

[90] See R. Alves, "Theology and the Liberation of Man" in *In Search of a Theology of Development*, pp. 75–92. Alves was associated with ISAL which had developed links with Catholic organizations between 1963 and 1967. However, Alves was in the United States for most of this period (at Princeton where he was very familiar with the work of Richard Shaull), and apparently, it was not until Cartigny that Gutiérrez and Alves actually met (see Smith, *The Emergence of Liberation Theology*, pp. 176 and 254 n. 45).

[91] This was published the following year but changed at the publisher's request to *A Theology of Human Hope* (Washington, D.C.: Corpus Books, 1969). In the Spanish trans-

Hugo Assmann, another Brazilian, also wrote on the limits of a theology of development in 1968.[92] The following year, Assmann produced a short pamphlet titled *A Prospective Evaluation of Liberation Theology* that he developed further in the early 1970s.[93] Meanwhile, in Uruguay, the Jesuit theologian Juan Luis Segundo continued his explorations into a more distinctively Latin American approach to theology. In 1968 and 1969, he published the first two volumes of his series *Theology for the Artisans of a New Humanity*, which explored fundamental theological themes in a new dialogical format based on the first of five annual seminars (1968–1972) for lay people.[94] In November 1969, the

---

lation, it changed again to *Opio o instrumento de liberación* (Montevideo: Tierra Nueva, 1970). In this work, Alves's theological resources are markedly Protestant in comparison with Gutiérrez, and it is notable that whereas the Catholic pioneers in liberation theology tended to receive graduate training in Europe, their Protestant counterparts such as Alves and Míguez-Bonino went to the U.S. In *A Theology of Human Hope*, Alves gave particular attention to the German theologians Karl Barth, Rudolf Bultmann, Dietrich Bonhoeffer, and Jürgen Moltmann. A few years later, he followed it with *Tomorrow's Child: Imagination, Creativity and Rebirth of Culture* (New York: Harper and Row, 1972). However, Alves's relation with the Brazilian Presbyterian church was not easy and after formally leaving the church, he published a book severely criticising its conservative stance on social issues. See Alves, *Protestantism and Repression: A Brazilian Case Study* (trans. J. Drury; Maryknoll, N.Y.: Orbis Books, 1985 [Portuguese orig. 1979]).

[92] H. Assmann, "Tareas e limitacões de uma teologia do desenvolvimento," *Vozes* 62 (1968), pp. 13–21.

[93] The pamphlet first appeared in 1969, but was not formally published until a year later, as H. Assmann, *Teología de la liberación: una evaluacion prospectiva* (Montevideo: MIEC-JECI, 1970). This was then developed and expanded into a larger volume (a collection of smaller writings), H. Assmann, *Opresión-liberación: Desafío a los cristianos* (Montevideo: Tierra Nueva, 1971). With further elaboration these became *Teología desde la praxis de la liberación. Ensayo teológico desde la América dependiente* (Salamanca: Sígueme 1973), pp. 27–102. A partial English translation of this was published in the U.K. as *A Practical Theology of Liberation* (trans. P. Burns; London: Search Press, 1975). Apparently Assmann objected to the translation of the title (saying that he did not know what practical theology was), and when it was published in the United States, it was titled *Theology for a Nomad Church* (Maryknoll, N.Y.: Orbis Books, 1976). Dussel also suggests that this prospective evaluation of liberation theology was "its first demarcation in relation to other theologies [and] its first clear epistemological definition" (*The Church in Latin America*, p. 393). According to Dussel, liberation theology was seen in relation to French theology, and it was important to situate it more clearly in relation to German theology. Although Alves had engaged with Moltmann's theology of hope, he had not given attention to the political theology of Metz.

[94] J. L. Segundo, *Theology for the Artisans of a New Humanity* (5 vols; trans. J. Drury; Maryknoll, N.Y.: Orbis Books, 1973–1974 [Spanish origs. 1968–1972]). The seminars were organised by the Peter Faber Pastoral Centre in Montevideo and focussed on the church (1968), grace (1969), God (1970), the sacraments (1971), and evolution and guilt (1972). Each chapter of the books stemmed from a four hour seminar. The first part of the seminar was a one-hour lecture, which is reprinted along with further clarifications. In the seminars, the lectures end with one or two questions that were used to stimulate an hour's discussion. These are given as appendices in the books alongside brief explanations of why these questions were chosen and other appendices

Mexican Theological Society held a Congress on "Faith and Development" in which the theme of liberation became central to the discussion.[95] Liberation theology was starting to coalesce as a cohesive and sophisticated theological movement, a joint venture of the progressive church and radicalised theologians in different Latin American countries.[96]

CONCLUSION

Latin America's continuing problems in the 1960s exposed the economic and political problems in the dominant development model and encouraged the search for radical new alternatives. The second half of the 1960s was a remarkable period of history across the world and the year of Medellín stands out for particularly memorable events. In the United States, assassins killed Robert Kennedy and Martin Luther King Jr. In Vietnam, the "Tet offensive" of the Chinese New Year showed that the Vietcong were still an effective military force, and that the escalation of United States troops in Vietnam since 1965 had not brought the end of war in sight. In Europe, students and workers took to the streets of Paris in a series of protests. Perhaps most significant of all, however, was the "Prague Spring" when the reformist agenda of the Czech administration was crushed by Soviet tanks. In Latin America, Institutional Act V in Brazil launched the era of hard dictatorships. Meanwhile, the massacre of students by riot police in Mexico City (apparently concerned to protect the city's image ahead of the Olympic games) confirmed that state violence was a feature of authoritarian regimes on the right as well as the left of politics.

During these years of ferment, voices in the church started to discuss liberation as a vital concept in the church's social mission and pastoral approach.

---

that provide further resources for the discussion. During the seminar discussion, the lay participants were encouraged to reflect on the lecture in the light of their own lived experiences. The third part of the seminar allowed the course leader to respond to the participants' discussion and comment on their views for a further hour. The final hour was usually reserved for more personal meditation or liturgical contemplation. There was also time for discussion of how the issues might be applied to the local social context. However, it is a pity that the books only preserve the first hour of these seminars. The discussion of the material, subsequent comments by the course leader, and any reference to social application are not included. Nonetheless, the books remain revealing studies of the sort of pastoral experimentation that was taking place.

[95] The proceedings were published as *Memoria del primer Congreso Nacional de teología: Fe y desarrollo* (2 vols; Mexico City: 1970).

[96] The United States government did not ignore these developments. In 1969, Nelson Rockefeller toured Latin America on President Nixon's behalf. He recognised the signs in the Medellín documents that the church in Latin America was taking a new stand on social justice and his influential report warned that this made it "vulnerable to subversive penetration"; see "Quality of Life in the Americas"—*A Report of a Presidential Mission for the Western Hemisphere*, Department of State Bulletin (8 December 1969), p. 18 (cited in Lernoux, *Cry of the People*, p. 59). The report strengthened United States support for the military in Brazil and for similarly repressive military regimes in Chile, Argentina, and Central America during the 1970s.

The actual birth of liberation theology and the church's option for the poor can be dated to mid-1968. The statements of the Jesuit Provincials in Rio de Janeiro in May and the bishops at Medellín in August showed evidence that a major conversion was under way amongst the guardians of the institutional church. The church was re-aligning itself with the poor majority. Gustavo Gutiérrez provided the theological support for this shift at Chimbote in July 1968. The following year, a number of theologians produced works that took liberation as a central theme and outlined a new political course for the church. By the end of the decade, liberation theology had consolidated its church and academic credentials sufficiently to ensure that it would not be a passing fad but the foundation of an important new movement.

Part 3

The Preferential Option
for the Poor
1970–1979

CHAPTER SIX

A New Way of
Doing Theology

> [T]he theology of liberation offers us not so much a new
> theme for reflection as a *new way* to do theology.
>
> Gustavo Guttiérez[1]

INTRODUCTION

In the early 1970s, many of the radical initiatives of the late 1960s finally crys-
tallised into the ecclesial and theological movement that would be known as
liberation theology. During 1970–1971 a number of conferences in different
Latin American countries took the liberation theme forward.[2] The focus of
papers at the conferences and other writings at the time all indicate the impact
that liberation terminology was having on theological thought.[3] The culmination

---

[1] G. Gutiérrez, *A Theology of Liberation: History, Politics and Salvation* (trans. and ed.
C. Inda and J. Eagleson; Maryknoll, N.Y.: Orbis Books, 1973; London: SCM Press, 1974
[Spanish orig. 1971]), p. 15. A slightly revised second edition was published in translation in 1988. To preserve the sense of historical progress, all quotes and page references in this chapter are from the first edition, and its occasionally exclusive language
has been left untouched.

[2] An important conference titled "Liberation: Option for the Church in the 1970s"
took place in Bogotá in March 1970. Other conferences and seminars included: "Exodus
and Liberation" (July 1970 in Buenos Aires); "Seminar on Liberation Theology" (October
1970 in Ciudad Juárez, Mexico); and "Liberation Theology and Pastoral Work" (December
1970 in Oruro, Bolivia). The meaning of liberation theology was also discussed in detail
at meetings sponsored by the Protestant organisation ISAL which Catholic theologians
attended and contributed to. These included: "Symposium on Liberation Theology" and
"The Theological Reality" (August 1970 and June 1971 in Buenos Aires); "Popular
Motivation and Christian Faith" (July 1971 in Nana, Peru); and "Methodology of Liberation Theology" (July 1971 in Bogotá). On the meetings in 1970–1971 see Smith, *The
Emergence of Liberation Theology*, pp. 177–179; Dussel, *A History of the Church in Latin
America*, pp. 244–247.

[3] For a list of papers presented at the conferences in June 1971 in Buenos Aires, and
July 1971 in Bogotá, see Smith, *The Emergence of Liberation Theology*, p. 179. See also

119

of these early works came in December 1971, when Gustavo Gutiérrez published his classic work A *Theology of Liberation*.[4]

Gutiérrez's book brought his previous short pieces into relation with each other, developed them at greater length and included extensive references to the intellectual influences that shaped his theology. Although the overall structure of the book was not always straightforward, three key elements from his earlier work were very clear.[5] First, his *methodological principle*, which was based on theology as critical reflection; second, the *terminological innovation*, which focussed on the theme of liberation; third, a *pastoral option of political commitment*, which addressed the challenges for the church in Latin America as it sought to move beyond New Christendom to express solidarity with the poor and protest against their poverty.[6] The result was the first systematic statement of liberation theology's agenda and it became one of the most influential works in twentieth-century Christian theology.[7]

---

the brief articles by CELAM secretary E. Pironio, 'Teología de la liberación,' *Criterio* 1607–1608 (Nov. 1970), pp. 783–790; and on the Protestant side, J. Míguez Bonino, "Teología de la liberación," *Actualidad Pastoral* 3 (1970), pp. 83–85.

[4] It was dedicated to one of the first martyrs of liberation theology—Câmara's assistant Henrique Pereira Neto (d. 1969)—and to the Peruvian writer José Maria Arguedas who had been a profound influence on Gutiérrez's thought. On Arguedas' work and influence on Gutiérrez, see R. M. Brown, *Gustavo Gutiérrez*, pp. 27–31.

[5] The presentation of each strand in the book does not always follow the expected chronological sequence. The book is organised in four parts and Part 4 (chapters 9–13), entitled "Perspectives," constitutes about half the book. The analysis in Part 4 sometimes repeats, sometimes extends, and at other times provides background to the argument in Parts 1–3.

[6] The methodology (see esp. A *Theology of Liberation*, chapter 1) and the terminology of liberation (see esp. chapters 2, 6, and 9) already found expression in Gutiérrez's papers at Chimbote (1968) and Cartigny (1969). The pastoral agenda (see esp. chapters 4, 5, 7, and 12) previously published in his *La Pastoral de la Iglesia en América Latina* (1968) was based on earlier talks in Montevideo (1967) and Petrópolis (1964). The political dimension to poverty (see esp. chapter 13) was developed in the course at Montreal (1967) and his contributions to Medellín (1968).

[7] Pablo Richard also offers an interpretation of Gutiérrez's development of thought in three-stages but it differs slightly from the framework offered here. For Richard, the three stages were characterised primarily by a developing understanding of practice. The first stage (illustrated in 1968 with *La Pastoral de la Iglesia en América Latina* and previously in university talks in 1964) was concerned with the pastoral practice of the church. The second stage focussed on the political practice of Christians. The third stage extended beyond the political practice of Christians to include the popular classes (see Richard, *Death of Christendom, Birth of the Church*, p. 147). Gibellini also offered a three-stage schema, but again it is slightly different (see The Liberation Theology Debate, p. 312). He saw the first stage as the meeting in Petrópolis (1964) organized by Illich, where Gutiérrez developed the epistemological theme of theology as critical reflection on praxis. Gibellini noted that the same theme appeared in *La Pastoral de la Iglesia en América Latina* and then chapter 1 of A *Theology of Liberation*. The second stage, Gibellini saw as starting in 1965 with the rise of a revolutionary movement prompting Gutiérrez to become more critical of inherited European theology and focus more attention on the social and political scene. The third stage, Gibellini traced to the course on poverty in

METHODOLOGICAL PRINCIPLE:
THEOLOGY AS CRITICAL REFLECTION ON PRAXIS

In *A Theology of Liberation* Gutiérrez challenged traditional theological approaches that distanced theology from everyday concerns and real life conflicts. As an alternative, *A Theology of Liberation* offered a theological approach that was rooted in the social context of faith and sought to respond to its contemporary challenges. For Gutiérrez theology was "a critical reflection on Christian praxis in the light of the Word."[8]

Gutiérrez presented the primary task of theology as the struggle with issues firmly located in human history. Theology does not take place in a social vacuum, but always arises in relation to particular historical contexts and social situations.[9] Unlike most of his predecessors in the Latin American church, Gutiérrez felt that theology could not escape its social context. Theologians should not treat social issues as a distraction to be ignored, but rather they should embrace them as historical realities to be pondered through theological reflection. He presented theology as both *reflection on* and *response to* the social situation confronting the theologian. In a particularly memorable passage, he commented:

Theology is reflection, a critical attitude. Theology follows; it is the second step. What Hegel used to say about philosophy can likewise be applied to theology: it rises only at sundown.[10]

In a later work, Gutiérrez repeated the same principle in a slightly different way:

The theological moment is one of critical reflection from within, and upon, concrete historical praxis, in confrontation with the word of the Lord as lived and accepted in faith . . .[11]

1967 in Montreal in which the poor came to be seen as both a social class and bearers of God's word, which Gutiérrez then developed in the concluding chapter of *A Theology of Liberation*.

[8] See Gutiérrez, *Theology of Liberation*, pp. 3–15 (esp. 13).

[9] For a forceful later statement by Gutiérrez along these lines, see Gutiérrez, *The Power of the Poor in History* (trans. R. R. Barr; Maryknoll, N.Y.: Orbis Books; London: SCM Press, 1983), p. 212.

[10] Gutiérrez, *Theology of Liberation*, p. 11. The phrase "rising at sundown" refers to Hegel's comment on philosophy as the owl of Minerva, the Goddess of wisdom. Other liberation theologians have followed Gutiérrez in arguing that their work begins with a recognition and response to the inhuman suffering of the Latin American people. For example, Míguez Bonino stated, "Latin American theology of liberation is beginning to emerge *after the fact*, as the reflection about facts and experiences which have already evoked a response from Christians"; J. Míguez Bonino, *Doing Theology in a Revolutionary Situation* (Philadelphia: Fortress Press, 1975), p. 61. However, some critics expressed doubts as to whether liberation theology actually struck the correct balance between its professed commitments and its critical reflection. For example, Spanish theologian Alfredo Fierro described it as a simple "profession of faith" rather than "critical reflection on faith" (Fierro, *The Militant Gospel: An Analysis of Contemporary Political Theologies* [trans. J. Drury; London: SCM Press, 1977], p. 328).

[11] Gutiérrez, *The Power of the Poor in History*, p. 200; see also chapter 5 on earlier variations.

Gutiérrez argued that in the Bible the knowledge of God is inseparable from action for justice, knowing God involves unity with God through action. The Christian is called to faith in action. As Gutiérrez put it: "... only by doing this truth will our faith be 'veri-fied,' in the etymological sense of the word."[12]

A new theological *method* was required in which understanding of the gospel was inseparable from an active response to it. Consciously echoing Marx's call to a praxis beyond Feuerbach's philosophical reflections, Gutiérrez wrote: "This is a theology which does not stop with reflecting on the world, but rather tries to be part of the process through which the world is transformed."[13]

To stress this theological shift Gutiérrez argued for orthopraxis to take precedence over orthodoxy. The term "praxis," derived from Marxist thought, is used to emphasize the dialectic of action and practice guided by reflection and thought. Orthodoxy, understood as the "proclamation and reflection on statements understood to be true," makes way for orthopraxis as the true criterion for liberation theology.[14]

Gutiérrez's commitment to action and social transformation, therefore involved a profound reorientation of the theological agenda. It should, however, be noted that while the reordering of priorities is certainly radical and Gutiérrez's call for it was very provocative, it would be mistaken to see Gutiérrez's shift from orthodoxy to orthopraxis as a denial of orthodoxy's importance. The emphasis on orthopraxis was an attempt to develop and enlarge orthodoxy, rather than replace it; or in other words, it comes not to abolish, but to fulfill orthodoxy.[15]

---

[12] A *Theology of Liberation*, p. 10; cf. Gutiérrez, *The Power of the Poor in History*, p. 201.

[13] Gutiérrez, *A Theology of Liberation*, p. 15.

[14] Gutiérrez, *A Theology of Liberation*, p. 10. Support for this came from other Latin American theologians. For example, the Uruguayan theologian Juan Luis Segundo agreed with Gutiérrez that orthopraxis should be seen as transcending orthodoxy: "... orthodoxy possesses no ultimate criterion in itself because being orthodox does not mean possessing the final truth. We only arrive at the latter by orthopraxis. It is the latter that is the ultimate criterion of the former, both in theology and in biblical interpretation. The truth is truth only when it serves as the basis for truly human attitudes" (J. L. Segundo, *The Liberation of Theology* [trans. J. Drury; Maryknoll, N.Y.: Orbis Books; 1976 (Spanish orig. 1975)], p. 32. Likewise Míguez Bonino (*Doing Theology in a Revolutionary Situation*, p. 81) argued: "Theology, as here conceived, is not an effort to give a correct understanding of God's attributes or actions but an effort to articulate the action of faith, the shape of praxis conceived and realized in obedience. As philosophy in Marx's famous *dictum*, theology has to stop explaining the world and start transforming it. *Orthopraxis*, rather than *orthodoxy*, becomes the criterion for theology." [Emphasis original]

[15] Gutiérrez was careful to state that his intention in drawing a distinction between orthopraxis and orthodoxy was not to deny the meaning of orthodoxy but: "to balance and even to reject the primacy and almost exclusiveness which doctrine has enjoyed in Christian life and above all to modify the emphasis, often obsessive, upon the attainment of an orthodoxy which is often no more than fidelity to an obsolete tradition or a debatable interpretation. In a more positive vein, the intention is to recognize the work and importance of concrete behaviour, of deeds, of action, of praxis in the Christian life"; *A Theology of Liberation*, p. 10.

Many of the pioneers of liberation theology shared this same orientation.[16] Reflection on social injustice should not just involve detached observation and abstract reflection followed by a purely academic exercise in theological thought.[17] A few years later, José Míguez Bonino (an Argentinean Protestant liberation theologian) echoed Gutiérrez's view that this liberation theology is primarily "a new way of 'doing theology.'"[18] The idea of doing theology serves as an effective reminder that theological thinking can never be separated from practice and action, and that this was the methodological foundation on which liberation theology was built.[19]

THEOLOGICAL TERMINOLOGY: LIBERATION

One of Gutiérrez's central concerns in *A Theology of Liberation* was to outline a new theological understanding of the relation between human history and salvation history. His stroke of genius was to show that given the social reality of Latin America the language of liberation offered the best insight into the process of salvation. Traditionally, the church had understood nature and grace to be separate states of being. However, Vatican II had endorsed moves towards understanding spiritual and secular domains in a more integral way. The Conciliar documents recognised the relationship between the two planes rather than just stressing their differences.[20] Gutiérrez drew on this significant shift in thought and put special emphasis on its insight into history as one. The integral relationship between salvation and history is a consistent theme throughout the book.[21] What made Gutiérrez's engagement with this issue so important was

---

[16] For example, Leonardo and Clodovis Boff later summarised the first step of liberation theology as "Liberating action or Libera(c)tion" and the second step as "faith reflecting on liberating practice"; L. Boff and C. Boff, *Introducing Liberation Theology*, pp. 4–9.

[17] Leonardo and Clodovis Boff argue that in view of the social injustices of Latin America the only response a Christian can make is a wholehearted commitment to the liberation of the oppressed: "How are we to be Christians in a world of destitution and injustice? There can be only one answer: we can be followers of Jesus and true Christians only by making common cause with the poor and working out the gospel of liberation" (L. and C. Boff, *Introducing Liberation Theology*, p. 7).

[18] Míguez Bonino, *Doing Theology in a Revolutionary Situation*, p. 82. The idea of doing theology was also mentioned by Assmann, *Practical Theology of Liberation*, p. 43.

[19] The Brazilian theologian Clodovis Boff summed up liberation theology as "reading of the praxis of Christians in the light of God's word"; see C. Boff, *Theology and Praxis: Epistemological Foundations* (trans. R. Barr; Maryknoll, N.Y.: Orbis Books, 1987 [Portuguese God's word"; see C. Boff, orig. 1978]) p. 139.

[20] Gutiérrez saw the Council as moving to embrace "salvation to all men and to the whole man" (Gutiérrez, *A Theology of Liberation*, p. 168). The wording of the Spanish reflects the close relation that Gutiérrez saw between these two concerns: "*a todos los hombres y a todo el hombre.*" Gutiérrez felt the church went much further in accepting the former (*a todos los hombres*) and understood himself as moving the focus onto the latter (*a todo el hombre*) on which the church was more reticent.

[21] The importance of the theme—and the sensitivity surrounding discussion of it— go a long way to explaining why at first glance the book appeared to have such a strange structure. Gutiérrez first raised the central question of the relationship between salvation and liberation in chapters 2–3 of the book and then returned to it in chapter 9

that he pressed for further development of Conciliar teaching on a closer engagement with society and argued for a more historical view of salvation, which demanded (rather than prohibited) Christian involvement in political issues.

Vatican II stressed the importance of integral *development* (economic and human) that was stressed in *Populorum Progressio* (§ 14). Gutiérrez argued that liberation offered a better framework for theological discussion. His approach captured the revolutionary spirit of the age. Developing a theology of liberation allowed Gutiérrez to express his theology in a new way, but still remain within the limits of orthodoxy on its understanding of salvation.

As seen in the previous chapter, Gutiérrez did not create the understanding of liberation *ex nihilo*. Other progressive thinkers in Latin America influenced Gutiérrez's advocacy of liberation during the 1960s. New ways of thinking in other academic disciplines created an atmosphere of liberation amongst intellectuals across the continent, and the terminology of liberation gained particularly strong currency in social sciences and educational theory. In left-wing circles, liberation came to be understood as implying an overturning (revolution) of existing procedures.[22] Gutiérrez was conscious of liberation's implications in dependency theory, radical pedagogy, and the cultural analysis (including Herbert Marcuse and Franz Fanon). He was convinced that theology could adopt and adapt it to address both Latin American society and tradition Christian doctrines in new ways.[23]

Some critics have said that Gutiérrez and other liberation theologians wished to fully equate salvation with *political* liberation. While this might have been how Gutiérrez's insights were mistakenly interpreted in some circles, it was never something that Gutiérrez advocated. He accepted the distinction between salvation and political liberation, but argued for an essential interrelationship. Where he appeared to equate salvation with liberation, it was not just political liberation he had in mind, but a wider sense of integral liberation on three different levels.

---

which is entitled "Liberation and Salvation." It is typical for him to deal with an issue in an introductory way and then return to it later in more detail in a different way. It is also typical of his style that he indicates his concerns by raising a question about a problem. Thus, he introduces chapter 9 with a question: "What is the relationship between salvation and the process of the liberation of man throughout history? Or more precisely, what is the meaning of the struggle against an unjust society and the creation of a new man in the light of the Word?" (p. 149). This echoes the start to chapter 3 (titled "The Problem," which constitutes a short first chapter in Part 2, "Posing the Problem"). At that point he had formulated it as: "To speak of a theology of liberation is to seek an answer to the following question: what relation is there between salvation and the historical process of the liberation of man?" (p. 45).

[22] See H. Assmann, *Theology of a Nomad Church* (Maryknoll, N.Y.: Orbis Books, 1976 [1971]), pp. 49–51.

[23] See esp. Gutiérrez, *A Theology of Liberation*, pp. 21–36, 91–92. On the history of the term liberation after 1965, see H. Assmann, *Practical Theology of Liberation*, pp. 45–46.

Twice in the book, he explicitly identified these three levels of liberation.[24] First, a liberation from economic exploitation, which Gutiérrez saw as the rightful aspiration of oppressed classes. Second, a liberation from fatalism, which would allow a people to take control over their own destiny. This existential liberation was concerned with truly personal freedom.[25] For Gutiérrez, it was complementary to liberation from exploitation, but at a different level to it. It was broader in scope and more universal in relevance than the liberation of oppressed classes. It could be applied to a whole understanding of history, in terms of humanity taking increasing responsibility for its own destiny and self-fulfillment. This liberation was a process of gradually overcoming historical constraints. Finally, there was liberation from sin, which permitted communion with God. At this level, unlike the term development, the term liberation offers a new approach to the biblical sources which present Christ as the Saviour who liberates humanity from sin.[26]

Gutiérrez explained that this "is not a matter of three parallel or chronologically successive processes, however. There are three levels of meaning of a single, complex process. . . ."[27] In using the term liberation he was trying to do justice to all three levels of the one salvation process and avoid "idealist or spiritualist approaches, which are nothing but ways of evading a harsh and demanding reality."[28] Gutiérrez did not intend to reduce the importance of liberation from sin, but to show the different ways in which sin had consequences.[29]

Gutiérrez's main point was that liberation was a better term than development for understanding and explaining the single complex process of salvation at a political, existential, and theological level. The term liberation gave insight into salvation because it incorporated all three salvific levels, while other terms tended to be understood at just one level.

Thus, at a political level, Gutiérrez saw the aspiration of oppressed classes to free themselves from exploitation as justified. In global terms, he also agreed

---

[24] The Spanish word he uses, *nivel* (level), makes this clear. See *A Theology of Liberation*, pp. 25–37 (esp. 36–37) and pp. 176–178.

[25] His emphasis on this second level seems to have been influenced by his early studies in psychology and existentialism. There were also echoes of Teilhard de Chardin's evolutionary vision of human progress.

[26] Gutiérrez, *A Theology of Liberation*, pp. 25–37 and 176–178.

[27] Gutiérrez, *A Theology of Liberation*, p. 37. On p. 176 he is equally clear: "These three levels mutually affect each other, but they are not the same. One is not present without the other, but they are distinct: they are all part of a single, all-encompassing salvific process, but they are to be found at different levels. Not only is the growth of the Kingdom not reduced to temporal progress; because of the Word accepted in faith, we see that the fundamental obstacle to the Kingdom, which is sin, is also the root of all misery and injustice; we see that the very meaning of the growth of the Kingdom is also the ultimate precondition for a just society and a new man."

[28] Gutiérrez, *A Theology of Liberation*, p. 37.

[29] Gutiérrez (*A Theology of Liberation*, p. 37) emphasized that "Christ the Savior liberates man from sin, which is the ultimate root of all disruption of friendship and of all injustice and oppression."

with dependency theorists that the dominant models of economic and political development were part of the problem, rather than part of the solution. The economic and political well-being of Latin America rested on rejection of such developmentalism. In both cases, national and international, the way forward was to be found in liberation from such development not reforms to it.[30]

At the existential level, the concept of liberation could be contrasted with inadequate concepts of personal development, which ignored the wider social context. Like Freire, Gutiérrez was sceptical of any personal development that did not promote true freedom. For example, if Freire was correct, the dominant models of education usually disempowered people. Instead of promoting personal growth, they undermined personal freedom.[31] Viewed from one perspective such education might be seen as evidence of personal development, but Freire argued that in fact it was a dehumanizing process in which human subjects are transformed into less than human objects.

Most importantly of all, at the third level, it is possible to speak theologically of liberation from sin, whereas it is inapproprate to speak of this in terms of development.[32] Christian orthodoxy rejects the belief that humanity can save itself from its sinful situation. Thinking of salvation in terms of development or reform runs the risk of underemphasizing the theological conviction that salvation is dependent on God's grace as well as human response. The term liberation captures the Christian understanding of sin as bondage requiring release.

Thus liberation was a more incisive term than development at each of the three levels.[33] Nonetheless, despite his careful argument Gutiérrez has frequently been criticized for oversimplifying the theological nature of salvation by representing it purely in terms of human liberation struggles and equating theology with politics. Part of the problem may be that in the 1970s, Gutiérrez's writings primarily dealt with liberation at the first (political) level. His understanding of the third (theological) level emphasized the integral relation between

---

[30] The influence of dependency theory on the early work of Gutiérrez and other liberation theologians needs to be recognised. However, dependency theory has come in for considerable criticism and later works in liberation theology put less emphasis on its theoretical analysis of economic and political development. Compared with A Theology of Liberation, Gutiérrez's later recent works gave dependency analysis much less prominence. For a discussion of current evaluations of dependency theory, see A. F. McGovern, Liberation Theology and Its Critics: Towards an Assessment (Maryknoll, N.Y.: Orbis Books, 1990), pp. 125–129, 156–176.

[31] See especially the discussion of "Banking Education" in Freire, Pedagogy of the Oppressed, pp. 57–61. Gutiérrez mentioned Freire in A Theology of Liberation, pp. 91–92, 213, 233–235.

[32] For a collection on the theology of development in English, see G. Bauer (ed.), Towards a Theology of Development (Geneva, WCC 1970). Some strands already influenced progressive theologians in Latin America, including: J. Comblin, Teología do desenvolvimento (Belo Horizonte, 1968); idem, Cristianismos y desarollo (Quito: 1970).

[33] See D. Brackley, Divine Revolution: Salvation and Liberation in Catholic Thought (Maryknoll, N.Y.: Orbis Books, 1996), esp. pp. 72–77.

the first and the third levels but there was relatively little explicit focus on the second (existential) level. Furthermore, Gutiérrez explicitly described his theology as a "political hermeneutics of the Gospel" and the boldness of this assertion was bound to create a reaction. However, in his defence Gutiérrez argued that his emphasis on politics was a corrective rather than a denial of the other concerns of theology.[34] In fact, Gutiérrez's analysis of salvation in which all three levels are *essential to* and *inseparable from* each other offered a very effective counter-critique to his critics. From this perspective, it was they who were reductionist (in ignoring the political level) rather than him.[35]

Gutiérrez presented human actions for political liberation (the first level) as an essential part of the overall liberation-salvation process, but not exhaustive of it. This supported his endorsement of human work towards a just society as part of a salvific process—and not just preparation for it—without equating human action (at the first or second level) with the fullness of salvation.[36] Within this carefully nuanced understanding, liberation and salvation were not alternative paths but alternative terminology for a single holistic process. The unified process can be referred to as either liberation or salvation, but whichever terminology is used at least three levels—political, existential, and theological—should be recognised in the single holistic unity of liberation-salvation.[37]

---

[34] See G. Gutiérrez, "Liberation Praxis and Christian Faith" in R. Gibellini (ed.), *Frontiers of Theology in Latin America* (Maryknoll, N.Y.: Orbis, 1979 [Italian orig. 1975]), pp. 1–33.

[35] As early as *A Theology of Liberation* Gutiérrez defended himself along these lines and attacked reductionist implications of the old dualistic thinking: "The very radicalness and totality of the salvific process require this relationship. Nothing escapes this process, nothing is outside the pale of the action of Christ and the gift of the Spirit. This gives human history its profound unity. Those who reduce the work of salvation are indeed those who limit it to the strictly 'religious' sphere and are not aware of the universality of the process. It is those who think that the work of Christ touches the social order in which we live only indirectly or tangentially, and not in its roots and basic structure. It is those who in order to protect salvation (or to protect their interests) lift salvation from the midst of history, where men and social classes struggle to liberate themselves from slavery and oppression to which other men and social classes have subjected them. It is those who refuse to see that the salvation of Christ is a radical liberation from all misery, all despoliation, all alienation. It is those who by trying to 'save' the work of Christ will 'lose' it." (pp. 177–178).

[36] "This is the reason why any effort to build a just society is liberation. And it has an indirect but effective impact on the fundamental alienation. It is a salvific work, although it is not all of salvation" (*A Theology of Liberation*, p. 177). In the Spanish version the rejection of the idea that human work is only preparation for salvation is even clearer. Gutiérrez's phrase "*es ya obra salvadora*" (translated in the ET as "It is a salvific work") could be more literally rendered as "It is *already* a salvific work."

[37] In his introduction to the second edition of *A Theology of Liberation*, Gutiérrez reiterated the importance of this threefold distinction and noted that Puebla took up his distinction and incorporated it into the final document. He also stressed the importance of the second level of liberation in any understanding of the whole.

To support his case, Gutiérrez argued that recent developments in Christian thinking on the unity of history and the nature of salvation provided a new framework to address political issues.[38] The more positive evaluation of human history—which recognised the unity between human history and salvation history—supported a new Christian attitude to politics.[39] To illustrate the theological foundations for this, he examined the biblical understanding of Exodus, Creation, and the work of Christ.

Gutiérrez noted that the Exodus theme was central to biblical theology.[40] It provided a theological norm for a liberating hermeneutics.[41] Gutiérrez wrote:

---

[38] "What we have recalled in the preceding paragraph leads us to affirm that, in fact, there are not two histories, one profane and one sacred, 'juxtaposed' or 'closely linked.' Rather there is only one human destiny, irreversibly assumed by Christ, the Lord of history. His redemptive work embraces all the dimensions of existence and brings them to their fullness. The history of salvation is the very heart of human history . . ." (Gutiérrez, A Theology of Liberation, p. 153).

[39] Gutiérrez's argument was on two fronts. First, that salvation history was inseparable from human history; second, that human history had to be viewed in a salvific perspective. This was because Gutiérrez defined himself against two opposite positions on the matter. On the one side, against traditionalists who denied the salvific value of human existence, he argued that "the salvific action of God underlies all human existence" (p. 153). On the other side, he suggested that those who were committed to social and political movements from a purely secular motivation needed a fuller conception of history that only a Christian salvation perspective provided: "The historical destiny of humanity must be placed definitively in the salvific horizon. Only thus will its true dimensions emerge and its deepest meanings be apparent" (A Theology of Liberation, p. 153).

[40] The exodus was mentioned at Medellín but not really developed as a biblical resource. It came to prominence in the 1970s when Gutiérrez's identified it as a paradigm for liberation theology. The first major study of the exodus was in the work of the Argentinean exegete, José Severino Croatto, Exodus: A Hermeneutics of Freedom (trans. S. Attanasio; Maryknoll N.Y.: Orbis Books, 1981 [Spanish orig. 1973]). Croatto was one of Latin America's most sophisticated hermeneutical scholars and his work on the exodus was primarily focussed on methodological issues rather than commentating on the exodus story itself. See also G. V. Pixley, On Exodus: A Liberation Perspective, (trans. R. R. Barr; Maryknoll, N.Y.: Orbis Books, 1987 [Spanish orig. 1983]).

[41] On Gutiérrez's treatment of the Exodus in later works, see The Power of the Poor in History, pp. 27–29, 118–119; We Drink from Our Own Wells: The Spiritual Journey of a People (trans. M. J. O'Connell; Maryknoll, N.Y.: Orbis Books; London: SCM Press, 1984), pp. 11, 73; and The God of Life (trans. M. O'Connell; Maryknoll, N.Y.: Orbis Books; London: SCM Press, 1991), pp. 4, 50. A helpful analysis of Gutiérrez's use of the bible is offered by Jeffrey Siker, "Uses of the Bible in the Theology of Gustavo Gutiérrez: Liberating Scriptures of the Poor," Biblical Interpretation 4 (1996), pp. 40–71. Siker's comments on the Exodus are particularly interesting in this regard (p. 44): "The story of the exodus (both in the book of Exodus proper and elsewhere in the OT, e.g., Deut. 6, 8) is also quite important for Gutiérrez, as the story identifies God as a liberating God. But the exodus story is not, I would argue, the crucial biblical story or theme underlying Gutiérrez's liberation theology, a misunderstanding that is often repeated in analyses of Gutiérrez's work." However, although Siker cautions against overemphasising Gutiérrez's reliance on Exodus, he recognises that the importance of the exodus story to Gutiérrez should not be underestimated either, and it is telling that Siker suggests that Gutiérrez later downplayed the significance of the exodus story in response to his critics (p. 68).

"The memory of the Exodus pervades the pages of the Bible and inspires one to reread often the Old as well as the New Testaments."[42] Gutiérrez showed how the Exodus was linked to creation in Genesis. Liberation as presented in Exodus provided the theological framework for reading divine creation and human labour in Genesis as salvific work.[43] Against this background, Gutiérrez presented Christ as the liberator who completed and fulfilled this work of creation/liberation.[44] However, to make clear the holistic sense of liberation as salvation, Gutiérrez argued that Christ is to be understood in all three levels of the liberation process—political, historical, and theological.

> In Christ the all-comprehensiveness of the liberating process reaches its fullest sense. His work encompasses the three levels of meaning which we mentioned above.[45]

Gutiérrez emphasised that theological reflection on human work and social praxis must be rooted in an affirmation of their salvific character.[46] Humans are challenged to follow the creative and liberative process that is indicated in the narrative from Genesis to Exodus, and is seen most clearly in Christ. Gutiérrez argued that human work in the political and social sphere was therefore part of the salvific process.[47] Subsequently, his work raised questions on the pastoral practices and political commitments of the church.

PASTORAL PRACTICE AND POLITICAL COMMITMENT: SOLIDARITY WITH THE POOR AND PROTEST AGAINST POVERTY

Gutiérrez explored the pastoral choices facing the church in the context of the church's political transition from Christendom to New Christendom. The New Christendom, according to Gutiérrez, rested on a "distinction of planes" that allowed greater lay involvement in social activities.[48] The distinction-of-planes

---

[42] Gutiérrez, *A Theology of Liberation*, p. 157. Gutiérrez also stressed the contemporary relevance of the Exodus: "The Exodus experience is paradigmatic. It remains vital and contemporary due to similar historical experiences which the People of God undergo" (p. 159).

[43] Human activity is included in this theological perspective since "Man is the crown and centre of the work of creation and is called to continue it through his labor . . ." (p. 158).

[44] Gutiérrez, *A Theology of Liberation*, pp. 175–178.

[45] Gutiérrez, *A Theology of Liberation*, p. 178.

[46] Gutiérrez, *A Theology of Liberation*, p. 160.

[47] Gutiérrez, *A Theology of Liberation*, pp. 159–160: "Consequently, when we assert that man fulfils himself by continuing the work of creation by means of his labor, we are saying that he places himself, by this very fact, within an all-embracing salvific process. To work, to transform this world, is to become a man and to build the human community; it is also to save. Likewise, to struggle against misery and exploitation and to build a just society is already to be part of the saving action, which is moving towards its complete fulfilment. All this means that building the temporal city is not simply a stage of 'humanization' or 'pre-evangelization' as was held in theology up until a few years ago. Rather it is to become part of a saving process which embraces the whole of man and all human history."

[48] *A Theology of Liberation*, pp. 53–58.

model divided sacred and secular history in a way that was an important step forward on old Christendom. It recognised the partial autonomy of the secular realm and allowed the laity limited engagement with social issues albeit in a closely supervised moral framework. However, Gutiérrez recognised that it remained a timid and ambiguous attempt to respond to pressing social challenges.

Moreover, Gutiérrez argued that inadequacies in the distinction-of-planes model had been exposed in practice when committed Christians took up the challenge to engage on social issues. Problems with the model arose when young people and lay movements tried to transform society in accordance with the moral teaching of the church, but without taking sides on political issues. Many progressive members of the laity found themselves radicalized by their engagement with social issues and became increasingly political in their understanding of them. In this process, they came to see the claim of the church that it was politically neutral as deeply misleading. The reticence to take sides and the rhetoric of neutrality concealed the ways in which the church was still closely linked to those in power and failed to address the needs of those who were exploited. Ironically, as the progressive laity started to take more radical political stances on the side of the oppressed, it was the "distinction of planes model" that was used to condemn their activities.[49]

At a theological level, assumptions about the distinction of planes that held up the New Christendom model were also under challenge. Challenges came from two opposite directions. Outside the church, the steady rise of secularization in modern societies could not be ignored. In a world "come of age" (a phrase Gutiérrez took from the German Lutheran Dietrich Bonhoeffer) the self-understanding of educated people changed. The church had to recognise the demands for human freedom and autonomy. Meanwhile, inside the church, Catholic theology moved from a position that emphasised the gulf between the two planes, to one that acknowledged a difference but stressed their integral relationship.[50]

How should the church in Latin America respond to this new understanding of the relationship between the church and world? Gutiérrez reviewed the more radical political positions that progressive Christians in Latin America— including laity, priests and religious, and bishops—had started to adopt and the opposition they faced. Gutiérrez stressed the need for a pastoral option based on solidarity or identification with the Latin American poor and their quest for liberation. This would involve more active political commitment by the church.[51] The practical outcome of Gutiérrez's theological discussion was clear.

---

[49] Gutiérrez notes: "The distinction of planes banner has changed hands. Until a few years ago it was defended by the vanguard; now it is held aloft by power groups, many of whom are in no way involved with any commitment to the Christian faith" (p. 65).

[50] Gutiérrez cites the important work of De Lubac and Rahner in this process and notes that the term integral achieved prominence at Vatican II (especially in *Gaudium et Spes*).

[51] See Gutiérrez, *A Theology of Liberation*, pp. 108–114.

The church should switch sides and be part the revolutionary process toward a socialist future in Latin America.[52]

Gutiérrez's sympathy for socialism and his willingness to draw on Marxist analysis inevitably attracted opposition.[53] Likewise, misunderstandings could easily arise from liberation theology's references to revolution. Liberation theology's talk of revolutionary commitments should not be seen as evidence that liberation theology advocated the violent overthrow of governments.[54] Gutiérrez's understanding of liberation theology as part of a move from developmentalism to social revolution was never a call to armed insurrection.[55] It was more a rejection of token reforms that did not address the real issues. In addition, it indicated in the terminology of the time the dramatic extent to which society had to change if it was to serve everyone and not just a small elite.[56] Talk of revolutionary change focussed attention on the need for structural social change, not just personal transformation. It highlighted the need for changes in politics and society and not just inner attitudes.

In this sense, liberation theology was rightly seen as a revolutionary movement. It hoped for a radical change in Latin American societies (a complete turnaround of political priorities) and a rejection of capitalist dependency. Gutiérrez and other liberation theologians referred to revolution in opposition to the ineffectual reform that they knew made so little difference in the past. Revolutionary commitment signified belief in social action and the urgency of dramatic change that went well beyond traditional mentalities of charity.[57] Certainly during the heady atmosphere of the late 1960s, there were a few highly publicized instances of priests like Camilo Torres joining guerrilla groups.[58] However, the vast majority of liberation theologians like Gutiérrez advocated revolution—at least in the most literal sense of the word—but firmly rejected armed struggle.[59]

---

[52] "In Latin America, the Church must place itself squarely within the process of revolution, amid the violence that is present in different ways" (Gutiérrez, *A Theology of Liberation*, p. 138).

[53] Liberation theology's relationship to socialist movements and Marxist analysis are discussed in greater length in the next chapter.

[54] Dominique Barbé describes it in terms of nonviolent revolution in D. Barbé, *Grace and Power: Base Communities and Non-violence in Brazil* (trans. J. P. Brown; Maryknoll, N.Y.: Orbis Books, 1987) pp. 39–40, 134–150.

[55] Gutiérrez, *A Theology of Liberation*, p. 25. On Gutiérrez and violence, see R. M. Brown, *Gustavo Gutiérrez*, p. 214; see further R. M. Brown, *Religion and Violence* (Philadelphia: Westminster Press, 2nd ed., 1987).

[56] On the relationship between liberation theologies and European theologies of revolution, see Gibellini, *The Liberation Theology Debate*, p. 16.

[57] See also Third World Bishops, "A Letter to the Peoples of the Third World," §§ 3–5.

[58] See Chapter 5 above. As noted in Chapter 5, Torres was very much the exception and should not be seen as in any way representative of liberation theology in his decision. In fact, it is better to see Torres and others who resigned the priesthood as the exceptions that proved the rule. The fact that they *left* the priesthood indicates the difference between them and the liberation theologians who remained within the church.

[59] Critics might object that to talk of revolution in this way gives a false impression

Some critics have suggested that liberation theology's sympathy to socialism and use of Marxist analysis meant at least an implict endorsement of violent revolution. However, liberation theologians consistently follow orthodox Catholic teaching on the use of violence. In the vast majority of cases this leads them to permit it in principle but to reject it in practice and explicitly distance themselves from it. For example, Gutiérrez accepted that in principle, armed struggle might be justifiable under certain conditions, but in practice he always rejected it as the wrong option.[60]

In the late 1970s, the issue of revolutionary struggle was given new prominence due to the active participation of Christians in social movements in Central America, especially the involvement of Nicaraguan Christians in the overthrow of Somoza in 1979 and the political repression in El Salvador that eventually led to civil war in the 1980s.[61] Many felt that the harm of a longstanding situation of oppression and the absence of other peaceable options (which are the circumstances recognised by Paul VI as making armed struggle permissible) justified Christian participation in attempts to overthrow the dictatorship. As a result, Christians participated in revolutionary movements in both Nicaragua and El Salvador. This included a number of priests who endorsed the Sandinista revolution in Nicaragua (but did not bear arms or join the fighting). In El Salvador, a few radicalised novices gave up their vocations to join guerrilla groups.

The majority of liberation theologians across the continent had considerable sympathy for these struggles but, like Gutiérrez, they were more willing to defend the aims of the struggle than the means. They tried to explain why Christians might feel forced into such actions, but they usually qualified their support in ways that showed that these actions were not choices that they would make themselves and were not necessarily applicable to other situations. For them, liberation theology's commitment to revolution was about a radical, but democratic transformation of society. The practical projects with which liberation theologians became involved—shanty town community groups, agricultural cooperatives, and movements claiming land for the landless were invariably much more modest and smaller in scale than the term revolutionary first suggests.

---

and might be irresponsible in the polarized societies of Latin America. However, the revolutionary language in liberation theology's early works offered an empowering vision of social change that fitted perfectly with the language of liberation. Furthermore, liberation theologians could reasonably wish to be judged primarily on what they actually wrote and not on what their critics supposed them to mean.

[60] It should also be remembered that at the other side of the political spectrum the Latin American church hierarchy usually had very close links with the armed forces. Military chaplains, who might hold high military ranks and even carry weapons, are far more common than guerrilla priests.

[61] See Berryman, *The Religious Roots of Rebellion*, pp. 51–89; A. Bradstock, *Saints and Sandinistas: The Catholic Church in Nicaragua and Its Response to the Revolution* (London: Epworth Press, 1987); T. Cabestrero, *Revolutionaries for the Gospel: Testimonies of Fifteen Christians in the Nicaraguan Government* (Maryknoll, N.Y.: Orbis Books, 1986).

Gutiérrez wrote *A Theology of Liberation* while a student adviser and parish priest in a working class neighbourhood in central Lima. With these experiences in mind, he took up the conclusions of Medellín on poverty to which he himself had contributed.[62] Gutiérrez started by noting the expectations created by Vatican II when John XXIII's message prior to the opening of the Council spoke of "a Church of a Poor."[63] However, he felt that the Council failed to live up to these initial expectations. Despite its references to poverty—most noticeably in *Lumen Gentium* (§ 16) and *Gaudium et Spes* (§ 14)—it failed to make poverty a major thrust of its work.[64] The problems therefore needed to be looked at again, and *A Theology of Liberation* offered Gutiérrez an opportunity to reflect on poverty in both its material and spiritual dimensions.

Gutiérrez presented material poverty as "the lack of economic goods necessary for a human life worthy of the name."[65] However, he added that the criteria for material poverty are in the process of change. In the modern world, they needed to include access to cultural, social, and political values, as well as its traditional economic dimension. Although it was widely accepted that poverty was degrading and something that must be rejected, Christians nonetheless had a tendency to idealise material poverty and give it a positive value. Gutiérrez saw this unresolved ambiguity in the attitude to poverty, as one of the most serious barriers to promoting an effective Christian social ethic.

A second element that Gutiérrez identified as important in this process was the shift from an individualistic to a structural understanding of the causes of poverty. Traditionally, poverty was seen as primarily a condition that affected individuals and made them objects of charity. He argued that this naive thinking about poverty would no longer do, because the victims of poverty were becoming conscious of poverty's structural elements and the need to struggle against these. He concluded:

> What we mean by poverty is a subhuman situation. As we shall see later, the Bible also considers it this way. Concretely, to be poor means to die of hunger, to be illiterate, to be exploited by others, not to know that you are being exploited, not to know that you are a person. It is in relation to this poverty—material and cultural, collective and militant—that evangelical poverty will have to define itself.[66]

Gutiérrez warned that the notion of spiritual poverty was less clear than material poverty and fraught with dangers of misunderstanding. He rejected any

---

[62] *A Theology of Liberation*, chapter 13.

[63] Radio message of 11 September 1962, in *The Pope Speaks* 8.4 (Spring 1963) p. 396, cited in *A Theology of Liberation*, p. 287.

[64] Gutiérrez acknowledged that *Populorum Progressio* is more concrete and clear on the subject of poverty, but said that "it will remain for the Church on a continent of misery and injustice to give the theme of poverty its proper importance" (*A Theology of Liberation*, p. 287).

[65] *A Theology of Liberation*, p. 288.

[66] *A Theology of Liberation*, p. 289.

spiritualistic account of poverty that treated poverty as an abstract ideal, rather than engaging with poverty as it was lived by the poor of Latin America. He argued that the ambiguities over spiritual poverty that arose from such abstract discussions had very harmful historical consequences.[67]

To clarify both the material and spiritual dimensions further, he then turned to the biblical meaning of poverty in the Bible and identified two basic senses: on the one hand, poverty as a scandalous condition, and on the other hand, poverty as spiritual childhood.[68] To explain this, Gutiérrez first offered an analysis of the words used in the Bible to describe the poor.[69] He saw the language of the Bible as a vigorous rejection of poverty and indignant protest against its causes. He concluded, "Indigent, weak, bent over, wretched are terms which well express a degrading human situation."[70] These terms indicated the biblical protest against material poverty as scandalous. The prophets Isaiah, Jeremiah, Amos, and Micah "condemn every kind of abuse, every form of keeping the poor in poverty or of creating new poor people."[71] Exodus, Leviticus, and Deuteronomy demanded positive and concrete measures to blunt the edges of poverty in the short-term and prevent poverty from becoming entrenched in the long-term.[72]

Gutiérrez concluded his analysis of biblical attitudes to the scandal of material poverty with a restatement of his belief in history as one. Human beings meet God in their encounter with other people. What they do unto others is what they do unto God. In terms of material poverty, this means that: "to oppress the poor is to offend God himself; to know God is to do justice among men."[73]

Then he turned to the Bible's understanding of spiritual poverty as spiritual childhood. In this sense, poverty was:

> . . . the ability to welcome God, an openness to God, a willingness to be used by God, a humility before God . . . Understood in this way poverty is opposed

---

[67] "We have also fallen into very vague terminology and a kind of sentimentalism which in the last analysis justifies the status quo. In situations like the present one in Latin America this is especially serious." A *Theology of Liberation*, p. 290.

[68] Gutiérrez took this distinction from A. Gelin, *The Poor of Yahweh* (trans. K. Sullivan; Collegeville, Minn.: The Liturgical Press, 1964), and drew on Gelin's work for his own analysis; A *Theology of Liberation*, p. 291 n. 11.

[69] These include the Old Testament terms, *rash*, *ébyôn*, *dal* and *anaw*, as well as the New Testament term *ptokós*. A *Theology of Liberation*, p. 291.

[70] A *Theology of Liberation*, p. 292.

[71] A *Theology of Liberation*, p. 293.

[72] Gutiérrez developed his account of material poverty as evil further, by identifying three biblical principles. First, the example set by Moses leading the people out of slavery and oppression so that they might inhabit a land where they could live with dignity. Second, the mandate of Genesis (1.26; 2.15), in which humanity was created in the image of God with a special place in creation. Finally, the Christian tradition that people are "the sacrament of God," a theme that Gutiérrez developed in more depth in chapter 10. See A *Theology of Liberation*, p. 295.

[73] A *Theology of Liberation*, p. 295.

to pride, to an attitude of self-sufficiency; on the other hand, it is synonymous with faith, with abandonment and trust in the Lord.[74]

He drew on the Psalms for this inspiration, but said that the idea found its highest expression in the New Testament Beatitudes. Thus, Gutiérrez saw the poverty described as blessed in Matthew 5.1 in terms of spiritual childhood. According to Gutiérrez "Blessed are the poor in spirit" refers, at a deeper level, to dependence on the will of God. He then examined different interpretations of Luke 6.20, "Blessed are the poor." He suggested that although this text refers to the materially poor, it should not be taken as the canonization of a social class or as an exhortation to accept social injustice for the sake of a future reward. On the contrary, Gutiérrez drew on Mark 1.15 to argue that Christ says that the poor are blessed because the Kingdom of God has begun, and therefore, their oppressive situation is about to change.[75]

Finally, having distinguished these two aspects of poverty and the biblical perspectives on them, Gutiérrez attempted to synthesise them. He introduced a third dimension to poverty as a basis for Christian commitment to solidarity and protest.[76] Gutiérrez saw this as the meaning of poverty for Christ and argued it offered the best model for the Latin American church. To support this, he drew on Paul's letters and argued that in christological perspective "poverty is an act of love and liberation."[77] For Gutiérrez "poverty has a redemptive value," but "it is not a question of idealizing poverty, but rather of taking it on as it is—an evil—to protest against it."[78] Then he turned to the ideal of the early church as represented in Acts 2.44 and 4.33. He argued that the intention behind the community of goods was not to erect poverty as an ideal but to eliminate poverty. On this basis, he concluded with a challenge to the church:

> Only by rejecting poverty and by making itself poor in order to protest against it can the Church preach something that is uniquely its own: 'spiritual poverty,' that is, the openness of man and history to the future promised by God . . . Only authentic solidarity with the poor and a real protest against the poverty of our time can provide the concrete, vital context necessary for a theological discussion of poverty.[79]

Gutiérrez's interpretation of poverty and the challenges that it presented to the church in Latin America and elsewhere amplified and explained the commitment taken at Medellín. The need for solidarity with the poor—and protest against their exploitation—pointed towards a radical transformation of the church.

---

[74] *A Theology of Liberation*, p. 296.

[75] *A Theology of Liberation*, p. 298.

[76] *A Theology of Liberation*, p. 299.

[77] *A Theology of Liberation*, p. 300.

[78] *A Theology of Liberation*, p. 300. Gutiérrez adds (pp. 300–301): "Christian poverty, an expression of love is solidarity with the poor and is a protest against poverty."

[79] *A Theology of Liberation*, pp. 301–302.

CONCLUSION

A *Theology of Liberation* did not come out of the blue, but built on various break-throughs made in the late 1960s. Nonetheless, as the first systematic exposition of many of liberation theology's key ideas, Gutiérrez's book is rightly seen as the movement's founding theological publication. Even though the component parts of liberation theology were born at Medellín and early formulations could be found in the work of different thinkers in the late 1960s—most notably Gutiérrez himself—they had attracted little attention outside a small circle and were almost unknown at the international level. Gutiérrez' book in 1971 served to baptise and name the newly born movement. It provided the firm theological foundation on which progressives in the church in Latin America could base their political option for the poor and ensured that liberation theology would come to the attention of a global audience.

The crucial contribution of A *Theology of Liberation* was that it set the key challenges facing the Latin American church into a powerful and well-integrated framework. First, *a new set of principles* for theology (theology as a second step and orientated to orthopraxis), which would govern its methodology. Second, *a distinctive new theological language* (liberation), which would provide the movement with a cohesive core and sense of self-identity. Third, *a new pastoral option and political commitment*—a commitment to serve the poor and a new solidarity in both thought and deed—which would provide the social impetus to liberation theology and the pastoral program for the church.

CHAPTER SEVEN

Justice, Socialism, and Revolution

> In the face of the present-day situation of the world, marked as it is by the grave sin of injustice, we recognise both our responsibility and our inability to overcome it by our strength. Such a situation urges us to listen with a humble and open heart to the word of God, as he shows us new paths toward action in the cause of justice in the world.
>
> The Synod of Bishops, *Justice in the World* (1971)[1]

INTRODUCTION

A Theology of Liberation and other early works of liberation theology focussed attention on the urgent need for social justice and suggested a more open attitude towards socialism and Marxist analysis. In Mexico, José Porfirio Miranda published his influential work *Marx and the Bible* (1971). In it he argued that Christianity and Marxism shared the same underlying concern for the economically oppressed. In Rome, the publication of *Octogesima Adveniens* (May 1971) and the bishops' synod on justice (November 1971) supported those in the church who wanted to make social justice a priority concern. However, it expressed concern over rapprochement with socialism or use of Marxism.

Just how far the church was open to an alliance with socialists was put to the test when the controversial Christians for Socialism movement emerged in Chile and other Latin American countries. Although the immediate controversy ended when Christians for Socialism in Chile came to an abrupt end after the 1973 coup, the issue remained deeply problematic for radical Christians involved in struggles for justice elsewhere.

---

[1] The Synod of Bishops, "Justice in the World" Statement, reprinted in O'Brien and Shannon (eds.), *Catholic Social Thought*, pp. 288–300 (293).

The early 1970s were very exciting times for liberation theology. In July 1972, many of liberation theology's leading advocates were invited to El Escorial Spain for a conference sponsored by the Institute of Faith and Secularization intended to introduce liberation theology to a European audience.[2] The papers presented at the conference showed the range and power of reflection that had already developed. In the same year, the Brazilian Leonardo Boff sought to build further foundations for liberation theology by grounding it on a more developed Christology. He took the term Jesus the Liberator and published a book of that title in 1972.[3] Jon Sobrino took this initiative further in 1976 with his *Christology at the Crossroads*. These two works added a new dimension to the liberation theology literature and offered further methodological principles for the movement to build upon in the future.

MARX AND THE BIBLE

José Miranda's book *Marx and the Bible* was published in Salamanca in 1971, a year before *A Theology of Liberation* was published in Spain.[4] Miranda was a former Jesuit with diverse academic interests and graduate training that ranged across philosophy, economics, and biblical studies. He worked as an adviser to student and worker groups in Mexico and wrote primarily as an independent scholar, rather than in service to the church. Nonetheless, his work had a major impact on how Europeans saw the emerging literature of liberation theology.

In *Marx and the Bible*, Miranda argued strongly that "to a great degree Marx coincides with the Bible."[5] A few years later and equally provocatively, he wrote in *The Bible and Communism*:

> for a Christian to claim to be anticommunist . . . without doubt constitutes the greatest scandal of our century . . . The notion of communism is in the New Testament, right down to the letter—and so well put that in the twenty centuries since it was written no one has come up with a better definition of communism than Luke in Acts 2.44–45 and 4.32–35.[6]

Such claims were clearly designed to be startling—especially in Mexico, where the church had a particularly conservative history—and it is hardly surprising that they stirred opposition. The book shaped perceptions of liberation theology as a whole, which was in some ways unfortunate, because his work was

---

[2] The papers of this important conference were published as Instituto Fe y Secularidad, *Fe cristiano y cambio social* (Encuentro de El Escorial, Spain, 1972; ed. J. Alvarez Bolardo; Salamanca: Sígueme, 1973).

[3] *Jesus Christ Liberator: A Critical Christology of Our Time* (trans. P. Hughes; Maryknoll, N.Y.: Orbis Books, 1978; London: SPCK, 1980 [Portuguese orig. 1972]).

[4] *A Theology of Liberation* was published in Spain in 1972, then translated into English and published in the U.S. in 1973 and the U.K. in 1974.

[5] Miranda, *Marx and the Bible*, p. xvii.

[6] J. P. Miranda, *Communism in the Bible* (trans. R. Barr; Maryknoll, N.Y.: Orbis Books, 1982 [Spanish orig. 1981]), pp. 1–2.

never representative of liberation theology. Nonetheless, Miranda's work offered a provocative reading of both Marx and the Bible, and although untypical, it would be wrong to dismiss his work simply as a naive baptism of Marx. In part, Miranda's work was significant because it showed just how far some of the radical ideas under discussion might be taken. Primarily, however, his importance lay in his consistent emphasis on the biblical concern for justice and the Bible's radical attitude to economic issues.[7]

Like Gutiérrez, Miranda drew on the Exodus narrative to illuminate the nature of God as liberator of the oppressed. He pointed out that the Bible presents the Exodus as the historical action in which God was revealed as Yahweh the deliverer of Israel (Exod. 6.6–7).[8] Miranda sees the Exodus as definitive of God's action: "He who reveals himself by intervening in our history is always Yahweh as savior of the oppressed and punisher of the oppressors."[9]

Miranda also made extensive use of the Prophetic books to argue that the Bible makes the understanding of God inseparable from the practice of justice.[10] He offered considerable biblical support for this. For example, Miranda refers to the statement in Jer. 22.16, "He judged the cause of the poor and the needy; then it was well. Is this not to know me? says the Lord," and comments:

> Here we have an explicit definition of what it is to know Yahweh. To know Yahweh is to achieve justice for the poor. Nothing authorises us to introduce a cause-effect relationship between 'to know Yahweh' and 'to practice justice.'[11]

Gutiérrez and other early liberation theologians also placed a very strong emphasis on justice, but Miranda appeared to go further than Gutiérrez.[12] Miranda stressed that the biblical view that "to know God is to do justice" was to be taken at absolute face value. According to Miranda, the message in this text was not that a causal connection existed between doing justice and knowing God, but that they were actually identical.

In effect, Miranda seemed to argue that in the Bible God *was* justice and vice-versa. This was a much more controversial claim than Gutiérrez's view that justice was a central and essential part of God's character and not a marginal

---

[7] Miranda makes much greater reference to biblical scholarship than to Marxist theory and this is reflected, for example, in many more entries in the index to the work of Old Testament scholar Gerhard von Rad than to Karl Marx.

[8] Miranda, *Marx and the Bible*, pp. 78–88. Like Gutiérrez, Miranda drew particularly on Gerhard Von Rad to link the exodus to creation (see esp. p. 77).

[9] Miranda, *Marx and the Bible*, p. 81.

[10] Miranda, *Marx and the Bible*, pp. 44–53. On the inseparability of God and justice, see also Miranda's follow-up work, idem, *Being and the Messiah: The Message of St. John* (Maryknoll, N.Y.: Orbis Books, 1977 [Spanish orig. 1973]), pp. 27–46, 137–140. For discussion, see P. Berryman, *Liberation Theology: The Essential Facts About Revolutionary Movements in Latin America and Beyond* (New York: Pantheon; London: Taurus; 1987), p. 148; A. F. McGovern, *Marxism: An American Christian Perspective*, pp. 190–194; idem, *Liberation Theology and its Critics*, p. 70.

[11] Miranda, *Marx and the Bible*, p. 44.

[12] For example, Gutiérrez, *The Power of the Poor in History*, pp. 7–8.

or accidental one. For Miranda, God should not be thought of as a being, nor did God have any existence except in the ethical imperative to justice. In effect, this de-ontologised the traditional theistic view of God and offered a radical ethic of justice in its place. Miranda saw God as justice in terms of being a summons to a better future.

This radical view of God's nature was closely associated with another distinctive feature in Miranda's work. Miranda rejected participation in what he called the *cultus* (the sphere of religious worship) as the basis for knowledge of God. This was because worship tended to separate knowing God from action for justice. He argued that it was only an idolatrous God that could be known in this way. Knowledge of the biblical God could not come through religion or religious actions of worship or contemplation, but only from the struggle for justice.

Miranda stood alone among Latin American theologians in his views, both in de-ontologising God into ethics and his rejection of worship. In fact, in adopting this approach, Miranda may have fed the fears of those that claimed that uncritically adopting Marxist categories of social analysis inevitably led to acceptance of an atheist outlook and antireligious ideology. Miranda raised important questions, but his negative view of traditional religious practice (and the church) and the provocative title of the book polarised debate. Many radical and progressives found it a fresh and powerful perspective. However, it was very easy for more conservative critics to dismiss it as partisan Marxism.[13] Unfortunately, the easy stereotyping of Miranda's work as Marxist reductionism consolidated the easy stereotyping of the whole liberation theology movement in the same terms. After the publication of *Marx and the Bible*, other works of liberation theology found charges of Marxist reductionism even harder to avoid; no matter how poorly and unreasonably such criticisms were referenced to the theologian or work in question.

OCTOGESIMA ADVENIENS AND THE SYNOD ON JUSTICE

In the same year that Gutiérrez and Miranda published their influential books, Paul VI elected against issuing a social encyclical to commemorate the 80th anniversary of *Rerum Novarum* and instead issued an apostolic letter, *Octogesima*

---

[13] In fact, Miranda's highly individualistic use of Marxist concepts and a Marxist framework for this task can hardly be described as uncritical Marxism. His subsequent work *Marx against the Marxists* was a sustained attack on common Marxist beliefs, and made clear that he was anything but an uncritical or orthodox Marxist; see J. P. Miranda, *Marx against the Marxists: The Christian Humanism of Karl Marx* (trans. J. Drury, Maryknoll, N.Y.: Orbis Books; London: SCM Press, 1980 [Spanish orig. 1978]). On Miranda's Marxism see A. Kee, *Marxism and the Failure of Liberation Theology* (London: SCM Press, 1990), p. 210; A. Fierro, *The Militant Gospel: An Analysis of Contemporary Political Theologies* (trans. J. Drury; Maryknoll, N.Y.: Orbis Books; London: SCM Press, 1977), p. 296.

Adveniens (*The Eightieth Anniversary*), on 14 May 1971.[14] The letter marked another significant step in defining the church's social responsibility in the contemporary world. It was of particular interest for its discussion of socialism and Marxism.

On socialism, it noted that some Christians were attracted to various different forms of socialism but cautioned that many of these drew inspiration from ideologies that were incompatible with Christian faith. It called for careful judgements that recognised the distinction between "the various levels of expression of socialism: as a generous aspiration and a seeking for a more just society, historical movements with a political organization and aim, and an ideology which aims to give a complete and self-sufficient picture of man."[15] It added that although these distinctions existed, the different levels were not completely separated from each other, and Christians needed to recognise the mutual influences between them "to see the degree of commitment possible along these lines, while safeguarding the values, especially those of liberty, responsibility, and openness to the spiritual, which guarantee the integral development of man."[16]

It then turned to Marxism and reviewed some of the different ways in which it might be seen before presenting a similar conclusion.

> While, through the concrete existing form of Marxism, one can distinguish these various aspects and the questions they pose for the reflection and activity of Christians, it would be illusory and dangerous to reach a point of forgetting the intimate link which radically binds them together, to accept the elements of Marxist analysis without recognizing their relationships with ideology, and to enter into the practice of class struggle and its Marxist interpretation, while failing to note the kind of totalitarian and violent society to which this process leads.[17]

Octogesima Adveniens supported local bishops who searched for contextual responses to the social challenges that they faced.[18] It recognised the autonomy of the national episcopates to develop their own pastoral programs in line with church teaching. In the 1970s, progressive episcopates such as those in Brazil, Peru, Chile (especially after 1973), and El Salvador (especially after 1977) took advantage of this official encouragement and promoted a wide range of social

---

[14] His previous encyclical *Humanae Vitae* (issued on 25 July 1968) had unexpectedly reaffirmed the traditional rejection of artificial contraception and generated considerable controversy. It was generally thought that this may have made him reluctant to issue another encyclical so soon. *Octogesima Adveniens* was issued as a letter to Cardinal Maurice Roy (president of the recently established Justice and Peace Commission) rather than as an official social encyclical; see O'Brien and Shannon (eds.), *Catholic Social Thought*, pp. 265–286.

[15] *Octogesima Adveniens*, § 31.

[16] *Octogesima Adveniens*, § 31.

[17] *Octogesima Adveniens*, §§ 32–34 (§ 34).

[18] On the legitimate pluralism of options see *Octogesima Adveniens*, § 50.

initiatives from the defence of Human Rights to demands for land reform.[19] At the bishops' synod in Rome, six months after the apostolic letter, they discussed social justice and the priesthood as the mission of the people of God.[20]

The Council for Justice and Peace handled preparations for the Synod's discussion of social justice.[21] In response to the challenge in *Gaudium et Spes* that Christians examine the signs of the times and detect their meaning, the synod addressed itself to social injustices in the light of the Catholic social tradition.[22] They took the challenges the church faced on urgent social issues as their starting point and drew on the existing social tradition. Their published statement "Justice in the World" recognised: "the serious injustices of men which are building around the world a network of domination, oppression, and abuses which stifle freedom."[23] They affirmed that "Action on behalf of justice and participation in the transformation of the world fully appear to us as a constitutive dimension of the preaching of the Gospel."[24] They recognised that promoting this social responsibility might require new roles and duties for the

---

[19] In 1978, the accession of John Paul II would start to reverse this regional autonomy and the recentralising process gathered speed in the 1980s. This created considerable tension between the Vatican and some national bishops conferences (and increased the tension within the conferences themselves), which was an important influence on the conflict over liberation theology in the 1980s.

[20] The 1971 Synod of Bishops was the third Synod held after Vatican II (in accordance with the Council's provisions for such meetings to be called by the Pope every two years after the Council). Much of the discussion at the conference focussed on priesthood and priestly discipline, but the conference is often referred to as the "Synod on Justice" because its statement on justice was subsequently published and made an important addition to the Catholic social tradition. See "Justice in the World" in O'Brien and Shannon (eds.), *Catholic Social Thought*, pp. 288–300. Furthermore, because the discussion of justice touched on such important issues, it was decided there should be further discussion at the 1974 Synod of Bishops.

[21] This body had been set up by Paul VI in 1967 to take forward the teaching of the Council in *Gaudium et Spes*. It had been the official Catholic body that sponsored cooperation with the World Council of Churches over the SODEPAX consultation at Cartigny in 1969 when Gutiérrez and Alves spoke of liberation.

[22] In the process, they provided a helpful summary of recent developments in the tradition in the previous decade: "As never before, the Church has, through the Second Vatican Council's constitution *Gaudium et Spes*, better understood the situation in the modern world, in which the Christian works out his salvation by deeds of justice. *Pacem in Terris* gave us an authentic charter of human rights. In *Mater et Magistra*, international justice begins to take first place; it finds more elaborate expression in *Populorum Progressio*, in the form of a true and suitable treatise on the right to development; and in *Octogesima Adveniens* is a summary of guidelines for political action" ("Justice in the World" in O'Brien and Shannon [eds.], *Catholic Social Thought*, pp. 296–297).

[23] "Justice in the World" in O'Brien and Shannon (eds.), *Catholic Social Thought*, p. 288. The rest of the document makes clear that this applied to both socialist and capitalist systems of domination.

[24] "Justice in the World" in O'Brien and Shannon (eds.), *Catholic Social Thought*, pp. 288 and 289.

church, and that these should be orientated especially to all those who are voiceless victims of injustice.[25] This endorsed the important shift—which liberation theology had already pioneered—away from the church calling on others to make a special social option for the poor and toward the church making the option its own responsibility.

Further echoes of liberation theology can be seen in the bishops' recognition that:

> In the Old Testament God reveals himself to us as the liberator of the oppressed and the defender of the poor, demanding from man faith in him and justice towards man's neighbour. It is only in the observance of the duties of justice that God is truly recognised as the liberator of the oppressed . . . Christ lived his life in the world as a total giving of himself to God for the salvation and liberation of men.[26]

However, the synod stopped well short of some of liberation theology's more radical aspects. For example, it condemned the problems created by colonialism and the danger that development might evolve into a new form of colonialism. However, the majority of bishops continued to speak of development as the way forward and liberation through development as the goal. The Peruvian bishops (influenced by Gutiérrez) offered a more outspoken contribution to the synod that included the explicit recognition of dependency and rejection of capitalism.[27] The synod was unwilling to go as far as the Peruvians, who pledged the Peruvian church to start: "opting for the oppressed and marginal peoples as personal and communal commitment."[28] The Peruvian contribution made explicit the idea of the church's social option for the poor. During the early 1970s, this phrase spread and became a shorthand summary of the social

---

[25] ". . . we must be prepared to take on new functions and new duties in every sector of world society, if justice is to be put into practice. Our action is to be directed above all at those men and nations which because of various forms of oppression and because of the present character of our society are silent, indeed voiceless victims of injustice" ("Justice in the World" in O'Brien and Shannon [eds.], *Catholic Social Thought*, p. 291).

[26] "Justice in the World" in O'Brien and Shannon (eds.), *Catholic Social Thought*, p. 293. In the 1960s what might be described—in dependency terms—as stimulus from the "theology of the centre" (Vatican II, *Populorum Progressio* and European political theology) influenced the "theology of the periphery." The 1971 Synod of Bishops and "Justice in the World" are important because they indicate the start of the reverse process in the early 1970s. They reflect the influence of the theology of the periphery on the theology of the centre.

[27] See Bishops of Peru, "Justice in the World," *IDOC* (December 1971), pp. 2–18; reprinted in Hennelly (ed.), *Liberation Theology*, pp. 125–136.

[28] See Bishops of Peru, "Justice in the World" (§ 8) in Hennelly, *Liberation Theology*, p. 128. The Synod, by encouraging episcopal conferences to pursue the Synod's discussion in the future at a local level, gave encouragement—or at least leeway—to those who took this more radical view, but the Synod itself stopped short of fully adopting its radical implications.

message of liberation theology. At the end of the decade at CELAM III (Puebla, Mexico), it found definitive expression in the bishops' famous references to a preferential option for the poor.[29]

CHRISTIANS FOR SOCIALISM

During the early 1970s, a basic consensus existed between liberation theologians and the Vatican on the importance of social justice, but a clear difference on the value of Marxism and danger of socialism. Gutiérrez's A Theology of Liberation stressed a commitment to social justice and the possibility of working with socialist and other groups already working to this end.[30] Hugo Assmann's Opresion-Liberación also offered a forceful statement on the urgency of social issues and a pro-Marxist analysis of what needed to be done.

On the other hand, the apostolic letter Octogesima Adveniens stressed the need for social justice, but rejected the principles of socialism. Likewise, "Justice in the World" had reinforced the urgency of social justice and called for the church to undertake new roles and duties, but said nothing about a new collaboration with socialists. Neither Octogesima Adveniens nor "Justice in the World" had been written directly about the situation in Latin America but they were both intended to apply there. In Latin America, the groups pressing for radical social change—as opposed to moderate reforms—were often inspired by socialism. Rejecting socialism (as demanded by Octogesima Adveniens) or ignoring it (as encouraged by "Justice in the World") presented a practical problem.

If the church's priority was social transformation, it made sense to collaborate with other groups committed to change. A church that maintained its distance from groups influenced by socialism—or denounced them outright—aroused suspicions that its own institutional interests, rather than social transformation, remained the priority. This tension might easily have remained at the level of a largely abstract debate. However, during the early 1970s, it was forcefully tested

---

[29] CELAM III, § 1134 (see chapter 8). The Peruvian bishops had clarified that the option for the poor was preferential and not exclusive in the very next sentence of their contribution: "This option does not exclude any individual from our charity; rather opting for those who today experience the most violent forms of oppression is for us an efficacious way of also loving those who, possibly unconsciously, are oppressed themselves by their very different situation of being oppressors" (§ 8). However, it was not until CELAM III at Puebla that the fully developed phrase "preferential option for the poor" would be officially sanctioned.

[30] Gutiérrez, influenced by the Peruvian socialist, José Mariátegui, hoped for a distinctively Latin American (or, as Mariátegui put it, "Indo-American") form of socialism; see A Theology of Liberation, pp. 88–92 (90). For a brief summary of Mariátegui's life and work, see S. B. Liss, Marxist Thought in Latin America (Berkeley: University of California Press, 1984), pp. 129–137. For an excellent discussion of the influence of Mariátegui on Gutiérrez (and Gutiérrez's attitude to socialism and Marxism) see C. Cadorette, From the Heart of the People: The Theology of Gustavo Gutiérrez (Oak Park, Ill.: Meyer-Stone, 1988), pp. 75–114. For Gutiérrez's position in relation to other liberation theologians, see McGovern, Liberation Theology and Its Critics, pp. 132–164.

by the rise of the Christians for Socialism movement in Chile and other Latin American countries. Christians for Socialism raised the questions of the church's relationship to socialism in a particularly controversial way. The publicity generated by the difficult relationship between the group and the Chilean hierarchy had a major impact on perceptions of the liberation theology as a militant movement.[31]

The election victory of the socialist Popular Unity Coalition with Salvador Allende as president of Chile in 1970 heralded a democratic revolution.[32] To Christians on the political left, this victory promised to fulfil the dreams of those who had worked to make the church more progressive in the late 1960s.[33] Under Allende, the land reforms initiated by Frei were extended and rapidly accelerated. For the brief period until the military coup of September 1973, Chile became the focus of revolutionary hopes for a democratic path to socialism.[34]

---

[31] For documents relating to the movement during its brief official lifespan, see J. Eagleson (ed.), *Christians for Socialism: Documentation of the Christians for Socialism Movement of Latin America* (Maryknoll, N.Y.: Orbis Books, 1975). For analysis, see B. Smith, *The Church and Politics in Chile: Challenges to Modern Catholicism* (Princeton, N.J.: Princeton University Press, 1982), pp. 230–280; A. F. McGovern, *Marxism*, pp. 210–242.

[32] Popular Unity was formed by a coalition of Communists, Socialists, Radicals, and other smaller groups in 1969 and contested the 1970 election against the incumbent Christian Democrat president Eduardo Frei. Frei won the 1964 election with support from the reformist wing of Catholicism including the Chilean church hierarchy. Frei promised a revolution in liberty and delivered a series of reforms that fitted the politically cautious hopes of the reformist church. However, his caution managed to simultaneously alienate the conservatives and failed to satisfy the political left. On Chile's post-Independence history, see S. Collier and W. F. Sater, *A History of Chile: 1808–1994* (New York: Cambridge University Press, 1996); on the Christian Democrat movement, M. Fleet, *The Rise and Fall of Chilean Democracy* (Princeton, N.J.: Princeton University Press, 1985).

[33] By the late 1960s, in Chile—as elsewhere in Latin America—a group of Christians emerged which was recognised in 1968 as the Young Church movement. This group pressed for much more radical social changes than the cautious reforms of Frei and later allied themselves to Allende's democratic socialism. From 1971, Allende's coalition government included the Christian Left in its short-lived democratic socialist experiment in Chile; see B. Pollack and H. Rosenkranz, *Revolutionary Social Democracy: The Chilean Socialist Party* (London: Frances Pinter, 1986); P. E. Sigmund, *The Overthrow of Allende and the Politics of Chile: 1964–1976* (Pittsburgh: University of Pittsburgh Press, 1977).

[34] Allende assumed the presidency on 3 November 1970, but his government lasted less than three years (sometimes referred to as "the 1,000 days") until it was toppled by a military coup led by General Augusto Pinochet on 10 September 1973. The coup inaugurated a seventeen-year period of repressive military under Pinochet, who eventually retired in 1990, after losing a plebiscite in 1988 (which forced him to call elections for 1989). On the Pinochet regime, see A. Valenzuela, *A Nation of Enemies: Chile under Pinochet* (New York: Norton, 1991); M. H. Spooner, *Soldiers in a Narrow Land: The Pinochet Regime in Chile* (Berkeley: University of California Press, 1994). For a recent work that covers his arrest in London in October 1998 for human rights abuses and the subsequent legal proceedings, see H. O'Shaugnessy, *Pinochet: The Politics of Torture* (London: Latin America Bureau, 2000).

A group of Chilean priests who were committed to living and working with the Chilean poor met in April 1971 to discuss Christian participation in the implementation of socialism in Chile. The workshop was billed as Christian Participation in the Task of Developing and Implementing Socialism in Chile. On 16 April the group issued a bold declaration known as the "Declaration of the 80" which advocated Christian commitment to socialist policies.[35]

> As Christians we do not see any incompatibility between Christianity and socialism. Quite the contrary is true. As the Cardinal of Santiago said last November: "There are more evangelical values in socialism than there are in capitalism."[36]

After the April meeting, this radical group together with some members of the Young Church and other supporters took the name Christians for Socialism. Gonzalo Arroyo became secretary and Sergio Torres and a small group of others became a steering group.

Since the priests referred to the words of the cardinal in their declaration, the Chilean church hierarchy felt it had to take a public stance on how they saw the movement.[37] On 22 April Cardinal Silva and the Chilean bishops responded with their "Declaration of the Bishops of Chile."[38] In the first part of the document, the bishops spoke positively of the urgent need for social trans-

---

[35] See "Declaration of the 80" in J. Eagleson (ed.), *Christians for Socialism: Documentation of the Christians for Socialism Movement of Latin America* (Maryknoll, N.Y.: Orbis Books, 1975), pp. 3–6.

[36] Eagleson (ed.), *Christians for Socialism*, p. 4. The group drew a distinction between Marxist analysis and the Marxist worldview that would be central to the recurrent debate on the relationships of liberation theology to Marxism. The group argued: "Thus it is necessary to destroy the prejudice and mistrust that exist between Christians and Marxists. To Marxists we say that authentic religion is not the opiate of the people. It is, on the contrary, a liberating stimulus to revivify and renew the world constantly. To Christians we offer a reminder that our God committed himself personally to the history of human beings. . . . There is a long road ahead for both Christians and Marxists. But the evolution that has taken place in Christians and Marxist circles permits them to engage in a joint effort on behalf of the historical project the country has set for itself. This collaboration will be facilitated to the extent that two things are done: 1) to the extent that Marxism presents itself more and more as an instrument for analyzing and transforming society; 2) to the extent that we as Christians proceed to purify our faith of everything that prevents us from shouldering real and effective commitment" (p. 4).

[37] Cardinal Raúl Silva Henríquez became one of General Pinochet's strongest and most outspoken critics. However, this reference to his views on socialism is misleading. Although Silva had been able to accept and work with Allende's government, he was never an active supporter of Allende's socialism. His outlook in 1971 was firmly New Christendom. He saw the role of the church, as the provider of moral guidance to whatever government was legitimately in power, socialist or free-market. The priests had cited his position very selectively with their suggestion that he favoured socialism. He merely affirmed the positive elements behind its ideals. The need to clarify this may have precipitated the bishops' swift response.

[38] "Declaration of the Bishops of Chile" in Eagleson (ed.), *Christians for Socialism*, pp. 12–15; reprinted in Hennelly, *Liberation Theology*, pp. 143–145.

formation but cautioned against "options for socialism with a Marxist cast."[39] In the second half—which turned directly to the "Declaration of the 80"— they stressed that priests must not involve themselves directly with politics.[40] Although it was permissible to provide moral guidance for the laity on political issues, the bishops cautioned against any suggestion that some political choices were the only ones available to Christians. The differences between the group and the bishops on this point were clear and reflected the crisis in Neo-Christendom theology as discussed by Gutiérrez. However, a generally polite tone was maintained in this early exchange.[41]

The bishops' response did not stop the Group of 80 from pressing their concerns and organising a meeting for a wider group of priests (referred to as "The 200") in preparation for the upcoming synod of the Chilean bishops. The document they issued after this meeting called for change within the church, but offered a less overtly political stance from the "Declaration of the 80."[42] It was broadly accepted by the bishops and added as an appendix to the documentation of the Chilean episcopate presented at their national synod.

Meanwhile, the core group of the Chilean Christian for Socialists started to make links with like-minded priests and laity from Argentina, Brazil, Bolivia, Colombia, and Peru. In December 1971, they decided to plan for a meeting of Christian socialists from across the continent and issued a "Draft Agenda of Proposed Convention" for "The First Latin American Convention of Christians for Socialism."[43] The timing of the convention (23–30 April 1972) was to coincide with the third meeting of United Nations Congress on Trade and Development (UNCTAD), which was scheduled for Santiago. The draft agenda stated three central objectives: to exchange; to analyze; and to probe more deeply into the experiences of Christians who are actively involved in the revolution to liberate Latin America.[44]

---

[39] See Eagleson (ed.), *Christians for Socialism*, p. 13.

[40] The bishops advise that: "like any citizen, a priest is entitled to have his own political option. But in no case should he give this option the moral backing that stems from his character as a priest. . . . We have always insisted, and we will continue to insist, that our priests abstain from taking partisan political positions in public. To act otherwise would be to revert to an outdated clericalism that no one wants to see again"; see Eagleson (ed.), *Christians for Socialism*, p. 14.

[41] For example, the bishops said: "The situation that has arisen does not affect our esteem for the priests in question. Nor does it diminish our high regard for the apostolic work they, along with many others, are performing"; see Eagleson (ed.), *Christians for Socialism*, p. 14.

[42] Eagleson (ed.), *Christians for Socialism*, p. 37.

[43] Issued 16 December 1971, see Eagleson (ed.), *Christians for Socialism*, pp. 19–31.

[44] Eagleson (ed.), *Christians for Socialism*, p. 21. To do this effectively at the convention, they called for national reports to be formulated in advance and then presented for further discussion at the meeting. For a selection of reports (including Chile, Peru, Puerto Rico, and Cuba), see Eagleson (ed.), *Christians for Socialism*, pp. 69–140.

In response to this proposal, Carlos Oviedo Cavada (auxiliary bishop of Concepción and secretary general of the Chilean Episcopal Conference) drew up a "Confidential Episcopal Memo on Upcoming Convention," which he circulated to the other Chilean bishops in January 1972.[45] The memo did not explicitly condemn the proposed convention, but it made clear that no episcopal approval for it had been sought or given.[46] In reply, Gonzalo Arroyo wrote to Cardinal Raúl Silva Henríquez on behalf of the organizing committee to invite him to the event.[47] On 3 March Cardinal Silva replied, but the tone was much less conciliatory than earlier exchanges, and he unequivocally rejected the proposed agenda.[48] Silva voiced particular concern over the group's attitude to Marxism. He acknowledged that the group's endorsement of Marxist thought was limited to its value as an analytical tool to identify the dialectic of class struggle. Nonetheless, he pointed to two concerns that had already been stressed by the bishops of Chile: neither the scientific validity of Marxist analysis as a sociological method, nor its inseparability from the overall Marxist theory were universally clear and self-evident. Silva went on to quote § 34 of *Octogesima Adveniens* and raised the concerns that the group had reduced Christianity to something that was purely sociological and had no element of mystery.[49]

In response, the coordinating committee sent a letter to the cardinal on 20 March 1972 signed by Arroyo and thirteen others, including Sergio Torres and Pablo Richard, which challenged his interpretation of the movement and sought to defend its stance.[50] With considerable grace, Silva accepted the substance

---

[45] "Confidential Episcopal Memo on Upcoming Convention" in Eagleson (ed.), *Christians for Socialism*, pp. 35–38.

[46] The memo gives background on the Christians for Socialism movement and states (p. 36) that although the priests in the 80 maintain relationships with their bishops, "the group known as the 80, as such, does not have the approbation of the Chilean episcopate."

[47] "Letter of Invitation to the Archbishop of Santiago" (dated 10 February 1972) in Eagleson (ed.), *Christians for Socialism*, pp. 39–40.

[48] "Initial Response of Silva to Gonzalo Arroyo" in Eagleson (ed.), *Christians for Socialism*, pp. 41–47.

[49] More specifically, Silva saw the danger of reductionism in: the reduction of Christianity to the revolutionary class struggle and to the historical situation; the reduction of theology to ideology in a superficial way; and the reduction of Christianity to a single dimension, socio-economic transformation. On a personal note, he ended by confessing that he was scandalized at Arroyo's efforts to promote the convention and suggested that Arroyo's institution (the Society of Jesus) betrayed the reasons for its existence in permitting him to do so (*Christians for Socialism*, pp. 44–46).

[50] "Response of the Coordinating Committee to Cardinal Silva" in Eagleson (ed.), *Christians for Socialism*, pp. 48–61. The writers expressed total disagreement with the personal reference at the end of the letter, and in turn, confessed themselves scandalized by such severe judgement by a pastor on a priest who struggled to bring the poor and oppressed to their liberation in Jesus Christ. They accepted that the Draft Agenda omitted "important features of Christian liberation, and that these are precisely the ones that you bring up in your six observations. But we do not deny what we have omitted.

of their remarks as intended to be positive and invited them to continue the conversation with him.[51] On 28 April he met with Fr Giulio Girardi of the Priest Secretariat to continue the dialogue and agreed on an "Authorized Summary of Cardinal Silva's Views" which restated his concerns, but generally offered a more positive view of the movement and its intentions.[52]

On the contrary we take these things for granted . . . So we spoke about things which were *new* to us and which therefore required greater elaboration: namely, *the sociological and political aspect of the Christian faith.*" (p. 49). They also suggested that: "The novel aspect of Paul VI's treatment of Marxism is his shift of emphasis from doctrine to concrete options. This shift was anticipated by John XXIII: 'It is perfectly legitimate to make a clear distinction between a false philosophy of the nature, origin, and purpose of men and the world, and economic, social, cultural and political undertakings— even when such undertakings draw their origin and inspiration from that philosophy. True, the philosophic formula does not change once it has been set down in precise terms, but the undertakings clearly cannot avoid being influenced to a certain extent by the changing conditions in which they have to operate (*Pacem in Terris*, n 159)'" (p. 53). They also quoted from *Octogesima Adveniens* § 31: "'Keen and discerning judgement is called for . . . Socialism finds expression in different ways: as a generous desire and a quest for a more just society, as an historical movement with a political organization aim, as a body of doctrine that professes to give an integral and independent consideration of man. Distinctions must be made between these forms of expressions, so that selectivity may be exercised in concrete circumstances . . . This discernment will enable Christians to appreciate to what extent they may involve themselves in these plans'" (p. 54). In this light, they suggested that "In the course of history Christians have taken over the most varied kinds of thought, some of them being greatly at variance with the Christian faith: e.g., gnosticism, pantheistic neoplatonism, Averroist aristotelianism, materialistic darwinism, atheistic psychoanalysis" (p. 54). On their own position, they confirmed that: "We agree . . . the Christian vision of liberation is more profound and complete than the Marxist vision . . . the Christian does go even deeper, planting and posing liberation in terms of man's relationship with God. On this level human beings do not simply liberate themselves; they integrate their efforts into the liberation achieved by Christ. But while Christianity does have a more clear-cut vision of the overall perspectives of liberation, it also has much to learn from Marxism, psychoanalysis, and other disciplines about their concrete mechanisms through which liberation works itself out at different levels" (pp. 55–56).

[51] "Response of Cardinal Silva to Coordianting Committee," 13 April 1972, in Eagleson (ed.), *Christians for Socialism*, pp. 62–63. Silva wrote: "Despite the polemical passages it contains, and despite the harsh and in my opinion unjust judgements it expresses, I accept the substance of it which strikes me as being quite positive" (p. 62). He went on to respond to some of their criticisms of him and reiterated the limits of permissible political engagement for a priest (p. 63).

[52] "Authorized Summary of Cardinal Silva's Views" in Eagleson (ed.), *Christians for Socialism*, pp. 64–66. On a positive note it indicated that Christians ought to involve themselves in the liberation of human beings and combat any and every oppressive structure (pp. 65–66). However, it continued to stress that: "in recognizing the fact of class struggle, the Christian cannot accept it as a permanent state of affairs. Rather, he must work to supersede it" (p. 64) and "As far as Marxism is concerned, they can utilize some of its features in the analysis of society. But they should maintain a critical attitude towards it, thus relativizing its tendency to absolutize economic factors and rectifying the materialist ideology that serves as its bases" (p. 65).

In April 1972, the convention took place as planned and approximately four hundred delegates attended. The majority were priest-members from Latin American organisations (Third World Priests, ONIS, etc.), but also present were some Protestant members (especially linked to ISAL).[53]

Sadly, by this time attitudes in the hierarchy to the movement had hardened. The bishops addressed many of the issues raised at their plenary meeting of the episcopal meeting at Punta de Tracla (6–11 April 1973) and concluded "No priest or religious can belong to the movement known as 'Christians for Socialism.'"[54] However, rather than make this public immediately, they convened a committee to make a more thorough study of the literature with a view to an official proclamation.

The official proclamation was ready by mid-August but was not scheduled for formal approval until a meeting a month later. By this time, Allende's government was in crisis under economic and political pressure from powerful business interests. As the problems deepened and concerns grew over the outbreak of chaos, a military coup—encouraged and assisted by the CIA—overthrew Allende's government on 11 September 1973. In the weeks that followed, a military junta headed by Augusto Pinochet imposed a harsh martial law as the basis for a new National Security State similar to Brazil. As a first step toward this, many of Allende's supporters (as well as Union leaders, community workers, and other potential subversives) were rounded up, tortured, and then executed. Christians for Socialism was outlawed and many members were disappeared or forced into exile.

Despite the new situation brought by the coup, the bishops decided to publish their proclamation as it stood in October. It included the prohibition on priests or members of religious order being members of Christians for Socialism.[55]

---

[53] A theological committee (including Giulio Girardi, Gustavo Gutiérrez, and Hugo Assmann) assisted the group's main committee. In addition to the informal opportunities to network, the formal business of the convention included an opening address from Arroyo, a visit by delegates to Salvador Allende and Cardinal Silva, a brief address from Sergio Méndez Arceo the Bishop of Cuernavaca, the reading of a message from President Salvador Allende, the submission of national reports, and debate of ideas for a "Final Document of the Convention"; see Eagleson (ed.), *Christians for Socialism*, pp. 143–175.

[54] Session XVI, 11 April 1973, in Eagleson (ed.), *Christians for Socialism*, p. 179, n. 139.

[55] "Christian Faith and Political Activity: Declaration of the Chilean Bishops" in Eagleson (ed.), *Christians for Socialism*, pp. 179–228. The main document started with a brief introduction on the situation in Chile under Allende and then turned to Christians for Socialism. It identified a number of positive contributions but had a longer section on its "Unjust Accusations against the Church" including its unacceptable and injurious statements (p. 191). It acknowledged that "There may well be an acceptable sense in which one can adopt certain elements of this methodology within a Christian vision of history, but it is not evident in the tack taken by these priests. In general, they do not give any indication that they posses the required theological, philosophical, and scientific training for such a task" (p. 192). The bishops add that they reject not the fact of class struggle, but the Marxist interpretation of it (p. 206). They complained that the leadership of Christians for Socialism contradicted the bishops' disciplinary endeavours

The short-lived experiment was thus at an end in Chile. Elsewhere, other countries in Latin America were also entering a new phase in which the atmosphere of liberation would be stifled by brutal repression. In this new context, liberation theology's optimism that democratic socialism could be a realistic path for Latin America seemed utopian. Unfortunately, for many critics of the movement, the association between liberation theology and some of the rhetorical excesses of Christians for Socialism had been firmly entrenched and was often encouraged in the media portrayals. The simplistic picture of Marxist priests made good headlines, but did little to address the underlying issues.

JESUS THE LIBERATOR

Gutiérrez's presentation of the exodus as political and theological liberation in *A Theology of Liberation* prompted further examination of the New Testament and especially the gospels from a similar perspective. In *A Theology of Liberation*, Gutiérrez included a short section on "Jesus the Liberator." The term liberator had a particular resonance in Latin America, not just because of its obvious link to liberation, but also because the term is widely used to refer to independence leaders such as Simón Bolívar and San Martín. It was therefore not surprising that it was chosen by Leonardo Boff as the title for his early christological work *Jesus Christ Liberator*.[56]

In applying the term liberator to Christ, Boff was consciously trying to redress the distorted picture of Christ that has been created by ignoring his political significance. Boff was as emphatic as Gutiérrez that political liberation did not exhaust the Christian message. In fact, the original version of Boff's book was quite tentative about the political and economic dimensions of liberation. It was published in Brazil in 1972, a time when some parts of the church were

---

in full view of the faithful and "For this reason, and in the light of what we have said above, we prohibit priests and religious from belonging to that organization; and also from carrying out the kinds of activity we have denounced in this document in any form whatsoever—institutional or individual, organised or unorganised" (p. 217).

The document then turned to "Other Groups of Christians" (pp. 217–223). In what (in view of the later clashes between the church and the Chilean military) seems an extraordinary statement, they asserted: "The utilization of the faith in the opposite direction is just as regrettable. But it does not call for such extensive examination for obvious reasons. It is not crystallized in organized groups, it does not have the same impact on public opinion, it does not invoke the label 'Christian' so explicitly, it does not entail militancy on the part of priests and religious, it is not formulated in written documents, it does not propound a distinct doctrine or vision of the Church, it does not call the fundamentals of the faith into question in the same way, and it does not oppose the ecclesiastical hierarchy in the same measure" (p. 217).

[56] L. Boff, *Jesus Christ Liberator: A Critical Christology of Our Time* (trans. P. Hughes; Maryknoll, N.Y.: Orbis Books, 1978; London: SPCK, 1980 [Portuguese orig. 1972]). For other contributions to Latin American Christology, see the collection in J. Míguez Bonino (ed.), *Faces of Jesus: Latin American Christologies* (trans. J. Drury; Maryknoll, N.Y.: Orbis Books, 1984 [Spanish orig. 1977]). See also C. Bussmann, *Who Do You Say? Jesus Christ in Latin American Theology* (Maryknoll, N.Y.: Orbis Books, 1985 [German orig. 1980]).

suffering harsh repression. Perhaps Boff would have wished to say more on these if his own situation had been different.[57] However, he rejected any suggestion that Jesus was to be seen as liberator only in terms of promising deliverance from foreign domination or economic oppression. He felt that such oversimplification failed to do justice to the Christian gospel in both first-century Palestine and twentieth-century Latin America. Boff emphasized that it was the human person, the society, and the totality of reality that all underwent God's transformation.[58]

Boff's work was subtitled A *Critical Christology of Our Time*. In it, Boff tried to move beyond the critical Christologies of Europe.[59] He wanted to develop a Latin American perspective that would broaden traditional dogmatic Christologies and reflect a more holistic concern with human life. In the process, he also hoped to provide a basis of hope for the present transformation of society. He wanted to challenge traditional dogmas that maintained the relationship between the church and political society in Latin America. He stressed the legitimate role of social concerns in theology and the need to restore right action and ethics (orthopraxis) as criteria for theology.[60]

Boff's doctoral studies in Germany had made him familiar with the debates over historical criticism, and in his first chapter he offered a summary of how discussion of the historical Jesus had developed. Boff's own emphasis on a human Jesus and his historical message reflected this scholarship to a significant degree. European hermeneutical approaches, such as existentialism, encouraged him to present the subjective and personal significance of Christ, as well as the historical aspects. However, Boff went beyond personal existential concerns to a more explicit political reading.[61]

Boff started with Jesus' proclamation of the kingdom of God. This he said was a message of integral liberation. He noted that the term kingdom of God occurs 122 times in the Gospels and 90 times on the lips of Jesus.[62] Supported

---

[57] As Boff notes in his preface to the English translation (p. xii), when the book was originally published in Brazil the word liberation was forbidden in all communications media. The epilogue added to the English translation (pp. 264–295) includes much more explicit attention to the political significance of liberation and its implications for Latin America.

[58] Boff, *Jesus Christ Liberator*, p. 55; cf. p. 105.

[59] Boff was aware that much of the literature with which he engaged was European but he stressed the distinctively Latin American nature of his enterprise: ". . . a Christology thought out and vitally tested in Latin America must have characteristics of its own. The attentive reader will perceive them throughout this book. The predominantly foreign literature that we cite ought not to delude anyone. It is with preoccupations that are ours alone, taken from our Latin American context, that we will reread not only the old texts of the New Testament but also the most recent commentaries written in Europe" (*Jesus Christ Liberator*, p. 43).

[60] Boff, *Jesus Christ Liberator*, pp. 43–47.

[61] Boff was aware that Moltmann and others had started to make this move in a European political theology (p. 300 n. 2), but he made little explicit reference to them.

[62] Boff, *Jesus Christ Liberator*, p. 52.

by a consensus amongst biblical scholars, he emphasised that the kingdom does not signify another world or territory, but the transformation of this world in terms of a new order.[63] He argued that this transformation should not be understood as exclusively political or exclusively spiritual, but represented "all reality in all its dimensions, cosmic, human and social."[64]

Boff also noted that Jesus proclaimed the kingdom through his actions as well as his preaching.[65] Acts of liberation (for example, healings and exorcisms) made the kingdom present.[66] For example, when the followers of John the Baptist questioned Jesus, Jesus replied by pointing to his actions towards the poor and oppressed (Lk. 7.18–23). Jesus was not only proclaiming the kingdom but also actually bringing it about by his presence (cf. Lk. 11.20; Lk. 17.21).[67]

For Boff, Jesus was an authority higher than the law, and therefore he could offer liberation from the law. Jesus liberated individuals to become new people governed by a new ethic of love and fraternity expressed in the Sermon on the Mount (Mt. 6.17–18). Jesus broke social conventions and stratifications to demonstrate this ethic in practice and teach total liberation from all forms of alienation.[68] Boff saw Jesus as a down-to-earth genius, whose simple, honest, and direct style forced people to make a decision before God. His life was characterised by the very human characteristics of anger, joy, goodness, strength, friendship, sorrow, and temptation that make him easily recognisable. Jesus had a sense of authority and creative imagination that marked him with a distinctive originality. His life realised the exemplary path that his contemporary disciples should choose to follow.[69] Ultimately, his work to liberate people from

---

[63] Boff, *Jesus Christ Liberator*, p. 55.

[64] Boff, *Jesus Christ Liberator*, p. 60. See also, "In a word, it could be said that the kingdom of God means a total, global, structural revolution of the old order, brought about by God and only by God" (*Jesus Christ Liberator*, pp. 63–64). This is entirely consistent with his later work where he restates the same position as: "The kingdom or reign of God means the full and total liberation of all creation, in the end, purified of all that oppresses it, transfigured by the full presence of God. No other theological or biblical concept is as close to the ideal of integral liberation as this concept of the kingdom of God" (L. and C. Boff, *Introducing Liberation Theology*, p. 52).

[65] For example, on Lk. 11.20, see Boff, *Jesus Christ Liberator*, p. 283.

[66] In his discussion of Jesus' words and actions it was hardly surprising that he paid particular attention to Luke's gospel. From the outset, Luke's gospel presents Jesus' mission in terms of liberation. For example, Luke's presentation of Jesus' reading from Isa. 61.1–2 in the synagogue at Nazareth (Lk. 4.16–21) identified the origins of Jesus' ministry as the proclamation of the kingdom of God and the Lord's year of favour: "The Spirit of the Lord is upon me, because he has anointed me to bring good news to the poor. He has sent me to proclaim release to the captives and recovery of sight to the blind, to let the oppressed go free, to proclaim the year of the Lord's favour" (NRSV). See also Luke's emphasis on the revolutionary challenge of the kingdom and its reversal of social roles so that the least is the greatest (Lk. 9.46–48; 22.25–26).

[67] On Lk. 17.21, see Boff, *Jesus Christ Liberator*, p. 280.

[68] Boff, *Jesus Christ Liberator*, pp. 64–79.

[69] Boff, *Jesus Christ Liberator*, pp. 80–90.

the constraints of society led to his death.[70] Then, because of the resurrection, the failure of death was transformed into triumph. In the resurrection, Boff saw the answer to all human hope because it showed the transfiguration of all human reality corporal and spiritual as a utopia realised in this world.[71]

Boff examined the later christological titles given to Jesus against this reading of the gospels. On this basis, he presented the church's christological tradition in terms of the human and divine capacity to give oneself to others.[72] This reading of Christology challenged Christians to discover Jesus anew in the world—especially in the presence of the poor. By understanding the world as open to transformation and fulfillment, Christians could try to reproduce Christ's example in their own lives.[73] In this process they might refer to Christ under different titles, including Christ as revolutionary and Christ as liberator.[74] However, it was not primarily through titles that Jesus was to be understood, but by trying to live as Jesus himself lived.[75]

The other major work of Latin American Christology in the 1970s was Jon Sobrino's *Christology at the Crossroads.*[76] Sobrino was a Basque Jesuit who worked in El Salvador for many years and recently returned from his doctoral studies in Frankfurt. His book was the result of a series of lecturers on Christology he gave at the Central American University in San Salvador.[77] His approach drew on the historical-critical method of Biblical Studies common in Europe.[78] However, he added two methodological principles that he saw as particularly

---

[70] Boff blamed Jesus' death on the fact that his work set all the authorities of the day against him. This included the Pharisees, scribes, Saduccees, Heriodians, and the Romans themselves; see Boff, *Jesus Christ Liberator,* p. 100.

[71] Boff, *Jesus Christ Liberator,* p. 135.

[72] Boff, *Jesus Christ Liberator,* p. 205.

[73] Boff, *Jesus Christ Liberator,* pp. 206–225.

[74] Boff, *Jesus Christ Liberator,* pp. 238–240. However, he always stressed that these titles must be understood in an integral way. For example, (Boff, *Jesus Christ Liberator,* p. 239): "It is not liberation from Roman subjugation, nor a shout of rebellion by the poor against Jewish landowners. It is total and complete liberation from all that alienates human beings, including sickness, death, and especially sin." Despite the efforts by Boff and Gutiérrez to stress their integral understanding of liberation, critics of liberation theology have continued to charge them with onesidedness in their approach.

[75] Boff, *Jesus Christ Liberator,* p. 245.

[76] J. Sobrino, *Christology at the Crossroads: A Latin American View* (trans. J. Drury; Maryknoll, N.Y.: Orbis Books; London: SCM Press, 1978 [Spanish orig. 1977]).

[77] Sobrino was born in Spain in 1938, but immediately after joining the Jesuits as a young man, he was dispatched to El Salvador in 1957. After five years of graduate studies in the United States and seven years in Germany completing his advanced studies, he described his return to El Salvador in 1974 as "awakening from the sleep of inhumanity" an "awakening to the reality of oppressed and subjugated world, a world whose liberation is the basic task of every human being, so that in this way human beings may finally come to be human" (J. Sobrino, *The Principle of Mercy: Taking the Crucified People from the Cross* [Maryknoll, N.Y.: Orbis Books, 1994 (Spanish orig. 1992)], p. 1).

[78] In particular, Sobrino stressed the kingdom of God as the centre of Jesus' message and Jesus' faith in God.

appropriate to Christian witness in Latin America. First, he affirmed a practical commitment to Christian discipleship. Second, he identified a similarity of situation between contemporary Latin America and first-century Palestine.

For Sobrino, a practical commitment to Jesus was crucial to an authentic Christology. Like Gutiérrez and Boff, Sobrino argued that the theological significance of the Gospels could not be discovered simply through detached reflection. An appropriate hermeneutic involved a commitment to following Christ in everyday engagement with the world in which one lived. In fact, the original Spanish title for *Christology at the Crossroads* was "Christology from Latin America: An Approach Based on Following the Historical Jesus."[79]

In the preface to the English translation, Sobrino emphasised that committed discipleship was more than a practical consequence of Christology; it was also a precondition for Christology.

> We can come to know Jesus as the Christ only insofar as we start a new life, break with the past and undergo conversion, engage in Christian practice and fight for the justice of God's kingdom. That is why I stress the following of the historical Jesus. . . . I stress the following of the historical Jesus here because it is only this that makes christological epistemology possible at all.[80]

Sobrino claimed that there is a decisive similarity between the historical situation in contemporary El Salvador and the historical situation of Jesus' day. As he saw it, they were both situations of sin that lead to death.[81] Since Sobrino's understanding of the similarity primarily in terms of sin (not politics) has not been widely recognized, it is worthwhile to quote Sobrino at length here:

> First of all, there is a clearly noticeable resemblance in the situation here in Latin America and that in which Jesus lived. Needless to say, we cannot interpret that resemblance in some ingenuous or anachronistic way. The following of Jesus cannot be any automatic process of imitation which pays no heed at all to our own concrete situation and bypasses political, anthropological, and socio-economic analysis. At bottom the resemblance lies in the fact that in Latin America, as opposed to other historical situations, the present condition is acutely felt and understood to be a sinful situation. Thus the resemblance does not lie solely in the objective conditions of poverty and exploitation that characterize Jesus' situation and ours, as well as many others throughout history. It lies primarily in the cognizance that is taken of the situation. In that respect there is a real historical coincidence between the situation of Jesus and that of our continent today, and it is more marked than in other places.[82]

These two hermeneutical principles, Christian commitment and the similarity of situations, allowed Sobrino to incorporate and go beyond the traditional

---

[79] *Cristología desde américa latina: esbozo a partir del seguimiento del Jesús histórico.*

[80] *Christology at the Crossroads*, p. xxiv.

[81] It is not simply that sin exists, but that it is clearly recognised as a cause of death that provides the similarity of situations.

[82] *Christology at the Crossroads*, pp. 12–13.

tools of academic historical-critical scholarship. As a result, the historical issues
that he addressed when using the Bible were not just those relating to past
history, the text and the events that gave rise to it, but also those relating to
present history, the context and its significance. According to Sobrino, if a
reader was socially committed and recognised the fundamental theological similarity between Latin America and Palestine, he or she did not need to subordinate concern for the historical Jesus beneath contemporary relevance. The
urgent needs of Latin America's sinful situation did not detract from the historical quest, but gave new insight into Jesus' life and teaching.

Sobrino's approach to Christology distilled many of the different facets of doing
theology into a practical principle—active discipleship of Jesus in one's own
social context as a necessary step for those who want to know Jesus. As such,
his book was a welcome addition to liberation theology but it raised concerns
at the Vatican.[83] In September 1977, the International Theological Commission
(ITC)—an advisory body to Paul VI—published a document titled "Human
Development and Christian Salvation" that was sympathetic to liberation theology's concern for the poor, but expressed reservations over the term social
sin, and warned against over-simplifying biblical themes in political terms.[84]
Given the difficult balancing act that this required of liberation theologians, it
was hardly surprising that the issue resurfaced even more forcefully during the
papacy of John Paul II.

CONCLUSION

In keeping with the radical atmosphere of the time, the early literature of liberation theology pointed to closer cooperation with socialist groups and more
positive use of Marxist analysis. Christians for Socialism in Chile demonstrated
how far some progressive priests were willing to extend this. However, neither the Vatican nor the Chilean hierarchy were willing to endorse such theoretical or practical experiments. The controversy over Christians for Socialism
resulted in making liberation theology's critics more suspicious of the movement and episcopal hierarchies even more cautious in their pronouncements
on socialism. After the premature end to Christians for Socialism in Chile, the
controversy fell out of the headlines for a few years. However, on the ground
in Latin America, relations with popular organisations committed to socialism

---

[83] The Congregation of Catholic Education expressed concern over alleged Marxist
and Protestant influences in the book, but when Sobrino made a written defence against
the charges and the matter appeared to be closed. In fact, Sobrino's book was notable
for its avoidance of Marxist analysis and terminology and the accusations seemed to be
more guilt by association rather than careful reading of the book. Nonetheless, the incident showed that differences over the influence of Marxism in liberation theology were
still unresolved.

[84] International Theological Commission, "Human Development and Christian
Salvation," *Origins* 7 (3 November 1977); reprinted in Hennelly (ed.), *Liberation Theology*,
pp. 205–219.

remained a contentious issue. Individual bishops, priests, religious, and laity had to deal with the issues as best they could in accordance with church teaching and their own experiences in the situations.

By about 1975, explicit discussions of dependency and revolution and the use of Marxist terminology and analysis decreased rapidly in the literature of liberation theology. An important factor in this was the imposition of National Security States. In contrast to the optimism over radical change in the 1960s, the outlook now seemed uncertain and the need for caution was greater.

On the positive side, by this time the literature of liberation theology was beginning to open up a whole variety of subjects for doing theology. The works of Boff and Sobrino on Christology showed that radical theological reflection on liberation could be done without references to the theoretical literature of dependency, ideological critiques or Marxism. Structural economic analysis started to receive less attention. This led to a marked change in the tone and style of later works in liberation theology when compared with the late 1960s and early 1970s. These changes would be further reinforced by the interaction of liberation theologians with the experiences of the so-called popular church and base communities.

CHAPTER EIGHT

The Church of the Poor

> The Church is beginning to be born at the grassroots,
> beginning to be born at the heart of God's People.
>
> Leonardo Boff[1]

INTRODUCTION

During the 1970s, with political repression on the rise across the continent, the Catholic church in Brazil, Nicaragua, El Salvador, and other countries in Latin America started to refashion itself as a church of the poor. The emergence of this popular church (as it was often known) was a response both to pastoral initiatives from above (taken by bishops and church hierarchies in the 1960s) and to grass-roots activism springing up from below. The most important influence varied from country to country and diocese to diocese; in some places it was "top-down," in others was "bottom-up," and in some it was equally both. Depending on which factors predominated and how these were directed, the pastoral renewal took different shape in different local contexts. Some of these communities were simply part of ecclesial renewal to meet local pastoral needs and offered little that was new in terms of social activism. Many others, however, were strongly marked by social concerns and readily identified with liberation theology. These socially active communities were the most tangible expressions of the pastoral vision and political option advocated by liberation theologians. At the same time, these base communities helped to reorientate liberation theology's option for the poor.

The base communities were sympathetic audiences for the radical ideas of liberation theologians. As social bodies, the base communities could work toward the transformations of society and the church in practical ways at local and national level. Their activities allowed the literature of liberation theology to have a practical outcome in the shaping of a mass movement. At the

---

[1] L. Boff, *Ecclesiogenesis: The Base Communities Reinvent the Church* (trans. R. Barr; Maryknoll, N.Y.: Orbis Books; London: Collins, 1986 [Portuguese orig. 1977]), p. 23.

same time, the experiences of the communities encouraged and supported more thoroughgoing and systematic theological work. In particular, the struggles of the communities challenged theologians to clarify and redefine their option to the poor. As the popular church suffered a period of fierce persecution in many countries, their experiences evangelized the theologians. In 1980, looking back on the seventies, Gutiérrez commented:

> After Vatican II and the stimulus of the Medellín Conference, we creatively reappropriated the gospel expression about evangelizing or 'preaching the good news to the poor.' Reinforced by an option for the oppressed and commitment of solidarity with them, a series of rich and promising initiatives took place all over Latin America. . . . Then came the irruption of the poor. At *a terrible price the common people began to become the active protagonists of history.* This fact gave us deeper insight into the whole matter of evangelization. Working in the midst of the poor, exploited people, whom we were supposedly going to evangelize, we came to realize that we were being evangelized by them.[2]

As the 1970s progressed, liberation theologians increased priority to the poor as the active authors of liberation theology and incorporated an epistemological/theological option for the poor into their methodology. Liberation theology set out to transform the lives of the poor but in this process the poor, transformed liberation theology.

REPRESSION AND PERSECUTION

During the early 1970s, Brazil positioned itself as regional policeman.[3] The Brazilian military successfully exported their National Security ideology to neighbouring militaries in the Southern Cone and Bolivia. Military coups in Bolivia (1971–1978), Chile (1973–1989), Uruguay (1973–1985), and Argentina (1976–1983) ensured that in the 1970s and early 1980s, almost the entire continent was under dictatorial rule.[4] Hard-line regimes willing to use torture and

---

[2] Gutiérrez, "The Irruption of the Poor in Latin America and the Christian Communities of the Common People" in S. Torres and J. Eagleson (eds.), *The Challenge of Basic Christian Communities* (EATWOT International Ecumenical Congress of Theology, São Paulo, Brazil, 20 February–2 March 1980; Maryknoll, N.Y.: Orbis Books, 1981), pp. 107–123 (120). At the same conference Sobrino noted: "Neither *Evangelii Nuntiandi* nor Medellín placed any stress on persecution or martyrdom either. They both re-emphasise the need for subjective witness in the evangelization process. Both, Medellín in particular, stress the need for poverty and the necessity of becoming poor in order to be in solidarity with the poor. But the essential nature of witness is not viewed in terms of persecution and martyrdom" (J. Sobrino, "The Witness of the Church in Latin America" in Torres and Eagleson [eds.], *The Challenge of Basic Christian Communities*, pp. 161–188 [171]).

[3] See Lernoux, *Cry of the People*, pp. 167–175.

[4] Paraguay, which was always viewed as a bit of a backwater, suffered the long-standing dictatorship of General Alfredo Stroessner from 1954 to 1989; see P. H. Lewis, *Paraguay under Stroessner* (Chapel Hill: University of North Carolina, 1980). However, Peru was an interesting exception in the early 1970s, because during the first phase of military

state terror as policies of social control replaced the so-called soft dictatorships of earlier decades. The church was often caught in the crossfire or deliberately targeted when it tried to intervene or protest.

In Brazil, Emílio Médici's regime (1969–1974) continued the hard-line tendency of his predecessor Costa e Silva (1967–1969). General Ernesto Giesel (1974–1979) relaxed the military's grip a little, but human rights abuses under his government remained high. Progressive priests in the Brazilian church were often targets for political violence. In 1976, three more priests were killed.[5] In the same year, Bishop Dom Adriano Hipólito was kidnapped in his diocese of Nova Iguaça on the outskirts of Rio de Janeiro. He was only released when he had been stripped, splashed with red paint, and humiliated in an attempt to defame his reputation.[6] Between 1968 and 1978, nine bishops, eighty-four priests, thirteen seminarians, and six women religious were imprisoned in Brazil along with 273 other pastoral agents (local lay leaders).[7] Ordinary laity of the base communities, who enjoyed less protection, suffered in untold numbers. In 1972, Cardinal Arns of São Paulo created a human rights agency for the church, which served as a precedent for similar initiatives in Chile and El Salvador a few years later.[8] As the decade progressed, the Brazilian bishops became more outspoken, especially under Aloísio Lorscheider's leadership of the CNBB.[9] In

---

rule, under General Juan Velasco Alvarado (1968–1975), the government sought progressive reforms rather than reactionary repression. As a result, the regime enjoyed positive relations with the Peruvian church, which at the time was one of the most progressive episcopates on the continent. It was not until the second phase of military rule, under General Francisco Morales Bermúdez, that Peru came under the influence of National Security Doctrine and repression started to escalate; see esp. J. Klaiber, *The Catholic Church in Peru, 1821–1985: A Social History* (Washington, D.C.: Catholic University of America Press, 1988), pp. 276–358.

[5] Frs. Rodolfo Llukembein, João Bosco Penido Burnier SJ, and A. Pierobon. See Lernoux, *Cry of the People*, p. 464.

[6] See Lernoux, *Cry of the People*, pp. 314–320.

[7] Archdiocese of São Paulo Human Rights Commission cited in Klaiber, *The Church, Dictatorships and Democracy in Latin America*, p. 35.

[8] The church's central Commission of Peace and Justice was originally created after Medellín, but it was based in Rio de Janeiro under the conservative oversight of Archbishop Eugênio de Araujo Sales. It was not until Arns developed a chapter in São Paulo (with independence after 1974) that the Brazilian church developed a serious role in recording and publicising human rights abuses. In the final years of the military regime, it was the São Paulo commission that organised the covert collection of copied military records for publication as Archdiocese of São Paulo, *Torture in Brazil: A Report by the Archdiocese of São Paulo* (trans. J. Wright; ed. J. Dassin; New York: Vintage Books, 1986 [Portuguese orig. 1985]). The amazing story of the ecumenical collaboration between Arns and the Presbyterian Jaime Wright on this project (supported by the WCC) is told in Lawrence Weschler, *A Miracle, A Universe: Settling Accounts with Torturers* (Chicago and London: University of Chicago Press, rev. ed. 1998 [1990]), pp. 7–77. For a wider overview of the church's involvement in human rights in Latin America, see E. L. Cleary, *The Struggle for Human Rights in Latin America* (Westport, Conn., and London: Praeger, 1997).

[9] Lorscheider was elected CNBB secretary in 1968. However, the early years of his

November 1976, the CNBB issued their outspoken "Pastoral Message to the People of God."

The situation in Chile was particularly severe. After the 1973 coup, the widely respected prelate, Cardinal Silva, responded to the torture and disappearance of thousands of Chileans by helping to establish the Committee for Cooperation for Peace in Chile. The committee provide legal and other assistance to victims of the Pinochet regime and documented the human rights abuses taking place.[10] When government pressure finally forced its closure at the end of 1975, Cardinal Silva responded immediately by establishing a Vicariate of Solidarity to continue its work.[11] Pinochet was furious at Silva's defiance and worked ceaselessly to intimidate and undermine him. Silva also faced considerable opposition from some of the other Chilean bishops, but other Latin American bishops rallied to his support.[12]

In fact, hostility towards the church was spreading across the continent and reaching the highest levels. In Bolivia, the government's Banzer Plan (named after the dictator) advocated covert actions to increase tension and widen divisions between different political factions in the church. The intention was to undermine and intimidate progressive bishops and harass and smear troublesome priests.[13] In many cases, harassment extended to physical beatings, death threats, and even murders. Missionary priests were liable for deportation or refused reentry if they travelled abroad.

While persecution was mainly at a local level, there were some very high profile exceptions. In August 1976, armed security forces in Ecuador broke up an international meeting of Latin American bishops and theologians in Riobamba

---

leadership were constrained by the conservative majority on the CNBB executive. The previous CNBB president, Agnelo Rossi, had been very cautious in relations with the government. However, when Rossi became Prefect of the Congregation for the Evangelization of Peoples in Rome in 1970, it allowed progressives to make critical headway in influence over the Brazilian church. Paulo Arns replaced him in São Paulo, and Lorscheider was elected as president of the CNBB in 1971. Aided by Ivo Lorscheiter who became CNBB secretary (and later succeded Lorscheider as CNBB president in 1979), the progressives had considerable influence on the leadership of the Brazilian church in the 1970s.

[10] It was an ecumenical venture with the Methodist, Lutheran, and some Pentecostal churches as well as the rabbinical college and World Council of Churches. See B. Smith, *The Church and Politics in Chile: Challenges to Modern Catholicism* (Princeton, N.J.: Princeton University Press, 1982).

[11] As a church office, the Vicariate came under Silva's direct protection and was located next to the cathedral in the central Plaza de Armas.

[12] Silva was known for his political moderation and diplomacy in dealing with Christians for Socialism and persuading Salvador Allende to back down over his policies on schools. Bishops elsewhere in Latin American responded cautiously to hostilities against bishops in Brazil who were seen as radicals (for example, Hélder Câmara and Pedro Casaldáliga). However, the campaign against Silva showed the extremity of the political forces that he and the Chilean church confronted and the need for a unified response.

[13] See Lernoux, *Cry of the People*, pp. 143–147.

and arrested them.[14] When the three Chilean bishops were finally allowed to return to Santiago, they were pelted with rocks in a demonstration orchestrated by Pinochet's security forces.[15]

The Riobamba affair suggested internationally organised harassment of the church.[16] The cooperation of the dictatorships in setting up national security states contributed to further collaboration between their security forces in eliminating political opposition. After 1976, state repression in Latin America became internationally organised, with political agreements by military regimes to collaborate with other. The most notorious example of this was the so-called Condor Plan, which allowed easy extradition of political refugees between collaborating security forces. Even more disturbingly, it allowed state-security forces to operate clandestinely in another member country to assassinate or disappear their targets without having to answer awkward questions.

In most countries, hostilities against the church did not reach the same severity as against other civil groups (for example, opposition politicians, union activists, or students), because the church's traditional status and international connections provided considerable protection. Nonetheless, the 1970s were an unprecedented period of church persecution across the continent. This deepened divisions in the church between those who had made the option for the poor and those who continued to opt for privilege.

After the coup in Argentina in March 1976, seventeen priests and nuns were murdered; thirty more were imprisoned by the end of the following year.[17] During the "dirty war" against internal dissent, most members of Argentinean church hierarchy actively supported the government or looked the other way and refused to speak.[18] An exception to this was Bishop Enrique

---

[14] Bishop Mariano Parra León in Venezuela had a heart attack while they were held in custody.

[15] Penny Lernoux offers a typically vivid account of the Riobamba incident and the bishops return to Chile in Cry of the People, pp. 137–142.

[16] Lernoux (Cry of the People, pp. 141–142) points out that the Ecuadoran military would probably not have acted on their own initiative, but at the instigation of Brazil or Chile. Some of the church participants at the Riobamba meeting had just attended a similar meeting in Brazil, and Chile had particularly close ties with Ecuadoran military.

[17] Lernoux, Cry of the People, p. 345. Right-wing violence against the Priests for the Third World by groups such as the Argentinean Anti-Communist Alliance (AAA) began a few years before this. This included the murder of the movement's most prominent representative, Carlos Mugica, in May 1974. Partly as a result of these attacks, by 1974 the movement had already split and ceased to function. Nonetheless, priests who had been members of the movement were still prime targets after the 1976 coup.

[18] For the official report on the military's war against its own citizenship issued after the return to democracy in 1983 (and proving to be a best-seller), see National Commission on Disappeared People, Nunca Más: A Report by Argentina's National Commission on Disappeared People (trans. Writers and Scholars International; Boston and London: Faber & Faber, 1986 [Spanish orig. 1984]); an interesting analysis on the paranoia behind the terror is given by M. Feitlowitz, A Lexicon of Terror: Argentina and the Legacies of Torture (Oxford: Oxford University Press, 1998). For a fascinating investi-

Angelleli of La Rioja in the rural northwest region. In July 1976, he was attempting to establish responsibility for the murder of two priests in his diocese—the evidence pointed to the military—when he himself was killed in an automobile accident in highly suspicious circumstances.

In Central America, the repression was just as bad.[19] In El Salvador, a small group of radical priests became active in the 1970s and the appointment of Bishop Oscar Romero as archbishop of San Salvador in 1977 was widely interpreted as a conservative move to bring them into line. Romero's appointment coincided with the fraudulent election of General Romero (no relation) as president and a clamp-down on the country's unions and political movements.[20] Perhaps because of the new archbishop's perceived conservatism, persecution of the Salvadoran church escalated dramatically in 1977 after his appointment.[21] Two priests—the Jesuit Rutilio Grande in March and the diocesan priest Alfonso Navarro in May—were killed and right-wing groups threatened to assassinate any Jesuits left in the country after 21 July 1977. In face of widespread condemnation, the threat went unfulfilled; but in the next three years, a further six priests were killed. This experience and the suffering of ordinary Christians in the base communities moved Archbishop Romero deeply. He became one of the most outspoken prophets of the Latin American church and—in fulfillment of the 1971 Synod of Bishops—became known as the voice of those without voice.[22] He was outspoken in condemning both the political violence that was becoming commonplace, and the economic injustices that were

---

gation of the religious dimension to dirty war torture, see F. Graziano, *Divine Violence: Spectacle, Psychosexuality, and Radical Christianity in the Argentine 'Dirty War'* (Boulder, Colo., and Oxford: Westview Press, 1992); for the wider background, see J. Burdick, *For God and Fatherland: Religion and Politics in Argentina* (Albany: State University of New York Press, 1996).

[19] Argentinean security agents actively collaborated with their Central American counterparts in Nicaragua, El Salvador, and Guatemala in setting up surveillance and security apparatus; see A. C. Armony, *Argentina, the United States and the Anti-Communist Crusade in Central America 1977–1984* (Athens: Ohio University Press, 1997), pp. 73–105.

[20] General Romero had been the hawkish defence minister for the previous president, General Molina (1972–1977). Since a communist uprising in 1932, El Salvador's military maintained a tight control on state security, and the 1972 and 1977 elections simply endorsed their nominated candidate. For an overview of the period in El Salvador, see P. Berryman, *The Religious Roots of Rebellion* (Maryknoll, N.Y.: Orbis Books; London: SCM Press, 1984), pp. 91–161; Lernoux, *Cry of the People*, pp. 61–80.

[21] Archbishop Romero was previously known for his political moderation and had been in conflict with the country's priests and Jesuits who advocated political engagement. On Romero's life see J. Brockman, *Romero: A Life* (Maryknoll, N.Y.: Orbis Books, 1989), and O. Romero, *Archbishop Oscar Romero: A Shepherd's Diary* (trans. I. B. Hodgson; London: Catholic Agency for Overseas Development and Catholic Institute for International Relations, 1993).

[22] For his homilies and pastoral messages, see O. Romero, *Voice of the Voiceless: The Four Pastoral Letters and Other Statements* (trans. M. Walsh; Maryknoll, N.Y.: Orbis Books, 1985 [Spanish orig. 1980]); *The Violence of Love: The Words of Oscar Romero* (trans. J. Brockman; New York: Harper & Row, 1988; London: Collins, 1989).

at the root of El Salvador's problems. In weekly homilies broadcast on the radio, he frequently committed the church to standing with the poor in their tribulations and finding its own salvation in solidarity with their suffering.

This prompted retaliation from his opponents. Bombs exploded at churches, the archdiocesan radio station, and the Catholic University. Romero himself was frequently threatened with death. In February 1980, he sent a letter to President Carter requesting a halt to further consignments of aid to El Salvador's security forces.[23] On 23 March 1980, Romero's sermon pleaded for an end to the violence with an appeal addressed directly at ordinary soldiers: "In the name of God, and in the name of this suffering people, whose laments rise to heaven each day more tumultuous, I beg you, I beseech you, I order you in the name of God: Stop the repression!"[24] The next day, he was assassinated as he celebrated mass in a hospital chapel. Within a year, El Salvador toppled into a full-scale civil war that brought untold misery and lasted throughout the following decade. This civil war dominated internal politics and everyday life in the 1980s and brought further persecution of the church.[25]

Meanwhile, in neighbouring Nicaragua, Anastasio Somoza won a staged election in 1974. Rejecting political pressures for overdue reforms, he chose instead to unleash the National Guard against his political opponents, union representatives, and peasant leaders.[26] Eventually, he united almost the whole country—including the business community and church hierarchy—against him.[27] In July 1979, a mass uprising led by the Sandinistas finally swept him from power. Thus, just as the decade began with Allende embarking on a socialist experiment in Chile, so it ended with the Sandinistas adopting a range of socialist

---

[23] See "Letter to President Carter" in O. Romero, *Voice of the Voiceless*, pp. 188–190. President Jimmy Carter rejected his plea, despite his 1976 election victory over Gerald Ford on a platform that promised honest government and concern for human rights in foreign policy. However, Carter's Democratic administration was at least more concerned for human rights in its foreign policy than the Republican period of Nixon and Ford in the early seventies. While Carter's professed concern for human rights did not prevent widespread human rights abuses in Latin America during 1976–1980, it at least moderated them to some extent. The night that the Republican candidate Ronald Reagan beat Carter in the 1980 election was a night of celebration for the right wing of Salvadoran politics. Two weeks later four U.S. women working in El Salvador—three U.S. nuns and one U.S. lay missionary—were raped and murdered by National Guard members who believed that they were now beyond any moral or political restraint.

[24] Brockman, *Romero*, p. 242.

[25] See A. L. Peterson, *Martyrdom and the Politics of Religion: Progressive Catholicism in El Salvador's Civil War* (Albany: State University of New York Press, 1997).

[26] This included particular persecution of grassroots Christian movements inspired by Capuchin priests. See Berryman, *The Religious Roots of Rebellion*, pp. 51–89; Lernoux, *Cry of the People*, pp. 81–107.

[27] See A. Bradstock, *Saints and Sandinistas: The Catholic Church in Nicaragua and its Response to the Revolution* (London: Epworth Press, 1987); J. M. Kirk, *Politics and the Catholic Church in Nicaragua* (Gainesville: University of Florida Press, 1992).

policies in Nicaragua.[28] However, during the 1980s, it would pay a high price—just as Allende's Chile had done—for its search for a political alternative.

THE BASE CHRISTIAN COMMUNITIES

One of the signs of the times recognised at Medellín was the potential importance of base communities in the Latin American church.[29] The base ecclesial communities (commonly referred to by their acronym in Spanish and Portuguese as CEBs) developed into impressive national movements in many countries, and especially in Nicaragua, Chile, Peru, El Salvador, and most of all Brazil.[30] For many progressives the CEBs pointed toward a grass-roots regeneration of the church in Latin America.[31]

The rest of this chapter focuses on the CEBs in Brazil in the 1970s and their role in integrating the ideas of liberation theology with a socially orientated pastoral practice. It has proved surprisingly hard to even estimate the number of CEBs or quantify the people involved with them.[32] It has become clear that

---

[28] It would, however, be quite wrong to think of the Sandinistas as hard-line Leninist-Marxist. There polices were a mix of free-market and state-planning intended to better the lot of the poor majority who had been impoverished under Somoza. They achieved notable success in raising standards of health and education, despite these projects being particular targets for U.S.-sponsored contras during the 1980s.

[29] Document 15, Pastoral de Conjunto, §§10–12; Document 1, Justice, §20; Document 6, Pastoral Popular, §13. Medellín refers to the communities as base Christian communities rather than base ecclesial communities, although it does describe the Christian base community as "the first and fundamental ecclesial unit" (Pastoral de Conjunto, §10) and speaks of "ecclesial communities in the parishes" (Pastoral Popular, §13). As the movement grew in strength it attracted attention outside Latin America and was supported in Paul VI's *Evangelii Nuntiandi* (8 December 1975) following the 1974 Synod of Bishops in Rome on "Evangelization in the Modern World." *Evangelli Nuntiandi* cautioned against a number of perceived dangers in base communities (§58.5–58.13), but gave the CEBs an important endorsement as "a hope for the universal Church." (§58.5). At Puebla, in 1979, considerable attention was given to the CEBs and their value and importance for the Latin American church was strongly reaffirmed (§629).

[30] The Portuguese *comunidades eclesiais de base* and the Spanish *comunidades eclesiales de base* are both commonly abbreviated to CEBs and translated as base church communities or basic christian communities in English. However, the communities are sometimes referred to as *comunidades Cristãs de base* (Portuguese) or *Comunidades Cristianas de base* (Spanish), which is more literally translated as base Christian communities.

[31] See S. Mainwaring, "Grass-Roots Catholic Groups and Politics in Brazil" in S. Mainwaring and A. Wilde (eds.), *The Progressive Church in Latin America* (Notre Dame, Ind.: University of Notre Dame Press, 1989), pp. 151–192 (151). It should also be noted that base communities also existed outside Latin America and were especially developed in the Philippines.

[32] There are a number of reasons why the figures need to be taken with some caution. First, the definition of what constitutes a base ecclesial community will alter the numbers significantly. Second, all the estimates are based on very partial samples, and therefore rest to a large extent on guesswork in assuming how representative these

despite the impression sometimes given, even in Brazil, the communities never represented the whole Brazilian church or even a majority of Brazilian Catholics.[33] Nonetheless, they were a very significant sector of the church. During the 1970s, they emerged from fairly modest early origins to become a focus of world attention and assume a position at the forefront of liberation theology.

The Distinctive Features of the CEBs

The CEBs were known as base level or basic communities because they were smaller subdivisions of the parish. A large or particularly active parish might be divided into many such communities.[34] Many CEBs were in poor rural areas or in the working-class and shanty-town areas (*favelas*) surrounding Brazilian cities.[35] In these areas CEB members were likely to work with their hands as poorly paid labourers. Many were near the base of the social pyramid and some

---

might be. Third, there is inevitable pressure for numbers to be reported favourably in areas supportive of the movement and down-played in areas where there is disapproval for them. The most frequently given numbers are based on a survey by the Centró de Estatística Religiosa e Investigações Sociais, which suggested that there were 40,000 CEBs in 1974, rising to 80,000 in 1980. Furthermore, it seems that the strength of the CEBs in Brazil and elsewhere peaked in the 1980s, and has been in decline since (although sometimes even higher numbers—100,000 or 120,000—are cited as the peak). Hewitt reviews different estimates of the number of CEBs and the difficulties in counting them in, W. E. Hewitt, *Base Christian Communities and Social Change in Brazil* (Lincoln: University of Nebraska Press, 1991), pp. 6–10. In terms of the number of people, Edward Cleary suggests that CEBs have approximately one million members in Brazil and at least as many in other Latin American countries (E. Cleary, *The Church in Latin America Today: Crisis and Change* [Maryknoll, N.Y.: Orbis Books, 1985] p. 104). Once again, however, others have estimated significantly higher than this, with some estimates for Brazil going as high as four million. Unfortunately, estimates of CEB membership have even more problems than estimates of the number of CEBs, since levels of membership need to be defined and accurately measured. Hewitt comments: "Although, consequently, two or perhaps three million Brazilians may participate in CEBs, the level at which they do so may disqualify many from actual CEB membership" (Hewitt, *Base Christian Communities and Social Change in Brazil*, p. 8).

[33] Scott Mainwaring suggests three factors in the Brazilian situation that help to explain why the church in Brazil took such a progressive and innovative lead. First, the initiatives of the 1950s that provided the foundation for the more radical approach in the 1970s. Second, the history of institutional weakness that encouraged innovation at grassroots level. Third, the absence of sustained persecution by liberalism, which encouraged a general openness to society. See S. Mainwaring, *The Catholic Church and Politics in Brazil, 1916–1985* (Stanford, Calif.: Stanford University Press, 1986), pp. 237–238).

[34] For insider accounts of particular communities in Brazil, see D. Barbé, *Grace and Power: Base Communities and Non-violence in Brazil* (trans. J. P. Brown; Maryknoll, N.Y.: Orbis Books, 1987); A. B. Fragoso, *Face of a Church* (trans. R. R. Barr; Maryknoll, N.Y.: Orbis Books, 1987); R. Rezende, *Rio Maria: Song of the Earth* (trans. and ed. M. Adriance; Maryknoll, N.Y.: Orbis Books; London: Catholic Institute for International Relations, 1994).

[35] Regrettably there is no single term that provides an adequate translation of the Portuguese and Spanish term *de base*. Each of these English variants captures a different nuance of what is meant by *de base*.

were only marginally literate. However, even in poor neighbourhoods, the membership was unlikely to be composed of the most destitute. Most community members had sufficient means to get by most of the time; and enough stability in life to attend meetings on a fairly regular basis. The dispossessed homeless or entirely disenfranchised poor were less well-represented than the working poor. Furthermore, the CEBs often included more financially secure members as well—teachers or white-collar municipal workers—who might provide lay leadership for the group.[36]

As ecclesial, the groups were part of the official pastoral work of the church. The strength of commitment to the groups varied from diocese to diocese and parish to parish, but in Brazil, at least the communities were a central part of the church's official national plan. When base communities first developed in the 1950s and 1960s, they found support from a wide variety of political positions in the church. As a way of extending church authority in society, they had a wide appeal amongst the episcopacy.

In 1975, crucial impetus to the term base ecclesial communities was given by Paul VI's Apostolic Exhortation *Evangelii Nuntiandi* (*Proclaiming the Gospel*) after the 1974 Synod of Bishops.[37] Not only did *Evangelii Nuntiandi* use the term basic ecclesial communities, but it distinguished between communities which were critical of the institutional church (referred to simply as basic communities) and those which were supportive (described as basic ecclesial communities).[38] Thus, the term CEB—base *ecclesial* community—reflected official church approval.[39] For many progressives in Brazil, the CEBs were more than just a legitimate part of the church, they were seen as essential to the church's future.[40]

---

[36] It would be mistaken to think that base communities only existed in the poorer neighbourhoods. However, in middle-class areas, the communities might have a less pronounced political edge and concentrate more on traditional charitable acts (see Hewitt, *Base Christian Communities and Social Change in Brazil*, pp. 60–72).

[37] Paul VI, *Evangelii Nuntiandi: Apostolic Exhortation on Evangelization in the Modern World* (1975). The Medellín document *Pastoral de Conjunto* (§§10–12) referred simply to base *Christian* communities without adding the term ecclesial.

[38] *Evangelii Nuntiandi*, §58. Azevedo (*Basic Ecclesial Communities in Brazil*, pp. 70–71) interprets this as a reference to the difference between communities in Brazil (which had support of the bishops), and communities in Europe and North America (which were not part of an episcopal strategy).

[39] Prominent writers in Brazil referred to the communities as ecclesial in the 1960s. For example, R. B. Caramuru, *Comunidade eclesial de base: uma opçã pastoral decisiva* (Petrópolis, R. J.: Editora Vozes, 1967), and J. Marins, *Comunidade eclesial da base* (São Paulo: Edições Paulinas, 1968). However, the CNBB was still referring simply to "communities from the base" in the early 1970s, for example in their study, *Comunidades: Igreja na Base*, (CNBB Studies, 3; São Paulo: Edições Paulinas, 1974). The term base ecclesial community became common in the literature after 1975; a similar CNBB document was titled *Comunidades eclesiais de base no Brasil*, (CNBB Studies, 3; São Paulo: Edições Paulinas, 1979) and likewise a subsequent study was *Comunidades Eclesiais de Base na Igreja do Brasil* (São Paulo: Edições Paulinas, 1982).

[40] The importance of the base ecclesial communities in this period is reflected in the

The Brazilian bishops' biennial plans of 1975–1977 and 1977–1979 placed the CEBs among the top four pastoral priorities. This meant practical support for the communities in terms of resources and expertise. Furthermore, the CNBB's endorsement of CEBs ensured that even if a local bishop was unsympathetic, the local CEBs could call on support from a national network.

As a community, the people might meet once a week in small groups (anything from six to over a hundred people) to reflect on the Bible in the light of their local situation and their own lives.[41] Active involvement of the laity was central to the CEBs.[42] CEBs usually had someone who acted as a facilitator or animator who need not be a priest.[43] More often, lay catechists took this role. The intention of the facilitator was not to instruct, but to provoke the discussion and dialogue.[44]

As noted below, it was not until the early 1970s that many of the communities—and especially those in dioceses with progressive bishops—became active agents for political change. However, when this happened, their communal emphasis meant that all members of the group were encouraged to express their views on contemporary issues. In the process of sharing experiences, a deeper awareness of common problems and their relation to wider causes often emerged. This process owed much to the pedagogical approach to consciousness-raising piloted in Brazil in the early 1960s by Paulo Freire. After discussing

---

national meetings of communities that started after 1975. The first national plan was "CEBs: Born of the People by the Spirit of God" (1975); next came "CEBs: The Church, a People Walk Together" (1976) and "CEBs: Church, A People Liberating Itself" (1978). The fourth meeting took place in 1981 as "CEBs: The Church, A People Who Have Organized Themselves for Liberation" and the fifth in 1983 as "CEBs: A United People, Seedbed of a New Society." See Azevedo pp. 99–100 n. 3.

[41] They are only residential communities in the sense that the members are likely to live fairly close together. They do not share a communal residence and although families often cooperate together, the CEBs are not communes where all possessions are held in common such as described in Acts.

[42] In most of Latin America, it was usual for progressive bishops to promote CEBs and conservative bishops to resist them. However, Brazil was unusual for the shared consensus between conservatives and progressives that the church should promote base communities. Support for base communities as a way of strengthening the church's presence in society was common in both the progressive and conservative wings of the Brazilian church. However, there was a marked difference on the social and political dimension to CEBs activity from diocese to diocese. For progressives, the orientation to social transformation was an integral part of the CEBs. For conservative critics, this politicisation was a serious deviation from the original purpose of the communities.

[43] Progressive women religious and/or the local priest were often critical in the establishment of a community, but as the CEB developed it was likely to become increasingly dependant on lay leadership.

[44] In practice, their effectiveness in this depended on their personalities, skills, and commitment to the participatory ideal. It would be naïve to believe that every CEB lived up to these high ideals in every situation, but it would be unduly cynical not to recognise the dramatic change toward more equal relationships created within the communities.

a problem and diagnosing its roots, the community could reflect on how they might solve it using their own means and initiatives.[45] Community level solutions could range from pooling resources into a small credit fund for members, working together to build a shared centre, organising a petition for traffic controls to protect pedestrians, or any manner of local community action.

The Historical Development of the CEBs

The political orientation of CEBs in the 1970s and 1980s did not materialise overnight. Base communities in Brazil were originally part of a nonpoliticised pastoral process in Brazil that predated the earliest publications in liberation theology. A number of early experiments in church renewal at a community level were made in the 1940s and 1950s. These provided a foundation for the emergence of the early base communities in the 1960s.[46] The ecclesial base communities extended this trend further in the late 1970s and early 1980s. After the mid-1980s, the momentum of the movement slowed, and after the return to formal democracy in 1985, the CEBs ceased to be the force they once were.[47]

To understand this history more precisely, a helpful distinction may be drawn between the early base communities of the 1960s and the later base *ecclesial* communities of the 1970s and 1980s.[48] In itself, the change in terminology did not mark a significant change in the nature of the communities, However, its timing overlapped with a more important change that was taking place, because in the early 1970s many base ecclesial communities were influenced by liberation theology. It was these activist communities—committed to social analysis and social transformation—that liberation theologians had in mind when they referred to CEBs in their work.[49]

---

[45] The Medellín document on education encouraged the adoption of Freire's approach with its references to liberating education (esp. §§ 7–9).

[46] For an excellent recent overview, see A. Dawson, "The Origins and Character of the Base Ecclesial Community: A Brazilian Perspective" in C. Rowland (ed.), *Cambridge Companion to Liberation Theology* (Cambridge: Cambridge University Press, 1999), pp. 109–128 (esp. 110–113).

[47] The conservative upswing in the church in the 1980s and the retirement of bishops who supported the CEBs (and their replacement with less sympathetic or actively hostile bishops) also had a signficiant impact and is discussed at greater length in Chapter 11.

[48] In the 1960s, the ecclesial nature of the base communities was certainly recognised (and the movement endorsed by the CNBB in their national plans), but the term that was used was base communities not base ecclesial communities. However, after 1975, formal references to the movement invariably referred to the base ecclesial communities (or frequently the acronym CEBs) even though it was common for these to be abbreviated to base communities or simply communities in less formal references.

[49] Although, as noted above, liberation theologians referred to the communities as base communities or base ecclesial communities, it was invariably the social activist CEBs of the 1970s, not their earlier predecessors, that they meant.

Forerunners in the 1940s and 1950s

Notable amongst the precedents for the CEBs were the ecclesiological innovations in the Northeast diocese of Barra do Piraí and especially the popular catechesis movement associated with Dom Agnelo Rossi. Beginning in the 1950s, popular catechism sought to "extend evangelization and the presence of the church."[50] Lay leaders would substitute for the priest in those roles that were open to them in the absence of the priest. Although it was impossible to celebrate mass in this way, other aspects of worship were possible including weekly meetings with reading of the Bible and prayers.[51] Likewise, in the Amazon area of Maranhão from 1952 onward, the bishop of São Luis (Dom José Delgado) decentralized parishes into chapels and encouraged lay leadership in them. To support this shift, his auxiliary bishop (Dom Antônio Fragoso) provided training courses for lay administrators and maintained contact with them.[52]

Tentative origins for the political dimension of the CEBs may also be discerned in this period. In the late 1940s, the movement for adult education in the Northeast diocese of Natal under Dom Eugênio Sales linked the traditional concerns of catechesis to integral concerns for the whole human being. A similar concern for the whole human being became increasingly prominent in the radio-broadcast movement that started in the Northeast in the late 1950s and the Base Education Movement with its commitment to conscientization built on this foundation in the 1960s.[53] The Movement for a Better World might also be noted here. It spread to Brazil from Rome in the late 1950s and influenced both priests and bishops. It stressed the importance and urgency of social issues. Its social programs were firmly anticommunist rather than politically progressive in inspiration, but at least they posed an implicit challenge to the fatalistic acceptance of poverty and misery.

Emergence of Base Communities in 1960s

Early base communities appeared in Brazil in the early 1960s.[54] The communities offered the chance for participation at a more personal level in a social community as Brazilian society became increasingly disrupted by the effects of migration and industrialization. National support for the base communities in Brazil was first indicated in the Emergency Plan of 1962 drawn up in response

---

[50] M. Azevedo, *Basic Ecclesial Communities in Brazil* trans. J. Drury; (Washington, D.C.: Georgetown University Press), p. 26.

[51] Azevedo, *Basic Ecclesial Communities in Brazil*, pp. 25–27.

[52] Although he was moved from this position in 1963, Dom Fragoso continued to play a prominent role as a leader of the progressive church as bishop of Crateus (also in northeast Brazil). His story and reflections on the church's role are offered in his book A. B. Fragoso, *Face of a Church* (trans. R. R. Barr; Maryknoll, N.Y.: Orbis Books, 1987).

[53] On Paulo Freire, conscientization and the Base Education Movement, see Chapter 3.

[54] At about the same time, base communities were also appearing elsewhere. For example, one of the earliest and most influential for Central America was San Miguelito in Panama City; see F. Bravo, *The Parish of San Miguelito in Panama* (Cuernavaca: Centro Intercultural de Documentación, 1966).

to a letter from John XXIII.[55] This was subsequently reaffirmed in the bishops' First Joint Pastoral Plan (1966–1970) with its recognition of the church as the people of God.[56]

The emphasis in Vatican II documents on active participation in the church (*Lumen Gentium*) and involvement with the world (*Gaudium et Spes*) gave the existing initiatives in Brazil official support and encouragement. In Brazil, the very process of disseminating Conciliar documents through courses, study sessions, and popularised publications started to build the new participatory pastoral model and take forward the existing experiments in lay participation in the church. This was a remarkable development in a church that had only just allowed the mass to be celebrated in the language of people attending and started to encourage people to read the Bible for themselves.

Throughout this period the role of base communities was understood in fairly traditional ways.[57] The relatively poor priest-to-population ratio in Brazil created a desperate need for more lay leadership if the church was to maintain its influence on society. The communities allowed the church to project its institutional presence, promote lay participation, and enrich relationships within the local church. The fact that evangelical churches and traditional Afro-Brazilian religions—both of which are significant in Brazil—have a much more participatory style may have encouraged the people of Brazil to support the base communities.

Radicalization of the CEBs in the 1970s

The CNBB, which was virtually silent on social matters since the 1964 coup, finally started to raise its voice in protest against the military regime in the 1970s.[58] By then, many leaders of the Brazilian church were progressively radicalized by the repressive measures of the military dictatorship, which were

---

[55] CNBB, *Plano de Emergência para a Igreja do Brasil* (Rio de Janeiro: Livraria Dom Bosco Editôra, 1963). It was formally adopted by the CNBB in 1963.

[56] CNBB, *Plano de Pastoral Conjunto 1966–70* (Rio de Janeiro: Livraria Dom Bosco Editôra, 1966). The plan recommended: "Our present parishes will or should be composed of various local communities and basic communities. . . . Thus it will be most important to undertake parish renewal through the creation of dynamization of these basic communities" (2nd ed. 1967, pp. 57–58; cited in Azevedo, *Basic Ecclesial Communities in Brazil* p. 46 n. 21).

[57] The relative readiness with which the Brazilian church contemplated changes in the 1960s has been interpreted by some as a survival mechanism, a response to the social and economic changes of the preceding three decades. Proponents of this view argue that industrialisation and mobilization eroded the traditional power of the church over the people, and the church was eager to restore its institutional role. In this interpretation, the changes undertaken in the 1960s were to undercut the appeal of socialism (on social concerns) and Pentecostalism (on lay participation). The CNBB integrated the nascent local movements into their national plans, and thereby made them into a concern for the Brazilian church as a whole.

[58] See esp. D. Regan, *Church for Liberation: A Pastoral Portrait of the Church in Brazil* (Leominster, Herefordshire: Fowler Wright Books, 1987).

at their height from 1968 to 1974.[59] Hand-in-hand with this radicalisation of many in the church hierarchy at a grass-roots level, the base communities movement also developed a more radical political outlook after 1968.[60]

On 6 May 1973, the bishops from the Northeast and Amazon regions both published documents that sharply condemned abuses by the military regime and its human rights violations, "I Have Heard the Cries of My People" and "Marginalization of the People, Cry of the Churches."[61] Although the bishops in the Northeast and Amazon were still ahead of the CNBB, by now the CNBB was becoming increasing critical of the military. It was starting to express public concern not just over individual cases of human rights, but also of the widespread and entrenched social poverty in Brazil's National Security State. In 1972 and again in 1973, the CNBB stated its support for the Amazonian bishops. Increasingly, CNBB statements started to address issues of poverty and commit the church to the poor.[62]

As the military clamped down on opposition organizations and prevented political meetings that might voice criticism of the regime, the base communities came to the fore as voices of protest on behalf of the poor majority in the 1970s.[63]

---

[59] Hélder Câmara and other outspoken bishops voiced criticism of the government on a number of occasions. The Dominican Affair of November 1969 was a particularly high-profile example of tensions with the church. On 4 November, Carlos Marighella (the leader of the guerrilla group Alliance for National Liberation, ALN) was caught in São Paulo and the church came under suspicion for helping him. A nationwide investigation eventually accused eleven Dominicans, one Jesuit, and two secular priests of aiding subversives. The Dominican Carlos Christo was arrested on 9 November and spent twenty-two months in trial before being sentenced in September 1971 to four more years in prison. Christo's writings in prison were published as C. Christo, *Against Principalities and Powers* (trans. J. Drury; Maryknoll, N.Y.: Orbis Books, 1977; U.K. ed., *Letters from a Prisoner of Conscience* [London: Lutterworth, 1978]). The shocking treatment of one jailed Dominican, Father Tito de Alençar (graphically described in a letter from the prison), led him to commit suicide on his release (see Lernoux, *Cry of the People*, pp. 321–324).

[60] Barbé (*Grace and Power*, p. 92) writes: "By Christmas of 1968, after the toughening of the regime in December of that year, the priests and religious—the 'agents of pastoral ministry'—had to make a choice: either join the guerrilla forces and the clandestine subversion, as urged by certain Marxist and even Christian elements of the middle class, or attach themselves, more seriously than before, to a pastoral labour at the base, in order to get close to the worker militants and peasants and form communities with them. Those options were never laid out with the clarity just used here, but they were real." The radicalization of Catholic Action and the MEB in the early 1960s provided a precursor to this shift in the base communities in the early 1970s.

[61] Mainwaring (*The Catholic Church*, p. 93) comments, "At the time, these two documents were probably the most radical statements ever issued by a group of bishops anywhere in the world."

[62] Mainwaring divides the CNBB's attitude to the dictatorship into three periods: "After virtually supporting the military regime (1964–1968), it raised a timid voice against the repressive excesses (1968–1972) and finally a much stronger voice against violations of human rights and authoritarian excesses (1972–1982)" (*The Catholic Church*, p. 112).

[63] An important precedent for this was the so-called Catholic Left, which was radicalized during the late 1950s and early 1960s. Within the Catholic Left, the Young Catholic

In the CEBs people were able to discuss politics in ways that were not possible elsewhere. This contributed to a self-reinforcing process by which the CEBSs increased in their importance for Brazilian society during the military dictatorships. They attracted involvement from those committed to social change, and became increasingly political in their outlook.

The more progressive leadership of the CNBB (elected in 1972) helped give the communities at least some protection. Meanwhile, liberation theology encouraged the communities to view their social involvement and political actions as promoting the kingdom of God and living out a new reality of being the church.[64]

THE SIGNIFICANCE OF THE CEBS

Church and Society

The CEBs changed the face of Brazilian society. Bible reading and discussions in the CEBs often generated community actions and social projects. Usually, these started at fairly modest local level with objectives that would directly benefit the local community (a daycare centre, a food cooperative, a school, or health

---

Students (JUC) and Popular Action deserve special mention as anticipations of the radicalization of the CNBB and the CEBs in the 1970s (see Mainwaring, *The Catholic Church*, pp. 60–75). The JUC began in the 1930s as part of Brazilian Catholic Action (a clerically controlled conservative movement addressed to the future elite of the nation). However, with the reorganistation of Brazilian Catholic Action in the late 1940s, the JUC became more independent of clerical control started to work more closely with the national student movement. By 1960, JUC was actively involved in student and national politics and was highly critical of the social problems facing Brazil. In 1961, the Brazilian hierarchy started to take sanctions against the movement and it was eventually disbanded in 1966. However, Popular Action (Ação Popular) quickly replaced JUC as the channel for radical Catholic political action. Popular Action was created in 1961 and became a small, but highly influential force in left-wing Brazilian politics. It favoured revolution and endorsed socialist policies more clearly than was ever the case in JUC, but it remained highly critical of the Soviet Union and insisted on the importance of freedom and pluralism. After the 1964 coup, it was forced underground and underwent a further sequence of radicalization that propelled it toward Maoism and armed struggle. By this time, it had moved away from its original Christian identity, and in 1973, its remaining members joined the Communist Party of Brazil.

[64] For liberationist ecclesiology of the CEBs, see L. Boff, *Church: Charism and Power: Liberation Theology and the Institutional Church* (trans. J. Diercksmeier; New York: Crossroad; London: SCM Press, 1985 [Portuguese orig. 1981]); P. Berryman, *Liberation Theology: The Essential Facts about the Revolutionary Movement in Latin America and Beyond* (New York: Pantheon, 1987), pp. 64–68; J. Marins, T. M. Trevisan and C. Chanona, *The Church from the Roots: Basic Ecclesial Communities* (London: Catholic Fund for Overseas Development, 1989 [ET 1983]); S. Torres and J. Eagleson (eds.), *The Challenge of Basic Christian Communities* (Papers from the International Ecumenical Congress of Theology, 1980, São Paulo, Brazil; trans. J. Drury; Maryknoll, N.Y.: Orbis Books, 1981). For a Protestant perspective, see G. Cook, *The Expectation of the Poor: Latin American Basic Ecclesial Communities in Protestant Perspective* (Maryknoll, N.Y.: Orbis Books, 1985).

clinics; electricity, water, sewer systems, and paved roads). In time, the community might develop and join with other communities to address more national and structural issues such as minimum wages, working conditions, land distribution, and political campaigns.

Equally important, the communities provided experience of a working democracy. This often had a profound effect on participants. They developed confidence, understanding, and practical skills that were transferable to other political projects as the basis for participation in long-term social transformation far beyond any immediate work of the CEBs. Many of those involved in the transition to democracy in Brazil in the 1980s developed their political awareness and leadership skills in the CEBs.

For the Brazilian church, the CEBs provided new energy and a new relevance in many working-class and rural areas. Furthermore, as the movement became part of a national pastoral plan, they prompted the institutional church to assert its role in national political life. The church—and the CEBs themselves—often paid a heavy price for these social initiatives. However, for the many participants involved, it gave a new sense of pride and value in the church's social role and gained admiration from around the world.

At an ecclesiological level, the CEBs were also significant because they modelled an alternative vision for the church's own institutional relations. The CEBs provided a model of lay leadership and democratic principles that raised questions about the appropriateness of existing church hierarchies. Analysis and criticism of power structures led thoughtful members to envisage alternative power structures within the church.

For the Roman *curia* this reinvention of church relations was a highly sensitive issue. In the 1980s, it was at the heart of the difficult relationship between the Brazilian church and the Vatican. Although the Vatican endorsed the CEBs and saw them as a valuable tool in promoting the active and energetic presence of the church in society, it was always concerned that the CEBs be kept under firm ecclesial control. As a result, the CEBs could have an uneasy relationship with institutional authorities. Although they officially operated within the structures of the institutional church, and at least in Brazil the CEBs were part of an officially endorsed pastoral plan, their democratic nature was an implicit critique of the hierarchical church.[65]

The Reorientation of Liberation Theology

The CEBs prompted profound changes in liberation theology as a theological movement. In the communities, liberation theology interacted with real people and their problems. This interaction gave the developing theology a much stronger popular base than is normally the case for an academic theology and encouraged a new methodological emphasis on dialogue and a new epistemo-

---

[65] Chapter 11 examines how this tension created in the 1970s became an open conflict in the 1980s.

logical interest in the experiences of the poor as the starting point for theology.

Engagement with the poor converted liberation theology much more profoundly than anyone expected. Everyday experiences of oppression started to take precedence as the starting point for theology. Liberation theologians started to recognise the struggles of the poor as a privileged *locus* of theology—a place were God was specially revealed in history. Gutiérrez's book *The Power of the Poor in History* and Sobrino's *The True Church and the Poor* both reflected this new outlook and provided its theological foundation.[66] This was not intended to romanticize either the poor or their state of poverty. Gutiérrez was clear that:

> The preference for the poor is based on the fact that God, as Christ shows us, loves them for their concrete, real condition of poverty, 'whatever may be' their moral or spiritual disposition.[67]

Liberation theologians started to engage in a genuine dialogue with the poor, so as to learn from them. Picking up the challenge laid down by Freire's work on dialogical education, liberation theologians sought to listen to the poor and be their partners in articulating their experiences and faith. As a result, liberation theology became distinctive in terms of *who* did theology. The common split between the academic theologian and the people was rejected; instead, the theologian was challenged to forge an organic solidarity with the people.[68] Thus, after the mid-1970s liberation theology would often take place in at least three different levels: the professional, the pastoral, and the popular. At each level, there was a different emphasis in the theological forms even though each level was interdependent on the others.[69] In a classic image, Leonardo and Clodovis Boff refer to the different parts of a tree to explain the different parts of this single process:

> Liberation theology could be compared to a tree. Those who see only professional theologians at work in it see only the branches of the tree. They fail to see the trunk which is the thinking of priests and other pastoral ministers, let alone the roots beneath the soil that hold the whole tree—trunk and branches—in place. The roots are the practical living and thinking—though submerged and anonymous—going on in tens of thousands of base communities living out their faith and thinking it in a liberating key.[70]

---

[66] Gutiérrez, *The Power of the Poor in History* (trans. R. R. Barr; Maryknoll, N.Y.: Orbis Books; London: SCM Press, 1983 [Spanish orig. 1979]); J. Sobrino, *The True Church and the Poor* (trans. Matthew O'Connell; Maryknoll, N.Y.: Orbis Books; London: SCM, 1984 [Spanish orig. 1981]).

[67] Gutiérrez, *The Power of the Poor in History*, p. 138; cp Sobrino. In locating the preference for the poor in their struggles with poverty and not in any merit that they have as people, Gutiérrez and Sobrino, p. 137, reaffirmed the line of teaching that went back to *Rerum Novarum* that there was nothing specially deserving about the poor as people but they should be given special consideration because of their situation (see p. 46).

[68] On the practical ways that such solidarity might be shown at different levels of commitment, see L. and C. Boff, *Introducing Liberation Theology*, p. 24.

[69] See the chart in L. and C. Boff, *Introducing Liberation Theology*, p. 13.

[70] L. and C. Boff, *Introducing Liberation Theology*, p. 12.

Not all of the earliest pioneers of liberation theology were unhappy with this new orientation. Juan Luis Segundo saw the shift in the 1970s as effectively creating two different theologies of liberation.[71] The first, which was prompted by work with students' movements, was concerned with the social function of ideologies. It critiqued the role of Christianity in Latin American class interests that Christianity traditionally served. Its purpose was to "de-idologise" Christianity by rigorous ideological suspicion.[72] Because the context of this work was the universities, those who first received it were not the oppressed, but middle-class students who were concerned with the liberation of the poor previously held back by oppressive elements that they saw as constituent parts of their faith.[73] In contrast to this, Segundo outlined the second type of liberation of theology arising from a new context for theologising: the common people.[74] This type of theology emphasised learning from the common people, structuring the common people's understanding of faith, and grounding the practices coming from this faith.

Segundo himself remained firmly in the former camp. He left open the extent to which the two approaches were complementary or opposed and simply wished to emphasise how deep the division between them went.[75]

CONCLUSION

To understand the development of liberation theology in the 1970s, it is essential to recognise this interaction between its academic literature and its ecclesial manifestations. The base communities that sprang up throughout Latin America, especially in Brazil and Central America, provided fertile soil for lib-

---

[71] J. L. Segundo, "Two Theologies of Liberation," *The Month* 17 (October 1984); reprinted in Hennelly (ed.), *Liberation Theology*, pp. 353–366.

[72] A classic example of this strand is J. L. Segundo, *The Liberation of Theology* (trans. J. Drury; Maryknoll, N.Y.: Orbis Books; 1976 [Spanish orig. 1976]). See also the five-volume Christology he wrote in the 1980s, *Jesus of Nazareth, Yesterday and Today* (5 vols., trans. J. Drury, Maryknoll, N.Y.: Orbis Books; London: Sheed and Ward; 1984–1989 [Spanish origs. 1982–1985]). For good overviews of Segundo's work, see Marsha Hewitt, *From Theology to Social Theory: Juan Luis Segundo and the Theology of Liberation* (New York: Peter Lang, 1990); A. T. Hennelly, *Theology for a Liberating Church: The New Praxis of Freedom* (Washington D.C.: Georgetown University Press, 1989).

[73] Segundo, "Two Theologies of Liberation," pp. 357–358.

[74] Segundo notes: "This context was already there in most Latin American countries, but it was discovered, so to speak, with the help of some popular or populist movements, which came to public attention in the early 1970s and still more openly in the late 1970s. . . . Thus, Enrique Dussel coined for theologians and pastoral agents the expression, the discipleship of the poor; Leonardo Boff spoke about a new 'ecclesiogenesis,' a church born from the poor; and Gustavo Gutiérrez chose as the title of his new book *The Power of the Poor in History*; Segundo, "Two Theologies of Liberation", pp. 358–360.

[75] Thus, he concluded: ". . . after twenty years at work, liberation theology is profoundly alive on our continent, although taking different forms in different classes or groups of society"; Segundo, "Two Theologies of Liberation," p. 365.

eration theology and ensured that the impact of liberation theology would spread much further than most theological movements. However, the CEBs were more than passive recipients of liberation theology.

The writing of liberation theologians stimulated and directed the growth of the popular church, and the needs and experiences of the popular church stimulated and redirected the writing of liberation theology. Theologians became actively engaged with CEBs and sought to engage with the concerns of CEBs. This had a profound effect on the style and focus of their theological work. The involvement of an increasingly mass popular movement in the vision of liberation theology started to transform the movement in the 1970s. The CEBs prompted many liberation theologians to focus on how their work could support the church at a popular level.

Whereas many of the early works in liberation theology prior to 1975 were clearly intended with a well-educated audience in mind, as the 1970s progressed, liberation theologians were prompted to reconsider the insights in the movement's earliest publications in the light of their creative theological partnership with the base communities and their readings of the Bible. In the process, they began to open up further theological avenues for exploration. It was this shift, which can be dated from 1975–1979 onward, that marked the transition from opting to write a theology *for* the poor to a theology *from* the poor. Liberation theologians engaged with the people's thoughts and ideas as they arose from everyday life in the light of Christian faith. In turn, they offered theological reflections intended to strengthen and sustain the people in their journey of faith as the people of God.

CHAPTER NINE

Reading the Word
and the World

> The liberation theologian goes to the scriptures bear-
> ing the whole weight of the problems, sorrows and hopes
> of the poor, seeking light and inspiration from the divine
> word. This is a new way of reading the Bible: the
> hermeneutics of liberation.
>
> Leonardo and Clodovis Boff[1]

INTRODUCTION

The CEBs helped liberation theologians to go further in their understanding
of the option for the poor. Base communities challenged some liberation theologians to involve the poor much more directly in the theological process
itself and discover God's presence in their lives. In the 1970s, many communities became co-participants with professional theologians in the theological
process. Liberation theologians came to value the experiences and insights
shared by community members as helpful starting points for their work. The
impact of this shift was particularly clear in liberation theology's adoption of a
hermeneutical circle for reading the Bible at a popular level.[2]

---

[1] See L. Boff and C. Boff, *Introducing Liberation Theology*, p. 32.

[2] The term hermeneutical meaning interpretation is derived from Hermes, the Greek
messenger God. On the hermeneutical method developed in Latin American liberation
theology, see esp. L. and C. Boff, *Introducing Liberation Theology*, pp. 22–42; cf. L. and
C. Boff, *Salvation and Liberation*, pp. 1–13. For practical examples, see esp. the communal readings of the Solentiname community in Nicaragua published as E. Cardenal,
The Gospel in Solentiname (trans. D. D. Walsh; 4 vols; Maryknoll, N.Y.: Orbis Books,
1976–1982 [Spanish origs. 1975–1977]); the readings and meditations of the Brazilian
bishop Hélder Câmara, *Through the Gospel with Dom Hélder Câmara* (trans. A. Neame;
Maryknoll, N.Y.: Orbis Books; London: Darton, Longman & Todd, 1986); and the more
recent meditations offered in G. Gutiérrez, *Sharing the Word through the Liturgical Year*
(Maryknoll, N.Y.: Orbis Books; London: Geoffrey Chapman, 1997 [Spanish orig. 1995]).

In the late 1960s and early 1970s, liberation theology was based on the political option for the poor, which closedly resembled radical versions of European political theology. How fundamental the differences actually were was an issue of some contention. It was certainly true that Latin American liberation theology was more rooted in the immediate realities of political oppression than the European political theology of the time. Likewise, in terms of methodology, liberation theology was also distinctive from the outset in its commitment to theology as a second step, as articulated by Gutiérrez and others in the late 1960s. Nonetheless, some observers felt that liberation theology was still firmly within the European tradition. However, in the second half of the 1970s, liberation's theology's epistemological option for the poor distinguished it far more sharply from European or North America theologies than the simply political option of the early years had done. Understanding the extension of the political option into an epistemological option (and therefore, a more truly theological option) is crucial to understanding the development of the liberation theology in the 1970s and the complexity of the movement as a whole.

By the end of the decade, liberation theology was a well-established theology and influential movement in church and society. Christians influenced by liberation theology constituted a civil opposition in many countries under military dictatorship. However, Latin American elites and conservative church figures were eager to blunt its edge, and hostility toward the movement grew and became better organised. The final part of this chapter examines this resistance in terms of the institutional intrigues of the third extraordinary bishops' meeting, CELAM III 1979, in Puebla (Mexico). The conflicts at Puebla offer insight into the battles being waged across the continent over the soul of the church at the close of the decade. In the end, the conflict at Puebla was indecisive. A determined defence of liberation theology by progressive bishops at the conference ensured that the conference did not bring the movement to an end. Nonetheless, it pointed to the fact that the main opposition that liberation theology might face in the future might be more to do with church authorities than with repressive governments.

THE HERMENEUTICAL CIRCLE

During the 1970s, leading figures in Brazilian liberation theology (which included the brothers Clodovis and Leonardo Boff and the Dutch Carmelite missionary Carlos Mesters) responded to the CEBs by fashioning a new way of reading the Bible.

According to Leonardo and Clodovis Boff, reading the Bible required an approach involving three different stages or mediations based on the see-judge-act methodology of Catholic Action.[3] The most theoretically advanced statement of this approach is given by Clodovis Boff in his work *Theology and Praxis*,

---

[3] As noted in Chapter 3, this form of Catholic Action was embraced throughout Latin America by the 1950s.

adapted from his doctoral dissertation and published in Brazil in 1978.[4] The
three steps were the social-analytical, hermeneutical, and practical mediations,
which were combined together in a circular process for reading the biblical word
and the social world.[5]

Social Analysis

The first step (or mediation) was social and historical analysis. Participants in
a Bible reading group addressed the social issues that affected their daily lives.
Discussion often began with members of the group to talking about the events
of everyday life, things that may have happened to them that week. More
expansively, they might retell the wider story of their lives and the personal
history that they have experienced. Recognising common elements in people's
histories and experiences provided the starting point for social analysis, which
could move beyond personal stories to raise structural issues. For example, discussion of hunger, personal poverty, and pressure on land might eventually lead
on to the consideration of the foreign debt, systems of world trade, and divisions in society.

For a deeper analysis of the social situation, the group's discussion might draw
upon concepts from social science. This was necessary if the group's social
understanding was to go beyond superficial symptoms to understanding the real
causes at the root of social issues.[6] However, since community members might
have only limited education (and in some cases many might be illiterate)
detailed discussion of Marxist theory (or other analytical tools) was never a
priority for the communities.

Interpretation

The Boffs called the second step of the circle the "hermeneutical mediation."
At this point, the community sought to read the Bible and understand Christian
tradition in accordance with the commitment to liberation and the preferential option for the poor. Some of the most important biblical material reflected
liberation theology's interest in the Exodus, the prophets in the Old Testament,
and the gospels in the New Testament.[7] The perspectives brought to the texts

---

[4] C. Boff, *Theology and Praxis: Epistemological Foundations* (trans. R. R. Barr; Maryknoll,
N.Y.: Orbis Books, 1987). The central elements of this approach are restated in a number of other places; an especially helpful version is offered in the outstanding introduction
to liberation theology written by Clodovis and Leonardo Boff a few years later, Boff and
Boff, *Introducing Liberation Theology*.

[5] This version of the hermeneutical circle should be distinguished from the one elab-
orated by Juan Segundo in *The Liberation of Theology* (trans. J. Drury; Maryknoll, N.Y.:
Orbis Books; 1976 [Spanish orig. 1975]).

[6] For a well-balanced discussion on liberation theology's relationship with the social
analysis, see McGovern, *Liberation Theology and its Critics*, pp. 105–176.

[7] It would, however, be mistaken to suggest that these are the sole sources of liberation readings. Leonardo and Clodovis Boff comment, "The hermeneutics of liberation
stresses these veins, but not to the exclusion of everything else" (Boff and Boff, *Introducing
Liberation Theology*, pp. 32–33).

by the community often opened up fresh perspectives on what seem to be less relevant texts. As Gutiérrez says, "When the reading of the Bible is done as a community, as a church, it is always an unexpected experience."[8]

Inevitably, such readings were always selective to some degree. However, selectivity is inevitable in any reading of the Bible. Reading the Bible in Latin America had always been selective, stretching back to Columbus and the conquistadors. The crucial issue was not the existence of selectivity, but who benefited from it.[9] Furthermore, within the CEBs, the Bible was to be interpreted by the community discussing the text together, rather than the individual extracting a meaning on their own. So, any interpretation had to be given some public justification. Each interpretation could be measured against the community's experience, as well as the individual's.

Action

After social analysis and hermeneutical mediation, the third step was practical action. The action element in the circle covers a wide variety of options, from very small-scale practical projects at a local level to participation in broad-based national movements. At a local level, projects might involve community members in organising a daycare centre for the children, a food cooperative, a local advice centre, or a primary health care facility. At a municipal level, the group might organise petitions and lobby local government for the provision of public services such as education, water, electricity, bus routes, or paved roads. Nationally, the group could contribute to national reform campaigns and join demonstrations for recognition of workers' rights, the minimum wage, and welfare legislation. Representatives might be chosen to attend regional or even national meetings of community groups where social issues were discussed and new initiatives started. In some cases, direct practical action such as land occupations took place. In both the cities (for housing) and the countryside (for farming), the conflicts over land can be intense.[10] In many countries the struggle for land was often the highest priority.

The practical mediation often brought the community into direct or indirect contact with political issues. All of the examples above had a political dimension to a greater or lesser extent. The Boffs described political action as a "true form of faith" even though they recognized that "faith cannot be reduced to

---

[8] G. Gutiérrez, *The God of Life* (trans. M. O'Connell; Maryknoll, N.Y.: Orbis Books; London: SCM Press, 1991 [Spanish orig. 1989]), p. xvii.

[9] Some critics of liberation theology accept that the Bible often speaks with more than one voice, and therefore agree that some hermeneutical selectivity is inevitable, but disagree with the reading proposed by liberation theologians. However, the Boffs argued that their interpretation had to be seen in terms of a prior ethical option for the poor and the Bible itself pointed toward this.

[10] The centrality of the land issue in Brazil was reflected in the establishment of the Pastoral Land Commission (*Comissão Pastoral da Terra* or CPT) to coordinate and promote activities around land reform.

action."[11] Actions that arose in the practical mediation completed the hermeneutical circle, but they did not end the circular process. The hope was that the community would be ready to restart the circle with a renewed commitment to the poor.[12]

THE ACADEMY OF THE POOR

Some academic critics have questioned the scholarship of liberation theology on the basis that liberation theologians were more concerned with the everyday lives of the poor than with the intellectual disciplines required for theology, especially in biblical studies.[13]

At one level, such criticism is justified. Many liberation theologians received their training in academic disciplines in the 1950s and 1960s.[14] Although they studied at major European centres of Catholic theology, much of what they learned was dated by the 1970s (and even more so in the 1980s).[15] Furthermore, systematic theology usually took pride of place in the theological curriculum, and the main proponents of liberation theology being referred to here are general theologians, not biblical experts. Leonardo and Clodovis Boff, Gutiérrez, and Jon Sobrino all make extensive use of the Bible at a professional level, but they are not specialists in biblical scholarship.[16] Their use of the Bible is invariably theological and there is relatively little sustained and detailed exegesis in their main works.[17] Most liberation theologians are aware of important shifts in biblical criticism, but have little time or opportunity to be abreast of recent biblical scholarship. Much of the recent historical scholarship is in English and the financial cost and time required to keep abreast of it in Latin America would be very considerable.

---

[11] See Boff and Boff, *Introducing Liberation Theology*, p. 39.

[12] Thus, Lenoardo and Clodovis Boff concluded: "Liberation theology is far from being an inconclusive theology. It starts from action and leads to action, a journey wholly impregnated by and bound up with the atmosphere of faith. From analysis of the reality of the oppressed, it passes through the word of God to arrive finally at specific action. 'Back to action' is a characteristic call of this theology. It seeks to be a militant, committed and liberating theology" (*Introducing Liberation Theology*, p. 39).

[13] Segundo records that in its early days liberation theology "clearly evoked a certain amount of academic disdain from the great centres of theological thought around the world . . . as a well-intentioned but rather naive and uncritical effort. . . ." (Segundo, *The Liberation of Theology*, p. 5).

[14] In biblical studies, this was often even before the new focus on biblical studies prompted by Vatican II had taken effect.

[15] For example, Gutiérrez studied at Louvain, Lyons, and Rome.

[16] In terms of the hermeneutical circle, concern for the Bible occurs mainly in the second mediation (hermeneutics) and even here, despite its obvious importance, it is not the only source for theological judgements. This discourages specialization in single academic disciplines.

[17] Even Gutiérrez's treatment of Job, his most sustained treatment of a biblical book, gives priority to theological questions over textual issues. See Gutiérrez, *On Job: God-talk and the Suffering of the Innocent* (trans. M. O'Connell; Maryknoll, N.Y.: Orbis Books, 1987 [Spanish orig. 1986]).

Most liberation theologians have access to universities or seminaries with a theological library, but they are unlikely to have anything that matches North American or British holdings in these areas. In some cases, it is a struggle to maintain and develop even basic theological collections and scholarly tools. For example, the Jesuit run Universidad Centroamericana in El Salvador was bombed repeatedly during the late 1970s and 1980s. In 1989, almost all the equipment and collections of the Pastoral Centre was destroyed by the armed forces. In view of such difficulties—and recognising the urgency of other tasks—there is an understandable temptation to underestimate the importance of academic biblical research.[18]

Nonetheless, the Bible was never the exclusive guide of Catholic theology. Church teaching and tradition was always an authoritative source alongside the scripture. By adding the experiences of the poor as a further privileged source, liberation theologians introduced a further partner to the dialogue, and clearly it would be unfair to judge them solely in terms of their biblical work. Criticisms of the way that liberation theology's social concerns have compromised the integrity of its scholarship are therefore often too simplistic. The accusation was frequently made as a self-evident assertion that any social involvement would be a subjective matter undermining academic objectivity. Liberation theologians responded to these suggestions by questioning the assumption that theology can or should ever be socially detached or value free. They point out that such attempts at neutrality or objectivity are likely to be both misleading and inappropriate. Claims that a theology is neutral or objective can hide a conservative acceptance of the *status quo*. In situations of flagrant social injustice, the failure to recognise and judge what is wrong is not a neutral stance, but collusion with the powers that be. Theological approaches that assert neutrality and objectivity above all else are often blind to their own covert participation in sinful situations. Liberation theologians argued that it is not a matter of theology taking sides, but of deciding which side it was on.[19]

Underlying much of the debate was the issue concerning to whom and to what theology should be accountable. Liberation theologians believed that previous academic theologies were not held sufficiently accountable to the poor for the political implications of their work. Theological reflection tended to be irresponsible in the sense of not answering—or feeling the need to answer—to a community or audience beyond the church or university. The idea that theology should be accountable to the poor, and tested in what might be described as "the academy of the poor" was a radical challenge. Yet the Boffs argued:

---

[18] For example, in addition to the moral ambiguities of emphasising the Exodus as a model for liberation another serious issue in works from the 1970s was the tendency to stigmatize Judaism (and especially the Pharisees); see M. Ellis, *Toward A Jewish Theology of Liberation* (Maryknoll, N.Y.: Orbis Books, 1987).

[19] More specifically, liberation theology asked whether theology should continue to support the *status quo*—however much this may be unintentional—or whether it should make a positive option for society's oppressed and try to change the *status quo*.

... anyone who wants to elaborate relevant liberation theology must be prepared to go into the 'examination hall' of the poor. Only after sitting on the benches of the humble will he or she be entitled to enter a school of 'higher learning.'[20]

These differences in theological priorities between liberation theologians and other academic approaches to the Bible emerged clearly in the work of Carlos Mesters. Mesters is a Dutch Carmelite, who worked extensively with communities in Brazil. In the Brazilian context, Mesters made explicit the theological priorities for a popular reading of the Bible:

The Bible is read and studied in order to know better the present situation and the calls from God that exist in it. The ultimate aim of the people's use of the Bible *is not so much to interpret the Bible, but to interpret their lives.*[21] [Emphasis original]

For Mesters, the Bible was a mirror of life. The story of the people of God in the Bible was a mirror for looking at their story in history.[22] Mesters argued that this approach was justified because the Bible's importance to life should take precedence over academic studies that are not orientated to application. He referred to this as putting the Bible in its proper place:

Finally, the common people are putting the Bible in its proper place, the place where God intended it to be. They are putting it in second place. Life takes first place! In so doing, the people are showing us the enormous importance of the Bible and, at the same time, its relative value—relative to life.[23]

For Mesters, the relative value given to traditional biblical scholarship was something to rejoice at rather than regret. He did not see this as a negation of the academic disciplines in biblical study, but a recognition that biblical interpretation demanded more than academic study. Authentic interpretation of the Bible in Latin America meant engaging with the people in interpreting the real life issues they were facing and not studying the text solely for scholarly interest.

Mesters argued that the exegete needed to do more than study the text if they were to read the Bible properly. He identified three forces that came into operation when the Bible was read in the base communities:

---

[20] Boff and Boff, *Introducing Liberation Theology*, p. 24.

[21] Mesters, *Defenseless Flower: A New Reading of the Bible* (Maryknoll, N.Y.: Orbis Books, 1989 [Portuguese orig. 1983]), p. 71.

[22] Mesters, *Defenseless Flower*, p. 2; cf. p. 70: "In the people's eyes the Bible and life are connected. When they open the Bible they want to find in it things directly related to their lives, and in their lives they want to find events and meanings that parallel those in the Bible. Spontaneously, they use the Bible as an image, symbol, or mirror of what is happening to them here and now."

[23] C. Mesters "The Use of the Bible in the Christian Communities of the Common People" in Torres and Eagleson (eds.), *The Challenge of Basic Christian Communities*, pp. 197–210 (209); cf. Mesters, *Defenseless Flower*, pp. 5–10.

Life, science, and faith. People, exegesis, and church. Three forces in constant tension, each with its defenders, attempting in its own way to make its contribution to the correct use of the Bible in the church.[24]

These three forces mixed together for mutual interference and illumination.[25] The contribution of expertise was in both directions. The community contributed expertise and insights derived from their experiences to challenge the way in which the professional theologian interpreted the Bible. Rather than being a threat to the academic integrity of biblical study, this two-way process could be a valuable balance and guide for it.

Mesters recognised that the people's contribution was far from infallible and that it could open the door to popular misinterpretation. The connections that the people made between the Bible and their own community might be arbitrary, and have no real basis in either the Bible or in their own lives. At times it could oversimplify deep and complex dynamics. Specialists in biblical studies therefore had an essential role in using their knowledge to guide the community's discussion. When used properly, biblical criticism could free the reader from the fundamentalist prison of the letter. However, concern for historicity did not and should not come first for the people of the communities. Mesters turned the tables on the critics and argued that it was they who were in danger of oversimplifying the complexity of the issues. Although historical questions were important in freeing the Bible from the chains of fundamentalist literalism, there was a danger that giving too much weight to historical enquiries will create a new prison of historicism.

Mesters claimed that at the popular level, the community intuitively took a way between these opposite dangers by interpreting the text in a symbolic way that was neither fundamentalist nor historicist. In defence of their approach, he argued that "a symbolic explanation of the facts is not always the product of a naive, uncritical, or prescientific understanding."[26] He described how the people followed their own priorities: "They try to be faithful, not primarily to the meaning the text has in itself (the historical and literal meaning), but to the meaning they discover in the text for their own lives."[27] Historical concerns for the original meaning of the text developed as the people reflected on and examined what they understood the Bible to be saying for their lives and struggles.[28] The people's reading was therefore, always an unfinished interpretation. Understanding was provisional on further experiences and remained open to revision in response to theological scholarship.

Despite the undoubted achievements of the scholarly tradition, the religiously learned never had a monopoly on religious truth. Mesters pointed to the conflicts

---

[24] Mesters, *Defenseless Flower*, p. 107.
[25] Mesters, *Defenseless Flower*, pp. 106–111.
[26] Mesters, *Defenseless Flower*, p. 6.
[27] Mesters, *Defenseless Flower*, p. 9.
[28] Mesters, *Defenseless Flower*, p. 9.

that Jesus provoked when he took the Scriptures away from the experts of his day and started to interpret them in a new way.[29] Jesus did not conduct theology or biblical studies in an academic institution, but through a passionate engagement with the real life issues of first-century Palestine. Liberation theologians would argue that detachment from worldly concerns is a more serious error than involvement with social issues and political struggles.[30] Thus for all its imperfections and potential dangers, Mesters insisted on the legitimacy of the people's reading.[31]

In some places, Mesters even went further and criticized academic exegesis for losing its sense of serving those who strive to live in faith. Whereas academic scholarship was once a radical challenge to the dogmatic use of the Bible, he argued that it has now lost its radical edge.

> Academic exegesis no longer has the courage it had in the first half of this century, when, with excellent results, it criticized the overly dogmatic use of the Bible in the church. Today it no longer has the same courage to see and criticize the overly dogmatic use of the Bible, both inside and outside the church.[32]

For Mesters, the scholarly work of the exegete was not determined by the norms of academia, but guided by the concerns of the communities and the contributions of the people. If liberation hermeneutics failed according to traditional academic standards, then conversely, those traditional academic standards failed according to the basic principles of liberation theology. Liberation theology pressed the church and the academy to choose the values that were most important in Latin America.

Liberation hermeneutics should be understood within the context of the 1970s two-fold option for the poor: political and epistemological. In retrospect, it is clear that liberation theology exaggerated and romanticised some of its own contributions arising from the poor and did not always give sufficient attention to other biblical research. However, as with any movement, failures to perfectly fulfill its ideals were not proof that the ideals were in themselves misguided or wrongheaded. If the liberation theology of the 1970s had flaws and weaknesses in its biblical work, it shared them with most other contemporary approaches to constructive theology. Furthermore, assessment of these weak-

---

[29] Mesters, *Defenseless Flower*, pp. 8–9; cf. Segundo's claim that in the New Testament: "It is an historical fact that the people who were *best informed about God's revelation in the Old Testament* let Jesus pass by and failed to see in him the new and definitive divine revelation. The Christian message has come down to us through the *amaretz* of Israel, that is, the people who were less knowledgeable about the law and its interpretation" (*The Liberation of Theology*, p. 82, emphasis original).

[30] Segundo puts it bluntly: "Indeed Jesus seems to go so far as to suggest that one cannot recognize Christ, and therefore come to know God, unless he or she is willing to start with a personal commitment to the oppressed" (*The Liberation of Theology*, p. 81).

[31] Mesters, *Defenseless Flower*, p. 71.

[32] Mesters, *Defenseless Flower*, p. 158.

nesses needs to be balanced against liberation theology's obvious strengths on relating the word to the world, which is likely to prove part of its most enduring legacy. Liberation theologians recognised that the Bible could illuminate and empower the struggle for justice in Latin America. Likewise, they saw that contemporary struggles for justice could illuminate the Bible and generate new insights into its message.[33]

FROM THE NONBELIEVER TO THE NONPERSON

In the 1970s, liberation theologians undertook a process of deepening their reflection on Christian commitment in Latin America and the meaning of liberation. The atmosphere of liberation that characterised the late 1960s deteriorated rapidly in the early 1970s. As the 1970s progressed, the confidence of the previous decade receded. The National Security State, with its apparatus of systematic terror, spread throughout the continent with terrible consequences for the poor and the progressive church. Enrique Dussel described the more cautious mood created by these harsh realities after 1972 at a major meeting of liberation theologians in Mexico in 1975 titled *Liberación y cautiverio* (Liberation and Captivity).[34]

In 1976, the retreat from the early hopes of liberation became even more apparent when Leonardo Boff published his *Teologia do cativeiro e da libertação* (*Theology of Captivity and Liberation*).[35] Speaking especially for Brazil, Boff confirmed: "there is no longer the euphoria of the 1960s, when it was possible to dream of popular liberation on a spectacular scale."[36]

While this shift within liberation theology was already in process, the differences between Latin American liberation and European theology—especially

---

[33] For my own attempt at a liberationist reading of the passion narratives in the light of human rights reports, see D. Tombs, "Crucifixion, State Terror and Sexual Abuse," *Union Seminary Quarterly Review* 53 (Autumn 1999), pp. 89–108.

[34] Nearly forty papers by leading liberation theologians involved at the conference are collected together in E. Ruiz Maldonado (ed.), *Liberación y cautivero: debates en torno al método de la Teología en América Latina* (Encuentro Latinoamericana de Teología. Ciudad México del 11 al 15 de agosto, 1975; Mexico, DF: Clavería, 1975). Dussel's contribution, "Sobre la historia de la teología en America Latina" (pp. 19–68 esp. 58), presented Latin American liberation theology according to three stages of evolution: a time of preparation, from the opening of Vatican II to Medellín (1962–1968); the formulation of a theology of liberation, from post-Medellín to Escorial (1968–1972); and a time of captivity and exile as periods of liberation (after 1972).

[35] The expression "with a white hand" in this chapter's opening citation from Gutiérrez is an acknowledged citation from Leonardo Boff's *Teologia do cativeiro e da libertação* (Lisbon: Multinova, 1976). As used by Gutiérrez and Boff, it was an appropriate shorthand for the political and racial interests of the European colonisers and their modern day descendants. In El Salvador in the late 1970s, it took on a particular ominous association as the name taken by the most brutal of the right-wing death squads that started to operate at this time.

[36] Boff, *Teologia do cativeiro e da libertação*, p. 9; cited in Gibellini, *The Liberation Theology Debate*, p. 2.

the issue of the originality of early works in liberation theology when compared with European political theology—became a subject of acute controversy.[37]

At the 1975 conference in Mexico, Jon Sobrino (a Basque Jesuit who has spent his working life in El Salvador, but completed doctoral studies in Frankfurt) suggested an important difference between European theology and the early works in the new theology coming to the fore in Latin America.[38] According to Sobrino, all modern Christian theology developed within the boundaries set by the Enlightenment, but European and liberation theology reflected responses to the two different phases of the Enlightenment. Sobrino saw the two phases as represented in two key figures: the first in Immanuel Kant; the second in Karl Marx. According to Sobrino, the first phase looked to "the liberation of reason from all authority," whereas the second looked to "not just a liberation of the mind, but a liberation from the misery of the real world."[39]

Six months after the conference, in March 1976, The German Lutheran theologian Jürgen Moltmann—whose work *The Crucified God* was a particular focus in Sobrino's dissertation—wrote "An Open Letter to José Míguez Bonino."[40] Míguez Bonino, an Argentinean Methodist, criticised Moltmann in his recently published *Doing Theology in a Revolutionary Situation*.[41] While he acknowledged that Moltmann's discussion of the liberation of man in *The Crucified God* was a brilliant argument, Míguez Bonino complained that despite Moltmann's deliberate attempt to dialogue with liberation theology, he failed to grasp the basic challenge of Latin American works. As a result, Míguez Bonino said, Moltmann's outlook remained within the circle of European polit-

---

[37] In the early 1970s, Latin American criticism of the failings of progressive European theologians—when read from a Latin American situation—already strained relations between the two groups. The split was particularly clear in Hugo Assmann's remarks at a WCC sponsored conference in Geneva in 1973. Moltmann and Metz already raised questions about liberation theology in a series of talks in Madrid in 1974.

[38] J. Sobrino, "El conocimiento teológico en la teología europea y latinoamericana" in Ruiz Maldonado (ed.), *Liberación y cautivero*, pp. 177–208; ET "Theological Understanding in European and Latin American Theology" in J. Sobrino, *The True Church and the Poor* (trans. M. O'Connell; Maryknoll, N.Y.: Orbis Books, 1984 [Spanish orig. 1981]), pp. 7–38. This conference marked Sobrino's first clear identification with liberation theology, and Dussel's paper credited him as one of the notable new figures in the movement on account of his work on the death of Christ (Dussel, "Sobre la historia de la teología en America Latina," p. 61).

[39] Sobrino, *The True Church and the Poor*, p. 11.

[40] J. Moltmann, "An Open Letter to José Míguez Bonino," *Christianity and Crisis* (29 March 1976), pp. 57–63; reprinted in Hennelly (ed.), *Liberation Theology*, pp. 195–204. Moltmann was well known for his influential works *Theology of Hope* (trans. J. W. Leitch; London: SCM Press, 1967 [German orig. 1964]) and *The Crucified God* (trans. R. A. Wilson and J. Bowden; London: SCM Press, 1974 [German orig. 1973]).

[41] Míguez Bonino picked out Moltmann's *Theology of Hope* and *The Crucified God* on the basis that "Moltmann is the theologian to whom the theology of liberation is most indebted theology and with whom it shares the clearest affinity," *Doing Theology in a Revolutionary Situation*, pp. 144–50 (144).

ical theology.[42] In particular, he complained that Moltmann did not give a tangible content to God's identification with the oppressed.[43] Moltmann addressed his response to Míguez Bonino as a friend.[44] However, there was no hiding the strong feelings in his frank and forceful response to the criticism of European political theology by Míguez Bonino and others.[45] First, he claimed that unlike the new challenges raised by African or Black theology, Latin American liberation theology did not introduce anything comparably new from Latin America. Instead, its novelty was in its use of Marx, as if Marx were a Latin American discovery, when in fact, Marx was European and already well-known to European theology.[46] Second, he argued that the Latin Americans claimed to have turned to the people, but in fact it was fairer to say that they had turned to Marx, and it was wrong to see the two things as the same.[47] On this basis, he praised liberation theology's ideals in its turn to the people, but argued that this was still a task that lay ahead of it and was certainly not a difference between its early works and European theology.

> Theology as pure theology, and even that has been extended and broadened to Marxism and socialism, remains in its own circle. The true radical change that is necessary is still ahead of both the 'political theologians' in the European context and the 'liberation theologians' in the Latin American context. In my opinion they can enter in a thoroughly mutual way into this change—namely, a radical turn toward the people.[48]

---

[42] Míguez Bonino, *Doing Theology in a Revolutionary Situation*, p. 146.

[43] To illustrate this, he cited Moltmann's statements that: "The crucified God is really a God without country and without class. But he is not an apolitical God; he is the God of the poor, of the oppressed, of the humiliated" (Moltmann, *The Crucified God*, p. 305). Then he noted: "But the poor, the oppressed, the humiliated *are a class* and *live in countries*" (emphasis orig., Míguez Bonino, *Doing Theology in a Revolutionary Situation*, p. 148).

[44] He started by saying that he read *Doing Theology in a Revolutionary Situation* in a single sitting and was "as deeply moved by it as I am disturbed" (Hennelly (ed.), *Liberation Theology*, p. 195).

[45] In addition to Moltmann's two main points discussed here—the European nature of Latin American liberation theology and its failure to truly turn to the people—he also defended European theology for its recognition that it did not exist in any sort of revolutionary or even pre-revolutionary context and argued for democratic socialism as the realistic political framework for social justice in Europe (Hennelly, *Liberation Theology*, pp. 200–203).

[46] Thus, he saw even Gutiérrez's *A Theology of Liberation* as offering very little that was distinctively Latin American. Moltmann asked: "Gutiérrez has written an invaluable contribution to European theology. But where is Latin America in it all?" (Hennelly, *Liberation Theology*, p. 195).

[47] "In them one reads more about the sociological theories of others, namely Western socialists, than about the history or the life and suffering of the Latin American people. . . . Marxism and sociology do not bring a theologian into the people but, at least at first, only into the company of Marxists and sociologists" (Hennelly, *Liberation Theology*, p. 199).

[48] Hennelly, *Liberation Theology*, p. 200.

Read in Latin America, the tone of Moltmann's letter seemed another example of arrogant Euro-centrism. He recognised how the early works of liberation theology remained largely dependent on the European tradition, but gave little attention to how liberation theologians were developing their thought through practical engagement with struggles for social justice and in the face of real dangers. His point that an option for Marx could only be an incomplete part of an option for the people was a fair critique of limitations in liberation theology's early works. However, the transition that Moltmann called for was already taking place in the 1970s. The radical turn toward the people that Moltmann challenged liberation theologians to embrace was already underway in liberation theology's extension of its option for the poor, from being a purely political option into a political and epistemological option. While this shift did not show up in the literature until the second part of the decade, it was already well underway after 1972 and had revolutionized liberation from within by 1979. Nonetheless, the exchange with Moltmann may have encouraged liberation theologians to make the shift more explicit and focus on it more directly in their writing from 1976 onwards.

A clear sign of the shift can be seen in August 1976 at the first meeting of the Ecumenical Association of Third World Theologians at Dar-es-Salaam (Tanzania). Gustavo Gutiérrez's paper "Two Theological Perspectives: Liberation Theology and Progressivist Theology" offered further clarification on how liberation theology was distinctive from European theology.[49] In this work, Gutiérrez addressed the strengths as well as the weaknesses of European political theology. His extended review of Metz's contributions—and to a lesser extent Moltmann's—located them in the broad sweep of European history and presented them as facing up to the questions of freedom, the Enlightenment, and a Marxist critique of religion that became so important in the European context. He also noted that after some uncomfortable early encounters, European political theology started to bring these aspects of its work into a fruitful dialogue with liberation theology.[50]

According to Gutiérrez, the fundamental problem that has influenced theology in developed Western nations has been the secular challenge to religious belief. The Christian gospel has been forced to demonstrate its credibility in

---

[49] G. Gutiérrez, "Two Theological Perspectives: Liberation Theology and Progressivist Theology" in S. Torres and V. Fabella (eds.), *The Emergent Gospel: Theology from the Underside of History* (EATWOT Dialogue held in Dar-es-Salaam, Tanzania, 5–12 August 1976; Maryknoll, N.Y.: Orbis Books, 1978), pp. 227–255. The following year he published it in revised form as *Teológia desde el reverso de la historia* (Lima: Centro de Estudios y Publicaciones, 1977); ET "Theology from the Underside of History" in Gutiérrez, *The Power of the Poor in History*, pp. 169–221. Gutiérrez noted that the most lethal assaults on liberation theology came from those who claimed to be concerned with orthodoxy and the magisterium of the church, and that in answering critics such as Moltmann, liberation theology should not lose sight of where the hardest battles were to be waged (p. 170).

[50] Gutiérrez, *The Power of the Poor in History*, p. 185.

the increasingly secularized culture that Bonhoeffer referred to as "a world come of age." Since Schleiermacher, the nonbeliever increasingly set the agenda for theology in Europe and North America.[51] Often, this pushed academic theology into sophisticated philosophical attempts to speak to the progressive modern spirit of nonbelief. Latin American theologians who completed their studies in Europe in the 1950s and 1960s followed this basic orientation.

However, on their return to Latin America the limitations of this outlook became apparent. The challenge of nonbelief that followed from the progressive modern spirit was not the same as the challenges to life experienced by the majority of the Latin American people.[52] As Gutiérrez and other liberation theologians came to see it, the most important concern for theology in Latin America was not the nonbeliever, but the nonperson: the millions who were deprived of basic physical necessities and elementary human rights. According to Gutiérrez:

> This is why our question is not how to speak of God in an adult world. That was the old question asked by progressivist theology. No, the interlocutor of the theology of liberation is the 'nonperson,' the human being who is not considered human by the present social order—the exploited social classes, marginalized ethnic groups, and despised cultures. Our question is how to tell the nonperson, the nonhuman, that God is love, and that this love makes us all brothers and sisters.[53]

Gutiérrez insisted that doing theology for the nonperson involved a rereading of history and Christian faith from the vantage point of the victim:

> History, where God reveals himself and where we proclaim him, must be *reread from the side of the poor*. The history of humanity has been written 'with a white hand,' from the side of the dominators. History's losers have another outlook. History must be read from a point of departure in their struggles, their resistance, their hopes.[54]

Gutiérrez's phrase "theology from the underside of history" signified this starting point in the lives of the marginalized—the epistemological option in which the lives of the poor were the *locus* of theology (see Chapter 8). Committing oneself to this option made a difference to which questions would be asked as well as to how they would be answered. Gutiérrez pointed out that the questions

---

[51] See F. D. Schleiermacher, *On Religion: Speeches to its Cultured Despisers* (trans. J. Oman; New York: Harper & Row, 1958 [ET 1894]).

[52] In as much as any social group in Latin America embodied the progressive modern spirit, it was the cultural elite who were much more likely to be part of the problem for the poor, rather than part of the solution. Speaking only to this elite about belief would have little value for the lives of the poor.

[53] Gutiérrez, *The Power of the Poor in History*, p. 193. Clodovis and Leonardo Boff made the same point when they said: "The gospel is not aimed chiefly at modern men and women with their critical spirit, but first and foremost at nonpersons, those whose basic dignity and rights are refused them" (*Introducing Liberation Theology*, p. 8).

[54] Gutiérrez, *The Power of the Poor in History*, p. 201.

and concerns of the marginalized often have less to do with abstract theology and more to do with practical social, economic, and political issues. A theology that is responsive to them would have to reflect this, but it is no less theological than one that is focussed on nonbelief.

CELAM III AND OPPOSITION IN THE CHURCH

A further factor in liberation theology's development in the 1970s was the growing opposition that it faced in some church circles. The 1971 and 1974 Synods of Bishops both stressed social justice. The papal documents related to the Synods, *Octogesima Adveniens* and *Evangelii Nuntiandi* were both broadly supportive of liberation theology. *Evangelii Nuntiandi* went even further than *Octogesima Adveniens* to use—and thereby at least implicitly endorse—the language of liberation. It stated:

> The Church, as the Bishops repeated, has the duty to proclaim the liberation of millions of human beings many of whom are her own children—the duty of assisting the birth of this liberation, of giving witness to it, of ensuring that it is complete.[55]

However, just as *Octogesima Adveniens* expressed cautions over the use of Marxism, in a similar way *Evangelii Nuntiandi* stressed that liberation must not be a reductionist concept.[56] Both documents rejected liberation theology's perceived endorsement of violence as a legitimate means of social change.[57] There was therefore a lack of clarity in the Vatican's position on liberation theology. Vatican social teaching emphasised support for concern for the poor and even adopted the language of liberation in some places, but it seemed that Latin American liberation theology was still viewed with extreme reservation.

Meanwhile, conservative opposition to liberation theology grew steadily in some Latin American church circles. In 1972 at the CELAM annual meeting in Sucre (Bolivia), a much more conservative wing within CELAM captured key administrative positions within the organisation. The Colombian bishop Alfonso López Trujillo was elected as secretary general and reshaped CELAM's previously progressive outlook to reflect his own conservatism. Together with the Belgian Jesuit Roger Vekemans, he set up a new conservative periodical, *Tierra Nueva* (Bogotá), which maintained a steady stream of fiercely critical arti-

---

[55] *Evangelii Nuntiandi*, § 30.

[56] "As the kernel and center of his Good News, Christ proclaims salvation, this great gift of God which is salvation from everything which oppresses man but which is above all liberation from sin and Evil One" (§ 9). Returning to the same theme later on *Evangelii Nuntiandi* emphasised that the liberation that evangelization proclaims "cannot be contained in the simple and restricted dimension of economics, politics, and social or cultural life; it must envisage the whole man, in all his aspects, right up to and including his openness to the absolute, even the divine Absolute" (§ 33).

[57] *Octogesima Adveniens* in *Catholic Social Thought*, pp. 294–295; *Evangelii Nuntiandi*, § 37. In both cases, Paul VI seemed to be backing away from recognising the possibilities described in *Populorum Progressio*, § 31.

cles against liberation theology.[58] With active support from the Vatican *curia*, Trujillo rose rapidly from auxiliary bishop to cardinal. For conservatives, the third extraordinary CELAM meeting (The Present and Future of Evangelization in Latin America) offered a decisive opportunity to reverse the direction taken at Medellín in 1968. After his election in 1972, López Trujillo worked hard to ensure that he and his allies would be in a strong enough position to outmanoeuvre the bishops who were more supportive of liberation theology.

CELAM III was originally scheduled for 1978, to mark the ten years since Medellín. In preparation for the conference, López Trujillo manoeuvred sympathetic bishops to key posts to chair committees and prepare draft documents.[59] To prevent the influence of progressive theologians who made such an impact at Medellín, he also took firm control of the official invitation list for theological advisers.[60] Finally, he also made arrangements to isolate the delegates at the conference from outside influences, and restricted the media's involvement to formal press briefings with questions submitted in writing in advance.

However, López Trujillo's careful preparations for the conference hit an early setback when his Consultative Document stirred strong reactions from progressive church leaders and community groups throughout the continent when it was published in 1977.[61] The Brazilian church led the protests and the president of CELAM—Cardinal Aloisio Lorscheider of Fortaleza in Brazil—commissioned a redrafted Working Document more acceptable to progressives.[62] Meanwhile, the deaths of Paul VI and John Paul I meant that the meeting had to be postponed until 1979. This gave the progressives a little more time to react to the developments to ensure that they would be ready to defend their positions when the conference finally met.[63]

In January 1979, John Paul II travelled to Mexico on a trip to inaugurate the CELAM meeting, three months after his election as the first non-Italian

---

[58] Vekemans had previously been an adviser to the government of Eduardo Frei in Chile and left shortly after Allende came to power. His opposition to Christians for Socialism and liberation theology was expressed in his lengthy, but untranslated book *Teología de la liberación y Cristianos por el Socialismo* (Bogotá: CEDIAL, 1976).

[59] Cardinal Sebastiano Baggio, who was president of the Pontifical Commission for Latin America, gave him influential support in this task.

[60] In total there were 350 participants, which included 175 elected bishops from national conferences, 12 bishops appointed by the Vatican, and 16 official theological advisers. The rest were representatives from religious orders, churches in other continents, or other denominations.

[61] CELAM, "Documento de Consulta" (Bogotá: CELAM, 1977).

[62] CELAM, "Documento de Trabajo" (Bogotá: CELAM, 1978). Lorscheider was one of the few progressives on the CELAM executive, but was nonetheless able to use his influence to great effect.

[63] On attitudes to the forthcoming conference amongst progressives, see esp. the collection of articles published together as "Puebla: Moment of Decision for the Latin American Church" as a special edition of the journal *Crosscurrents* 28.1 (1978), pp. 1–103.

Pope for 455 years. At the famous shrine of Guadalupe (about twelve miles north of Mexico City), John Paul II concelebrated mass with the Latin American bishops.[64] In his homily, the Pope affirmed Medellín and its teaching on integral liberation as "a call of hope towards more Christian and more human goals."[65] However, he also told the bishops that at times the interpretations of this had not been beneficial to the church and he stressed that the option for the poor was preferential not exclusive.

Later the same day—in an address to the priests and religious of Mexico—he cautioned them against understanding themselves as social and political leaders and repeated his concern that an exaggerated interest in temporal problems could easily be a source of division.[66]

The following day, the Pope gave a lengthy address at the opening session of the conference itself in the small city of Puebla de Los Angeles (about 70 miles southeast of Mexico City). He encouraged the bishops to take the positive elements of Medellín as their starting point, but to let their debates be guided by the Puebla Working Document so as avoid incorrect interpretations.[67] He instructed the bishops that they could not keep silent when rereadings of Christ created confusion about the Gospel.[68] In a clear warning to the progressives—and as a prequel to the confrontations of the 1980s—the Pope put particular stress on the importance of church unity.[69] After establishing these guides the Pope discussed the challenges to the church as "Defenders and Promoters of Human Dignity."[70] He drew on his predecessor's *Evangelii Nuntiandi* to affirm that a correct and nonreductionist understanding of the Christian idea of liberation was essential.

---

[64] An account of the Pope's journey to Mexico and the entire text of his speeches may be found in *John Paul II in Mexico: His Collected Speeches* (London: Collins, 1979). His homily at Guadalupe and addresses at Puebla are also included—in an alternative translation—in CELAM, *Puebla: Evangelization at Present and in the Future of Latin America: Conclusions* (Official English Edition of the Third General Conference of Latin American Bishops, Puebla, Mexico, 1979; Slough: St. Paul Publications; London: Catholic Institute for International Relations, 1980 [Spanish orig. 1979]), pp. 1–26.

[65] *John Paul II in Mexico*, pp. 39–46 (44).

[66] *John Paul II in Mexico*, pp. 47–50. Likewise, in his address to the women's religous orders that followed he warned against options for the poor that arise from socio-political options rather than the gospel (see *John Paul II in Mexico*, pp. 51–52).

[67] See *John Paul II in Mexico*, pp. 66–83 (67). Later in his speech the Pope emphasised the importance of a solid Christology for their work. He did not mention any names, but he pointed to specific errors to be avoided. For example: "In some cases Christ's divinity, is passed over in silence. . . . In other cases, people claim to show Jesus as politically committed, as one who fought against oppression and the authorities, and also as one involved in the class struggle. The idea of Christ as a political figure, a revolutionary, as the subversive man from Nazareth, does not tally with the Church's catechesis" (p. 69).

[68] *John Paul II in Mexico*, p. 71.

[69] *John Paul II in Mexico*, pp. 75–76.

[70] *John Paul II in Mexico*, pp. 78–82.

While none of these addresses made an explicit condemnation of liberation theology, many media reports focussed almost exclusively on his words of caution, rather than those parts of the speeches that might be seen as offering some support.[71] Given the expectations at the time, it was hardly surprising that the concerns the Pope raised and the way in which he presented them were widely seen as a straightforward rebuke of liberation theology. For liberation theologians, it was an inauspicious start to an already difficult meeting.

Gutiérrez and other liberation theologians that attended Medelin in the capacity of theological advisers were pointedly excluded from invitation to the meeting at Puebla. López Trujillo was determined to restrict access to the proceediongs. However, a number of them travelled anyway and set up an office in the town. At first, it seemed that there was little that the uninvited advisers could do. Security at the high-walled Palafoxian Major Seminary on the outskirts of the town was tight and outsiders were turned away. However, this did not stop some progressive bishops from ignoring requests to remain within the seminary walls and visiting them outside. A pattern quickly developed in which some bishops visited the group and showed them copies of documents under discussion. The theological advisers then worked at night to discuss and respond to conference drafts and provide new material for the bishops in the morning. Some of their work then made its way into the conference discussions and final documents.

As the conference progressed, the strict security loosened and contact between those outside and those inside the seminary increased. Whereas the Medellín conference attracted little attention outside the church, the media interest at Puebla was intense with up to 4000 journalists present. López Trujillo's attempts to isolate the bishops from the media had a major setback when shortly before the conference, he inadvertently handed a journalist a tape which included comments outlining his strategy for the Puebla meeting. The tape included a frank discussion of his hopes to manipulate the proceedings and derisory comments about a number of progressive bishops including his predecessor Eduardo Pironio and the Jesuit General Superior, Pedro Arrupe. When the Mexican newspaper *Uno Más Uno* published his comments he was forced to take a much lower profile, and his ability to enforce his plan was severely weakened.[72]

On top of this, at the outset of the conference the bishops themselves rejected López Trujillo's plans to appoint CELAM staff to the steering committee

---

[71] A little later during his visit—when speaking to poor *campesinos* (peasant farmers) in Oaxaca—the Pope was equally strong in advocating the importance of social concerns in Christian life. Here, it might seem that liberation theology's strong stance on social justice was not wrong in itself. Rather, the problem appeared to be its political implications, especially the way that liberation theology stressed the political implications and the Marxist elements in their early works.

[72] See J. Filochowski, "Medellin to Puebla" in Catholic Institute for International Relations (ed.), *Reflections on Puebla* (London: Catholic Institute for International Relations, 1980), pp. 19–21 (esp. 15–16).

for the 21 commissions that worked on the documents. Instead, the bishops elected five of their own number for this task. The progressive Archbishop of Panama, Marcos McGrath, was then elected as their head, ensuring a much greater balance of power between the different wings of the church. Although the progressives still did not have anything like the influence they had at Medellín, they at least had a much stronger position than was expected. This helped to ensure that the conference would not result in a flat condemnation of liberation theology or the popular church.[73]

In general, the final Puebla statements offered a more cautious perspective than those at Medellin. For example, the passages on the use of Marxism drew attention to the dangers of Marxist analysis that assumed aspects of a Marxist world-view that are not compatible with a Christian vision.[74] They reaffirmed Paul VI's teaching at the beginning of the decade in *Octogesima Adveniens* (14 May 1971).[75] Although liberation theology after 1976 showed clear signs of a switch in emphasis, the continuing fear of Marx's influence indicated some of the problems that still lay ahead for liberation theologians in the 1980s.

However, many of the documents were inconsistent in their emphasis.[76] In fact, a number of key phrases appeared in the final documents that reflected the concerns of liberation theology and gave strong endorsement to the option for the poor and the base communities. The most significant of these is "A Preferential Option for the Poor" (chapter 1 of part 4 in the final conclusions) in the context of "A Missionary Church Serving Evangelization in Latin America." This starts with the bold statements:

> With renewed hope in the vivifying power of the Spirit, we are going to take up once again the position of the Second General Conference of the Latin American episcopate in Medellín, which adopted a clear and prophetic option expressing preference for, and solidarity with, the poor. We do this despite the distortions and interpretations of some, who vitiate the spirit of Medellín, and despite the disregard and even hostility of others. We affirm the need for conversion on the part of the whole Church to a preferential option for the poor, an option aimed at their integral liberation (§ 1134).

---

[73] Newspaper accounts often offered simplistic versions of the conference as a rejection of liberation theology, and the Pope's speeches were usually cited in support of this. However, the Pope's activities and speeches during his visit reveal a much more complex position than some newspaper accounts suggested.

[74] Puebla, §§ 544–545.

[75] Puebla, §§ 544, citing *Octogesima Adveniens* § 34 (see Chapter 6).

[76] The actual influence of liberation theology on the final documents is also open to debate. For example, Edward Cleary, suggests that Boff and Sobrino's work on Christology had a significant impact on Puebla where—unlike Medellín—Christology suffuses the final document (E. Cleary, *The Church in Latin America Today*, p. 97). However, Phillip Berryman argues that although Puebla is marked by a Christology, it is a traditional view of Christ in glory, rather than a liberationist Christ in conflict that is most marked and that this could only have been deliberate.

In a footnote to the next section, § 1135, the bishops listed more specifically who they principally identified as the poor in terms broader than economic poverty. These included:

> our indigenous peoples, peasants, manual laborers, marginalized urban dwellers and, in particular the women of these social groups. The women are doubly oppressed and marginalized.

They thereby endorsed the extension of the social/political option for the poor that emerged between *Rerum Novarum* and Medellín to a more inclusive application for other oppressed social groups.[77] In addition, Puebla reflected the developments of the 1970s in which the option for the poor became a process by which the church was converted by the poor and reoriented around the poor. The second new attitude shown to the poor was also shown here:

> Commitment to the poor and oppressed and the rise of the grassroots communities have helped the Church to discover the evangelizing potential of the poor. For the poor challenge the Church constantly, summoning it to conversion.[78]

Lumen Gentium said that the church recognised "in those who are poor and who suffer, the image of her founder."[79] Some passages at Puebla, perhaps influenced by new work in Latin America, made this even more emphatic. For example:

> This situation of pervasive extreme poverty takes on very concrete faces in real life. In these faces we ought to recognize the suffering features of Christ the Lord, who questions and challenges us.[80]

The immediate aftermath of Puebla was marked by the same divisions and mixed results.[81] On the progressive side, liberation theologians took great satisfaction from turning a difficult situation into at least partial victory by avoiding clear condemnation. They were also able to interpret the meeting as an endorsement of the option for the poor and repeat important phrases from the documents.[82] However, it was equally clear that considerable opposition to

---

[77] *Rerum Novarum* suggested that the poor have a special claim for consideration, but only discussed its relevance in terms of the state's duties. Medellín pointed to the special claims of the poor as an option for the church.

[78] Puebla, § 1147. *Rerum Novarum*, §29; see also *Quadragesimo Anno*, §25.

[79] *Lumen Gentium*, § 8 (see Chapter 4).

[80] § 31. The social groups that are especially identified include: "the faces of young children, struck down by poverty ... the faces of young people, who are disorientated because they cannot find their place in society ... the faces of indigenous peoples, and frequently of the Afro-Americans ... the faces of the peasants ... the faces of laborers ... the faces of the underemployed and unemployed ... the faces of the marginalized and overcrowded urban dwellers ... the faces of old people" (§§ 32–39).

[81] For a collection of generally positive views on Puebla, see John Eagleson and Philip Scharper (eds.), *Puebla and Beyond: Documentation and Commentary* (trans. John Drury; Maryknoll, N.Y.: Orbis Books, 1980).

[82] For example, in El Salvador, Archbishop Romero drew on Puebla's assessment of

liberation theology remained amongst many bishops. Furthermore, conservative opponents of liberation theology within the church were more determined than ever to oppose it. In March 1979, López Trujillo (who had been Secretary of CELAM since 1972) defeated the progressive Archbishop McGrath of Panama in the elections for Lorscheider's successor as President of CELAM. The result ensured that it would be a more conservative CELAM in the next decade, and this meant that liberation theologians would have to work within a more difficult context within the church.

CONCLUSION

The communal readings of the Bible offered in base communities generated new interpretations of the Bible that theologians drew on in their own understanding of the reality of faith in Latin America. This meant that liberation theology would not be a scholarly exercise undertaken by professional theologians and then offered to the poor. The active participation of the poor would be necessary if the church was to be not just for the poor, but also a church of the poor. The dialogical methodology that developed in response to this was an important advance on Catholic Action's pastoral circle of see-judge-act. Liberation theology's hermeneutical circle radicalized the potentially conservative tendencies of the earlier model in each of its mediations: it extended the field of concerns from the personal to the communal and political; it emphasized the importance of a deeper social analysis; and it included active participation in the struggle against social injustice as an essential part of the process.

In the 1990s, commentators on the CEBs asked searching questions about whether their numerical strength and democratic egalitarianism had been exaggerated and the extent of their biblical insights romanticised.[83] It is certainly important to recognise that the account of the hermeneutical circle given in this chapter—based on the Boffs—is more at the level of theoretical ideal than actual practice. Caution in judging how well liberation theology lived up to its own ideals is important if overestimating its achievements is to be avoided. Nonetheless, the way that the Bible was read in the CEBs offered a practical way to incarnate both the political and epistemological options for the poor in

---

the social injustice in Latin America for his fourth Pastoral Letter (6 August 1979). Addressing the Salvadoran people, Romero stated: "That 'muted cry' of wretchedness that Medellín heard ten years ago, Puebla now describes as 'loud and clear, increasing in intensity, and at times full of menace' (§ 89). It calls the characteristics that delineate this situation of injustice 'the most devastating and humiliating kind of scourge' (§29). They are infant mortality, the housing shortage, health problems, starvation wages, unemployment, malnutrition, no job security and so on." See Romero, *Voice of the Voiceless*, pp. 114–161.

[83] See, for example, P. Berryman, *Religion in the Megacity: Catholic and Protestant Portraits from Latin America* (Maryknoll, N.Y.: Orbis Books, 1996); J. Burdick, *Looking for God in Brazil: The Progressive Catholic Church in Urban Brazil's Religious Arena* (Berkeley: University of California Press, 1993).

a way that gave new dignity and hope for thousands of Christians in Latin America.

Looking back over the whole decade, a clear shift can be discerned. In the early years, Gutiérrez and others developed the insights from the 1960s into a methodological principle (theology as critical reflection on action), linked to the powerful terminology of liberation and based on a political commitment to a new pastoral approach (solidarity with the poor and protest against their poverty). The emergence of base communities as a social network orientated to social transformation gave liberation theology a social outlet at a popular level. However, as time passed, work with the communities started to reorien- ate liberation theologians. As repression and persecution increased, the poor started to convert liberation theology. After 1975, publications put less emphasis on the radical analysis and revolutionary message and started to focus on God's special presence in the suffering and struggles of the poor as a distinctive epis- temological principle.

Part 4

The God of Life
1980–1989

CHAPTER TEN

Deepening the Commitment and Expanding the View

> How are we to do theology *while Ayacucho lasts?* How are we to speak of the God of life when cruel murder on a massive scale goes on in 'the corner of the dead'? How are we to preach the love of God amid such profound contempt for human life?
>
> Gustavo Gutiérrez[1]

INTRODUCTION

In the 1980s, liberation theology's preferential option for the poor began to face a new range of challenges. At a political level, the decade was notable for a transition to democracy in many countries.[2] However, despite the return to civilian rule in most countries, hopes of economic and political liberation faded. The 1980s have been described as the lost decade for development. Silent revolutions ushered in neo-liberal free-market policies across the region.[3] The gap

---

[1] G. Gutiérrez, *On Job*, p. 102 (emphasis original).

[2] Democracy was restored in Argentina in 1983. After defeat in the Malvinas/Falkland Islands War with Britain in 1982, the military were so discredited that they were forced to accept a speedy return to civilian rule. Raúl Alfonsín won the October 1983 election and was inaugurated as president in December 1983. In Brazil, General João Baptista Figueiredo (1979–1985) continued the slow process of *abertura* (opening up) initiated by his predecessor General Geisel (1974–1979) and allowed more political parties to participate in elections, although still under very restricted conditions. In January 1985, the opposition party candidate Tancredo Neves was the surprise winner of an indirect election for president in the electoral college. The military accepted the result with some reluctance and Brazil prepared for a return to full democracy after over twenty years of military rule. When Neves died before he could assume the presidency his more conservative deputy, José Sarney (1985–1990), took his place.

[3] For an accessible discussion of the silent revolutions and their impact, see D. Green, *Silent Revolution: The Rise of Market Economics in Latin America* (London: Cassell and Latin America Bureau, 1995).

between rich countries and poor countries widened, and the standard of living of many in Latin America actually fell over the course of the decade.

At an economic level, the foreign debt crisis proved a disaster for Latin America. The total debt for Latin America and the Caribbean was under $300 billion in 1981. It grew to $450 billion by 1990.[4] Many of the loans were first taken out at low interest in the 1970s when Western banks encouraged reckless borrowing to recycle the petro-dollars built up after the 1973 price rises in oil. Often, this money was wasted through inappropriate projects, military spending, and simple corruption. It did little to promote efficient long-term productive capacity. In the 1980s, interest rates soared, and Latin American countries found themselves sinking into a debt trap with escalating and unpayable debts.

New Latin American governments found that they could not escape the legacy of their predecessors. To make their payments, they slashed subsidies on goods the poor needed to survive (such as food and transport subsidies) and cut back welfare services such as education and health. When even this failed to resolve the problem, some—most famously Mexico and Peru—reneged on the debt and refused to pay. However, they faced harsh sanctions from the international community that quickly forced them back into line. Others desperate to maintain their international creditworthiness turned instead to the International Monetary Fund (IMF). This helped to restructure the debt at the cost of following stringent measures imposed to cut essential services yet further.

To add to the difficulties, civil conflicts in Central America and Peru wreaked havoc on the already strained social fabric and economic infrastructure. In Peru, the Maoist guerrilla movement, Shining Path (Sendero Luminoso), and the government's counter-insurgency inflicted untold misery on thousands of innocent victims and anyone who actively sought to hold a middle ground.[5] In Nicaragua, the U.S.-backed "contras" operating from Honduras blew up schools and medical clinics built by the new Sandinista government. In El Salvador, a full-scale civil war broke out between the U.S.-backed government and a coalition of guerrilla groups united under the title of Farabundo Martí National Liberation Front (FMLN).[6] In Guatemala, state violence against indigenous Mayan communities reached genocidal proportions in the period 1981–1983.

---

[4] Data from U.N. Economic Commission for Latin American and Caribbean cited in Green, *Silent Revolutions*, p. 68.

[5] On Shining Path, see D. Poole and G. Rénique, *Peru: Time of Fear* (London: Latin America Bureau, 1992); D. S. Palmer (ed.), *Shining Path of Peru* (London: Hurst and Company, 1992).

[6] Martí was a leader in El Salvador's communist led peasant uprising of 1932, the first communist revolt in the hemisphere. However, the 1932 revolt failed and the brutal reprisals (in which 30,000 peasants were massacred) left a deep scar in Salvadoran society; see T. P. Anderson, *Matanza: El Salvador's Communist Revolt* (Lincoln: University of Nebraska Press, 1971). On the civil war in El Salvador in the 1980s, see J. Dunkerley, *Power in the Isthmus: A Political History of Modern Central America* (London: Verso, 1988), pp. 267–333.

Meanwhile, the literature of liberation in the 1980s moved on to explore new areas as it continued the post-1975 trend from explicitly political to more directly pastoral reflection. The commitment to the poor remained, but the tone was significantly less polemical and militant. Gutiérrez's books put less emphasis on political theory and social analysis and more on spirituality and contemplation. When Gutiérrez republished a revised version of *A Theology of Liberation* in 1988, this shift in tone and expression became even clearer.[7] His introduction to the revised edition clarified the key changes addressed in this chapter and concluded with an anecdotal story that reflected the continuity and change in his thinking.

Some years ago, a journalist asked whether I would write *A Theology of Liberation* today as I had two decades earlier. In answer I said that though the years passed by, the book remained the same, whereas I was alive and therefore changing and moving forward thanks to experiences, to observations made on the book, and to lectures and discussions. When he persisted, I asked whether in a love letter to his wife today he would use the same language that he used twenty years ago; he said he would not, but he acknowledged that his love perdured. My book is a love letter to God, to the church, and to the people to which I belong. Love remains alive, but it grows deeper and changes its manner of expression.[8]

THE GOD OF LIFE AND SPIRITUALITY OF LIBERATION

The insurgency and counter-insurgency that convulsed Peru in the 1980s had a profound effect on Gutiérrez's work. Increasingly, he reflected on the mystery of what he called "the God of Life" in a society characterised by unjust and premature death.[9]

His *God of Life* was first published in 1982 and then reissued in a substantially expanded version in 1989. The later version opened with the words of two representatives from Villa El Salvador (a shantytown close to Lima) who addressed John Paul II on his visit to Peru.[10] Gutiérrez recalled their words of greeting to the Pope: "Holy Father, we are hungry. . . . We suffer affliction, we

---

[7] G. Gutiérrez, *A Theology of Liberation: History, Politics and Salvation* (trans. and ed. C. Inda and J. Eagleson; Maryknoll, N.Y.: Orbis Books; London: SCM Press, 2nd ed., 1988). This allowed the language to be updated to become more gender inclusive and some other minor changes to the text. For example, the section in chapter 12 that was previously "Christian Brotherhood and Class Struggle" (pp. 272–279) was updated and reformulated as "Faith and Social Conflict" (pp. 156–161), but the basic stance remained the same.

[8] Gutiérrez, *The God of Life*, p. xlvi.

[9] "Human life unfolds within an option for death or an option for life," G. Gutiérrez, *We Drink from Our Own Wells*, pp. 69–70.

[10] The papacy of John Paul II has been particular noteworthy for the energy and frequency of his international visits. His 1985 visit to Latin America lasted 11 days (26 January–6 February) and included visits to Venezuela, Ecuador, Peru, and Trinidad and Tobago.

lack work, we are sick. Our hearts are crushed by suffering as we see our tuber-
cular wives giving birth, our children dying, our sons and daughters growing
up weak and without a future." Gutiérrez noted: "The simplicity and fright-
fulness of these opening words set the tone for all that follows. . . . The reality
of unjust and premature death is described in utterly unadorned language. Out
of it comes, with renewed force, a profession of faith: But despite all this, *we
believe in the God of life.*"[11]

Gutiérrez's style of reflection in the book is markedly different from *A Theology
of Liberation*. In *The God of Life* Gutiérrez drew almost exclusively on biblical
texts in the light of the Latin American situation and church teaching. There
was minimal reference to the social sciences or philosophical influences. Throughout the work, Gutiérrez pointed to the biblical understanding of God as liberator and protector of the poor. In a particularly helpful section on idolatry,
Gutiérrez contrasted the God of life with the idol worship that the Bible condemns.[12] He noted that the Bible saw idolatry—not atheism—as the rejection
of God. He observed that Latin America claimed to be a Christian continent,
but it was the only continent where the majority were at the same time Christian
and poor.[13] The continent's rich elite claimed to serve God, but Gutiérrez
claimed that their real commitments were to the modern idols of death. Their
true loyalties were to mammon and worldly power.

Gutiérrez's understanding of idolatry—as a yearning for power and money
that stops at nothing—offered a powerful critique of Latin America's sinful situation. Idolatrous competitors replaced the God of life in the hearts of the powerful. Material wealth and false security were prized above the true God of justice
and life. Gutiérrez saw the biblical condemnation of idols as a rejection of
human powers when they were raised above God's powers of creation. He
exposed and condemned the same mentality amongst the powerful of Latin
America. Their idolatrous concern for wealth stemmed from a self-idolatry
regarding their own power. Idolatry was on the side of death against life because
"idolatry is a murderous god."[14] Gutiérrez pointed to the suffering of the poor
that resulted from different idolatries in the Bible and showed how the idolatry
of money demanded human victims.

> The idolatry of money, of this fetish produced by the work of human hands,
> is indissolubly and causally connected with the death of the poor. If we thus
> go to the root of the matter, idolatry reveals its full meaning: it works against
> the God of the Bible, who is a God of life. Idolatry is death; God is life.[15]

At the 1980 International Ecumenical Congress of Theology (held in São Paulo
under the auspices of the Ecumenical Association of Third World Theologians),

---

[11] G. Gutiérrez, *The God of Life*, p. xi.
[12] Gutiérrez, *The God of Life*, pp. 48–64.
[13] Gutiérrez, *The God of Life*, p. 48.
[14] Gutiérrez, *The God of Life*, p. 53.
[15] Gutiérrez, *The God of Life*, p. 56.

the collective group of Latin American theologians (both Protestant and Catholic) spoke clearly of the importance of spirituality and the need for it to be taken up in the future writings, meetings, and events.[16] Not surprisingly, works on spirituality were one of the distinctive features of liberation theology in the 1980s, and both Gutiérrez and Sobrino were particularly prominent.[17]

Gutiérrez already spoke in *A Theology of Liberation* of the "great need for a spirituality of liberation."[18] His book *We Drink from Our Own Wells* was an opportunity to work this out in much more detail and signalled many of the significant new themes and ideas that would be important in his 1980s publications.[19] It seems that Gutiérrez wrote the book in some haste, and it has been suggested that one of his concerns was to head-off criticism from conservative traditionalists and critics in the Vatican (who claimed that his work reduced theology to politics and ignored spiritual concerns). However, many of the themes were important for him from the very beginning. It would be quite wrong to think of spirituality as a belated introduction into Gutiérrez's political outlook for purely pragmatic reasons.[20] Gutiérrez's work as a pastor always kept him rooted in a concern for spirituality, and the suggestion that he replaced spirituality with politics in the 1970s does not do justice to his continuing commitment, despite his international prominence, to the everyday life of his parish.

---

[16] The International Ecumenical Congress of Theology, São Paulo, Brazil, 20 February– 2 March 1980; see "Final Document" in Torres and Eagleson, *The Challenge of Basic Christian Communities*, pp. 231–246. For more on the conference and the role of EAT-WOT, see below.

[17] See also S. Galilea, "The Spirituality of Liberation," *The Way* 25.3 (July 1985), pp. 186–194.

[18] Gutiérrez, *A Theology of Liberation*, p. 136.

[19] G. Gutiérrez, *We Drink from Our Own Wells*. The book came out of the lectures Gutiérrez gave at the XII Jornadas de Reflexión Teológica (a theology summer school organized by the Catholic University of Peru in Lima, 8–19 February 1982). A recollection of the summer school (and especially Gutiérrez's lectures on spirituality) is offered in H. Nouwen, *¡Gracias!: A Latin American Journal* (Maryknoll, N.Y.: Orbis Books, 2nd ed. 1993 [1983]), pp. 132–146; Nouwen also contributed a foreword to *We Drink from Our Own Wells* (pp. xii–xxi). Some of the material in *We Drink from Our Own Wells* was published in a slightly earlier form in the article by Gutiérrez, "Drink from Your Own Well," *Concilium*, 159 (1982), pp. 38–45.

[20] The explicit emphasis was certainly new when compared to the 1970s, but the differences should not be overstated for either Gutiérrez or the liberation theology movement as a whole. In a footnote, Gutiérrez (*We Drink from Our Own Wells*, p. 1 n. 2) mentioned significant works on liberation spirituality that had already been published, for example, L. Boff, *Vida segundo o espiritu* (Petrópolis, RJ: Editora Vozes, 1982). Furthermore, attention to spirituality was already featured as a section in *A Theology of Liberation*, pp. 203–208, and in his first footnote (*We Drink from Our Own Wells*, p. 1) Gutiérrez explained that "Ever since I published that book [*A Theology of Liberation*] I have been intending to develop the theme of these pages more fully. Only now has it been possible for me to do so; the delay has the advantage that I can now draw on the experiences and reflections of so many others in recent years."

For Gutiérrez, spirituality was the following of Jesus in everyday life. This required action and prayer being kept together.[21] As in A *Theology of Liberation*, he insisted on the integral nature of liberation and the essential connection between spirituality and the social and political sphere.[22] He rejected notions of spirituality that separated the spirit from the body and argued that:

> Life according to the Spirit is therefore not an existence at the level of the soul and in opposition to or apart from the body; it is an existence *in accord with life*, love, peace, and justice (the great values of the reign of God) and *against death*.[23]

The sources of an authentic Latin American spirituality—the wells from which he encouraged people to drink—were the historical struggles against oppression and testimonies of hope and resurrection that occupied the faithful in Latin America.[24] The starting point for this spirituality was the experiences of the poor and those who stood by them. Gutiérrez wished to root spirituality in the life, struggles, and hopes of those who worked for the kingdom of God in Latin America. Within this framework, Gutiérrez repeatedly returned to the premature and unjust deaths of the poor and the challenges that they posed. He interwove reflection on their experiences with biblical reflections and Christian tradition. Latin American sources—ranging from the unpublished testimonies of base community members at meetings to the publications of Latin American bishops—shape the distinctively Latin America ethos of the work.[25]

Authentic spirituality is following Jesus in contemplation and action, solidarity with the oppressed, hope in a world of suffering, the option for life in the face of death, and faith in resurrection. Authentic spirituality, however, must have a social and communal dimension. It is not just something within the inner life of the individual. Gutiérrez made this clear in the final paragraph of the book:

---

[21] Gutiérrez, *We Drink from Our Own Wells*, p. 5 and p. 37. Gutiérrez criticised approaches to spirituality that failed to promote this essential link and noted two particularly common mistakes. First, to see spirituality as a matter for a relative minority, either those called to life in religious orders or laity who turned away from the everyday activities of the world. Second, to see spirituality as an individual and interior matter of people for whom intentions took precedence over outcomes and often with little concern for the outside world. He notes that these traits make possible what Puebla referred to as "the spirituality of evasion" (*Puebla*, § 826).

[22] See Gutiérrez, *We Drink from Our Own Wells*, p. 29 n. 16, where Gutiérrez refers back to his formulation of this in A *Theology of Liberation*, pp. 36–37, 143–144 (see above).

[23] Gutiérrez, *We Drink from Our Own Wells*, p. 71.

[24] Gutiérrez's title deliberately echoes the words of St. Bernard of Clairvaux in *De Consideratione* that when it comes to spirituality everyone "must drink from their own well."

[25] Because it takes the ordinary and the everyday as its starting point, the Spanish liberation theologian Pedro Trigo SJ (who studied under Gutiérrez in Lima and worked with base communities in Ecuador and Venezuela) described *We Drink from Our Own Wells*, rather than A *Theology of Liberation*, as the "first stammerings" of liberation theology (cited in P. Berryman, *Religion in the Megacity*, p. 118).

Spirituality is a community enterprise. It is a passage of a people through the solitude and dangers of the desert, as it carves out its own way in the following of Jesus Christ. This spiritual experience is the well from which we must drink. From it we draw the promise of resurrection.[26]

The focus on spiritual experience helped Gutiérrez's to sharpen his methodology in the 1980s.[27] Gutiérrez saw spirituality as more than an additional theme for liberation theology. It was fundamental to the very methodology of liberation theology.[28] He did not contradict his earlier focus on theology as a second step, but he clarified the importance of contemplation and silence as preconditions of theology.

Discourse on faith is a second stage in relation to the life of faith itself. This methodological statement is a central one in the theology of liberation. But the statement does not imply a separation of the two stages or aspects. Its point is simply to emphasize the fact that authentic theological reflection has its basis in contemplation and in practice. Talk about God (theo-logy) comes after the silence of prayer and after commitment. Theology is discourse that is continually enriched by silence.[29]

This development in his methodology was further clarified in Gutiérrez's other major works of the 1980s. In his introduction to *On Job: God-Talk and the Suffering of the Innocent* Gutiérrez provided one of the clearest statements of his approach.

God is first contemplated when we do God's will and allow God to reign; only after that do we think about God. To use familiar categories, contemplation and practice make up a first *act*; theologizing is a *second act*. We must first establish ourselves on the terrain of spirituality and practice; only subsequently is it possible to formulate discourse on God in an authentic and respectful way.[30]

---

[26] Gutiérrez, *We Drink from Our Own Wells*, p. 137.

[27] Gutiérrez argues that spirituality always precedes theology. He points to this as the historical course in all of what he calls the "great spiritualities" including Anselm (c. 1033–1109) and Thomas Aquinas (c. 1225–1274). Thus he insists: "The solidity and energy of theological thought depend precisely on the spiritual experience that supports it. This experience takes the form, first and foremost, of a profound encounter with God and God's will. Any discourse on faith starts from, and takes its bearings from, the Christian life of the community. Any reflection that does not help in living according to the Spirit is not a Christian Theology. When all is said and done, then, all authentic theology is spiritual theology. This fact does not weaken the rigorously scientific character of the theology; it does, however, properly situate it." Gutiérrez, *We Drink from Our Own Wells*, pp. 36–37.

[28] Gutiérrez notes at the start: "Since the very first days of the theology of liberation, the question of spirituality (specifically: the following of Jesus) has been of deep concern. Moreover, the kind of reflection that the theology of liberation represents is conscious of the fact that it was, and continues to be, preceded by the spiritual experience of Christians who are committed to the process of liberation." Gutiérrez, *We Drink from Our Own Wells*, p. 1.

[29] Gutiérrez, *We Drink from Our Own Wells*, p. 136.

[30] Gutiérrez, *On Job*, p. xiii.

Like *The God of Life* and *We Drink from Our Own Wells*, Gutiérrez's book *On Job* was a notable contrast in style to *A Theology of Liberation*. It drew on Job's situation for a profound meditative reflection on the challenge of evil for Christian faith. The book was dedicated jointly to Gutiérrez's parents, who first spoke of God to him. It was also dedicated to the people of Ayacucho who were at the centre of the political violence claiming thousands of innocent lives and making hundreds of thousands homeless. Gutiérrez wanted to find a way to talk about God when the innocent continued to suffer in Ayacucho. He noted that Johannes Baptist Metz in Germany previously asked how theology could be done *after* Auschwitz. In Latin America, Gutierrez said, the challenge came from the present as well as the past. Gutiérrez summed up the challenge in a critical question: "How are we to do theology *while Ayacucho lasts?*"[31] This question leads to many others: How could theology speak of the God of life in the face of murder on a massive scale? How could the church preach the love of God amid such profound contempt for human life? How could Christians have faith in the resurrection when death reigned, and especially the death of children, women, the poor, the indigenous, and the other "unimportant" members of our society?[32]

For Gutiérrez, this was only possible by keeping faith with the profound mystery of the God of life and maintaining active solidarity with those who suffered. Liberation theology advocated sharing the suffering of the poor while protesting against it, and during the 1980s, this commitment was tested to the extreme in Peru.

A Theology of Liberation exuded energy and optimism; liberation seemed to be close at hand. Gutiérrez's work in the 1980s arose from the same solidarity with the poor that marked his work since the 1960s, but they expressed it very differently. *A God of Life*, *We Drink from Our Own Wells*, and *On Job* were more cautious about political change and much more direct in the pastoral anguish. They gave less reason for immediate hope, but perhaps more reason for long-term faith.

Jon Sobrino's work in El Salvador during the 1980s also stimulated reflection on a liberative spirituality that was largely complementary to Gutiérrez's. A collection of Sobrino's writings on this theme was published as *Spirituality of Liberation*.[33] Like Gutiérrez, Sobrino saw liberation spirituality as life lived as a following of Jesus. He described it as life "lived in a particular spirit—specifically, in the case of Christian spiritual life, life lived in the spirit of Jesus."[34] Sobrino stressed that the spiritual was in essential relation to the historical rather than in isolation from it. He commented, "there is no spiritual life without actual,

---

[31] Emphasis original. Gutiérrez, *On Job*, p. 102.
[32] Emphasis original. Gutiérrez, *On Job*, p. 102.
[33] J. Sobrino, *Spirituality of Liberation: Towards a Political Holiness* (trans. Robert R. Barr; Maryknoll, N.Y.: Orbis Books, 1988 [Spanish orig. 1985]).
[34] Sobrino, *Spirituality of Liberation*, p. 2.

historical life. It is impossible to live with spirit unless that spirit becomes flesh."[35] In this historicized sense, spirituality (the integral reality to which liberation is directed) was the guiding light of liberation theology's very earliest origins.

Sobrino's title for the Spanish version of his work was *Liberación con espíritu* (*Liberation with Spirit*). This phrase echoed the terminology of his close friend and colleague, Ignacio Ellacuría, the rector of San Salvador's Central American University. Ellacuría suggested the phrase "poor with spirit" as a way to synthesise the differences in the first Beatitudes of Matthew and Luke.[36] Matthew's "Blessed are the poor in spirit" (Mt. 5.3) and Luke's "Blessed are you who are poor" (Lk 6.20) have often been seen as pointing in opposite directions. Luke's phrase has often been an excuse to focus on abstract spiritual poverty at the expense of the material poverty indicated by Matthew. However, for Ellacuría, both material and spiritual poverty are important; the phrase poor with spirit indicated their integral character. It also captured the faith of the Salvadoran communities that in a decade of civil war managed to maintain their spiritual journey of faith.[37]

Ignacio Ellacuría, and then Jon Sobrino, also took up and developed earlier insights on the close relation between Christ's suffering and the plight of the Salvadoran poor. More than four hundred years earlier, Bartolomé de Las Casas discerned Christ's presence in the suffering Indians of the sixteenth century. Gutiérrez—who was particularly inspired by Las Casas—had already drawn attention to this in the 1970s.[38] It was an insight that El Salvador's archbishop—Oscar Romero—also came to in 1977. In one instance, the village of Aguilares was occupied by the military, and the villagers suffered great violence. As they reclaimed their town and church, Romero addressed them in his homily as images of Christ, crucified on the cross.[39]

In the late 1970s, Ellacuría started to use the image to reflect on El Salvador's conflict and the relationship between the crucified Christ, and "the crucified

---

[35] Sobrino, *Spirituality of Liberation*, p. 4.

[36] Unfortunately Ellacuría's distinctive phrase is sometimes missed in English translations. For example, *Spirituality of Liberation* (p. 25) references the phrase "*pobres con espíritu*" to Ellacuría, but mistranslates it as "poor in spirit" not "poor with spirit."

[37] For a good overview on the progressive church in this period, see S. Wright, *Promised Land: Death and Life in El Salvador* (Maryknoll, N.Y.: Orbis Books, 1994). See also M. López Vigil, *Death and Life in Morazan: A Priest's Testimony from a War-Zone in El Salvador: Father Rogelio Ponseele Talks to María López Vigil* (trans. D. Livingstone; London: Catholic Institute for International Relations, 1989 [Spanish orig. 1989]).

[38] Gutiérrez especially drew attention to the links Las Casas made in his letter to the king, which proclaimed that natives in the Indies were like "Jesus Christ, our God, scourged and afflicted and crucified, not once, but millions of times." Las Casas, "Historia de las Indias," *Obras Escogidas* 2: 356, cited in Gutiérrez, *Power of the Poor in History*, p. 197.

[39] O. Romero, "Homilia en Aguilares" in J. Sobrino, I. Martín-Baró y R. Cardenal (eds.), *La voz de los sin voz* (San Salvador: UCA Editores, 1980), p. 208.

people" became central to Sobrino's christological reflection in the 1980s.[40] The image drew on Paul's theology of the church as the body of Christ, which could be creatively revitalised in the light of post-Conciliar understanding of sacred and secular history. The violence directed against ordinary Salvadoran Christians, they said, was violence directed against Jesus. The identification of Christ with the suffering poor of Latin America provided a powerful statement on the religious significance of social injustice.

For Ellacuría, the suffering of the people of El Salvador (in English the name means the Saviour) was related historically and theologically to the suffering of Christ.[41] An understanding of the crucified people could therefore deepen an understanding of the suffering of the historical Jesus.[42]

Sobrino's reflections on the crucified people sought to balance the hope of Latin American Christologies of "Jesus the liberator" with the pain of the contemporary presence of Christ in the world. The poignancy of the crucified people in Sobrino's work took on an awful new level when Ellacuría and five other Jesuits that he lived with (as well as their housekeeper and daughter) were murdered in November 1989. Sobrino only escaped because he was out of the country at a conference in Thailand.[43]

Sobrino's grief and shock at the murders was directed into his theological work. His writing was marked by intensified reflection on the crucified people and on the theological significance of martyrdom in his struggle to understand faith in a God of life when the idols of death prove so strong. As Sobrino has explained, the term "crucified people" is not hyperbolic exaggeration, but a necessary attempt to describe a horrifying social reality:

> Crucified peoples is useful and necessary language at the real level of fact, because cross means death, and death is what the Latin American peoples are subjected to in thousands of ways. It is slow but real death caused by

---

[40] Ellacuría and Sobrino had a particularly close friendship and work life at the Jesuit run Central American University in San Salvador. They shared a common background as Basque Jesuits and they both devoted their lives to work in El Salvador.

[41] Ellacuría first presented on this topic at a conference in Mexico as part of preparation for CELAM III at Puebla. It was published as "Pueblo crucificado: ensayo de soteriologia historica" in na, *Cruz y resurrección* (Mexico: Centro de Reflexión Teológica, 1978), pp. 49–82; ET "The Crucified People" in Ellacuría and Sobrino, *Mysterium Liberationis: Fundamental Concepts of Liberation Theology* (Maryknoll, N.Y.: Orbis Books, 1993 [Spanish orig. 1990]), pp. 580–604. For Sobrino's development of the theme, see J. Sobrino, *Jesus in Latin America* (trans. various; Maryknoll, N.Y.: Orbis Books, 1987 [Spanish orig. 1982]), esp. pp. 148–165.

[42] Speaking of the Salvadoran poor as a crucified people Jon Sobrino noted: "If they resist, they are crucified suddenly and violently. If they do not resist, they are crucified gradually and slowly" (*Spirituality of Liberation*, p. 30).

[43] See esp. Whitfield, *Paying the Price*. On the false accusation of Ellacuría's Marxism that accompanied the murders, see D. Tombs, "The Legacy of Ignacio Ellacuría for Liberation Theology in a 'Post-Marxist' Age," *Journal of Hispanic/Latino Theology* 8.1 (2000), pp. 38–53.

the poverty generated by unjust structures—'insitutionalised violence': the poor are those who die before their time. It is swift, violent death, caused by repression and wars, when the poor threaten these unjust structures. And it is indirect but effective death when peoples are deprived even of their cultures in order to weaken their identities and make them more defenseless.[44]

EXPANDING THE VIEW

At the same time that Latin American liberation theologians deepened their reflection on spirituality and suffering, they also extended their horizons outwards with a wider concern for oppression. Gutiérrez described many of these changes in an introductory chapter titled "Expanding the View" for the 1988 edition of *A Theology of Liberation*. He noted:

> Black, Hispanic, and Amerindian theologies in the United States, theologies arising in the complex contexts of Africa, Asia and the South Pacific, and especially fruitful thinking of those who have adopted a feminist perspective— all these have meant that for the first time in many centuries theology is being done outside the customary European and North American centres.[45]

Latin American theologians were not the only ones to search for new directions in theology in the 1970s. In the United States, Black theologians began to focus on race and racism in the churches and society as long neglected issues in theology. Meanwhile, in Africa, theologians started to search for a theology beyond the shackles of Eurocentrism and cultural imperialism. Likewise, in Asia, Christian theologians were exploring new approaches to dialogue with the other major religious faiths. However, in the early 1970s there was very little contact between these developing movements. It was not until the Theology in the Americas conferences in Detroit (1975) and Ecumenical Dialogue of Third World Theologians at Dar-es-Salaam (Tanzania) in 1976 that Latin American liberation theologians even began to address other liberation theologies. Unfortunately, the distinctiveness of each movement made initial attempts to dialogue with each other difficult. Instead of building solidarity these early contacts often ended in misunderstanding and mutual suspicion.

It was only after 1980 that serious dialogue with liberation theologies from other social contexts helped the Latin Americans recognise the importance of social dynamics other than poverty. As the 1980s progressed, African inculturationism, Asian pluralism, and the racial justice emphasis of Black theology all influenced Latin American liberation theology. Furthermore, the ecumenical setting of these dialogues also contributed to greater awareness amongst Latin

---

[44] Sobrino, *The Principle of Mercy*, p. 50.
[45] Gutiérrez, *A Theology of Liberation* 2nd ed., p. xix. The same phrase was used for a collection of papers given at a conference at Maryknoll, New York, in 1988 to mark the new edition of *A Theology of Liberation*, the twentieth anniversary of Medellín and Gutiérrez's sixtieth birthday; see M. Ellis and O. Maduro (eds.), *Expanding the View: Gustavo Gutiérrez and the Future of Liberation Theology* (Maryknoll, N.Y.: Orbis Books, 1990).

American Catholic theologians of the need to address liberation within an ecumenical framework.

Black liberation theology appeared in the United States at almost exactly the same time that Latin American liberation theology was emerging at the end of the 1960s. Black theology was not a derivative of Latin American liberation theology.[46] It was rooted instead in the distinctive experiences of African Americans in the United Sates, especially in the Civil Rights movement and Black Power movements of the 1950s and 1960s.[47] Theologians from Latin America met with their North American colleagues for the first time at the Theology in the Americas conference in Detroit, August 1975.[48] Although they shared much in common, in terms of engaging with contextual experience and taking social liberation as central to their work, they were also deeply divided on some issues. Some Latin Americans saw Black North Americans as fighting to take an equal place in U.S. society, while being uncritical of the global injustices that the U.S. economy created. On the other side, Black theologians felt that Latin Americans placed too much emphasis on economic class and ignored issues of race and colour.[49] Likewise, the North American feminists felt that the Latin American's commitment to liberation did not address sexism and

---

[46] James Cone served as a foundational figure for the literature of Black theology in an even more significant way than Gutiérrez was for Latin American liberation theology. Cone's two earliest works were both published before Gutiérrez's A Theology of Liberation; see J. H. Cone, Black Theology and Black Power (New York: Seabury Press, 1969); J. H. Cone, A Black Theology of Liberation (Philadelphia: Lipincott, 1970). Since it has sometimes been mistakenly suggested that all other liberation theologies are derivative from Latin American liberation theology, it should be noted that Cone did not read Spanish and the earliest published version of Gutiérrez's thought available in English was in Theological Studies 1970. Gutiérrez's book was not published in English until 1973, which was the same year that Cone's A Black Theology of Liberation was translated into Spanish. In May 1973, the WCC organised a symposium in Geneva to address Latin American and Black theology which included Paulo Freire, Hugo Assmann, and James Cone and is reported in Risk 9.2 (1973).

[47] On the development of his liberation approach, see J. H. Cone My Soul Looks Back (Nashville: Abingdon, 1982); For My People: Black Theology and the Black Church (Bishop Henry McNeal Turner Studies in North American Black Religion, 1; Maryknoll, N.Y.: Orbis Books, 1984); Speaking the Truth (Grand Rapids, Mich: Eerdmans, 1986).

[48] See, S. Torres and J. Eagleson (eds.), Theology in the Americas (Papers from the Theology in the Americas Conference, Detroit, August 1975; trans. J. Drury; Maryknoll, N.Y.: Orbis Books, 1976). Some progressive North American theologians sympathetic to liberation concerns also participated.

[49] See Cone, For My People, pp. 72–74. The tension would resurface a number of times in dialogues at EATWOT. Cone discusses the relations of Black theology with other Third World theologies at EATWOT in My Soul Looks Back, pp. 93–113. The fact that many of the Latin American liberation theologians were lighter skinned and often had European family backgrounds added to the feelings of Black theologians that they did not adequately address issues of race. The one exception to this was Gutiérrez who may have had deeper insight into the issues (and perhaps given more respect by Black theologians) because of his own Indian background.

the liberation of women. In view of the different agendas, it was hardly surprising that the meeting created strong feelings; but it served a useful purpose. It showed that the different contextual theologies needed to talk to each other and enrich and challenge each other with their insights. The Ecumenical Association of Third World Theologians (EATWOT) proved an excellent forum for this dialogue.

EATWOT was intended to promote direct contact between theologians of the Third World.[50] In the late 1960s and early 1970s, although Third World liberation theologians were invited to dialogues sponsored by the World Council of Churches (WCC) or other bodies (for example the SODEPAX Conference in Cartigny), their dialogue tended to be mediated by the concerns of the host organisations in New York, Geneva, or Rome. EATWOT encouraged Latin Americans, Africans, Asians, and U.S. minorities to talk to each other directly about their own agendas. At EATWOT conferences Black theologians from North America and South Africa challenged the Latin Americans to take seriously issues of race and ethnicity, especially in countries like Brazil. Theologians from Africa and Asia also challenged theologians in Latin America to extend their theological awareness to issues of indigenous culture and relations with non-Christian religious traditions.[51] Debates over the relationship of Christianity

---

[50] The term Third World in EATWOT's title is significant. Talk of a Third World came to prominence in the 1950s and the acceptance of the term is especially associated with the Afro-Asian Conference at Bandung (Indonesia) in 1955, which was one of the first attempts at independent inter-regional organisation; see R. Wright, *The Colour Curtain: Report on the Bandung Conference* (New York: The World, 1956). In this original sense, the term was adopted as a positive self-designation to indicate non-alignment with both the First World (the political and economic systems of capitalist North America and Europe) and the Second World (the socialism of the former Soviet Union and Eastern Europe). Regrettably the original intentions behind the name are often forgotten, perhaps because a third way for nonaligned countries has proved elusive. As a result, the term Third World often simply implies a negative economic status as underdeveloped (a term that has its own history of disputed meaning). In the papers of the first conference, Torres noted that some prefer not to use the term Third World (S. Torres, "Introduction," Torres and Fabella (eds.), *The Emergent Gospel*, pp. vii–xxii [xxii]), but the Final Statement adopted the term for countries in Asia, Africa, Latin America, and the Caribbean outside the industrialized First World (including Japan, Australia, and New Zealand) and Second World regardless of whether they were free-market or socialist. Typically, these Third World countries shared social indicators of low economic standards of living, limited technological advances, over-reliance on agricultural production, unfavourable trade balances, and often large external debts. See "Final Statement of the Ecumenical Dialogue of Third World Theologians," Dar-es-Salaam, August 5–12, 1976, in Torres and Fabella (eds.), *The Emergent Gospel*, pp. 259–271 (260). The demise of the so-called Second World made the problems with the terminology particularly awkward. Some have suggested that in terms of both landmass and population, references to Africa, Asia, and Latin America as the "Two-Third World" would be much more appropriate. Others suggest that it would be better simply to talk of the North and the South.

[51] The gradual development of a distinctive contextual theology in Africa paralleled

with indigenous cultures in Africa and other religions in Asia stimulated similar discussion amongst Latin Americans about their implications for indigenous American traditions.[52]

Dar-es-Salaam (1976), Accra (1977), and Wennappuwa (1979)

The new organisation was launched with a conference of Ecumenical Dialogue to which delegates from Africa, Asia, and Latin America were invited.[53] Twenty-two theologians attended the first meeting in Dar-es-Salaam, Tanzania. Of the published papers, seven were from Africa, five from Asia, and three from Latin America by Enrique Dussel, Gustavo Gutiérrez, and Beatriz Couch.[54] Participants at the conference decided to make the conference the beginning rather than the end of the process of dialogue and agreed to a sequence of further events. A series of three continental conferences was planned to recognise the distinctive features of theology on the different continents—Africa, Asia, and Latin America.

---

the progressive emergence of liberation theology in Latin America in a number of ways. Decolonization in Africa during the 1950s was accompanied by the recognition that much of the theological culture inherited from European missionaries was alien in the newly independent countries. This encouraged new pastoral innovations, and a consultation of African theologians at Ibadan (Nigeria) in 1958 brought together many of those who started to address the future direction of Christianity in Africa. Five years later, the All Africa Conference of Churches (AACC) was inaugurated in 1963 in Kampala (Uganda); see AACC, *The Drumbeats from Kampala* (London: Lutterworth Press, 1963). During the 1960s, African theologians explored the issues of indigenization and inculturation especially in the liturgical field; see, for example, E. B. Idowu, *Towards An Indigenous Church* (London: Oxford University Press, 1965). The AACC held its second meeting at Abidjan (Ivory Coast) in 1969, and the papers were published as K. Dickson and P. Ellingworth (eds.), *Biblical Revelation and African Beliefs* (London: Lutterworth Press, 1969; Maryknoll, N.Y.: Orbis Books, 1971). In the same year, Paul VI gave encouragement to these developments when he endorsed the African liturgical renewal in an address to the Ugandan bishops in which he praised "a certain pluralism [which] is not only legitimate but desirable ... [and] favoured by the church. The liturgical renewal is a living example of this. And in this sense you may and you must have an African Christianity"; cited in A. Shorter, *African Culture and the Christian Church* (London: Geoffrey Chapman, 1973). Meanwhile, John Mbiti published his influential work *African Religions and Philosophy* (London: Heinemann, 1969; New York: Doubleday, 1970). However, it was not till the early 1970s that the first English-language articles to use the term African theology started to appear; see G. H. Muzorewa, *The Origins and Development of African Theology* (Maryknoll, N.Y.: Orbis Books, 1985).

[52] See L. Boff, *Good News to the Poor: A New Evangelization* (trans. R. Barr; Maryknoll, N.Y.: Orbis Books; Tunbridge Wells: Burns & Oates, 1992 [Portuguese orig. 1990]), pp. 95–114.

[53] A representative of U.S. Black minorities was also invited, but surprisingly there was no invitation for Black theology's most prominent spokesperson, James Cone.

[54] However, the final document—largely the work of the Chilean Sergio Torres, who was Secretary to EATWOT—paid particular attention to economic and political oppression; S. Torres and Virginia Fabella (eds.), *The Emergent Gospel: Theology from the Underside of History* (EATWOT Dialogue held in Dar-es-Salaam, Tanzania, 5–12 August, 1976; Maryknoll, N.Y.: Orbis Books, 1978).

In each case, the main body of participants would come from the continent concerned, while representatives from other continents would contribute their insights and critique the approach.

The first of the regional conferences—the Pan-African Conference—took place the following year at Accra, Ghana. About two-thirds of the nearly one hundred participants were from Africa with only seven from Latin America.[55] At this meeting, only six Latin Americans were present (including Gutiérrez and Míguez Bonino) and they were outnumbered by representatives of North American minorities which included a number of prominent Black theologians including James Cone, Gayraud Wilmore, and Jacquelyn Grant.[56] The relatively low profile of the Latin American contribution may have reflected the feeling of African and other members—that the Latin Americans should not become too dominant in setting the agenda of the organisation.[57] Differences of opinion with the Latin Americans over indigenization and inculturation were particularly noticeable at Accra and remained the key difference between Latin American and African theologians in future conferences.[58] The final communiqué of the document suggested both the value and the limits of Latin American liberation theology as a model of African theology.[59]

---

[55] These were Sergio Torres, Enrique Dussel, José Míguez Bonino, who was also and present at Dar-es-Salaam, plus Gustavo Gutiérrez, Julia Campos (Mexico), Candido Padin (Brazil), and Sergio Arce (Cuba).

[56] The decision to increase the number of representatives from black churches in the U.S. is discussed in a paper by Gayraud Wilmore which was written after the conference but included in the published papers as, G. Wilmore, "The Role of Afro-America in the Rise of Two-Third World Theology: A Historical Reappraisal" in K. Appiah-Kubi and S. Torres (eds.), *African Theology En Route* (EATWOT Pan-African Conference of Third World Theologians held in Accra, Ghana, 17–23 December 1977; Maryknoll, N.Y.: Orbis Books, 1979) pp. 196–208. It should be noted that some African theologians felt that the political liberation agenda of Black theology was as equally alien to the African concern for inculturation as the Latin American political emphasis. Perhaps the most prominent example of this view is John Mbiti. See James Cone's response to Mbiti's criticisms in "A Black American Perspective on the Future of African Theology" in Appiah-Kubi and Torres (eds.), *African Theology En Route*, pp. 176–186. The tensions between the concerns for inculturation and black liberation are clear in a number of the papers. One positive outcome of the conference for the future direction of African theology was the establishment of the Ecumenical Association of African Theologians (EAAT).

[57] Sergio Torres gave the opening address, but all the papers came from Africans, except one from James Cone. The importance of African theology's distinctive concerns is clear in the documents. The published papers are notable for a number of features that found little place in the Latin American approach. First, the African stress on culture and the importance of affirming indigenous African culture in reaction to past European colonialism and continuing neo-colonialism. Second, the recognition of the antiracist thrust in Black theology stressed by theologians facing apartheid in South Africa.

[58] Many African theologians felt that Latin American was essentially another Western theology. Three years previously, the third meeting of the AACC at Lusaka (Zambia) called for a moratorium on the sending of Western missionaries to Africa; see AACC, *The Struggle Continues* (Nairobi: AACC, 1975).

[59] It suggested that African theology arising from a commitment to African freedom

The next conference, the Asian Theological Conference, took place at Wennappuwa in Sri Lanka in January 1979 (a few weeks prior to CELAM III at Puebla).[60] The eighty participants (62 men and 18 women) were from ten Asian countries with eight fraternal delegates from other continents including only two from Latin America (Torres and Dussel).[61] All participants spent three days immediately prior to the formal conference as a "live-in period" to experience the Asian situations of oppression first hand and to root their reflections during discussions at the conference.[62] The similarities and differences in the approaches developed in different continents found clear expression in the papers evaluating the conference from an African, Latin American, and Black American perspective that were included in the published book.[63]

The major issues at the conference arose from the dual concerns of Asian Christian cultural identity (especially vis-à-vis the other major world faiths in Asia) and social liberation. The Latin American emphasis on social political liberation found strong support amongst many of the Filipino delegates.[64]

---

struggles in culture and politics would have three characteristics. First, it would be *contextual* and accountable to its African context. Second, "because oppression is found not only in culture but also in political and economic structures and the dominant mass media, African theology must also be *liberation* theology." Third, it would need to struggle against *sexism*. The recognition of contextuality ahead of the liberation and the recognition of cultural imperialism as the first of the issues from which liberation was required showed both the similarities and differences with the Latin Americans. See "Pan-African Conference of Third World Theologians: Final Communiqué" in Appiah-Kubi and Torres (eds.), *African Theology En Route*, pp. 189–195 (194).

[60] See V. Fabella (ed.), *Asia's Struggle for Full Humanity: Towards a Relevant Theology* (EATWOT Asian Theological Conference, Wennappuwa, Sri Lanka, 7–20 January 1979; Maryknoll, N.Y.: Orbis Books, 1979). At this time Asian Christian theology had already developed a distinctive contextual identity, which in some ways predated both Latin American and African versions. As in Africa, the decolonisation process prompted reexamination of the traditions derived from missionary theology in a number of countries. The WCC assemblies in Amsterdam 1948, Evanston 1954, and New Delhi 1961 stimulated discussion on the relationship between Asian churches and other Asian religions. A special note should be taken of the distinctive Minjung theology in Korea that dates from the early 1970s; see D. K. S. Suh, "Korean Theological Development in the 1970s" in CTC and CCA, *Minjung theology: People as the Subjects of History* (Singapore: CCA; Maryknoll, N.Y.: Orbis Books; London: Zed Books, 1981), pp. 38–43.

[61] The other delegates were two Black theologians from the U.S. (James Cone and Cecil Corbett), three from Africa (Rose Zoé-Obianga, Kofi Appiah-Kubi, and Ngindu Mushete), and one from the Caribbean (Eunice Santana de Velez).

[62] See V. Fabella (ed.), *Asia's Struggle for Full Humanity*, pp. 39–56.

[63] See R. Zoé-Obianga, "From Accra to Wennappuwa: What is New? What is More?" and J. Cone, "A Black American Perspective on the Asian Search for Full Humanity," and S. Torres, "A Latin American View of the Asian Theological Conference" in Fabella (ed.), *Asia's Struggle for Full Humanity: Towards a Relevant Theology*, pp. 171–176, 177–190, and 191–197 respectively.

[64] See especially C. H. Abesamis, "Faith and Life Reflection from the Grassroots in the Philippines" in Fabella (ed.), *Asia's Struggle for Full Humanity*, pp. 123–139. The Philippines are culturally much closer to the Latin American context than other Asian

However, others saw the primary issue in terms of cultural identity and relation to other faiths.[65] In an especially interesting paper, the Sri Lankan Jesuit Aloysius Pieris tried to prevent this either/or debate with an argument that made each thrust inseparable from the other.[66] Pieris argued for an Asian liberation theology in which "the common denominator between Asia and the rest of the Third World is its overwhelming poverty; the specific character which defines Asia within the other poor countries is its multifaceted religiosity."[67] In many ways, his words were of their time and hard for others to hear. However, in retrospect Pieris's presentation at Wennappuwa—and his equally important paper two years later in Delhi—can be seen as some of the most creative thinking on the challenges facing the Christian church in Asia. Pieris's critique of poverty was as profound as anything in Latin America, while his focus on world religions gave it a global dimension that Latin American theologians had hardly yet touched upon.[68]

São Paulo (1980)

The limited numbers of Latin Americans who could attend at Dar-es-Salaam, Accra and Wennappuwa meant that despite EATWOT's first three meetings, few of the Latin Americans had direct experience of Third World theologies in other contexts.[69] Prior to 1980, Latin American theologians might have read EATWOT conference reports and publications, but the theologies they represented remained news from foreign lands. Other contextual theologies made little impact on their own work. It was, therefore, only in the 1980s that the challenge of other Third World theologies started to come home to Latin Americans. The starting point for this was EATWOT's Latin American conference

---

countries. Its large Catholic majority (c. 85%) and the colonial history of the Philippines under the Spanish (starting gradually in 1542 and not ending until 1898) is exceptional for Asia.

[65] Regrettably, the Minjung theologians of South Korea—who might have bridged both perspectives—were prevented from attending the conference by the Korean government. Nonetheless, a Korean contribution to the conference papers was published as "Reflections by Korean Theologians on the Final Statement of the Asian Theological Conference" in Fabella (ed.), *Asia's Struggle for Full Humanity*, pp. 167–170.

[66] A. Pieris, "Towards an Asian Theology of Liberation: Some Religio-Cultural Guidelines" in Fabella (ed.), *Asia's Struggle for Full Humanity*, pp. 75–95. Although this paper was not successful in preventing polarisation at the conference, it has nonetheless been recognised as a significant potential framework for addressing the tensions raised at the conference.

[67] Pieris, "Towards an Asian Theology of Liberation," p. 75.

[68] For an overview of the challenges presented in Pieris's work, see "Liberating Christology: Images of Christ in the Work of Aloysius Pieris" in S. E. Porter, M. A. Hayes, and D. Tombs (eds.), *Images of Christ: Ancient and Modern* (STS 2 and RILP 4; Sheffield: Sheffield Academic Press, 1997), pp. 173–188.

[69] Those involved in one or more previous EATWOT gatherings included Sergio Torres, Enrique Dussel, Gustavo Gutiérrez, Beatriz Couch, Julia Campos, Candido Padin, and Sergio Arce.

in São Paulo billed as "An International Ecumenical Congress of Theology."[70] Because the conference was under the auspices of EATWOT rather than CELAM, it was particularly notable for the role of Latin American Protestants alongside their Catholic colleagues. The Methodist bishop of Rio de Janeiro, Paulo Ayres Mattos, was president of the organizing committee, and Beatriz Melano Couch (a professor at the Protestant Seminary in Buenos Aires) presided over the conference itself.[71]

The conference (20 February–2 March 1980) came at a time of enormous upheaval in Central America. The group met six months after the Sandinista revolution had driven Somoza from Nicaragua. Meanwhile, in El Salvador and Guatemala the repression was escalating to new levels of ferocity.[72] However, the surprisingly successful defence of the progressive church at Puebla the previous year, meant that most liberation theologians were in a positive mood.

Sergio Torres gave an opening address, which set out the conference's focus on the ecclesiology of the popular Christian communities.[73] Many of the papers presented were outstanding contributions to the new understanding of the base communities and their role in the evangelizaton of the church. The shift from a church that opted for the poor ethically and politically in the late 1960s and early 1970s, to a church that opted for the poor epistemologically and methodologically as the 1970s progressed was particularly clear in a number of contributions.[74] Conference participants made visits to local CEBs and public lectures in the evenings at a local university attracted enthusiastic crowds.

In response to criticisms over deficiencies in the Latin American approach raised at previous EATWOT conferences, three special preparatory seminars were arranged. These included one on women (Tepeyac, Mexico, 1–5 October 1979), one on indigenous peoples (San Cristobal de Las Casas, Mexico, 3–7 September 1979), and one on race (Kingston, Jamaica, 27–31 December 1979). Representatives who attended these seminars then presented papers to the larger conference in São Paulo.

Despite the importance of these meetings, their overall impact on reorientating traditional concerns was fairly marginal. For example, Mauro Batista, a black Catholic priest from São Paulo, addressed race and racism in Brazil with a review of Brazilian slavery and its legacy.[75] In the years 1530 to 1850, slave

---

[70] The papers were published as S. Torres and J. Eagleson (eds.), *The Challenge of Basic Christian Communities*.

[71] Her opening welcome is included in Torres and Eagleson (eds.), *The Challenge of Basic Christian Communities*, pp. xix–xx.

[72] Archbishop Romero was assassinated three weeks after the end of the conference on 24 March 1980.

[73] S. Torres, "Introduction" in Torres and Eagleson (eds.), *The Challenge of Basic Christian Communities*, pp. 1–10.

[74] See especially the various papers grouped in Part II, pp. 77–197.

[75] See M. Batista, "Black and Christian in Brazil" in Torres and Eagleson (eds.), *The Challenge of Basic Christian Communities*, pp. 50–54.

traders brought between four and six million Africans to Brazil and millions more died on the journey. The population census of 1872 showed that people of African and mixed race descent were the majority of the population and it was only the later waves of European migration to the southern states that changed the demographic distribution. However, despite the myth that Brazil is a colour-blind society and a racial democracy, it remains stratified by the colour of skin.[76] The estimated 40–50 million Afro-Brazilian minority community—much bigger than the entire population in many African countries— remains disadvantaged in many ways. The Catholic church hardly started to address issues of race in its work for social justice in the 1970s.[77] Most Latin American liberation theologians dismissed the problem of racism as not really a problem for Latin America, while others only considered race as a contributory factor to class.[78]

The tension between the more traditional Latin American liberation view that focussed on class issues and the more recent concerns about race were reflected in the final statement. Despite its acknowledgement of race, the emphasis in the Final Document was on political and economic oppression. It acknowledged that: "It is important to stress the implacability of a whole series of mechanisms of a more subtle domination, often underestimated in the analyses, which produce forms of inequality and discrimination among blacks, indigenous peoples, and women," but did not do much to engage with these.[79] Some of the observers from other continents felt they had to remind the Latin Americans that they had insights to learn as well as insights to offer. For their part, the Latin Americans acknowledged their lack of awareness of issues facing

---

[76] For example, the world famous football player Pelé—who served as extraordinary minister for sport (1995–1999)—was the first-ever Black minister in Brazilian government.

[77] The significance of race and ethnicity and race in colonial Latin America was reflected in the terms used to describe different social groups: peninsulares, Iberians born in Spain/Portugal but working in America; creoles (*criollos*), Iberians born in America; mestizos, mixed Iberian and Indian; Blacks, slaves and freemen of African descent. Under the Treaty of Tordesillas, the future territories of Africa were awarded to Portugal. Portuguese Angola was therefore the departure point for the trans-Atlantic slave trade to Latin America in the sixteenth century. The first slaves to serve on Brazilian sugar plantations arrived in 1538, and the number of slaves involved in this trade increased dramatically after 1595 when the Spanish crown commissioned the Portuguese to supply African slaves to Spanish America. During the seventeenth century, the English, French, and Dutch joined the Portuguese. Slaves were taken to both Spanish America and the Caribbean islands that England, France, and the Dutch acquired in the sixteenth century. In all cases, the conditions on the trans-Atlantic voyages were horrific. The Anglo-Brazilian Treaty of 1826 agreed a ban to the slave trade, but it was only after 1850 that the trade finally came to an end. It was even later (1888) that Brazil became one of the last countries in the world to formally abolish slavery as an institution.

[78] The document from the women's seminar will be discussed in the next chapter.

[79] "Final Document" in Torres and Eagleson (eds.), *The Challenge of Basic Christian Communities*, pp. 231–246 (234).

the churches of Asia, Africa, the Caribbean, and the ethnic minorities of the U.S. and committed themselves to improving communication with them.[80]

New Delhi (1981)

With the three continental conferences completed, New Delhi marked a new stage in the dialogue. It was intended to synthesize some of the developments from the previous five years and deepen the dialogue between the different theologies.[81] National consultations in 1980–1981 prepared regional reports to be presented at the conference. The fifty participants—which included both theologians and activists—included roughly equal numbers from Asia, Africa, and Latin America as well as representatives from Black and Hispanic minorities in the U.S. and one representative from the Caribbean. The scale of destitution in India was an eye-opening experience for many of the Latin Americans. Indian poverty challenged them to understand Latin American poverty in a clearer global context.[82] The conference itself raised further challenges to different aspects of their work.

As at Wennappuwa, the Sri Lankan Jesuit Aloysius Pieris presented an influential paper on engagement with non-Christian religions in the Christian struggle for liberation.[83] Pieris incorporated a strong liberation stance, but was cautious about how adequate the Latin American model could be in Asia. He pointed out that the majority of the Third World was non-Christian, and that a truly liberative theology needed to extend the boundaries of orthodoxy to address this.[84] Pieris did not criticise Latin American theology, but felt it had been uncritically imported into Asia. Implicitly his paper also suggested that the Latin Americans were in danger of an uncritical rejection of folk religion, indigenous culture, and popular spirituality.[85]

---

[80] See Torres and Eagleson (eds.), *The Challenge of Basic Christian Communities*, pp. 253–281 (esp. p. 244).

[81] V. Fabella and S. Torres (eds.), *Irruption of the Third World* (Fifth International Conference and First General Assembly of EATWOT, New Delhi, India, 17–29 August 1981; Maryknoll, N.Y.: Orbis Books, 1983).

[82] The conference included a three-day program of contact with Indian society. At the time, India had a population of 700 million of whom 65% lived below the poverty line. For the Latin American report on this experience, see I. Gebara and Z. Dias, "Everyday Life in India" in Fabella and Torres (eds.), *Irruption of the Third World*, pp. 171–180.

[83] A. Pieris, "The Place of Non-Christian Religions and Cultures in the Evolution of Third World Theology" in Fabella and S. Torres, *Irruption of the Third World*, pp. 113–139.

[84] A. Pieris, "The Place of Non-Christian Religions and Cultures in the Evolution of Third World Theology," p. 114.

[85] Pieris picked out José Miranda and to a lesser extent Jon Sobrino as examples of this ("The Place of Non-Christian Religions and Cultures in the Evolution of Third World Theology," p. 115). According to Pieris, support for this rejection of religion is based on "the two Karls of 'dialectical' fame, that is Karl Marx and Karl Barth." Pieris suggests that although their reasons for a rejection of religion are very different, in both cases there is a similar Western bias and risk of crypto-colonialism. For more on Pieris's work and his thought-provoking insights on liberation, see D. Tombs, "Liberating

A different type of challenge came from the Cameroonian Jesuit Englebert Mveng. Mveng, who was the executive secretary of the Association of African Theologians, criticised the way that some Latin Americans dominated the institutional workings of EATWOT.[86] He then suggested that the Latin Americans were uncritical of the destructive Western assumptions in their vision of human beings.

> We thank our colleagues for sharing with us, over the years, their Marxist analysis, their socialist projections for the society of the future, and their contextual reading of the bible. But we are not satisfied. First of all, the basic problem remains the foundations of Western anthropology, which would impose themselves upon the world. The concept of the human being that the West seeks to export to us is based on domination, power, death struggle, and so on—the triumph of death over life.[87]

A third criticism of limitations in Latin American theology (which applied to other Third World theologies as well) was given by Mercy Amba Oduyoye, who criticised the marginalisation of women in the church and in society, including the EATWOT conferences. The conference was intended to formulate a common statement from Asia, Africa, and Latin America that outlined the "irruption of the Third World" in global affairs and theological reflection. As Oduyoye pointed out, within this irruption was a further irruption—the irruption of women's voices which her male colleagues were slow to hear. Until they recognised the influence of sexism in church, society, and theology, EATWOT's theology would fail to address the complexity of oppression in the Third World and elsewhere.

Oaxtepec (1986)

The New Delhi conference drew the first and most intensive stage of EATWOT's work to an end. During the 1980s, EATWOT's work was more focussed on regional conferences than on major international gatherings.[88] The next major

---

Christology: Images of Christ in the Work of Aloysius Pieris" in S. E. Porter, M. Hayes, and D. Tombs (eds.), *Images of Christ: Ancient and Modern* (RILP 2; Sheffield: Sheffield Academic Press, 1997) pp. 173–188.

[86] E. Mveng, "Third World Theology—What Theology? What Third World?: Evaluation by an African Delegate" in Fabella and Torres (eds.), *Irruption of the Third World*, pp. 217–221. His complaints included concerns about the way that the statutes of the association were applied (or rather, not applied), and the way that Africa seemed to be marginalized at the expense of Latin America. Others in Africa and Asia seem to have felt similar frustration. For example, Preman Niles did not attend further conferences after the meeting in São Paulo. Elections for a new executive at New Delhi (the first committee had served their five year term) reduced some of the discontent and spread control of the conference a little more evenly. The Methodist bishop of Luanda (Angola), Emílio de Carvalho, was elected as President (and replaced J. R. Chandran of India), Torres moved to the vice-presidency, and Virginia Fabella took over as treasurer/secretary.

[87] E. Mveng, "Third World Theology," p. 220.

[88] During this new stage in EATWOT's work, there was an important conference in Geneva in January 1983. This was the first time that First World theologians from

EATWOT gathering was December 1986 in Oaxtepec, Mexico. The Oaxtepec meeting marked EATWOT's ten year anniversary, and coming five years after New Delhi, it was an appropriate opportunity to review what progress had been made since the initial sequence of meetings from 1976 to 1981. It was a major landmark in EATWOT's history, with fifty-six Third World theologians attending including more women than ever before. The theme of the meeting was designated as the commonalities and divergences in Third World theologies.

Published papers from the meeting suggested that Latin Americans took some of the previous challenges to heart.[89] Maria Clara Bingemer's introduction described Latin America's continual concern for social, economic, and political liberation, but recognised the much greater attention now given to race, indigenous issues, and gender.[90] José Míguez Bonino showed that Latin America shared with other Third World contexts a colonial/neo-colonial history that served as the backdrop for the struggle for life against systems of death. In this struggle, the God of life—to be encountered in other religious traditions as well as Christianity—was the basis of a new spirituality that serves to strengthen all those who stand in solidarity with the oppressed.[91] Sergio Torres's examination of divergences was a marked contrast to the ambiguities of the Final Statement at São Paulo that he drafted. He struck a much more modest tone with the admission that:

> ... it is essential to keep in mind that the majority of the oppressed people of the Third World are not Christians. And we have to be aware also that universal liberation will not be achieved with the contribution of Christians alone, but especially with the contribution of the main non-Christian religions. This makes our contribution somewhat relative and places us in a more humble and modest position.[92]

Europe and North America theologians were invited to join EATWOT's discussion and share their contributions on liberation. Many of the First World guests were activists rather than professional theologians and shared concrete experiences of struggle in labour movements or peace organisations. The contributions of a number of First World women theologians further reinforced the importance of feminist theology for any theology that espoused liberation. See R. R. Ruether, "A Feminist Perspective," and D. Sölle, "Dialectics of Enlightenment: Reflections of a European Theologian," and L. Russell, "A First World Perspective" in Virginia Fabella and Sergio Torres (eds.), *Doing Theology in a Divided World* (Sixth International Conference of EATWOT, Geneva, Switzerland, 5–13 January 1983; Maryknoll, N.Y.: Orbis Books, 1985), pp. 65–71, 79–84, and 206–211. Pablo Richard, "Nicaragua: Base Church Communities in a Revolutionary Situation," Julio de Santa Ana, "The Perspective of Economic Analysis," and Elsa Tamez, "Letter to Job," each contributed a Latin American perspective (pp. 28–32, 59–64, and 174–176).

[89] K. C. Abraham (ed.), *Third World Theologies: Commonalities and Divergences* (Second General Assembly of EATWOT, Oaxtepec, Mexico, 7–14 December 1986; Maryknoll, N.Y.: Orbis Books, 1990).

[90] M. C. Bingemer, "Preface" in Abraham (ed.), *Third World Theologies*, pp. vii–xiii.

[91] J. Míguez Bonino, "Commonalities: A Latin American Perspective" in Abraham (ed.), *Third World Theologies*, pp. 105–110.

[92] S. Torres, "Divergences: A Latin American Perspective" in Abraham (ed.), *Third World Theologies*, pp. 120–126.

Elsa Tamez—who explored the cross-fertilization that had taken place—noted that African and Asian theology encouraged Latin Americans to take Latin American culture more seriously (including its diversity) and especially the myths and symbols of indigenous religions.[93] Pablo Richard, who wrote the Latin American evaluation of the conference, echoed the same view. He described Latin America's awareness of its colonial history and the need for indigenization as the most important discovery that the Latin Americans gained from the dialogue.[94]

In the Introduction to the second edition of A *Theology of Liberation*, Gutiérrez expressed the same concerns:

> One of our social lies has been the claim that there is no racism in Latin America. . . . The marginalization of Amerindian and black populations, and the contempt in which they are held, are situations we cannot accept as human beings, much less as Christians.[95]

However, beyond these statements of intent the response of Latin American liberation theologians to these challenges was mixed. Very little was actually done to carry these projects forward. In retrospect, it is clear that engaging with an extended view of oppression was a much harder step for many theologians than the original commitment to the poor in the 1960s and conversion by the poor in the 1970s. Two crucial factors provided the foundations for the original focus on the poor: support by the church's magisterium and personal experience through vows of poverty and work with poor communities. These elements made much less impact on culture and race.[96] Some of the exchanges in EATWOT's early discussions during the 1970s were dismissive of such concerns and over defensive of the Latin American focus on class. As the 1980s progressed, this gradually changed and there was more emphasis on complementarily and convergence (rather than opposition and difference), but little substantive progress.

CONCLUSION

The 1980s saw most countries in Latin America moving away from dictatorship and the return of what might be called "low intensity democracy." However, despite improvements on the political side, the economic situation remained difficult and many countries faced crippling external debts. Silent revolutions and structural adjustment plans shifted Latin American economies away from state intervention to reliance on the free-market. Subsidies on basic goods and

---

[93] E. Tamez, "A Latin American Perspective" in Abraham (ed.), *Third World Theologies*, pp. 134–138 (esp. 137).

[94] P. Richard, "A Latin American Evaluation of Oaxtepec" in Abraham (ed.), *Third World Theologies*, pp. 170–173 (esp. 171).

[95] Gutiérrez, A *Theology of Liberation* (2nd ed.), p. xxii.

[96] Gutiérrez's Indian background distinguished him from the majority of liberation theologians, many of whom were either born in Europe or had recent European ancestry.

services were slashed leaving the poor to work harder than ever before just to stand still.

If the influential paradigm in the 1970s was exodus, the challenge of the 1980s was the continuing struggle between life and death. The new context encouraged more explicit emphasis on spirituality, highlighted the place of contemplative silence in liberation theology's methodological approach, and shifted attention to new biblical themes such as the cross and the suffering servant. It should, however, be stressed that these shifts were a change in emphasis and focus rather than a complete change of subject. As well as the obvious differences between the 1980s and the 1970s, there is also clear continuity with the earlier works. The insights of the 1980s were all at least implicit in the works of the 1970s, but are not given sustained liberationist treatments until the 1980s.

At the same time as this deepening was taking place there was also a broadening of outlook but with much more limited success. The option for the poor was always an option for the oppressed, but liberation theology's understanding of oppression in the 1980s became much wider than its vision in the 1970s. Dialogues within EATWOT prompted some liberation theologians to broaden their awareness of oppression and engage more with the challenges posed by ethnicity and race. However, it was hard for the liberation theologians that were at the forefront of the movement in the 1970s to sustain the same depth and insight on race and ethnicity that they had shown on politics and economics. Beyond the level of generalities, they offered little by way of creative theological response. This failure, coupled with the absence of enough new voices able to fulfill this important role, signalled the serious problems facing the movement in the longer term.

CHAPTER ELEVEN

Defending the Faith

> The Gospel of Jesus Christ is a message of freedom and
> a force for liberation. In recent years this essential truth
> has become the object of reflection for theologians, with
> a new kind of attention which itself is full of promise.
> *Instruction on Certain Aspects of Liberation Theology* (1984)[1]

INTRODUCTION

The 1980s was marked by more conservative pressure on the progressive church.[2]
Nelson Rockefeller's report on Latin America for the U.S. Republican party in
1969 questioned the future reliability of the church. During the 1970s, liberation theology fulfilled many of the fears of its right-wing critics. In 1980, a committee of Ronald Reagan's advisers met in Santa Fe (New Mexico) to discuss
hemispheric policy for what was destined to become the Republican Reagan-
Bush era.[3] Their report identified liberation theology as a particular threat to
U.S. commercial interests in Latin America and suggested measures to discredit
its reputation and counter the impact of its critique of capitalism.[4] During the
1980s, the statements and briefings of the neo-conservative Institute for Religion

---

[1] Congregation for the Doctrine of the Faith, *Instruction on Certain Aspects of "The
Theology of Liberation"* (Vatican City: 1984), Introduction; reprinted in Hennelly (ed.),
Liberation Theology, pp. 393–413 (393).
[2] For an excellent overview of events and the politics behind them, see P. Lernoux,
People of God: The Struggle for World Catholicism (New York: Viking, 1989).
[3] U.S. politics in the 1980s matched a generally Democratic Congress against the
Republican presidencies of Ronald Reagan (1980–1988) and George Bush (1989–1992).
[4] Santa Fe Committee, *A New Inter-American Policy for the 80s* (Washington, D.C.:
1980). The Santa Fe Document (as it is usually called) made clear that "U.S. foreign
policy should begin to confront liberation theology (and not just react after the fact). . . .
In Latin America, the role of the Church is vital to the concept of political freedom.
Unfortunately, Marxist-Leninist forces have used the Church as a political weapon
against private ownership and the capitalist system of production, infiltrating the religious community with ideas that are more communist than Christian"; cited in M. Löwy,
The War of the Gods: Religion and Politics in Latin America (London: Verso, 1996), p. 66.

and Democracy (founded in 1981) took up this challenge with sustained attacks on liberation theology and the progressive church, especially in Central America.[5]

Meanwhile, opposition to liberation theology was mounting in both Rome and Latin America. Powerful sectors in the Latin American church hierarchy were determined to succeed where Puebla had failed and bring liberation theology to a decisive end. The Vatican also renewed its interest in the work of some of the leading liberation theologians. After the election of Karol Wojtyla as John Paul II in October 1978, the pressure started to increase significantly.[6]

John Paul's experience in Poland of the church's opposition to state socialism influenced his attitude to liberation theology in two ways. First, it confirmed his hostility to socialism as an oppressive system of power and increased his suspicion of liberation theology's relationship with Marxism. He saw socialism rather than capitalism as the major threat to the Christian vision of life. Second, the strength of the Polish church that he had led was based on a tight-knit unity under a hierarchical leadership. A firm chain of command and strict obedience to authority were the military-style values that helped the Polish church defend itself against the hostile state. John Paul sought to transfer this to the worldwide Catholic church. His policy has been called a restoration because it sought to vigorously reassert Catholic influence in society.[7] Restoration was seen in traditional terms of Catholic leadership and moral authority, and in this regard was a significant change of direction from the emphasis at Vatican II on cooperation and partnership or dialogue with the world.

The concern for a restoration of church influence and authority helps to explain many of the points that might otherwise seem as contradictions in John Paul

---

[5] Although private, the institute had close ties to the Reagan administration and held a controversial conference sponsored by the State Department in 1985. Figures associated with the institute included Michael Novak, Peter Berger, Richard Neuhaus, and James Schall. For their attitudes to liberation theology, see M. Novak, *Will It Liberate?* (Mahwah, N.J.: Paulist Press, 1986); P. Berger, *Pyramids of Sacrifice: Political Ethics and Social Change* (Garden City, N.Y.: Doubleday Anchor, 1974); R. J. Neuhaus, *The Naked Public Square* (Grand Rapids, Mich.: Eerdmans, 1984); J. V. Schall (ed.), *Liberation Theology in Latin America* (San Francisco: Ignatius Press, 1982). On the institute itself, see Lernoux, *People of God: The Struggle for World Catholicism* (New York: Viking, 1989), pp. 176–177 and 400–403. For wider overviews of North American criticisms of liberation theology on political and other grounds, see Sigmund, *Liberation Theology at the Crossroads* (Oxford: Oxford University Press, 1990), pp. 134–153; McGovern, *Liberation Theology and Its Critics*, pp. 55–58. For a lengthier analysis, see C. L. Nessan, *Orthopraxis or Heresy: The North American Theological Response to Latin American Liberation Theology* (Atlanta: Scholars Press, 1989).

[6] Karol Wojtyla was elected on 16 October and installed on 22 October. At 58 he was the youngest Pope since Pius IX, and the first non-Italian Pope for four centuries. His predecessor Albino Luciani (John Paul I) succeeded Paul VI in August 1978, but died after only 33 days. For a well balanced biography and assessment of his papacy, see M. Walsh, *John Paul II: A Biography* (London: Fount, 1994).

[7] On the restoration policy of John Paul II and its implications for liberation theology, see R. Della Cava, "Vatican Policy, 1978–1990: An Updated Review" in *Social Research* 59.1 (Spring 1992), pp. 169–199.

II's papacy. For example, he went further than any previous pope in his endorsement of social justice as a necessary part of faith.[8] His teachings on many social issues have shared the same passion for justice that motivated liberation theologians.[9] However, he was also determined to bring unity to the church, reassert traditional authority over political issues, and curb any moves to engage with Marxism or socialism.[10] Furthermore, he has also been very sympathetic to conservative movements such as *Opus Dei* and "Communion and Liberation," and his readiness to listen to their leaders' opinions increased his suspicions of liberation theology.[11]

During the 1980s, Vatican suspicion of liberation theology developed into open opposition and high-profile confrontation. After his speeches in Mexico at the opening of Puebla, the Pope gave a further indication of his concern in the early 1980s. In 1980, he requested that Cardinal Arns explain the church's role in an auto-workers strike in São Paulo. The following year, when the Jesuit Superior General Pedro Arrupe suffered a serious stroke, the Pope intervened and appointed Paola Dezza as interim successor.[12] Arrupe was elected in 1965 in the aftermath of Vatican II and had overseen a period in which the Jesuits' commitment to social justice put them at the forefront of liberation theology.[13] Arrupe's December 1980 letter to Latin American provincials and its discussion

---

[8] For helpful overviews, see I. Linden, "People before Profit: The Early Social Doctrine of John Paul II," and C. Longley, "Structures of Sin and the Free Market: John Paul II on Capitalism" in Vallely (ed.), *The New Politics*, pp. 84–96 and 97–113. For papal social teaching in the 1980s, see especially *Laborem Exercens: On Human Work* (14 September 1981) and *Sollicitudo Rei Socialis* (30 December 1987).

[9] It might also be noted that John Paul II has been very conservative on women and gender issues, but sadly this is a viewpoint that is also shared by many male liberation theologians (see Chapter 12).

[10] His visits to Latin America have frequently shown both sides of this social teaching. In the 1980s these visits included Brazil (1980), Argentina (1982), Central America (1983), Dominican Republic and Puerto Rico (1984), Venezuela, Peru, and Ecuador (1985), Colombia (1986), Uruguay, Chile, and Argentina (1987), Uruguay, Bolivia, Peru, and Paraguay (1988). See M. Walsh, *John Paul II*, pp. 83–85, 108, 117–121, 142–143, 144–145, 169–170, 192–194.

[11] *Opus Dei* was founded in Spain in 1928 by Josémaria Escrivá de Balaguer y Albás and has since spread worldwide. Pius XII granted it recognition in 1950, and in 1982 John Paul II elevated the movement into a personal prelacy. It has been particularly active in Latin America and consistent in its opposition to liberation theology. "Communion and Liberation" is a similarly conservative movement (but less secretive and more focussed on youth) that developed in Italy in 1954 under the leadership of Luigi Giussani. For overviews of both movements and the influence on world Catholicism, see Lernoux, *People of God*, pp. 302–338.

[12] Arrupe's relation with the Pope had been difficult before this and he already told the Pope of his wish to resign but was asked to delay. See M. Walsh, *John Paul II*, pp. 97–98; P. Hebblethwaite, *In the Vatican* (Oxford: Oxford University Press, 1986), pp. 138–140.

[13] Arrupe had also been president of the Conference of Major Superiors (heads of religious orders) in Rome, and therefore in an influential role for other religious orders as well.

of Marxism (see below) provoked particular hostility from López Trujillo and his relations with some of the *curia* were also difficult.[14] Dezza's appointment seemed to be a reverse on Arrupe's vigorous leadership. Dezza was 79 years old and spent most of his time in Rome where he had previously been Rector of the Gregorian University (1941–1951). The Pope's apparently hostile move strained relations with the Jesuits, but their loyal obedience to papal authority (Jesuits make a special oath of obedience) prevented public protests. The crisis was eventually resolved when the Pope sanctioned the election of Peter-Hans Kolvenbach at the thirty-second General Congregation in September 1983.

By this time the Pope's moves to restoration were already well underway. In November 1981, he appointed Cardinal Joseph Ratzinger of Munich to succeed Cardinal Franjo Seper as prefect of the Congregation for the Doctrine of Faith, the most powerful body in the Vatican (and the descendant of the Inquisition).[15] Ratzinger had taught theology in German universities and attended Vatican II as an adviser to Cardinal Frings. In the 1960s, Ratzinger was seen as a liberal, and he was a founding member of *Concilium* in 1967.[16] However, his time at Tübingen overlapped with the student unrest in the late 1960s, and his experiences there contributed to the much more conservative direction of his theology in the 1970s.[17] In the 1970s, Ratzinger was associated with the more conservative *Communio*.[18] He was made archbishop of Munich in 1977 and elevated to cardinal soon afterwards. In cooperation with Cardinal Höffner of Cologne he worked to reestablish more conservative control on the West German church.[19] In his new position as prefect, he enjoyed the Pope's firm support for stopping what they saw as the excesses that followed from the opti-

---

[14] There was particular trouble with the Pontifical Commission for Latin America. The commission was under Cardinal Sebastian Baggio (the Vatican's prefect of the Congregation for Bishops from 1973–1984), who was sympathetic to the *Opus Dei* movement and had previously served as nuncio in Chile and Brazil where he developed close links with conservative Latin American bishops.

[15] When it was originally set up in 1542 the congregation was known as the Congregation of the Holy Inquisition of Heretical Error. In 1908, it became known as the Holy Office and as part of the renewal of Vatican II, Paul VI renamed it the Congregation for the Doctrine of the Faith in 1965. The International Theological Commission was created in 1969 to aid its work.

[16] *Concilium* was established after Vatican II and quickly became an important forum for progressive Catholic theology.

[17] During this period, he also clashed with the prominent Swiss theologian Hans Küng. Küng was one of the most progressive theologians at Tübingen and his popularity extended beyond the university to a sizeable public audience. His work had long been seen as controversial, and he clashed with Georg Moser (the bishop for Rottenburg-Stuttgart) and Joseph Höffner (the influential cardinal in Cologne). The Congregation for the Doctrine of Faith withdrew Küng's licence to teach as a Catholic theologian in December 1979.

[18] *Communio* was established in the 1970s to offer a more conservative counterpoint to *Concilium*.

[19] The German church was also in a strong position to influence the church in other countries due to the size of its financial donations. Höffner was able to exercise considerable influence over Vatican finances.

mism of Vatican II.[20] Ratzinger took a strong personal interest in liberation theology and his determination to bring it under closer Vatican control soon became clear.[21]

The progress of the conflict can be divided into at least three periods. First, the growing tension in 1980–1983, marked by concerns with the church in post-revolution Nicaragua and investigations into Sobrino, Boff, and Gutiérrez. Second, the period of acute conflict in 1984–1985, when the Vatican published its highly critical *Instruction on Liberation Theology* and silenced Leonardo Boff. Third, attempts on both sides to improve relations beginning in 1986, which included the Vatican's second and more positive *Instruction* on liberation theology. This prepared the way for the uneasy relationship that followed, during which the Vatican toned down but did not stop its direct confrontations with prominent liberation theologians and maintained a consistent policy of appointing conservative figures to Latin American dioceses where liberation theology had previously been strong. At the same time, however, the Vatican sought to make the language and themes of liberation theology its own while purifying them of previous errors.

GROWING TENSION (1980–1983)

Nicaragua and the Sandinistas

The revolution in Nicaragua in July 1979 brought the left-wing Sandinistas to power on a wave of popular support for wide-reaching social changes.[22] The Sandinistas took their name from Augusto Sandino, who led the revolt by

---

[20] The Pope began this process for the church in Europe at the January 1980 synod of the Dutch church. The Dutch church was widely perceived as one of the most advanced in its promotion of Vatican II reforms.

[21] In February 1983, the Pope elevated López Trujillo to cardinal. Ratzinger appointed him to the Congregation for the Doctrine of the Faith where he joined the archbishop of Brasília, José Freire Falcão, who was seen as sympathetic to Opus Dei.

[22] On the church in Nicaragua, see C. Jerez, *The Church and the Nicaraguan Revolution* (London: Catholic Institute for International Relations, 1984); T. Caberstreo, *Ministers of God, Ministers of the People: Testimonies of Faith in Nicaragua* (trans. R. R. Barr; Maryknoll, N.Y.: Orbis Books; London: Zed Books, 1986); A. Bradstock, *Saints and Sandinistas: The Catholic Church in Nicaragua and its Response to the Revolution* (London: Epworth Press, 1987); P. Casaldáliga, *Prophets in Combat: The Nicaraguan Journal of Bishop Pedro Casaldáliga* (Oak Park, Ill.: Meyer-Stone Books; London: Catholic Institute for International Relations, 1987); R. N. Lancaster, *Thanks to God and the Revolution: Popular Religion and Class Consciousness in the New Nicaragua* (New York: Columbia University Press, 1988); G. Girardi, *Faith and Revolution in Nicaragua: Convergence and Contradictions* (trans. P. Berryman; Maryknoll, N.Y.: Orbis Books, 1989); J. Medcalf, *Letters from Nicaragua* (London: Catholic Institute for International Relations, 1988); P. J. Williams, *The Catholic Church and Politics in Nicaragua and Costa Rica* (London: Macmillan, 1989); M. Foroorhar, *The Catholic Church and Social Change in Nicaragua* (Albany: State University of New York Press, 1989); M. Dodson and L. Nuzzi O'Shaughnessy, *Nicaragua's Other Revolution: Religious Faith and Political Survival* (Chapel Hill: University of North Carolina Press, 1990); J. M. Kirk, *Politics and the Catholic Church in Nicaragua* (Gainesville: University of Florida Press, 1992).

nationalist Nicaraguans against occupying U.S. Marines in the 1930s. Inspired by his nationalist ideology, the Sandinistas of the 1970s overthrew Somoza's corrupt government and sought to end outside interference and exploitation. Politically, they opted for a broadly democratic socialism. Their economic policy was a mixed free-market and state direction; indeed as time passed the emphasis shifted more to the former than the latter. The main expressions of their socialism were in the areas of health and education, in which they made huge strides against difficult odds.

The Sandinista government was certainly not perfect on every democratic criterion. As U.S. sabotage against their revolution grew, they also tightened state control over parts of the media. Their concern for security and the need for unity to confront counter-revolutionaries did not sufficiently respect the rights of all minorities. For example, they had a disturbing conflict with indigenous communities on the Caribbean Miskito coast. Nonetheless, the Sandinistas were undoubtedly a great improvement on the repressive dictatorship that went before which the United States enthusiastically supported. Compared to what was happening in nearby El Salvador and Guatemala, the Sandinistas were far ahead on any human rights criteria.

The Nicaraguan revolution posed difficult questions for Latin American Christians: how could they best work out a practical relationship with left-wing political parties? A wide cross-section of the church supported the revolution and early government initiatives.[23] Many in the base communities were particularly committed to new government's program of land reform, basic education, and primary health care. However, the Vatican was deeply concerned about the influence of Marxism in the Sandinista government and worried that cooperation might seem to endorse it. The Reagan administration took every opportunity to encourage the Vatican's fears by projecting their own concerns that the Sandinistas were a hostile Marxist-Leninist force.

The extraordinary alliance between the Sandinista party and the popular church was exemplified when four of Nicaragua's most prominent radical priests became government ministers.[24] However, as time passed, the bishops led by Archbishop Obando y Bravo, found themselves in increasing opposition to the Sandinistas and were critical of the direction the revolution had taken. The bishops gave the priests an ultimatum to resign in July 1981, but a compromise was reached according to which they could remain if they desisted from priestly duties during this time. However, during 1982, relations between the

---

[23] Bishops of Nicaragua, "Christian Commitment for a New Nicaragua, 17 November 1979," *LADOC* 10 (March–April 1979), pp. 1–4; reprinted in Hennelly (ed.), *Liberation Theology*, pp. 282–291.

[24] These were: Ernesto Cardenal (minister of culture) and Edgar Parrales (minister of social welfare and then ambassador to OAS), who were both diocesan priests; Miguel D'Escoto (foreign minister), a Maryknoll Father; and Fernando Cardenal (coordinator of Literacy Crusade), a Jesuit. Canon law at the time allowed priests to participate in politics in extraordinary circumstances.

government and the Vatican continued to deteriorate. As the gap between the bishops and the government widened, the position of the four priests serving in the government remained highly sensitive.

John Paul II was concerned that the tension between the popular church and the hierarchy would create a serious division in the church and was determined to restore order and authority through the bishops.[25] During the Pope's visit to Nicaragua in 1983, he sought to emphasise the importance of unity for the Nicaraguan church.[26] However, the trip served to increase rather than reduce his concerns.

The Pope's trip got off to a poor start after confusion at the airport scuppered careful arrangements to prevent embarrassment on either side. One of the government's reception party mistakenly stepped forward to greet the Pope and so the Pope proceeded to greet all those present in the line. However, this led to the anticipated problem when he reached the rebel priest Ernesto Cardenal. When Ernesto Cardenal bent forward to kiss the papal ring the Pope issued a firm and very public televised rebuke, wagging his finger and instructing Cardenal to regularize his position with the church.[27]

The papal Mass attended by a huge crowd in Managua compounded this inauspicious start. As the Pope's sermon on unity drew toward an end, a number of voices started to call for him to make a plea for peace and offer a prayer for the dead. Some press reports suggested a deliberate Sandinista plan, but other observers say it originated spontaneously. The commotion started in an area reserved for relatives of those who had lost family members in raids by the U.S.-backed contras, and then spread to others in the crowd. The Pope had to shout "silence" a number of times before he could proceed and seemed shaken by the experience.[28]

Ill-feeling over the visit heightened the tension between the Vatican and the four priests who had taken government posts under the Sandinistas. In November 1983, a new canon law was passed that prevented all participation of priests in government. The effect of this was to undermine the compromise that had

---

[25] López Trujillo organised a CELAM report prior to his visit that warned of serious problems posed by liberation theology in the Central American churches. The report of *Pax Christi* that put the church's struggles for justice in a more positive light carried less weight.

[26] His sermon "Unity of the Church" was delivered in the central Plaza 19 de Julio in Managua on 4 March 1983 (*The Pope Speaks* 28 [1983], pp. 206–210, reprinted in Hennelly [ed.], *Liberation Theology*, pp. 329–334). The message came as no surprise since he had already indicated concern over divisions in a previous message to the Nicaraguan bishops ("The Bishop: Principle of Unity," 29 June 1982, in *The Pope Speaks* 27, pp. 338–343; reprinted in Hennelly [ed.], *Liberation Theology*, pp. 323–328).

[27] Ernesto Cardenal's reputation in Nicaragua was especially high due to his accomplishments as a poet as well as his life as a priest. The televised pictures of the Pope's rebuke shocked many within the base communities.

[28] See International Observers, "Open Letter Regarding the Papal Mass" in Hennelly (ed.), *Liberation Theology*, pp. 335–337.

existed since 1981 between the four priests and the Nicaraguan bishops. Fernando
Cardenal was expelled from the Jesuits on 10 December 1984, and all four priests
were suspended from the priesthood on 19 January 1985.[29]

The Pope's concerns over Nicaragua typified his concern over liberation theology in general. First, he saw the popular church as a threat to the unity of
the church and the traditional authority of Rome. Second, he worried over the
relationship between priests and the Marxists in the Nicaraguan government.
Ever since the fourteenth ordinary meeting of CELAM at Sucre (1972), conservative Latin American church leaders sought to resist the changes signalled
at Medellín and return the church to its previous neutrality on political issues.[30]
They were delighted by the new Pope's attitude and seized the situation in
Nicaragua as proof of the dangers that liberation theology posed to the church
throughout the continent.

Marxist Analysis and Marxist Philosophy

The appropriate relationship of Christianity and Marxist analysis in Latin
America had not been properly resolved in the 1970s. While developments
within liberation theology meant that the issue was far less significant in
most writing than it had been in the early 1970s, the issues raised by the
Sandinista revolution made it a growing concern for church authorities once
again. It is therefore helpful to review a nuanced discussion of the dangers from
Marxist analysis, outlined in a letter to Jesuit superiors in Latin America after
the Puebla conference.[31] The General Superior of the Jesuits, Pedro Arrupe,
wrote the letter in response to §§ 544–555 of the Puebla document on the
dangers of Marxism. Arrupe's letter offered advice on the appropriate attitude
to Marxist analysis. Specifically, he discussed whether Marxist analysis could be
embraced while maintaining a rejection of other aspects of a Marxist world-
view such as atheism.

Arrupe avoided a blanket rejection of Marxist ideas and offered cautious
approval of what Marxist viewpoints might offer. He said, "we can accept a
certain number of methodological viewpoints which to a greater or lesser extent
arise from Marxist analysis, as long as we do not attribute an exclusive character to them."[32] He seemed to agree—at least in principle—that it was possible to use Marxist analysis while rejecting Marxist philosophy. However, Arrupe

---

[29] See Bradstock, *Saints and Sandinistas*, pp. 59–69. For Fernando Cardenal's views
on events see F. Cardenal, "A Letter to My Friends" in *The National Catholic Reporter*
(11 January 1985), pp. 1, 6–8; reprinted in Hennelly (ed.), *Liberation Theology*, pp. 341–347.

[30] In addition to the election of Archbishop Alfonso López Trujillo as the new
Secretary General of CELAM, other conservatives elected in key posts included Bishop
Luciano Duarteas, President of Social Action, and Bishop Antonio Quarricino to the
Department of the Laity.

[31] P. Arrupe, "Marxist Analysis by Christians," *Origins* 10 (16 April 1981), pp. 689–693;
reprinted in Hennelly (ed.), *Liberation Theology*, pp. 307–313.

[32] Arrupe, "Marxist Analysis by Christians," § 5.

went on to reject attempts to draw a simple distinction between Marxist analysis and other parts of Marxist philosophy. The letter argued that Marxist analysis could not usually be isolated in this way and stressed that uncritical acceptance of Marxist analysis was likely to have negative consequences for theology. For example, that "Marxist social analysis contains as an essential element a radical theory of antagonism and class struggle."[33] According to Arrupe: "In practice, however, the adoption of Marxist analysis is rarely the adoption of only a method or an 'approach.' Usually it means accepting the substance of the explanations Marx provided for the social reality of his time and applying them to that of our time."[34] He therefore concluded that Marxist analysis *as a whole* cannot be acceptable to Christian theology:

> In brief, although Marxist analysis does not directly imply acceptance of Marxist philosophy as a whole—and still less of dialectical materialism as such—as it is normally understood it implies in fact a concept of human history which contradicts the Christian view of humankind and society, and leads to strategies which threaten Christian values and attitudes.... To adopt therefore not just some elements or some methodological insights, but Marxist analysis as a whole, is something we cannot accept.[35]

Arrupe's views were a careful and balanced development of issues touched on in *Octogesima Adveniens* and the controversy over Christians for Socialism in Chile in the early 1970s. He gave an endorsement of the critical use of some aspects of Marxism, but rejected any thorough-going Marxist analysis.[36] The simplistic suggestion that if other aspects of Marxist philosophy are rejected, then Marxist analysis can be whole-heartedly embraced was rejected. However, while ruling out a full adoption of Marxist analysis, he left the door open for the continued critical use of Marxist thought in liberation theology.

Arrupe's letter raised important issues that could have provided a deeper framework for the discussions of Marxism in liberation theology and promoted more balanced critiques of the some of the publications in the 1970s. Unfortunately, as the decade progressed, the conversation usually moved backward rather than forward. Arrupe's careful statement was swept aside by more polemical works that made it harder rather than easier to evaluate the role of Marxism in liberation theology. Discussion was made even more difficult by the tendency of critics to speak of liberation theology in very general terms, which failed to recognised the dramatic changes that had taken place in its methodological approach during the 1970s.

---

[33] Arrupe, "Marxist Analysis by Christians," § 11.

[34] Arrupe, "Marxist Analysis by Christians," § 6.

[35] Arrupe, "Marxist Analysis by Christians," §§ 13 and 15.

[36] Furthermore, Arrupe noted the difficulties in making any *a priori* judgement on this matter. He also acknowledged that those outside the situation might see the main problem as theoretical compatibility at an ideological level, while those dealing with the issues on the ground might have much more modest goals of determing guidelines for practical partnership.

Investigations into Sobrino, Gutiérrez, and Boff

In 1980, continuing on from the Pope's warnings on Christology at Puebla, Cardinal Franjo Seper (Ratzinger's predecessor as prefect of the Congregation for the Doctrine of Faith) reopened the Sobrino case that had first been prompted by the 1977 publication of *Christology at the Crossroads*. Seper examined the response that Sobrino had previously given to the Congregation for Education and decided it required further clarifications. Sobrino sent a new response to Rome and it arrived shortly after Ratzinger took over. In 1982, Ratzinger asked the Jesuits to make a further enquiry on the matter. This was effectively the third investigation of Sobrino and was conducted by Juan Alfaro SJ in 1982–1983.[37] Alfaro's firm support for Sobrino ended the sequence. Meanwhile, Ratzinger was ready to move on to other inquiries, in particular on his former student—Leonardo Boff—and on the influential figurehead of liberation theology Gustavo Gutiérrez.

In 1981, Boff published a collection of his previous work on the church as *Church: Charism and Power*.[38] The underlying concern over Boff's work was that he had applied a social analysis of power relations to the working of the church. The newly formed archdiocesan Commission for the Doctrine of Faith of Rio de Janeiro (which operated under the auspices of the city's conservative archbishop, Eugênio de Araujo Sales) promptly seized its contents as a dangerous distortion of the church's orthodox doctrine.[39] The commission launched an examination of the book under the leadership of Bishop Karl Joseph Romer. This began with a critical review of the book by Father Urbano Zilles published in the *Boletim da Revista do Clero* in February 1982.

Boff responded to the criticisms with an article for the April 1982 edition of *Boletim da Revista do Clero*.[40] He also sent copies of his reply and the original criticisms to Rome.[41] However, the *Boletim da Revista do Clero* printed

---

[37] See J. Alfaro, "Foreword" in J. Sobrino, *Jesus in Latin America* (trans. various; Maryknoll, N.Y.: Orbis Books, 1987 [ET 1982]), pp. ix–xiii.

[38] L. Boff, *Church: Charism and Power: Liberation Theology and the Institutional Church* (trans. J. Diercksmeier; New York: Crossroad; London: SCM Press, 1985 [Portuguese orig. 1981]). Since Boff was responsible for the religious section of Vozes (a Brazilian publishing company) he was involved not just as the author, but also the publisher of this work. On the controversy and its background, see esp. H. Cox, *The Silencing of Leonardo Boff: The Vatican and the Future of World Christianity* (Oak Park, Ill.: Meyer-Stone Books, 1988) and P. Lernoux, *People of God: The Struggle of World Catholicism* (New York: Penguin, 1989), pp. 89–115.

[39] When Eugênio Sales established the commission one of its central aims was to tackle liberation theology in his archdiocese since he had failed to persuade the national commission undertake the task. He also banned Clodovis Boff from instructing in schools or universities under his jurisdiction (Lernoux, *People of God*, p. 106).

[40] See Cox, *The Silencing of Leonardo Boff*, pp. 22–23.

[41] In retrospect, this may have been a crucial mistake. It allowed Rome to claim an interest and oversight in the case. Cardinal Rossi (the former Archbishop of São Paulo) who worked in the *curia* was concerned at the way liberation theology—and especially

Boff's article along with a further rejoinder from Zilles. When Boff responded to the rejoinder (in the journal *Grande Sinal*) it was again matched by another attack, this time from Fr. Estevo Bettancourt who was also a member of Rio de Janeiro Commission for the Doctrine of Faith. In addition, Boff's fellow Franciscan Bonaventura Kloppenburg (who was also another of his former theological teachers) published a critical review of the book in *Communio*.[42]

Kloppenburg's article in an international Catholic journal provided a convenient opportunity for Cardinal Ratzinger himself to enter directly into the controversy. On 14 April 1982, Ratzinger wrote to Boff to say the material that Boff sent had been received. He also asked Boff to make a formal response to Kloppenburg's criticisms as well, since this was not included in what Boff had previously sent.[43] Boff sent back his response as requested and also published it in the June 1982 edition of *Revista Eclesiástica Brasileira*, the influential journal for which he was editor.[44] Boff then waited until both the accusations and responses had been studied and a decision made. This proved a protracted process of almost two years.

During this time, the tension within the Brazilian church over liberation theology surfaced at the Bishop's Synod in Rome, which met on the theme of penance and reconciliation (September–October 1983). Cardinal Arns spoke on the significance of social sin and Cardinal Lorscheider criticised the false interpretations and suspicions of heresy raised against liberation theology. However, Cardinal Sales who represented the opposite tendency responded and was supported by Bishop Duarte of Aracaju and López Trujillo.[45] López Trujillo,

---

Boff's work—posed a threat to the church's traditional hierarchical authority. Rossi was an early supporter of base communities in São Paulo, but these were within the framework of a very traditional ecclesiology, and not—as Boff advocated—a new way of being church.

[42] Kloppenburg had particular influence as a member of the International Theological Commission and Boff had previously served as his secretary. Kloppenburg had already attacked liberation theology and the popular church in his book *The People's Church: A Defense of My Church* (trans. M. J. O'Connell; Chicago: Franciscan Herald Press, 1978 [Portuguese orig. 1977]).

[43] Ratzinger refused the Brazilian bishops' request that they conduct their own investigation of Boff under Cardinal Lorscheider. Ratzinger's justification of direct intervention was that Boff's work had been translated (and thus became an international matter), and that Boff sent copies of the original exchange with Zilles to Rome.

[44] At the same time, Kloppenberg's article was reprinted in the newspaper *Jornal do Brasil* and generated further publicity for the dispute.

[45] Whereas the CNNB elected most representatives that were present, the Vatican invited López Trujillo and Dom Duarte, the Brazilian Archbishop of Aracaju. A few months later Dom Duarte made a highly publicised attack on the popular church in Brazil through a T.V. and newspaper interview at the CNBB Assembly (6–15 April 1983). He alleged that many bishops opposed the Pope, complained about the influence of Marxism in the church, condemned the independence of the popular church from the bishops, and suggested that papal intervention might be needed. Ironically, it may have been such a blatant attack that swung support for progressives (including the outgoing President of CNBB Dom Ivo Lorscheiter) in the elections of the CNBB executive. The

who was particularly hostile to Arns and Lorscheider after their defence of liberation theology at Puebla, claimed that the focus on social sin in Latin America
reduced personal sin to second place. The synod's message reflected the views
of Arns (who was elected to the drafting committee) more than López Trujillo.
Nonetheless, the Pope's final speech was critical of social sin as anything more
than an analogy.[46] This concern would resurface in later Vatican pronouncements in the 1980s.

Meanwhile the Commission for Doctrine and Faith were also exerting pressure on the Peruvian bishops to discipline Gutiérrez. In March 1983, Cardinal
Ratzinger issued a highly critical document entitled "Ten Observations on the
Theology of Gustavo Gutiérrez."[47] The allegations made against Gutiérrez—
which claim to be based on A Theology of Liberation and The Power of the Poor
in History—were not referenced to any specific passages, and therefore very hard
to counter.[48] Other theologians in Latin America and elsewhere voiced strong
support for him during this process. The German theologian Karl Rahner, who
had been so influential in determining the more open theology of Vatican II,
wrote to Cardinal Landázuri Ricketts of Lima to voice his conviction that the
liberation theology that Gutiérrez represents was thoroughly orthodox.[49]

Although the Peruvian bishops conference became more conservative, the
opponents of liberation theology were not yet strong enough to overrule those
who valued Gutiérrez's work. Cardinal Ricketts and a number of other bishops
protected Gutiérrez from those who wanted to publicly condemn his work in
accordance with the Observations. After twelve months, the deadlocked Peruvian
bishops were not able to resolve the problem when Ratzinger called the Doctrinal
Commissions of the National Latin American Bishops Conferences to a joint
meeting in Bogotá in March 1984. At the meeting he denounced the Marxist
affinities of liberation theology and its ecclesiological errors. However, it was
still not enough to provoke a clear condemnation of liberation theology by the

---

progressive slant of the CNBB was to have important consequences in the tensions between
the Vatican and Leonardo Boff in the mid-1980s. See D. Regan, Church for Liberation:
A Pastoral Portrait of the Church in Brazil (Dublin: Dominican Publications, 1987), pp.
1–15 (esp. 3).

[46] See Walsh, John Paul II, p. 127.

[47] Commission for the Doctrine of the Faith, "Ten Observations on the Theology of
Gustavo Gutiérrez" (March 1983); reprinted Hennelly (ed.), Liberation Theology, pp.
348–350.

[48] For a very helpful overview of criticisms of Gutiérrez, see Brown, Gustavo Gutiérrez,
pp. 131–156, and especially pp. 137–138 for a summary of the Observations.

[49] K. Rahner, "Letter to Cardinal Juan Landázuri Ricketts of Lima," 16 March 1984,
in Hennelly (ed.), Liberation Theology, pp. 351–352. This was not the first time that Rahner
voiced strong support for liberation theology. Along with other prominent German theologians (including Herbert Vorgrimler, Johannes Metz, Martin Niemoller, and Ernst
Kasemann) he publicly protested attacks on liberation theology in a statement published in November 1977 and translated into English as German Theologians, "We Must
Protest," Cross Currents 28 (1978) pp. 66–70. For discussion of this article, see G. Baum,
"German Theologians and Liberation Theology," The Ecumenist 16 (1978), pp. 49–51;
reprinted in Hennelly (ed.), Liberation Theology, pp. 220–224.

Peruvians.[50] Eventually, they sent two contradictory assessments of Gutiérrez back to the Vatican, which were little use to Ratzinger.[51] Nonetheless, responding to the ten observations occupied a great deal of Gutiérrez's energy for the best part of two years and eventually found careful expression in his work "Theology and the Social Sciences."[52]

March 1984 also saw further pressure on liberation theology when the Italian magazine *30 Giorno* featured an article claiming to reveal Ratzinger's personal concerns over liberation theology and its relationship to Marxism.[53] The article was apparently based on Ratzinger's confidential papers that he claimed were used without his permission.[54] How such a provocative article came to be published at such a sensitive time remains unclear, but it seemed to genuinely describe his feelings and left little doubt on his fierce opposition to liberation theology. Jon Sobrino and Ignacio Ellacuría were picked out as explicit targets (the only liberation theologians that were named, although Ratzinger presumably had Gutiérrez and Boff very much in mind as well), and the influence of Rudolf Bultmann and scientific exegesis were also heavily criticised. The article ended with his comment "if one thinks how radical this interpretation of Christianity that derives from it really is, the problem of what one can and must do about it [liberation theology] becomes even more urgent."[55]

Two months later, Ratzinger finally responded to Boff on the controversy surrounding *Church: Charism and Power*. Ratzinger's letter, dated 15 May 1984, gave a number of criticisms of the book and suggested that Boff come to Rome for a colloquy (conversation) to discuss them further. Boff requested that the discussion take place in Brazil, but when this was rejected, he accepted Ratzinger's invitation.[56] News of the colloquy added to Ratzinger's comments in *30 Giorno*

---

[50] See Brown, *Gustavo Gutiérrez*, p. 138. In comparing the situations of Gutiérrez and Boff, it is significant to note that both the Peruvian and Brazilian bishops' conferences were split at a national level; Gutiérrez's enjoyed the local support of his archbishop, whereas Leonardo Boff did not (Cardinal Sales was an active opponent of liberation theology).

[51] Ratzinger increased the pressure on the Peruvian episcopal conference with a personal visit in April 1984, but the Peruvians remained split and Gutiérrez remained safe.

[52] This was first published in the Peruvian journal *Paginas*, pp. 63–64 (September 1984), and included as a chapter in Gustavo Gutiérrez, *The Truth Shall Make You Free: Confrontations* (trans. M. J. O'Connell; Maryknoll, N.Y.: Orbis Books, 1990), pp. 53–84.

[53] J. Ratzinger, "Liberation Theology" (March 1984); reprinted in Hennelly (ed.), *Liberation Theology*, pp. 367–374.

[54] *30 Giorni* was a relaunched version of the magazine *Incontri*. The conservative Italian based organisation "Communion and Liberation" established *Incontri* in 1981 as a vehicle to express their views on the church, and its targets included liberation theology and the popular church in Latin America (see Lernoux, *People of God*, pp. 330–333).

[55] Hennelly (ed.), *Liberation Theology*, p. 374.

[56] Previous investigations into the Swiss theologian Hans Küng and the Belgian theologian Edward Schillebeeckx suggested that this was a prudent course. Küng refused to go to Rome and was condemned in his absence. The CDF condemned him in 1979, and the German bishops withdrew his license to teach in 1980. By contrast, Schillebeeckx agreed to go and escaped with a reprimand.

and the preparation of the *Instruction* all pointed to a clampdown on liberation theology. Concern over the direction of events prompted the editorial board of *Concilium*—an international journal to which Boff had close ties—to issue a statement of solidarity with liberation theologians in June 1984.[57]

At about the same time, Ratzinger's close ally and colleague on the Commission for the Doctrine of Faith, Cardinal Höffner of Cologne visited São Paulo to review the seminary and its training of priests. While in Brazil with Cardinal Arns Höffner appeared generally positive on what he saw. However, after his return to Europe, he published a strong attack and warned against liberationist presentations of Christ as a revolutionary figure.[58]

Meanwhile, Boff spent the next months preparing for his visit to Rome and thinking through his replies to Ratzinger's concerns. To give support, Bishop José Ivo Lorscheiter (president of the CNBB), Cardinal Aloísio Lorscheider (president of the CNBB Commission on Doctrine and former president of the CNBB and CELAM), and Cardinal Paulo Evaristo Arns (archbishop of São Paulo) all arranged to be in Rome at the same time as Boff. Although they would officially be in Rome on other business, they took a close interest in the upcoming colloquy and the two cardinals arranged to be present for the second half of it.[59] Since Boff's conformity with ecclesial authority was at stake, the presence of the two cardinals was an important part of Boff's defence. Boff was eager to show that he was in line with the pastoral policies of the CNBB and had their authority. For their part, Arns, Lorscheiter, and Lorscheider had good reason to interpret the investigation of Boff as part of an open Vatican assault on the direction of the Brazilian church under their leadership.[60]

---

[57] *Concilium* Editorial Board, "Statement of Solidarity with Liberation Theologians, 24 June 1984"; reprinted in Hennelly (ed.), *Liberation Theology*, pp. 390–392. Boff was on the editorial board of *Concilium* and responsible for the Brazilian edition. In addition, he contributed a significant number of articles to the journal in the 1980s, including: Boff, "Martyrdom: An Attempt at Systematic Reflection," *Concilium* 163 (1983), pp. 12–17; "A Theological Examination of the Terms 'People of God' and 'Popular Church,'" *Concilium* 176 (1984), pp. 89–98; "The Poor Judge: The Magisterium and the Liberation Theologians," *Concilium* 192 (1987), pp. xi–xiii; "What are Third World Theologies?" *Concilium* 199 (1988), pp. 3–13; "Anti-Communism: End of an Industry," *Concilium* 205 (1989), pp. xi–xiii. He also served as a co-editor for volumes on important themes in liberation theology, including: L. Boff and J. Elizondo (eds.), *La Iglesia Popular: Between Fear and Hope* (*Concilium* 176; New York: Seabury; Edinburgh: T & T Clark, 1984); L. Boff and J. Elizondo (eds.), *Option for the Poor: Challenge for the Rich Countries* (*Concilium* 187; Edinburgh: T & T Clark, 1986); L. Boff and J. Elizondo (eds.), *Theologies of the Third World: Convergences and Differences* (*Concilium* 199; Edinburgh: T & T Clark, 1988).

[58] See Lernoux, *People of God*, p. 44; Hewitt, *Base Christian Communities*, p. 100.

[59] Both cardinals had been elected at the Synod of Bishops in Rome the previous year to represent the Americas (along with Cardinal Bernardin of Chicago) on the Council of the Synod's General Secretariat.

[60] During the same year, the Vatican undertook a review of seminary training in São Paulo and other dioceses. Cardinal Josef Höffner of the Sacred Congregation for Catholic Education warned against presentations of Christ as a revolutionary figure (see W. E.

ACUTE CONFLICT (1984–1985)

Boff arrived in Rome on 2 September and was greeted by his brother Clodovis and his sister Lina who were both already there. The very next day the long-awaited Vatican *Instruction* on liberation theology (dated 6 August) was finally issued. The Vatican spokesmen claimed that this was entirely coincidental, but the delay in publication, until Boff was in Rome, certainly increased the pressure on Boff and the *Instruction's* high-handed criticisms were an ominous indication of the Vatican's attitude.[61]

The 1984 "Instruction on Certain Aspects of Liberation Theology"

Libertatis Nuntius or the *Instruction on Certain Aspects of the Theology of Liberation* set out Ratzinger's concerns on liberation theology at some length.[62] The publication of the *Instruction* was clearly intended to bring liberation theologians into line with ecclesial authority, but its message was not completely straightforward. Some passages in the *Instruction* read as if they might have been written by liberation theologians themselves. Thus, the *Instruction* opens with the surprisingly positive passage cited more fully at the start of this chapter, "The Gospel of Jesus Christ is a message of freedom and a force for liberation."[63] At a later point, in a forceful statement of issues central to liberation theology it states: "Justice as regards God and justice as regards man are inseparable. God is the defender and liberator of the poor" (§ 4.6).

However, despite taking over the language of liberation in some regards, the *Instruction* was clearly intended as a fierce attack on Latin American liberation theology.[64] It expressed particular concern over two closely related failures of

---

Hewitt, *Base Christian Communities*, p. 100). Cardinal Arns may have taken the investigation into Boff personally, since he was a fellow Franciscan and Arns had overseen part of Boff's training.

[61] The delay also permitted an additional statement of Ratzinger's views prior to the official *Instruction*. Toward the end of August, Ratzinger gave a sequence of candid interviews to the respected Italian journalist Vittorio Messori that Messori recorded for later publication. Extracts were published in the magazine *Jesus* the following year while the case against Boff was still being decided. The full interview was subsequently published as V. Messori, *The Ratzinger Report: An Exclusive Interview on the State of the Church* (trans. Salvator Attansio and Graham Harrison; San Francisco: Ignatius Press, 1985).

[62] CDF, *Instruction on Certain Aspects of the Theology of Liberation* (Vatican City: 1984), Intro. Juan Segundo offers a detailed critique of the *Instruction* in Segundo, *Theology and the Church: A Response to Cardinal Ratzinger and a Warning to the Whole Church* (trans. J. Diercksmeier; Minneapolis, Minn.: Winston Press; London: Geoffrey Chapman, 1985).

[63] *Instruction*, § Intro. See also: "Justice as regards God and justice as regards man are inseparable. God is the defender and liberator of the poor" (§ 4.6).

[64] Section 3 of the *Instruction* is devoted to liberation as a Christian theme. While it recognises liberation as "fundamental to the Old and New Testament" and describes the term theology of liberation as "a thoroughly valid term," it insists that "the two can be understood only in light of the specific message of revelation, authentically interpreted by the magisterium of the church" (*Instruction* § 3.4). Segundo (*The Liberation*

liberation theologians. First, it claimed that they gave one-sided attention to earthly and temporal matters. For example, it charged liberation theologians with minimising the importance of liberation from sin. Second, the *Instruction* claimed that liberation theologians used borrowed concepts (presumably a reference to Marxism) without "sufficient critical caution."[65] Both criticisms were raised in the third paragraph of the Introduction and permeated the whole *Instruction*. Since, Marxism was the connecting link at the heart of both these concerns, the focus on Marxism in much of the *Instruction* was easily understandable. This was made clear at the outset when the *Instruction* presented its intention as:

> to draw the attention of pastors, theologians and all the faithful to the deviations and risks of deviation, damaging to the faith and to Christian living, that are brought about by certain forms of liberation theology which use, in an insufficiently critical manner, concepts borrowed from various currents of Marxist thought.[66]

The *Instruction* could therefore move quickly from approval for the Christian heritage behind the term liberation when used correctly, to a sweeping condemnation of the corruptive influence of Marxism in the way that liberation theologians used the term.[67]

The main body of the document was split into two parts of roughly equal length, §§ 1–6 and 7–12. The first six sections alternate between an affirmation of the theme of liberation in principle (§§ 1, 3, and 5) and a warning about liberation theology in practice (§§ 2, 4, and 6). Thus § 1, titled "An Aspiration," described "the powerful and almost irresistible" aspiration for liberation as "one of the principle signs of the times." Section 2, "Expressions of this Aspiration," then warned that this aspiration often finds itself captive of ideologies which hide or pervert its meaning (§ 2.3) and lead to violence (§ 2.4). Likewise, § 3 on "Liberation: A Christian Theme" recognised that "In itself, the expression 'theology of liberation' is a thoroughly valid term" (§ 3.4); but § 4 on "Biblical Foundations" warned against a reduction of liberation to something which is "principally or exclusively political in nature" (§ 4.3). It

---

of Theology, p. 4) warned of this danger back in the early 1970s: "ecclesiastical authorities themselves have adopted the terminology of liberation. Gradually this has led to a watering down of its content, so that the language of liberation is emptied of all real meaning." Likewise, Gutiérrez mentions the dangers of "attempts to apply the cosmetic vocabulary of 'liberation' to old pastoral and theological stances"; see Gutiérrez, *The Power of the Poor in History*, p. 64.

[65] The *Instruction* warns that "It is difficult, and perhaps impossible, to purify these borrowed concepts of an ideological inspiration which is incompatible with Christian faith and the ethical requirements which flow from it." *Instruction*, § Intro., in Hennelly (ed.), *Liberation Theology*, pp. 393–394.

[66] *Instruction*, § Intro., in Hennelly (ed.), *Liberation Theology*, p. 394.

[67] For example: "But the 'theologies of liberation,' which deserve credit for restoring to a place of honour the great texts of the prophets and of the Gospel in the defence of the poor, go on to make a disastrous confusion between the poor of the scripture and the proletariat of Marx" (*Instruction*, § 9.10).

emphasised that "The first liberation, to which all others must make reference, is that from sin" (§ 4.12). "The Voice of the Magisterium" (§ 5) recalled the interventions of the church's magisterium "to awaken Christian consciences to a sense of justice, social responsibility, and solidarity with the poor and oppressed" (§ 5.2). "A New Interpretation of Christianity" (§ 6) contrasted this with the warning that for some "the necessary struggle for human justice and freedom in the economic and political sense constitutes the whole essence of salvation. For them, the Gospel is reduced to a purely earthly gospel" (§ 6.3).[68]

The final paragraphs of § 6 emphasised that not all liberation theologies are guilty of these dangers. It also made explicit the need to speak of liberation theologies in the plural rather than just liberation theology in the singular. The different theologies of liberation are divided "between the preferential option for the poor forcefully reaffirmed without ambiguity after Medellín at the conference of Puebla on the one hand, and the temptation to reduce the Gospel to an earthly gospel on the other" (§ 6.5). It then went on to say that it would restrict its focus to the latter.[69]

Specific allegations against the use of Marxist analysis arose in § 10 of the *Instruction*. These included a number of related concerns. First, that some liberation theologies adopted *a priori* a classist viewpoint which has come to function as a determining principle. Second, that they wrongly committed themselves to the idea of class conflict and the necessity of violence as presented in Marxist social analysis.[70] Finally, that they accepted ideas from Marxist social analysis that committed them to an atheistic philosophy and "a reductionist reading of the Bible."[71] Like the earlier Observations on Gutiérrez, the *Instruction* seemed to assume that any liberation theology that utilised Marxist analysis necessarily led to these problems. The sweeping version of the argument in the *Instruction* facilitated denunciations of liberation theology, but hindered the clear assessment of liberation theologians on the real issues outlined by in Arrupe's document. Liberation theologians inevitably assumed that this was deliberate. The priority was more to denounce liberation theology than promote a careful evaluation.[72]

---

[68] Segundo describes this alternation as a "see-saw" and gives further elaboration on its stages in Segundo, *Theology and the Church*, pp. 24–26. After the initial appearance of the *Instruction* it was widely rumoured that more positive sections of the early pages had been added by the Pope because he felt the draft shown him struck too negative a tone (see Cox, *The Silencing of Leonardo Boff*, p. 109). In a letter describing his visit to the Vatican in 1988, Bishop Casaldáliga suggests that the first five sections came from the Pope. However, it is clear that Ratzinger refused to concede this claim (see Hennelly [ed.], *Liberation Theology*, pp. 532–540 [534]).

[69] "In the present document, we will only be discussing developments of that current thought which, under the name 'theology of liberation,' proposes a novel interpretation of both the content of faith and of Christian existence which seriously departs from the faith of the church and, in fact, actually constitutes a practical negation" (§ VI.9).

[70] *Instruction*, § 10.1.

[71] *Instruction*, § 10.5.

[72] The *Instruction* explicitly stated two limitations in its scope. First, that not all

The *Instruction* met with a predictably mixed reception. Since the *Instruction* did not name particular theologians, it was hard to respond to or defend against. It might be possible, in principle, to read the *Instruction* as an attack on only unusual variants of liberation theology like Miranda's work on Christianity and Marxism.[73] However, there is little doubt that the *Instruction* was targeted at leading liberation theologians, such as Gustavo Gutiérrez and Leonardo Boff. Opponents of liberation theology welcomed the *Instruction* and saw it as clearly aimed against the leading proponents of the movement and not just marginal examples.[74]

To deflect its criticism Boff and Gutiérrez argued that the positions described in the *Instruction* did not reflect their published work or thought.[75] In an interview with the Peruvian newspaper *La República*, Gutiérrez struck a particularly positive note by focusing on the *Instruction's* affirmation of the term liberation.[76] However, it was hard to deny that it was clearly directed against them, and it prepared the way for Ratzinger to make further attacks on both of them.

---

liberation theologies should be seen as flawed in this way. The use of the plural, theologies of liberation, appeared to recognise the diversity in liberation theologies. In particular, it suggested that liberation theologies must correctly follow the church's teaching at Medellín and Puebla. This implies that some were guilty on the matters criticised, while others were not, and that there were fairly clear criteria by which to make this judgement. Second, that it acknowledged that it was mainly concerned with the dangers and negative aspects of liberation theology and promised a more positive treatment of the liberation theme in a subsequent document (*Instruction*, § Intro.). On both matters, however, there was more to the matter than was immediately apparent.

[73] However, because Miranda is a lay academic, he does not seem to have worried the Vatican.

[74] In Latin America, Cardinal López Trujillo, Bishop Bonaventura Kloppenburg, and others gathered in July 1985 at a conference sponsored by *Communio* in Los Andes, Chile (see "Declaration of Los Andes," *CELAM* 24 [October–November 1985] pp. 5–9; reprinted in Hennelly [ed.], *Liberation Theology*, pp. 444–450). *Communio* was a journal that was founded to provide a conservative counterweight to the progressive ethos of *Concilium*. The conference issued a ringing endorsement of the *Instruction* and asserted that: "the positions described in parts VI to X of the *Instruction* are not hypothetical constructs, but real pronouncements contained in numerous books, essays, and articles that circulate throughout Latin America" (§ 3). The Chilean liberation theologian Ronaldo Muñoz wrote a reply to the Andes Declaration in "An Open Reply to Cardinal López Trujillo," in *LADOC* 16 (November–December 1985), pp. 40–43; reprinted in Hennelly (ed.), *Liberation Theology*, pp. 451–453.

[75] For Boff's response, originally printed in the Brazilian newspaper *Folha de São Paulo*, see L. Boff, "Vatican Instruction Reflects European Mind-Set" in *LADOC* 15 (January–February 1985), pp. 8–12; reprinted in Hennelly (ed.), *Liberation Theology*, pp. 415–418. Gutiérrez responds further to the *Instruction* in "The Truth Shall Make You Free," in Gutiérrez, *The Truth Shall Make You Free: Confrontations*, pp. 85–200.

[76] Gutiérrez pointed out: "The document declares that the Christian message is 'a message of freedom and a force for liberation.' It also affirms that aspirations to liberation are a sign of our times that must be analyzed in the light of the gospel. It explicitly states that 'the expression liberation theology is a totally valid expression.'" He also

Silencing of Leonardo Boff and Pressuring Gutiérrez

The conflict with Boff was particularly sensitive because the issues that Boff raised went directly to the Vatican's authority.[77] Boff's work on ecclesiology raised questions on the nature of the church and the Pope's restoration of church order much more directly than Gutiérrez.[78] Boff's tenacious commitment to his position exemplified precisely the problem that the *curia* identified in his work—a failure to accept proper ecclesial authority.

Ratzinger's conversation with Boff finally took place on 7 September. It was an awkward meeting between former student and former teacher who were both committed to a defence of the faith, as they understood it. Boff read his prepared answer and then discussion of his ecclesiology followed.[79] Some of the tension was eased when Cardinals Arns and Lorscheider joined them for the second part of the session, and the talk moved away from Boff's book to a friendlier and less formal discussion of the church in Brazil.[80] After the meeting, Boff stayed on in Rome for awhile before he returned to Brazil in October.

Back in Brazil, Boff had to wait six months before he was informed on the outcome of the meeting. In the meantime, Ratzinger tried to use the publication of the *Instruction* to pressure the Peruvian bishops to issue their own condemnation of Gutiérrez. He called the Peruvian bishops to Rome in October 1984 to discuss the case further.[81] When they arrived, Ratzinger presented a

---

explicitly referred to Arrupe's statement on Marxist analysis. He appears to accept Arrupe's view that Marxist analysis can have an exclusive character and agrees with Arrupe that therefore cannot be accepted in its entirety. However, he argues that the Marxist analysis that it rejects is certainly not the attitude that he takes in his work. He distinguishes carefully between the "critical use of social sciences" which he sees as legitimate and contrasts it with "the adoption of Marxist analysis in its entirety, with all the ideological presuppositions that implies." Reprinted as Gutiérrez, "Criticism Will Deepen, Clarify Liberation Theology," *LADOC* 15 (January–February 1985), pp. 2–7; also in Hennelly (ed.), *Liberation Theology*, pp. 419–424 (esp. 421–423).

[77] Gutiérrez's alleged errors were on the more complex methodological issue that only raised issues of authority indirectly.

[78] On the role of Marxism in his methodology, Boff like Gutiérrez had a sufficiently complicated stance to make a clear condemnation awkward. On the one hand, Boff may have had a personal sympathy to socialism, and the Marxist model of dialectical social science is given an important place in the social science perspectives that he uses (see L. and C. Boff, *Introducing Liberation Theology*, p. 28). On the other hand, explicit references to Marx or Marxist ideas are virtually nonexistent in Boff's work. Accusations on Marxism were very hard to corroborate from his published work, although there was concern about the allegedly Marxist reference to the church's "system of religious production."

[79] On their actual conversation, see Lernoux, *People of God*, pp. 108–109; Cox, *The Silencing of Leonardo Boff*, pp. 98–101. Cox suggests that a surprisingly important topic was discussion over *Lumen Gentium's* understanding of how the church of Christ subsists in (*subsistit in*) the Catholic church.

[80] Lorscheiter had also been in Rome as agreed, but due to the presence of the two cardinals, he was able to return.

[81] Lernoux, *People of God*, pp. 100–102; Brown, *Gustavo Gutiérrez*, pp. 145–146.

document that condemned Gutiérrez and liberation theology in unequivocal terms and pressed the Peruvians to endorse it. However, Cardinal Landázuri once again mounted a determined defence of Gutiérrez. The compromise document that the bishops published the next month did not include the condemnations that Ratzinger sought. It affirmed the validity of liberation theology, but acknowledged the authority of the *Instruction* in its warning over distortions.[82]

On the issue of Marxism, there was no doubt that Gutiérrez's writings in the 1970s made fairly extensive reference to Marxist thought, particularly the French Marxist Althusser and the Peruvian José Mariátegui.[83] However, Gutiérrez always claimed that he put them at the service of liberation theology rather than vice-versa. Marxism was not used because of an uncritical allegiance to its philosophy. It is only drawn upon when its analysis serves the cause of the poor by illuminating the real causes of their oppression.[84] Míguez Bonino describes the social analysis of Gutiérrez's A *Theology of Liberation* as "avowedly Marxist" but makes clear that this is by no means an uncritical acceptance of a dogmatic Marxism, but a selective use of certain Marxist ideas.[85] Besides this, Gutiérrez's work since then had already adopted a less Marxist tone. As long as he was careful, (and enjoyed the support of Cardinal Landázuri Ricketts) Gutiérrez was therefore able to defend himself from Ratzinger's criticisms.

A few months after the conversation with Boff and the visit of the Peruvian bishops to Rome, further light was shed on Ratzinger's personal views on liberation theology. The Italian magazine *Jesus* published selected extracts from the interviews that Ratzinger had given to Vittorio Messori in August 1984.[86] These reinforced the perception that Ratzinger was determined to correct what he saw as the distortions in liberation theology. It was therefore no surprise that Ratzinger wrote an official notification dated 11 March 1985 to confirm that Boff's written responses and the discussion in the colloquy had not adequately satisfied the Vatican on the points that had been raised. This was then made public, along with Ratzinger's letter to Boff of 15 May 1984.[87] At the

---

[82] Peruvian Episcopal Conference, "A Challenge to Faith: 26 November 1984," *Paginas* (November/September, 1984).

[83] Concern with Marxism had been particularly strong in the seventh of the ten observations, which detailed a number of highly negative points that it claims flow from this.

[84] Gutiérrez's essay "Theology and the Social Sciences," in his book *The Truth Shall Make You Free* (pp. 53–84), offers an extensive discussion of the role of social analysis in general and Marxism in particular.

[85] Míguez Bonino, *Doing Theology in a Revolutionary Situation*, p. 71.

[86] See note 61 above. The full version later appeared as *Rapporto sulla fede* (Milan: Paoline, 1985) which was translated as V. Messori, *The Ratzinger Report: An Exclusive Interview on the State of the Church* (trans. S. Attanasio and G. Harrison; San Francisco: Ignatius Press, 1985). Ratzinger also consented to the inclusion of the unauthorised 30 Giorno article at the end of the book (pp. 174–186).

[87] CDF, "Notification sent to Fr. Leonardo Boff regarding Errors in his Book, Church: Charism and Power," *Origins* 14 (4 April 1985) pp. 638–687; reprinted in Hennelly (ed.), *Liberation Theology*, pp. 425–430.

time, it seemed that no further action would be taken beyond this censure. Boff accepted it graciously with the remark that "he preferred to walk with the church rather than alone with my theology."[88]

Boff and most others hoped that this ended the matter, but there was worse to come. Two months later, on 9 May 1985, the Vatican announced that Boff was to observe a "period of obedient silence" for an unspecified duration that would "permit Friar Boff a time for serious reflection" and disqualified him from publishing or public speaking.[89]

In Latin American and elsewhere, some church leaders welcomed this further indication of Vatican censure for liberation theology. Others saw it as ill-deserved and rallied quickly to Boff's support.[90] Boff himself accepted the silence in a dignified manner, but was deeply saddened and discouraged at the turn of events.

In the same month that Boff received his silence, Gustavo Gutiérrez travelled to Europe to make a defence of his work. However, unlike Boff, Gutiérrez went to Lyons, not Rome, and his defence was to university academics, not to Ratzinger and his curial colleagues.[91] The occasion was a *viva* exam for the award of a doctorate for published work. Gutiérrez discussed all his works and especially his recent reply to Ratzinger's Observations in his paper "Theology and the Social Sciences."[92] The award of the doctorate—at the highest level of distinction—helped to strengthen Gutiérrez's position against further attacks.

UNEASY STANDOFF (1986 ONWARDS)

The Pope was determined to prevent the appearance of open division in the church. However, in view of the high-profile support for Boff from within the Brazilian church—and the oft-stated argument that Boff's work was in support of the National Pastoral Plan—it seemed to many in Brazil that the Vatican acted in too high-handed a way. The action against Boff suggested that the national leadership of the Brazilian bishops were not capable of self-determination in leading the Brazilian church. Many moderates joined the progressives in their concern over events. This ensured that divisions within the Brazilian church remained open and a continuing concern for the Vatican.

---

[88] Cited in Cox, *The Silencing of Leonardo Boff*, p. 105.

[89] Cox, *The Silencing of Leonardo Boff*, p. 3.

[90] Cox describes the meeting of a significant group of liberation theologians for this purpose. The meeting in Rio was ostensibly intended to plan the *Theology and Liberation Series* (TLS). However, Cox says that to show with Boff the participants all found their way to nearby Petrópolis.

[91] The discussion is printed in G. Gutiérrez, *The Truth Shall Make You Free: Confrontations*, pp. 1–52. Gutiérrez's examiners were all respected academics and some had roles within the official magisterium, including Bernard Sesboüé SJ (a member of the ITC) and Vincent Cosmao (a member of the Pontifical Commission for Justice and Peace). After his morning lecture and afternoon defence, he was awarded the doctorate with highest distinction (see Gutiérrez, *The Truth Shall Make You Free*, pp. 1–2).

[92] Gutiérrez, *The Truth Shall Make You Free*, pp. 53–84.

The Vatican's attempts to enforce unity risked creating a conflict between the Vatican and the Brazilian church that was even more serious than the earlier division that had been created within the Nicaraguan church.[93] The Vatican had a much more difficult task in dealing with the Brazilian leadership than it had faced in Nicaragua. The Brazilian church has the largest number of Catholics in the world, and over three hundred and fifty bishops. The Brazilian hierarchy was much more powerful than in Nicaragua, and many in the national leadership were sympathetic to liberation theology rather than united in opposition to it.

Since Boff's supporters in the Brazilian church showed no signs of backing down, further efforts to enforce discipline looked likely to make divisions worse rather than better. To avoid the embarrassment of public division, a new phase of reconciliation was required—at least temporarily.

Lifting the Silence and the Second Instruction on Liberation Theology (1986)

In March 1986, a group of twenty-one Brazilian bishops visited Rome, for their scheduled *ad limina* (regular five-yearly) visit with the Pope. The group included all the Brazilian Cardinals, and therefore reflected the different factions in the Brazilian church, from the committed supporters of liberation theology such as Cardinals Arns and Lorscheider to its outspoken opponents such as Cardinal Eugênio de Arauyo Sales. The Pope took the chance to listen to both sides and stressed the need for church unity.[94] Little was settled at the three-day meeting (13–15 March) beyond a plea for better relations and dialogue on both sides. However, progressives took comfort that the Pope had not taken sides and that they had not been attacked as the cause of the problem.[95] Furthermore, Ratzinger presented a draft of the document dealing with the most positive aspects of liberation, which was now very close to its planned publication. This was promised when the first *Instruction* had been published, but there were concerns that the delay in publication signalled that it might not ever be completed.

---

[93] Sharp divisions also remained in the Nicaraguan church. This may be seen in the bishops of Nicaragua, "Call to Dialogue," *Origins* 14 (26 July 1984), pp. 131–134, and the reply to it by the Maryknoll lay missionary Patricia Hynds, "Bishops Letter Deepens Church-State Estrangement," *Latinamerica Press*, 24 May 1984; both reprinted in Hennelly (ed.), *Liberation Theology*, pp. 375–380 and 381–384. However, in Nicaragua the church hierarchy became united against the popular church, whereas in Brazil the hierarchy was itself split. The Vatican was therefore able to address the situation in Nicaragua simply by strengthening the hierarchy, whereas it needed to be more cautious in its approach to Brazil.

[94] The Vatican's secretary of state, Cardinal Casaroli (who had been quite critical of the first *Instruction*), may have been influential in encouraging this rapprochement. Harvey Cox also suggests that the Pope believed that Ratzinger consulted widely with the Brazilian bishops in advance of the *Instruction* and was therefore surprised at the level of official disquiet that it caused (*The Silencing of Leonardo Boff*, p. 109).

[95] See Lernoux, *People of God*, pp. 110–113.

Shortly after their return to Brazil, there was further news for the bishops and for Boff. On Easter Saturday (29 March 1986) the Vatican lifted its period of imposed silence and Boff said he received it "as an Easter present." The timing of the news before the annual assembly of the CNBB in mid-April was particularly significant. It seemed to be intended to help gain a positive reception for the imminent publication of the second Vatican document on liberation theology and heal some of the divisions amongst Brazilian bishops.

Sure enough, the second document was finally published on 5 April 1986.[96] To further aid a positive reception for it, the Pope followed it with a warm letter to the Brazilian bishops on 9 April 1986, which Cardinal Bernardin Gantín personally presented to the CNBB assembly.[97] The letter clarified that both *Instructions* carried the Pope's explicit approval. It also indicated that as long as liberation theology remained "consistent and coherent with the teachings of the gospel of the living tradition and the ongoing magisterium of the church" it was "not only timely but useful and necessary" and "should be seen as a new stage . . . of the church's social teaching as set forth in documents from *Rerum Novarum* to *Laborem Exercens*.[98]

The second *Instruction* (titled *Libertatis Conscientia* or *Instruction on Christian Freedom and Liberation*) voiced similar concerns to the first, but as expected, its tone was much more positive.[99] It acknowledged that modern liberation movements had brought social and political freedoms (§§ 5–24), but questioned their success in bringing inner freedom (§ 9) and warned against the alienation and moral relativism that often comes with such developments (§§ 18–19). Although it recognised the legitimacy of speaking theologically in terms of liberation, it repeatedly stressed the primacy of redemption from sin for any true understanding salvation as liberation (§ 3).[100] Unlike the 1984 *Instruction*, for the most part the 1986 *Instruction* made little direct reference to Latin American liberation theology. Instead, it offered its own treatment of liberation themes in ways that corresponded either more or less closely with Latin American

---

[96] CDF, *Instruction on Christian Freedom and Liberation* (Vatican City: Libreria Editrice Vaticana, 1986); ET in *Origins* 15 (17 April 1986), pp. 115–128; reprinted in Hennelly (ed.), *Liberation Theology*, pp. 461–497. It was dated 22 March and scheduled for publication on Easter Sunday (30 March), but then delayed for further revision. Just as the CDF claimed that it was entirely coincidental that the first *Instruction* had been published the day after Boff arrived in Rome, so it insisted that the lifting of the silence the day before the expected publication of the second *Instruction* was equally coincidental.

[97] John Paul II, "Letter to the Brazilian Bishops," *L'Osservatore Romano* (English ed.; 28 April 1986), pp. 6–7; reprinted in Hennelly (ed.), *Liberation Theology*, pp. 498–506. Gantín succeeded Cardinal Baggio in 1984 as the Vatican's prefect of the Congregation for Bishops and met the Brazilian bishops during their visit the previous month.

[98] "Letter to Brazilian Bishops," § 5.

[99] Hennelly provides his own careful analysis of it as "The Red-Hot Issue of Liberation Theology," *America* (24 May 1986), pp. 425–425; reprinted in Hennelly (ed.), *Liberation Theology*, pp. 507–513.

[100] See also §§ 23, 37–42, and 71.

perspectives. It affirmed that "those oppressed by poverty are the object of a love of preference on the part of the church" (§ 68).[101] It endorsed the base communities, but warned that they should be in unity with the local and universal church (§ 69) and warned church pastors against direct intervention into politics (§ 80). It ended with a reflection on Mary's Magnificat as the basis for a theology of liberation.

On the whole it received a generally favourable response. There were new hopes that the conflicts of the past could be brought to an end. Gutiérrez welcomed it as closing a chapter and opening a new and more positive period. However, behind the scenes the Vatican was anxious to find less public ways to confront what it still saw as the dangers of liberation theology.

The Vatican's Consolidation of Control

Just as the attempt of Latin American conservatives to blunt liberation theology in the 1970s only partially succeeded at Puebla, so the direct confrontations between the Vatican and liberation theology in the first half of the 1980s met with only partial success. The Vatican was able to impose its discipline, but only at a cost in terms of church unity. The Boff case magnified an underlying rift with the Brazilian church. By the mid-1980s, a new approach was needed.

On the face of it the second *Instruction* signalled a rapprochement between the Vatican and liberation theology. Behind the scenes, however, the Vatican was busy in consolidating its control over the Latin American church. First, they gave careful thought to new Episcopal appointments. Second, they tried to take more discrete disciplinary actions against key theologians and church leaders. Third, they appropriated the language of liberation for an orthodox liberation theology.

Episcopal Appointments

From the start of his papacy, John Paul appointed and promoted Latin American bishops who were known to be hostile to the liberation movement or, at very least, were expected to be loyal to the Vatican's views. In this way, conservatives grew in influence on national episcopates and supported the Vatican's efforts by imposing their authority on their own dioceses and national policies.[102]

---

[101] It promptly clarified that "The special option for the poor, far from being a sign of particularism or sectarianism, manifests the universality of the church's being and mission. The option excludes no one" (§ 68).

[102] Hennelly (*Liberation Theology*, p. 459) notes that this was not limited to Latin America and cites the protest of 163 European theologians—including such eminent names as Hans Küng, Johannes Metz, and Edward Schillebeeckx—in what is known as the "Cologne Declaration." The declaration is dated 27 January 1989 (a translation is given in *The Tablet* (4 Feb 1989), pp. 140–141) and was precipitated by the Vatican's appointment of the new bishop for Cologne. The signatories complain that "The Roman Curia is energetically filling Episcopal sees throughout the world without respecting the sug-

It was much harder for the progressives to combat this second and more discreet attack. Although the direct confrontations with the Vatican of 1983–1986 had a much higher public profile, the shifting power in national bishop's conference was an equally significant part of the restoration policy.

Areas where liberation theology had been strong were the focus of special attention when as new bishops were appointed or promoted. For example, the archbishop of Managua, Obando y Bravo, was appointed cardinal in 1985 ahead of Archbishop Rivera y Damas of San Salvador, a more progressive bishop who was appointed to head the Salvadoran church in the difficult period following the assassination of Romero. In Chile, Cardinal Silva was a forceful critic of the military government of General Pinochet after the 1973 coup, but when he retired in 1983, his replacement as archbishop of Santiago was Juan Francisco Fresno.[103] Fresno's more cautious approach gained him the nickname of Cardinal "Fresnos" (the Spanish word for "brakes") amongst progressive clergy.[104] Pinochet's wife was widely cited as describing Fresno as an answer to prayers, although conflicts that he had with the government meant that he became more outspoken on occasion than many anticipated. When Fresno retired in 1989, an even more conservative choice was made in Antofagasta Carlos Oviedo.[105]

In Brazil, Bonaventura Kloppenburg became auxiliary of Salvador Bahía in 1983 (a year after his public criticism of Boff). In May 1984, another known opponent of liberation theology, José Freire Falcão was appointed archbishop of the politically sensitive archdiocese of Brasília. Another conservative, Dom Clóvis Frainer took over as archbishop of Manaus in 1984. The change in direction for the church in the Northeast was further marked when the conservative Lucas Moreira Neves was named archbishop of Salvador in Bahía (the official primacy of the Brazilian church) in September 1987 and soon afterwards elevated to cardinal.[106] He previously served as secretary to the Congregation for Bishops in Rome and was sympathetic to *Opus Dei*.[107]

When Ivo Lorscheiter (who had been a leader of the CNBB since 1970) was passed over for the archdiocese of Pôrto Alegre it was generally seen as

---

gestions of local churches and neglecting their established rights" (p. 140). For a response by Bishop Karl Lehman, president of the German Bishops Conference, see *The Tablet* (4 Feb 1989), pp. 141–142.

[103] Silva offered his resignation in 1982—at the customary age of 75—and was apparently very saddened by the alacrity with which it was accepted.

[104] Lernoux, *People of God*, pp. 141–152.

[105] The progressives feared that an even more conservative appointment was intended. Bishop Jorge Medina, who was seen by many as too close to the military, was spoken of in this regard. As a result, when Oviedo was appointed instead, it was seen almost as a victory for the progressives.

[106] See A. Riding, "Pope Shifts Brazilian Church to the Right," *New York Times* (8 June 1988); reprinted in Hennelly (ed.), *Liberation Theology*, pp. 529–531.

[107] Sympathy for *Opus Dei* was especially strong amongst the Peruvian episcopacy and Archbishop Ricardo Durand (who replaced Landázuri Ricketts) was a known opponent of Gutiérrez.

move against the progressive church.[108] Most significant of all was the retirement of Hélder Câmara in 1985. This allowed the Vatican to appoint the conservative José Cardoso Sobrinho to Recife. In September 1989, he collaborated with the Vatican's Congregation for Catholic Education to close two theological institutions in northeastern Brazil that had been at the forefront of promoting liberation theology at a pastoral level: the ITER (Theological Institute of Recife) and SERENE II (Seminary of the Northeast Region II).[109]

The wish to influence key Latin American dioceses extended beyond new appointments. In September 1988, the President of the CNBB and auxiliary bishop of São Paulo, Luciano Mendes de Almeida, was relocated to a conservative diocese in Minas Gerias. The following year, Brazil's largest archdiocese—Cardinal Arns's archdiocese of São Paulo—was split into four subunits. Leaders of the base community movement interpreted this change as a move to reduce their influence.

Disciplinary Actions

After 1986, disciplinary actions were more rare but did not cease. As soon as the silence was lifted, Boff published the work he completed under it, resulting in further conflict over his writing. There was also high-profile conflict with the Brazilian bishop Pedro Casaldáliga, a Spaniard who had been bishop of São Felix since 1971. Casaldáliga was a committed advocate of liberation theology in Brazil and also known for his solidarity with the popular church in Central America. Ratzinger objected to his description of the uncanonized Oscar Romero as a martyr and saint, and his bold attempt to inculturate the mass in indigenous traditions. Casaldáliga's trip to Nicaragua in July–August 1985 to support the hunger strike of Miguel D'Escoto (one of the priests who had been a government minister) was seen as especially provocative.[110] In June 1988, Cardinals Ratzinger and Gantín summoned him to Rome.[111]

In seventeen years, Casaldáliga had avoided the required *ad limina* visits to Rome and therefore travelled very reluctantly to Rome. On 16 June, Cardinals Ratzinger and Gantín quizzed him on a number of issues. These included: his acceptance of Vatican documents on liberation theology; his understanding of the poor in class terms; his preaching on social sin; and his references to

---

[108] See Mainwaring, *The Catholic Church and Politics in Brazil*, p. 249.

[109] One of the archbishop's particularly high profile struggles with a community influenced by liberation theology is described in R. Nagle, *Claiming the Virgin: The Broken Promise of Liberation Theology in Brazil* (New York and London: Routledge, 1997).

[110] On D'Escoto's hunger strike in protest at the *contra* war, see Kirk, *Politics and the Catholic Church in Nicaragua*, pp. 185–187; on Casaldáliga's visit, see P. Casaldáliga, *Prophets in Combat: The Nicaraguan Journal of Bishop Pedro Casaldáliga*.

[111] For his account of his trip to Rome, see P. Casaldáliga, "Letter to Brazilian Bishops," *National Catholic Reporter*, 11 November 1988, pp. 9–11; reprinted in Hennelly (ed.), *Liberation Theology*, pp. 532–540.

Romero and Camilo Torres as martyrs. His meeting with the Pope on 21 June was more cordial, but Cardinal Gantín made his displeasure with Casaldáliga evident at a second meeting before he returned to Brazil on 27 June. It therefore came as little surprise that in September 1988, the Vatican censured him and put restrictions on his speeches and travel.

The Language of Liberation

During the 1980s, the Vatican continued to adopt the language of liberation for a true liberation theology, in implied contrast to the reductionist language of Latin American liberation theologians such as Gutiérrez and Boff. While this assimilation of the term liberation in both *Instructions* was positive for liberation theologians in some ways—since it allowed them to claim official endorsement of their terminology—in the longer term it undermined the distinctive challenges of their work.[112]

In his response to the first *Instruction*, Boff argued that the document revealed a European mindset and methodology. He distinguished between the *Instruction* as an example of the treatment of liberation in a traditional way (which treated liberation only as a theological theme), and works in liberation theology (which also involved a new method of doing theology). The crucial difference, as Boff saw it, was that the former was possible for anyone through the conventional methods of intellectual study whereas the latter depended on the distinctive methodology that required practical participation in liberative action.

John Paul's willingness to use the language of liberation was particular clear in his encyclical *Sollicitudo Rei Socialis* (*On Social Concern*) at the end of 1987.[113] Once again, the Pope offered forceful teaching on social justice. For example, he repeated his message from Puebla that all property is under a "social mortgage" (§ 42). He also incorporated key phrases from Latin American liberation theology and acknowledged Latin American efforts to make liberation the fundamental category and first principle of action. However, he pointed to the recent teaching of the magisterium on the positive values as well as the deviations and risks of deviation on these issues (§ 46). His terminology of "true liberation" and "authentic liberation" may reflect these concerns. He therefore repeated the message of the 1986 *Instruction* (§§ 38 and 42) that sin is the primary barrier to liberation and spoke of structures produced by sin rather than sinful structures.[114] Another notable feature was the way that liberation was

---

[112] This strengthened a tendency that had its roots in the 1970s. Paul VI previously promoted the corrected interpretation of liberation theology in *Evangelii Nuntiandi* and Alfonso López Trujillo and Roger Vekemans attempted to adopt the language of liberation (as a deliberate strategy to oppose the radical social message of Gutiérrez and others) in the 1970s.

[113] The encyclical was a slightly belated marker for the twentieth anniversary of *Populorum Progressio* (which appeared in March 1967).

[114] "The sinful obstacle to overcome on the way to authentic liberation is sin and structures produced by sin as it multiplies and spreads" (§ 46).

so closely linked to development. John Paul put the two together and spoke of the intimate connection between them. Furthermore, instead of the simple phrase "option for the poor" he introduced the qualifier "option or love of preference for the poor." His affirmation of this option is further qualified by his interpretation of it simply as "a special form of primacy in the exercise of Christian charity" (§ 42). The term charity seemed to be a deliberate move back to the time before liberationists spoke of a political option and solidarity.

CONCLUSION

The dispute between the Vatican and liberation theology went through a number of stages in the 1980s, during which both sides were determined to defend the faith as they saw it. After an initial period of escalating tension (1980–1983), the Vatican's aggressive attempts to preserve unity and enforce its authority (1984–1986) were successful in most countries, but threatened to make things worse rather than better in Brazil. A period of rapprochement followed in which the Vatican worked more discretely by nominating conservative bishops for important appointments. As the decade progressed, the Vatican took over some of the language of liberation but rejected the distinctive method that has been used in Latin America.

The issues on which the Vatican and Latin American liberation theology clashed were ecclesiological, terminological, and methodological. On ecclesiology, Boff and other advocates of the popular church sought to extend their criticism of society to the workings of the church itself. The democratic nature of the people of God expressed in the base communities raised questions over the traditional hierarchical authority of the magisterium. On terminology, the Vatican remained convinced that the language of liberation used by liberation theologians was reductionist and needed to be reclaimed if the spiritual element was to be preserved. On methodology, the Vatican saw liberation theology's starting point in the commitment to the poor as dangerous and divisive and its acceptance of Marxist social analysis in early works as seriously flawed.

These three concerns were closely interrelated. For the Vatican, the Marxist influence in the language of liberation inevitably resulted in a reduction of theology to politics and a reduction of salvation from sin to political freedom and economic liberation. This in turn created division within the church, especially when the church as an institution became the focus of social criticism as happened with Boff.

Whatever might be said about the Vatican's ecclesiological and terminological concerns it is important to see that on the methodological points, the disputes over Marxism in works of liberation theology in the 1970s were already something of an anachronism in the mid-1980s. Changes in liberation theology's social setting and primary partner of dialogue during the 1970s—a move away from the universities and the radical literature of social sciences and into the "academy of the poor," and the experiences of poverty and injustice at an everyday level—meant much less attention to Marxist analysis after the mid-1970s.

As a result, the most contentious issue of the controversy—whether Marxist ideas and analysis could help theologians in the task of social analysis (as practiced in early works of liberation theology) without entailing determinism, atheism, and other aspects of Marxist philosophy (as the Vatican feared)—could only distract attention from a proper assessment of liberation theology. Liberation theologians continued to argue that using Marxist analysis was not in itself a flaw (although particular uses of it might be). However, Marxism was no longer central to their work and they denied that they had ever reduced the gospel to Marxism.

CHAPTER TWELVE

Facing the Feminist Challenge

> Mary is ever present in the daily lives of women of the
> *povo*. Brazilian women can identify with her—she is one
> of them: she is poor, her husband is a simple craftsman;
> she has no home in which to bear her child, but gives
> birth in a hut, she is a migrant from the interior and
> has to go to Bethlehem, from there to flee to Egypt.
> Mary is a woman of the *povo*; black, starving, strug-
> gling. Mary is pregnant 'out of wedlock,' exposed to the
> scorn of society. Mary is a mother.
>
> Caipora Women's Group[1]

INTRODUCTION

In the 1960s and 1970s, most male liberation theologians had not even begun
to address the oppression of women under patriarchy. Despite some efforts to
rectify this in the 1980s, attention to gender issues was never a strong part of
their work. Although women were often the most affected by poverty—and faced
multiple other problems in Latin America—male liberation theologians rarely
did more than lip-service to this as a serious theological concern.

It was Latin American women, rather than men, who struggled to put gender issues and sexism on the theological agenda in the 1980s.[2] Despite the creative and prophetic work of Latin America's leading women theologians, their
male colleagues often saw the struggle against sexism as an irrelevancy or at
best a secondary issue to the struggle against poverty.[3]

---

[1] Caipora Women's Group, *Women in Brazil* (London: Latin America Bureau, 1983),
p. 68.

[2] For a brief overview of the issues, see the set of interviews by K. O'Brien, "Feminists
to Liberation Theologians: 'Challenge Church on Sexism,'" *Latinamerica Press* (23 January
1986), pp. 5–6.

[3] The tendency to see gender issues as peripheral matters is well illustrated in the
attitudes of the priest that Dorothee Sölle records as "Wanda Tells How She Became a
Feminist" in *Celebrating Resistance: The Way of the Cross in Latin America* (trans. J. Irwin;
Minneapolis: Augsburg Fortress Press; London: Mowbray, 1993) pp. 1–2.

THE EMERGENCE OF WOMEN'S VOICES

The United Nations Decade for Women (1975–1985) addressed the marginalization of women at a global level. In Latin America, patriarchal attitudes ran as deep as anywhere. The spirit of the *conquistadores* and the social ideal of a patron of the *hacienda* (the male lord of the family and local community) shaped gender relations as much as labour relations. Latin American women frequently face discrimination for being women as well as poor, every day of their lives. The church in Latin America has done much more to reinforce the sharp gender divisions in Latin American societies than reduce them, for example, by its teaching that God has sanctioned a woman's subservience to her father or husband.

Published works of feminist liberation theology emerged in North America in the early 1970s almost immediately after the first works of Latin American liberation theology and Black liberation theology appeared.[4] By the early 1970s, feminist theology achieved a growing prominence in North America and later in Europe. These early works largely focussed on the situation of First World women (and the issues facing the white middle-class to which the authors belonged). However, they played a vital role in deconstructing patriarchal influences in the church and theology and putting the marginalisation of women firmly on the theological agenda.

North American feminists, such as Rosemary Ruether, participated at the Theology in the Americas Conference (Detroit 1975), but male Latin American liberation theologians in the 1970s showed minimal evidence of feminist

---

[4] See, for example, R. R. Ruether, *Liberation Theology* (New York: Paulist Press, 1972); idem, "Outlines for a Theology of Liberation," *Dialog* 11 (Autumn 1972), pp. 252–257; idem, "Sexism and the Theology of Liberation" in *Christianity and Crisis* 90 (12 December 1973), pp. 1224–1229; M. Daly, *Beyond God the Father: Towards a Philosophy of Women's Liberation* (Boston: Beacon Press, 1973); L. M. Russell, *Human Liberation in a Feminist Perspective: A Theology* (Philadelphia: Westminster Press, 1974). Some of these writers deliberately sought to make links with other liberation theologies in their understanding of different forms of oppression (see, for example, Russell, *Human Liberation in a Feminist Perspective*, pp. 50–71); others tended to focus more exclusively on the distinctiveness of sexism and the oppression of women under patriarchy (see, for example, Mary Daly, *Beyond God the Father*). For a helpful survey of the early 1970s see C. P. Christ, "The New Feminist Theology: A Review of the Literature" in *Religious Studies Review* 3.4 (1977), pp. 203–212. It should also be noted that as with the other liberation movements there were also a number of important publications during the 1960s that prepared the way for these fuller statements of a liberation perspective in the 1970s. See in particular, M. Daly, *The Church and the Second Sex* (New York: Harper & Row, 1968); V. Saiving, "The Human Situation: A Feminine View" in *The Journal of Religion* (April 1960), reprinted in C. P. Christ and J. Plaskow, *Womanspirit Rising: A Feminist Reader in Religion* (San Francisco: Harper & Row, 1979), pp. 25–42. For accounts of the longer history of women's theological work, see M. J. Selvidge, *Notorious Voices: Feminist Biblical Interpretation 1500–1920* (London: SCM Press, 1996), and many of the contributions in E. Schüssler Fiorenza (ed.), *Searching the Scriptures: A Feminist Introduction* (New York: Crossroad, 1993; London: SCM Press, 1994).

concerns. As men—who mostly worked in the male world of the churches—it was easy for the pioneers of liberation theology in Latin America to ignore the patriarchal context that affected both church and society. Whereas Catholic social teaching provided liberation theology with firm foundations on economic rights, it offered very little in terms of women's rights. *Rerum Novarum* had scarcely mentioned women. In the one place where it did address the issue it was in the context of child labour and simply stated that "Women . . . are not suited to certain trades; for a woman is by nature fitted for home work, and it is that which is best adapted at once to preserve her modesty, and to promote the good bringing up of children and the well-being of the family."[5] It was not until *Pacem in Terris* that John XXIII noted as one of the three distinctive characteristics of the age that:

> . . . women are now taking part in public life. This is happening more rapidly perhaps in nations of Christian civilization, and, more slowly, but broadly, among peoples who have inherited other traditions or cultures. Since women are becoming ever more conscious of their human dignity, they will not tolerate being treated as mere material instruments, but demand rights befitting a human person both in domestic and in public life.[6]

Medellín had made no more than the most fleeting of references to women. In "Message to the Peoples of Latin America" it referred to "woman and her irreplaceable function in the society" and although it acknowledged that women were demanding their right to a legitimate equality with men, there was little detail on what this meant in practice or how the church might promote it.[7] The document on the family criticised the vicious circle of underdevelopment, poor living conditions, and low sanitary conditions that so many families faced. However, it interpreted the roles of women in the family in traditional terms and did not address the social injustices experienced by women with reference to gender or in the context of patriarchy.

Puebla referred to women as "doubly oppressed and marginalized"—that is oppressed as women as well as oppressed as poor—but it is hard to tell whether its status as the only footnote in 1310 sections of text made this observation more significant or more marginal.[8] Whatever the case with this strange footnote, the bishops still did not offer any discussion of patriarchy or attempt to address sexism at a theological level. Furthermore, the Puebla meeting was

---

[5] *Rerum Novarum*, § 33.

[6] *Pacem in Terris*, § 41.

[7] "Message to the Peoples of Latin America" in CELAM, *The Church in the Present-Day Transformation of Latin America in the Light of the Council*.

[8] CELAM, *Puebla*, § 1135; see p. 197 above. In an interview, Elsa Tamez Gutiérrez said that the bishops at the conference intended it to be part of the main text, but it was made into a footnote in the editing process after the conference ended; see E. Tamez, *Against Machismo: Rubem Alves, Leonardo Boff, Gustavo Gutiérrez, José Míguez Bonino, Juan Luis Segundo and Others Talk about the Struggle of Women* (Oak Park, Ill: Meyer-Stone Books, 1987 [Spanish orig. 1986]), pp. 39–49 (40).

notable for the fact that although women's experiences were mentioned, women were still largely excluded from the theological discussion. At Puebla, the Mexican women's documentation centre *Mujeres para el Dialogo* (Women for Dialogue) offered meetings and conferences to the CELAM delegates but the impact these could make was limited. However, the quality and energy of their work did not go entirely unnoticed. The EATWOT steering group asked them to arrange a meeting for women from all over Latin America in preparation for the 1980 International Congress of Theology at São Paulo.[9] This meeting took place later that year near Tepeyac in Mexico under the title "The Latin American Woman: The Praxis and Theology of Liberation."[10]

Mary Judith Rees traces the beginning of the feminist challenge in Latin America to this meeting in Tepeyac.[11] In much the same way that from the outset liberation theology proclaimed itself as not just a topic within theology, but a distinctive new way of doing theology, the women at the meeting also emphasised that what was needed was not just women as a topic of concern for theology, but a new approach to the whole of theology from women's perspective.[12]

Elsa Tamez (a Methodist working in Costa Rica) and Ivone Gebara (a Brazilian Catholic) both took part at the EATWOT meeting in New Delhi (1981) and contributed to what Oduyoye described as the "irruption within the

---

[9] See Chapter 10.

[10] See Mujeres para el Dialogo, "Women, Praxis and Liberation Theology: Tepeyac, Mexico, 1–5 October 1979" in *Voices from the Third World* 2, 2 (1979), pp. 12–18. Their report was also presented at the International Congress of Theology at São Paulo; see C. Ferro, "The Latin American Woman: The Praxis and Theology of Liberation" in Torres and J. Eagleson (eds.), *The Challenge of Basic Christian Communities*, pp. 24–37. See also their later work, Mujeres para el Dialogo, *Mujer Latinoamericana, Iglesia y Teología* (Mexico: n.p., 1981).

[11] See her account of the meeting and its significance in M. J. Ress, "Feminist Theologians Challenge Churches," *Latinamerica Press* (31 May 1984); reprinted in Hennelly, *Liberation Theology*, pp. 385–392 (385). However, a number of historical precedents could be seen as much earlier beginnings for the movement. For example, Beatriz Couch recalls the contribution of the poet Sor Juana Inés de la Cruz in colonial Mexico (1651–1695) in B. M. Couch, "Sor Juana Inés de la Cruz: The First Woman Theologian in the Americas" in J. C. B. and E. L. Webster (eds.), *The Church and Women in the Third World* (Philadelphia: Westminster Press, 1985). For a selection of Sor Juana's poetry, see *A Sor Juana Anthology* (trans. A. S. Trueblood; Cambridge, Mass.: Harvard University Press, 1988); on her life and work, see O. Paz, *Sor Juana Inés de la Cruz: Her Life and World* (trans M. S. Peden; London: Faber and Faber, 1988).

[12] Rees comments: "It is here that feminist liberation theologians offer a challenge to their male counterparts. They argue that the very methodology of liberation theology—reflection on the praxis of liberation within a faith perspective—demands that the situation of women be a constitutive element, not just one more theme, within liberation theology. They maintain that to make the situation of poor women a central concern is indispensable to liberation theology if it is to be lifegiving to all the continent's marginated people"; "Feminist Theologians Challenge Churches," in Hennelly, *Liberation Theology*, p. 387.

irruption."[13] Tamez and the Korean woman theologian Sun Ai Park organised the main worship session with readings from Gen. 21.8–20 (Abraham driving out Hagar) and Lk. 1.46–55 (Mary's Magnificat).[14] Tamez's reflection on Hagar drew together the different dimensions of oppression that others were reluctant to recognise:

> Hagar is a woman who suffers a threefold oppression, like many women in the Third World. Hagar is thrice oppressed: because of her class (she is a slave); because of her race (she is an Egyptian, an impure race according to the Hebrews); and because of her sex (she is a woman).[15]

Tamez noted that when Hagar and Ishmael were driven into the desert and feared for the life of her son, she called on the God of Israel for deliverance. God appeared to her, saved her and her son and delivered them from slavery. This episode, Tamez said, was the only biblically recorded epiphany to a woman. If the Bible showed God in such dramatic solidarity with a slave-woman from a despised race in biblical times, then Tamez argued, God remained in solidarity with despised races, ethnic minorities, and oppressed women in the Third World.[16]

Tamez's contribution at New Delhi confirmed her status as one of the most promising women liberation theologians in Latin America.[17] When the Women's Commission of EATWOT created a regional department of Latin American women theologians in 1983, they asked Tamez to act as a coordinator. One of the most significant achievements of this new body was to organise a Continental Consultation in Buenos Aires in 1985. More than twenty years after the first significant meeting of male liberation theologians at Petrópolis, this continent-wide meeting of Latin American women did much to raise the profile of gender issues in theology. A number of influential papers—from figures such as Ana María Bidegain (Uruguayan working in Colombia), Ivone Gebara, Alida Verhoeven (Dutch working in Argentina), María Clara Bingemer (Colombia), Nelly Ritchie (Argentinean), Aracely de Rocchietti (Uruguay), Tereza Cavalcanti (Brazil), Consuelo del Prado (Peru), and Tamez herself—outlined the agenda for women's theology in Latin America.[18] Tamez's introductory contribution to the volume "The Power of the Naked" is an evocative synthesis of feminist

---

[13] See p. 223 above.

[14] E. Tamez, S. A. Park, and others, "Worship Service: This Hour of History" in Fabella and Torres, *Irruption of the Third World*, pp. 181–187.

[15] E. Tamez, "Reflections by Elsa Tamez" in Fabella and Torres, *Irruption of the Third World*, pp. 183–185 (184).

[16] Tamez, "Reflections by Elsa Tamez," p. 184.

[17] Her previous work included *Bible of the Oppressed* (trans. M. O'Connell; Maryknoll, N.Y.: Orbis Books, 1982 [Spanish orig. 1979]). Her Protestant background is particularly clear in her later work *The Amnesty of Grace: Justification by Faith from a Latin American Perspective* (trans. Sharon Ringe; Nashville: Abingdon Press, 1993 [Spanish orig. 1991]).

[18] Many of the papers have been published in E. Tamez (ed.), *Through Her Eyes: Women's Theology from Latin America* (Maryknoll, N.Y.: Orbis Books, 1989).

thought, liberation theology, and indigenous mythology that represents Latin American women's theology at its most courageous and innovative.[19]

The following year EATWOT's International Women's Conference took place at Oaxtepec (Mexico, December 1986). Latin American women joined with representatives from Africa and Asia in exploring their similarities and differences as Third World women liberation theologians prior to the EATWOT meeting the following week.[20] Latin American women at the conference included: Ivone Gebara, Luiz Beatriz Arellano (Nicaragua), Nelly Ritchie, María Pilar Aquino (originally from Mexico and working in California), Ana Maria Tepedino (Brazil), and Elsa Tamez.[21] Partly because of this meeting, women were much better represented and organised at the Oaxtepec meeting and their contribution to the final publication was much stronger than previous conferences.[22]

The conferences in Buenos Aires and Oaxtepec marked the formal emergence of Latin American women's liberation theology as an organised movement across the continent. Since these conferences, the publications by women Latin American theologians have multiplied and in many cases become more radical in the late 1980s and 1990s.[23] Since the mid-1980s, much of the most creative and challenging work in liberation theology has been by Latin American feminist theologians.[24] They have often offered more sophisticated and nuanced

---

[19] E. Tamez, "The Power of the Naked" in idem (ed.), *Through Her Eyes*, pp. 1–14.

[20] V. Fabella and M. A. Oduyoye (eds.), *With Passion and Compassion: Third World Women Doing Theology* (Reflections from the Women's Commission of EATWOT, 1985–1986; Maryknoll, N.Y.: Orbis Books, 1988). A good collection of Third World women's theology is offered U. King (ed.), *Feminist Theology from the Third World: A Reader* (London: SPCK, 1994).

[21] Their papers were published in Fabella and Oduyoye (eds.), *With Passion and Compassion*, pp. 125–180.

[22] See M. C. Bingemer, "Third World Theologies: Conversion to Others," and E. Tamez "A Latin American Perspective" in Abraham (ed.), *Third World Theologies*, pp. vii–xiii and 134–138.

[23] For example, Janet Reedy argues that women's theological production in Brazil went through three stages: first, the early pioneers such as María Clara Bingemer and others associated with the Pontifical University in Rio de Janeiro (1980–1985); second, more national networks of women and publications (1987–1990); third, the more mature and thematically diverse writings of the 1990s linked with a more radical group located primarily in São Paulo. See J. Reedy, "Pacifist Pioneers and Second-Generation Rebels: The State of Women Theologians in Brazil Today," paper presented in the Religion in Latin America and Caribbean Group at the American Academy of Religion Annual Meeting, Orlando, Florida, 1998.

[24] In the earlier years, Latin American women tended to avoid identifying themselves as feminist. The term was seen as too closely identified with the women's movement in North America or Europe and focussed on different concerns to those of Latin American women. Others avoided it simply to avoid problems with misinterpretation. Although this is still the case for many women in the base communities, more recently the term feminist theology has found growing acceptance in written works during the 1990s. See, for example, M. Pilar Aquino, *Our Cry for Life: Feminist Theology from Latin America* (trans. D. Livingstone; Maryknoll, N.Y.: Orbis Books, 1993 [Spanish orig. 1992]); "Latin American Feminist Theology," *Journal of Feminist Studies in Religion* 14.1, pp. 89–107.

interpretations of the oppression than male colleagues who rely primarily on class analysis. Their success in incorporating gender issues into a liberationist framework pointed a possible way forward for liberation theology as a whole—regrettably few of their male colleagues followed their lead.

During the 1980s, male theologians became more assiduous in paying lip service to the oppression of women.[25] However, they left it to their female colleagues to develop serious theological reflection on this. Their writings often referred to it as an issue, but did not take it as a starting point for their work. At one level, this was understandable. It was right for women to take the lead in articulating women's theology and reflecting on women's experience. However, male theologians tended to use this as an excuse to evade the real challenges posed by their patriarchal context. Rather than seeing gender as something that affected them as men just as it affected women as women, they saw gender as exclusively a women's issue. The fact that many male theologians were celibate clergy doubtless encouraged this mistaken belief.[26]

As a result, efforts by male liberation theologians to go beyond simply mentioning the oppression of women were pretty rare and amongst those that tried, the results were usually disappointing. When male writers addressed the distinctive contribution of women, they invariably presented women's perspective in terms of sensitivity, tenderness, and closeness to the cosmos. Women's roles continued to be as mothers and providers for the family; masculine and feminine were not viewed as socially constructed nor the traditional divisions as part of the patriarchal process.

For example, Leonardo Boff—who went much further than others in extolling the theological contribution of women—nonetheless seemed to assume an essentialist understanding of women's nature and roles.[27] Likewise, during the 1980s, Gutiérrez wrote an extensive chapter on Mary in *God of Life*.[28] It offered a radical interpretation of Mary in the struggle against poverty, but did not adequately recognise the deeper issues in the discussion of gender and patriarchy.

---

[25] For example, Gutierrez's work in the 1980s stressed the much more inclusive sense of the poor than was apparent in the 1970s. For example, he noted: "When I speak of conflict in history I always mention different aspects of it. That is why I continually refer to races discriminated against, despised cultures, exploited classes, and the condition of women, especially in those sectors of society where women are 'doubly oppressed and marginalized' (Puebla, no. 1134, note)" (*The Truth Shall Set You Free*, p. 70). Even in 1971, Gutiérrez introduced *A Theology of Liberation* as "based on the Gospel and the experiences of men *and* women committed to the process of liberation" (*A Theology of Liberation*, p. ix, emphasis added). However, Gutiérrez's work shows little sign of taking patriarchy as central as poverty in his analysis of Peruvian society.

[26] The sensitivities surrounding gender issues within the church and the extreme pressures that many of them already faced from suspicious church authorities should also be recognised as at least partly responsible.

[27] L. Boff, *The Maternal Face of God: The Feminine and its Religious Expressions* (trans. R. R. Barr & J. W. Diercksmeier; San Francisco: Harper and Row; London: Collins, 1987 [Spanish orig. 1979]).

[28] Gutiérrez, *God of Life*, pp. 164–186.

This failure of male theologians to address gender issues was especially significant because professional women theologians were not only quite rare, but also often strongly disadvantaged in getting their work published, especially if they offered a strong gender perspective. As a result, liberation theology as a movement remained very limited in its gender analysis.

MARY

Whatever the limitations of Gutiérrez's rereading of Mary it did at least reflect an awareness of her significance in the lives of women. A number of women Latin American liberation theologians have found rereadings of Mary to be particularly important in the quest for more liberative role models for Latin American women today. While it would be completely mistaken to think that women's liberation theology in Latin America is only about Mary, there are good reasons why Mary has assumed particular prominence in many works.

Devotion to Mary is a key feature in the popular religious rituals on the continent and the traditional view of Mary as virgin and mother provided a very influential gender stereotype for women's behaviour in Latin American society. Often, the Marian stereotype supported a very conservative ideology. The Caipora Women's Group from Brazil summarise the impact of Marian images on Brazilian society as follows: "The European image of Mary was exported to Brazil along with the Roman Catholic church: the holy, entranced, blue-eyed, obedient, asexual Mary. For centuries the church used this image of ideal womanhood to foster the subordinate role of women."[29] Women's subordination is also seen in the restricted social roles to which women are expected to conform. Ana María Bidegain observes that in the machista framework, "the only two vocations available to woman since the nineteenth century have been motherhood and consecrated virginity," and these are the two roles that are represented in traditional Christian images of Mary.[30] At the meeting of women theologians at Tepeyac, Mexico (October 1979) the Costa Rican feminist theologian Corra Ferro made the same point with some force:

> [a woman's] role is to accompany man. As such, she must be married to God (virgin) or to a man (wife). If not she is considered to be married to the devil. The church offers us the model of Mary as virgin and mother. Sanctity, we are told, is found not in anything we do, but in the acceptance of one or other state in life.[31]

The identity of women as primarily virgins or mothers has been termed "marianismo."[32] As a female foil to machismo, marianismo perpetuates a patriarchal

---

[29] Caipora Women's Group, *Women in Brazil*, p. 68.

[30] A. M. Bidegain, "Women and the Theology of Liberation" in M. H. Ellis and O. Maduro (eds.), *The Future of Liberation Theology: Essays in Honour of Gustavo Gutiérrez* (Maryknoll, N.Y.: Orbis Books, 1989), pp. 105–120 (108–109).

[31] Cited in M. J. Ress, "Feminist Theologians Challenge Churches," *Latinamerica Press*, (31 May 1984); reprinted in Hennelly, *Liberation Theology*, pp. 385–392 (386).

[32] See E. P. Stevens, "Machismo and Marianismo," *Society* 10.6 (1973), pp. 57–63, and

interpretation of Mary and exalts it as the model for Latin American women to follow. This contributes to the exploitation of women that remains widespread in Latin American society. Because machismo is based on male power over women—and marianismo exalts female submission to this—machista/marianista ideology provides a framework in which domestic violence can be sparked by the most trivial of incidents. The legal system is usually heavily biased toward leniency for an aggrieved man and often offers little protection to battered women.[33] Furthermore, in common with the rest of the world, during times of war and civil protest the violence against women can be particularly horrific.

The church's teachings on sexuality long supported this history of oppression and helped legitimate machista/marianista ideologies. Despite this history, the women theologians who met at Tepeyac felt the legacy of Mary could also be liberating. Cora Ferro acknowledged the implications of the traditional image as offering only the limited roles of virgin and mother, but then went on to observe:

> This attitude overlooks Mary's defiant song of liberation in the Magnificat and her stance at the foot of the cross, which was a defiant political act.[34]

Ferro's work signalled the beginning of more extensive studies in the next decade. The most extensive of these was *Mary, Mother of God, Mother of the Poor* by Ivone Gebara (a woman religious) and María Clara Bingemer (a laywoman) who both worked in Brazil.[35] Their experience with the popular church and base communities convinced them that "one cannot speak about the church

---

idem "Marianismo: The Other Face of Machismo in Latin America," in A. Pescatello (ed.), *Female and Male in Latin America* (London and Pittsburgh: University of Pittsburgh Press, 1973), pp. 91–101. According to Stevens, marianismo is the female foil to male machismo. Marianismo reinforces the machista system by exalting a traditional understanding of Mary—as submissive, asexual, and domestic—as the ideal qualities for all women. The marianista woman is the long-suffering partner of the machista man. The man is to dominate and the woman is to submit; the man is to demand and the woman is to give; the man is to be lustful and the woman is to be chaste. Marianismo co-opts women into machista society by giving pseudo-value to the patient endurance of oppression as women's divinely ordained imitation of Mary.

[33] For example, machista values influence legislation on rape; in fourteen Latin American countries a man may legally rape his fiancée or wife and in some countries—including Chile and Argentina—a rapist need only propose marriage to his victim to escape prosecution; see S. Boyd, "Rape Laws Offer Women Scant Protection," *Latinamerica Press*, 29.28 (1997), p. 2.

[34] Cited in M. J. Rees, "Feminist Theologians Challenge Churches" in Hennelly, *Liberation Theology*, p. 386.

[35] I. Gebara and M. C. Bingemer, *Mary, Mother of God, Mother of the Poor* (trans. P. Berryman; Maryknoll, N.Y.: Orbis Books; Tunbridge Wells, Kent: Burns & Oates, 1989 [Portuguese orig. 1987]). A summarized version of the book is offered by their chapter "Mary" in I. Ellacuria and J. Sobrino (eds.), *Mysterium Liberationis*, pp. 482–495. Bingemer develops further thoughts on Marian devotion in M. C. Bingemer, "Woman: Time and Eternity: The Eternal Woman and the Feminine Face of God," *Concilium* 6 (1991), pp. 98–107.

of the poor or of pastoral work among the popular classes without dealing with the figure of this woman."[36]

Gebara and Bingemer examined Mary with reference to the social context of Latin America's troubled history and showed that images of Mary reflected the interests of the different groups that claim them.[37] In the first years of the conquest, Mary belonged to the Spanish conquistadors who claimed that their success was due to Mary's assistance against the infidels.[38] Yet within a short time of the conquest the indigenous people absorbed Mary into their own religious practices. In 1531 on the hill of Tepeyac near Mexico City, the Indian peasant Juan Diego had an apparition of Mary in which she addressed him in his own language.[39] The legend of the Virgin of Guadalupe that grew out of this story elevated Mary to a special place in Latin American culture, which she continues to hold, especially for Latin American women.[40] For millions of women, Mary is an intimate friend and fellow-worker who struggled with the challenges of day-to-day life and understands its difficulties. From Mexico to the Southern Cone women share their worries and joy with Mary: over their food, shelter, birth, and bereavement. In particular, as a mother, Mary is seen as the friend and protector of other women who provide for their families. In Brazil, Mary is often referred to as the *mae do povo*—"mother of the people."

Based on their review of this popular devotion, Gebara and Bingemer argue that "When it comes to experiencing faith in Mary, the people are way ahead of any theological endeavours. Their experience is primary, and it is what generates subsequent reflection and the new formulations emerging from that

---

[36] Gebara and Bingemer, *Mary, Mother of God*, p. 159. As Gebara and Bingemer note, the prevalence of women in base communities gives particular significance to their work on Mary; Gebara and Bingemer, *Mary, Mother of God*, pp. 160–164. The Caipora Women's Group also indicate the important role of base communities in promoting a more liberating view of Mary: "As the base Christian communities spread and raise awareness among the poor, this image of Mary is gaining in importance; a woman from the *povo*, always present in the daily lives of Brazilian women" (*Women in Brazil*, p. 69).

[37] The ambivalence of Mary's image is emphasized by Gebara and Bingemer (*Mary, Mother of God*, p. 128): "Conquerors and conquered, owners and workers, religious and lay people have experienced their relationship with Mary over the centuries-long history of Christian faith in Latin America. Impelled by its own interests, each group has claimed Mary for its own, and so she has taken part in the conflicts of life and death, and victory and defeat of different groups within the complex Latin American social fabric."

[38] See Gebara and Bingemer, *Mary, Mother of God*, pp. 129–131.

[39] See Chapter 1; for Gebara and Bingemer's reading of this tradition, see *Mary, Mother of God*, pp. 144–154. Brazilian tradition also tells of the Paraíba River where Mary showed solidarity with the poor and racially oppressed of Brazil as Our Lady Aparecida (*Mary, Mother of God*, pp. 154–158).

[40] See V. Elizondo and V. P. Elizondo, *Guadalupe: Mother of the New Creation* (Maryknoll, N.Y.: Orbis Books, 1997). For Mary's influence on Mexican-American women, see J. Rodriguez and V. P. Elizondo, *Our Lady of Guadalupe: Faith and Empowerment Among Mexican-American Women* (Austin: University of Texas Press, 1994).

reflection."[41] They refer to the popular traditions that have grown up around Mary in this devotion as "the people's dogmatics,"[42] in which Mary is the "Mother of the Oppressed," "Our Lady of Latin America," and "Mother of the Forgotten."[43]

In the Magnificat (Lk. 1.46–55), Mary's song of liberation celebrates the events in which she is an active participant. God is worshipped as one who has raised the lowly and brought down the powerful from their thrones (Lk. 1.55). They see the revolutionary thrust of the song as diametrically opposed to the passive and submissive marianista ideology. As a woman of the people who was active in God's work for liberation in first-century Palestine, Mary can empower Christians in Latin America to continue the struggle for the kingdom of God today.

Even Mary's traditional image as the Virgin can be understood in a radically new way. Rather than rejecting human sexuality, it can be seen as a witness to a woman's control over her own sexuality. The Caipora group write:

> Nor does Mary's virginity any longer merely symbolise her asexuality and there-fore her distance from the reality of other women's lives. For women who all too often experience sexuality as violence, as rape, Mary's virginity sym-bolises the dream of physical autonomy.[44]

Latin American women theologians draw attention to Mary's positive decision for action in accepting God's task for her to carry and give birth to Christ (Lk. 1.38).[45] The Spirit makes her pregnant only because she has given her positive assent as co-worker in salvation history.[46]

While many women have welcomed this type of rereading, more radical feminists have remained sceptical.[47] The Argentinean theologian Marcella Althaus-Reid criticises the work of Gebara and Bingemer as failing to develop a feminist materialist approach.[48] As a result, she argues that their reading of Mary is not really on the historical plane, but only in terms of a religious sym-bol. She concludes:

---

[41] Gebara and Bingemer, Mary Mother of God, p. 127.

[42] On the relationship between popular dogmatics and the institutional church, see Gebara and Bingemer, Mary, Mother of God, pp. 125–127.

[43] Gebara and Bingemer, Mary Mother of God, p. 163.

[44] Caipora Women's Group, Women in Brazil, p. 68.

[45] For example, Bidegain, "Women and the Theology of Liberation," p. 116; Gebara and Bingemer, Mary, Mother of God, p. 69.

[46] By contrast, many Latin American women complain that they cannot limit their family size through sexual abstinence since their husbands insist on sexual relations and beat them if they refuse too often.

[47] Part of the difference in perspective is a result of different social context. Gebara and Bingemer's work reflects their work with church orientated women in rural com-munities. More radical feminists, such as Althaus-Reid, often articulate the attitudes of educated urban women who are much more critical of the church.

[48] M. Althaus-Reid, Indecent Theology: Theological Perversions in Sex, Gender and Politics (London and New York: Routledge, 2000), pp. 40–44.

Re-readings of the Bible, important as they may be, cannot unmask the fact that women have concrete lives ruled by Marian performances. If Mary is a symbol for the Latin American women's liberation movement, how is it that in 500 years we have seen exactly the opposite? Where does *Marianismo* come from then, if not from Mariology and popular Mariology?[49]

WOMEN AND THE BASE COMMUNITIES

Just as women were in the overwhelming majority as active participants in church congregations throughout Latin America, likewise they were usually the backbone of base community membership. In the 1980s, Julio Santa Ana estimated that 80–85% of members of base communities in Brazil were women.[50] Furthermore, women in religious orders were often vital in initiating and sustaining the communities. As teachers, counsellors, and facilitators the critical roles of women in religious orders was often an unacknowledged aspect of the liberation theology movement. Madeleine Adriance suggests that in Brazil women religious are the largest group of pastoral agents who work with the CEBs, and that they outnumber the priests by three-to-one.[51] Women embraced the base communities as a chance for a more authentic participation in the church.

Based on her study of base communities in rural areas in Amazonia, Adriance argued that the women she interviewed felt that their participation in the community changed their relationships in the family in a positive way.[52] The participation in the communities and the opportunities this provided for travel outside the community to regional and even national meetings develop women's leadership confidence and expectations of change in their own households. Furthermore, Adriance noted that the positive identification placed on motherhood by the church is one with which the women she studied positively identified with; it was not just a burden placed on them by the church.[53]

However, a number of critics have noted that despite the promise of the base communities and the numerical presence of women in them, the base communities

---

[49] Althaus-Reid, *Indecent Theology*, p. 44. See further, C. R. Boxer, *Mary and Misogyny: Women in Iberian Expansion Overseas, 1414–1815: Some Facts, Fancies and Personalities* (London: Duckworth, 1975), pp. 103–106.

[50] See his comments in E. Tamez, *Against Machismo*, p. 18; see also the comments of Leonardo Boff in Tamez, *Against Machismo*, p. 97.

[51] M. Adriance, "Agents of Change: Priests, Sisters, and Lay Workers in the Grassroots Catholic Church in Brazil," *Journal for Scientific Study of Religion* 30 (1991) pp. 292–305. The role of women religious in promoting and sustaining the CEBs has received relatively little attention, but may prove particularly important to understanding the success of the movement.

[52] M. Adriance, *Promised Land: Base Christian Communities and the Struggle for the Amazon* (Albany: State University of New York Press, 1995), pp. 145–149.

[53] Adriance, *Promised Land*, pp. 142–143. Adriance claimed that this is true even for women in São Paulo and in support, she cited the study in São Paulo by C. Drogus, "Reconstructing the Feminine: Women in São Paulo's CEBs," *Extrait des archives de sciences soicales des religions* 17 (1990), pp. 63–74.

often still reflected the gender inequality that characterises other social and ecclesial structures.[54] It is unusual for women's experiences and problems to be consciously promoted as central to the CEBs' agenda.[55]

The ambivalence of the CEBs on the status of women was noted at the meeting of Latin America women at Tepeyac in 1979. On the one hand, most participants welcomed the participatory model of the communities and women's
presence in them. One of the consequences of the participatory ethos was to
reduce the influence of hierarchical authority structures including patriarchy.
However, they deplored the frequent absence of women in charting the course
for the CEB movement. The women at the meeting noted:

> For the most part, women are still second-class citizens in the CEBs, where
> male-centred traditions continue to persist. For instance, CEB leadership is
> usually male as are those who represent the community to the larger church.
> It is most often a man who leads the liturgy in the absence of a priest or
> pastor. Male opinions tend to be given more weight in community reflection,
> and women are more often than not assigned the tasks that have to do with
> childcare, the preparation of food, setting up the chapel for worship, and clean-
> up afterwards.[56]

At a methodological level, the more spontaneous and experiential approaches
to theology that found expression in the CEBs were seen as reflecting feminist
challenges to more traditional, male-oriented, and systematic models. However,
these methodological principles were not always properly observed in practice,
and this prevented women's experiences from becoming central and constitutive to the CEBs.

Sonia Alvarez has argued that the CEBs failed in relation to women's experiences. Alvarez's study of two working-class areas of the Brazilian capital São
Paulo argued that:

> ... women have been differentially incorporated into the grassroots organi-
> zations of the People's Church in São Paulo. That is, although laywomen have
> been granted more active public roles within church-linked organizations,
> these roles are too often mere extensions of women's roles in the family. The
> incorporation of women into the new People's Church, then, may be rein-
> forcing rather than challenging unequal gender power relations at the com-
> munity level.[57]

---

[54] See the detailed study on women and the popular church by C. A. Drogus, *Women,
Religion and Social Change in Brazil's Popular Church* (Notre Dame, Ind.: University of
Notre Dame Press, 1997), esp. 151–171.

[55] The same point could be made for other countries. Just because the majority of
active church members are women, does not mean that women's experiences have been
normative for the church.

[56] See Ress, "Feminist Theologians Challenge Churches" in Hennelly, *Liberation
Theology*, p. 387.

[57] S. E. Alvarez, "Women's participation in the Brazilian 'People's Church': A Critical
Appraisal," *Feminist Studies* 16, 2 (1990), pp. 381–408 (382).

Alvarez also criticised the Brazilian church for failing to extend its progressive social commitments to areas of gender and sexuality. The church gave support to women's rights in politics and economics, but it remained traditional in its views of personal morality. Its teachings on sexual behaviour, contraception, and divorce were not influenced by feminist critiques of Catholic teaching. Even where the church stands in support of social causes that are important to women—such as opposition to violence—it does not necessarily address women's distinctive concerns and experiences in relation to them.[58] Alvarez argued that it was when women in the base communities sought for more autonomy for women on sexuality and reproduction issues that tension developed with priests who otherwise supported the communities.

In Brazil, as elsewhere, a particularly sensitive area in the church's position on reproduction rights and the issue of abortion. Alvarez observed that Brazil's anti-abortion laws are widely flouted by women of all social classes. There are as many as three million illegal abortions a year, often at great risk to the women concerned.[59] She suggested that the church's position in support of the laws was made very clear in its "prolife, profamily" campaign to influence the Constituent Assembly in 1987–1988. Alvarez saw this as symptomatic of the church's failure to respond to women's concerns on sexuality and reproduction.[60]

John Burdick's study in São Jorge (a small settlement in Baixada Fluminese about 20 miles north of Rio de Janeiro) added a further perspective to the debate.[61] Burdick's experiences of life in São Jorge suggested some serious limitations in the ways that CEBs have addressed gender issues. Burdick suggested that the CEBs adopted too narrow a position on politics which limited it to the public sphere outside the home. As a result, it offered little to women members who face problems in their family lives at home. He suggested that both the Afro-Brazilian spirit religion of Umbanda and the local Pentecostal church often offered more effective support for women who were dealing with domestic conflict, adulterous or abusive husbands and the stresses of sustaining a family.[62]

---

[58] Alvarez noted that in 1983, although Dom Paulo Evaristo Arns proclaimed a year-long pastoral campaign against violence, the issue of sexual violence against women was not adequately addressed; Alvarez, "Women's participation in the Brazilian 'People's Church,'" p. 389.

[59] Adriance suggested that abortion is more likely to be an issue for urban women since rural women put a high value on fertility (*Promised Land*, p. 154).

[60] Some of the differences between Adriance and Alvarez were probably due to the different social context in which they worked: rural Amazonia versus urban São Paulo. Adriance criticised Alvarez for adopting a too narrow—and middle-class based—position on women's rights in terms of contraception and abortion. Adriance argued that rural poor women are much closer to the church's traditional teaching on these issues, and that Alvarez was unfair on the impact of women in the base communities by suggesting that the church has not shifted on such issues.

[61] J. Burdick, *Looking for God in Brazil: The Progressive Catholic Church in Urban Brazil's Religious Arena* (Berkeley: University of California Press, 1993).

[62] On Brazil's African religions, see R. Bastide, *The African Religions of Brazil* (Baltimore,

Burdick's account agreed with Alavarez that the conception of politics in the CEBs fails to address women's distinctive concerns, but whereas Alvarez presented these more in terms of reproduction and sexuality, Burdick looks more at how women try to cope with domestic conflict. In either case, the potential of the CEBs to offer a less patriarchal agenda than the institutional church failed to materialise. The CEBs may have been good news for poor women, but they have been better news for them as "poor" than as "women." Like the theological literature of male theologians, they have yet to fully respond to the challenges posed by Latin American women.

CONCLUSION

The dialogues with other Third World theologians in the early 1980s exposed and helped start to correct some of the limitations that marked the writings of the 1970s. Despite the difficulties that many Latin American theologians had in accepting these criticisms, during the 1980s, there was a noticeable shift to at least acknowledge them more openly. Likewise, the other new horizon that liberation theology needed to address—women's liberation from patriarchy—was also increasingly acknowledged during the 1980s, but the response was quite limited.

On the one hand, a small number of Latin American women theologians creatively integrated Latin American liberation theology with concerns for gender and sexual equality to generate new theological insights and broaden the scope of liberation theology. However, such women were relatively rare and few male liberation theologians responded to the feminist challenge at anything more than a token level.

Although both women and men were always included in the option for the poor—despite the exclusivist language that characterised many of the earlier works—many male theologians seemed indifferent to the influences of gender on economic oppression and unaware of sexism and patriarchy as oppressive realities in their own right. The works of Latin American women showed that there was no need to choose between a concern for poverty and a concern for gender. The two should belong together, and when analysed together, they enriched each other. Thus, feminist perspectives could deepen the liberationist concern for poverty and vice-versa. While most male liberation theologians gradually came to acknowledge this, it nonetheless seemed to make minimal difference to their work. Overall, liberation theology as a movement therefore remained weak on gender issues and the CEBs continued to reflect largely male concerns.

Md.: Johns Hopkins University Press, 1978). For a very positive evaluation of evangelical churches on womens' lives, see E. Brusco, *The Reformation of Machismo: Evangelical Conversion and Gender in Colombia* (Austin: University of Texas Press, 1995).

Part 5

Crisis of Hope
The 1990s

CHAPTER THIRTEEN

End of an Era?

> These Five hundred years have been times of shadows
> and of light, of sin and of grace.
>
> Latin American Religious Conference[1]

INTRODUCTION

At a meeting in Petrópolis in 1985, a group of liberation theologians led by Leonardo Boff started to plan a new series that would systematise liberation theology's insights on different doctrinal issues. The plan was to produce a comprehensive fifty volume collection known as the *Theology and Liberation Series*. Leonardo Boff wrote the first volume in the series, *Introducing Liberation Theology* (which he co-authored with his brother Clodovis), as well as the second, *Trinity and Society*, during his period of Vatican imposed silence. They were both published soon after the silence was lifted in April 1986 and translated into English the following year.[2] In El Salvador, Jon Sobrino and Ignacio Ellacuría collaborated on a two-volume collection of fifty chapters devoted to systematic survey of liberation theology from contributors all over Latin America.[3] When

---

[1] "Message of the XI General Assembly of the Latin American Religious Conference (CLAR) to the Native and Afro-American Sisters and Brothers of Latin America and the Caribbean," *LADOC* 22 (September–October 1991), p. 16.

[2] *Introducing Liberation Theology*, which has been used in earlier chapters of this work, was a superb summary of the theological challenges raised by liberation theology, and remains the best introduction currently available; the second volume on the trinity was a bold attempt to develop a social understanding of trinitarian doctrine, L. Boff, *Trinity and Society* (trans. P. Burns; TLS 2; Maryknoll, N.Y.: Orbis Books; Tunbridge Wells, Kent: Burns and Oates, 1988 [Portuguese orig. 1986]).

[3] I. Ellacuría and J. Sobrino (eds.), *Mysterium liberationis: conceptos fundamentales de la teología de la liberación* (2 vols; San Salvador: UCA Editores, 1990), available in English in abridged form as *Mysterium Liberationis: Fundamental Concepts of Liberation Theology* (Maryknoll, N.Y.: Orbis Books, 1993) and in the U.K. in an even more abridged form as *Systematic Theology: Perspectives from Liberation Theology* (London: SCM Press, 1996).

it was published in 1990, it ran to over 1,300 pages and presented the mature work of many of liberation theology's leading advocates. Taken together, the two projects marked a remarkable overview of the scope and challenge of liberation theology as it had developed during the 1980s.

However, in retrospect they also indicated some of the problems that lay ahead. The first eleven volumes of the *Theology and Liberation Series* volumes were published between 1986 and 1988, but sales were poor.[4] Commercial concerns—coupled with pressure from the Vatican—led to the suspension of the project with only twelve volumes complete.[5] Liberation theology had been very much in the spotlight in the 1970s and early 1980s, and by the end of the 1980s its literature was more extensive than ever. However, support and interest seemed to be fading. In the 1990s, serious questions were asked about the future of the movement.[6]

Critics claimed that the movement had run its course and could only play a very marginal role in the post-Marxist era that would follow the fall of the Berlin Wall.[7] Advocates of liberation theology rejected such easy dismissals and pointed to the many areas in which their work remained important. There was some further important work in extending liberation theology's brief—by incorporating a more explicit ecological dimension—but there was a much less confident feel to work of liberation theologians than in previous decades. It was hard to find new ways to theologically confront the political and economic

---

[4] The other volumes were: E. Dussel, *Ethics and Community* (trans. R. R. Barr; *TLS* 3; Maryknoll, N.Y.: Orbis Books; Tunbridge Wells, Kent: Burns and Oates, 1988 [Spanish orig. 1986]); J. Comblin, *The Holy Spirit and Liberation* (trans. P. Burns; *TLS* 4; Maryknoll, N.Y.: Orbis Books; Tunbridge Wells, Kent: Burns and Oates, 1989 [Portuguese orig. 1986]); J. Pixley and C. Boff, *The Bible, the Church and the Poor* (trans. P. Burns; *TLS*, 6; Maryknoll, N.Y.: Orbis Books; Tunbridge Wells: Burns and Oates, 1989 [Spanish and Portuguese origs. 1987]); I. Gebara and M. C. Bingemer, *Mary, Mother of God, Mother of the Poor* (trans. P. Berryman; *TLS* 7; Maryknoll, N.Y.: Orbis Books; Tunbridge Wells: Burns and Oates, 1989 [Portuguese orig. 1987]); J. Comblin, *Being Human: A Christian Anthropology* (trans. R. R. Barr; *TLS* 8; Maryknoll, N.Y.: Orbis Books; Tunbridge Wells, Kent: Burns and Oates, 1990 [Portuguese orig. 1987]); A. Moser and B. Leers, *Moral Theology: Dead Ends and Ways Forward* (trans. P. Burns; *TLS* 9; Maryknoll, N.Y.: Orbis Books; Tunbridge Wells, Kent: Burns and Oates, 1990 [Portuguese orig. 1987]); P. Trigo, *Creation and History* (trans. R. R. Barr; *TLS* 10; Maryknoll, N.Y.: Orbis Books; Tunbridge Wells, Kent: Burns and Oates, 1992); R. Muñoz, *The God of Christians* (trans. P. Burns; *TLS* 11; Maryknoll, N.Y.: Orbis Books; Tunbridge Wells, Kent: Burns and Oates, 1991 [Spanish orig. 1988]).

[5] The twelfth volume (published five years after the eleventh) was P. Casaldáliga and J. M. Vigil, *Political Holiness: Spirituality of Liberation* (trans. P. Burns and F. McDonagh; *TLS* 12; Maryknoll, N.Y.: Orbis Books; Tunbridge Wells, Kent: Burns and Oates, 1994 [Portuguese orig. 1993]).

[6] For a brief response to some of these, see D. H. Levine, "On Premature Reports of the Death of Liberation Theology," *The Review of Politics* 57, 1 (1995), p. 105.

[7] Cuba remained an exception to the general trend, but it was no longer an inspiring example. Without the support of the Soviet Union, the hardships created by the unforgiving economic blockade imposed by the United States were even more glaring.

forces of the 1990s, and the old ways now seemed dated. Meanwhile, the progressive church was in retreat. At an institutional level, the Vatican continued its policy of appointing conservative bishops to important positions. At a grassroots level, the energetic spread of Pentecostal churches contrasted with an apparent decline in the CEBs. The 1990s marked the end of liberation theology as a vibrant and organised theological movement. Individual theologians continued to engage with the challenges posed by the New World Order, but had much less impact than in the past.

THE NEW WORLD ORDER

The dramatic political transformation of 1989–1990 was widely heralded as the end of Marxism and the triumph of capitalism.[8] The fall of the Berlin Wall, the collapse of the Eastern Block, and the electoral defeat of the Nicaraguan Sandinistas in February 1990 prompted critics of liberation theology to pronounce the movement dead.

Such superficial dismissals of liberation theology were very unfair and reflected a distorted understanding of liberation theology as a Marxist movement of political revolutions. In response, Leonardo Boff noted: "Marx was neither the father nor the godfather of liberation theology. This theology never opted for Marxism or for socialism; its option was for the poor. It saw socialism as a means of improving the lives of and achieving greater justice for the oppressed."[9] As noted above, many of pioneers of liberation theology had been attracted by Marxist analysis in the late 1960s and early 1970s, but liberation theology changed a great deal since then. The basic insight that poverty was the result of exploitative social relations remained a central conviction in their work, but to think of them as Marxist because of this would be very misleading.[10]

Nonetheless, the political shifts at the end of the Cold War focussed attention on the apparent triumph of the free markets in Latin America. Since the 1980s, the silent revolutions had transformed Latin American societies with neoliberal policies and now the same thing seemed to be happening on a global scale. In the 1970s, the sides of the struggle in Latin America remained basically clear-cut—on the one side, the poor majority struggling to survive; on the

---

[8] For a brief, but very helpful overview of the collapse and its historical background, see R. Pearson, *The Rise and Fall of the Soviet Empire* (London: Macmillan Press, 1998).

[9] Boff, *Ecology and Liberation*, p. 120.

[10] In fact, Alistair Kee has argued at some length that liberation theology's greatest failure was in not embracing Marxism sufficiently. Kee argues that Marx's metaphysical critique of religion as reversal has been completely ignored by liberation theologians; see *Marx and the Failure of Liberation Theology* (London: SCM Press, 1990). In their defence, liberation theologians might point to the more immediate concerns in the 1970s and 1980s that made their choice of priorities understandable. However, the issues Kee raises cannot be dismissed as an irrelevant diversion or First World luxury. No matter how politically progressive a religious movement might be, it can only be truly liberating if it is true to reality at the deepest level.

other side, the highly privileged economic elites becoming ever richer with the support of repressive military governments. The silent revolutions and the restoration of democracies deepened inequalities and economic polarisation continued, but the sides of the struggle became less clear.

One result of this was that the central terminology of liberation became much more problematic in the 1980s. To some extent, this had been offset by new emphasis on terms like the "God of life" and "crucified people," but for liberation theology as a movement, the difficulties with the language of liberation were potentially very serious. At the same time, they were diversifying their analysis of oppression beyond politics and economics into other issues, including race, culture, and gender. However, since the late 1970s, the primary thrust had been to approach this task in conversation with the poor rather than through a theoretical analysis. This allowed liberation theologians to deepen their sense of what poverty meant in the lives of the poor and to encounter God in new ways in the lives of the poor. However, they had done little to develop a theoretical analysis of the new economic situation or consider alternatives. During the 1980s, these weaknesses were not yet a crisis. However, in the 1990s, after events in Eastern Europe prompted talk of the triumph of capitalism (and even the end of history) the language of liberation suddenly seemed very dated. It was inevitable that questions would be asked about the ongoing relevance of liberation theology.

José Comblin outlined how liberation theology might respond to the new context in his book *Called to Freedom*.[11] Looking back on the last thirty years, he noted the irony that:

> We are in a new phase of social history in Latin America. What seemed obvious thirty years ago has become incomprehensible today, and what was rejected then is now esteemed. At that time you could not speak of reform; you had to be pursuing a revolution. Today no one speaks of revolution anymore, not even the Zapatista army in Mexico; everyone is seeking reform. Thirty years ago 'reformism' was a bad word; today it is the vogue word amongst the most progressive.[12]

Comblin's emphasis on political freedom was timely. During the 1990s, peace negotiations brought the longstanding conflicts in El Salvador (1980–1992) and Guatemala (1960–1996) to an end.[13] He rightly observed:

> Today, it makes no sense to reject the freedoms of the democratic system. They offer many more possibilities for the struggle of the poor than the alternatives that Latin America has witnessed. . . . There is no point in standing

---

[11] J. Comblin, *Called for Freedom: The Changing Context of Liberation Theology* (trans. P. Berryman; Maryknoll, N.Y.: Orbis Books, 1998 [Portuguese orig. 1996]).

[12] Comblin, *Called for Freedom*, p. 64.

[13] See the excellent collection by Cynthia Arnson (ed.), *Comparative Peace Processes in Latin America* (Washington D.C.: Woodrow Wilson Centre Press; Stanford, Calif.: Stanford University Press, 1999).

outside the contemporary world, by rejecting the whole language of freedom. It is within this modern language that we must situate the Christian message of the call to freedom.[14]

However, as Comblin recognised, the economic issues were intractable.[15] In the 1990s, there was more freedom than ever before to operate within a global market, but there was little hope of freedom from the market. Even when the problems within neo-liberalism started to surface after 1995 (with a serious monetary crisis in Mexico), dependency on the capitalist global system was so entrenched that talk of liberation seemed unrealistically utopian.[16] In 1994, when the first serious economic shocks started to hit Mexico, Latin America's total external debt had climbed over $525 billion (up from $450 in 1990).[17] As in the 1980s, the burden of servicing this debt fell primarily on the poor. In 1998, the United Nations estimated that over one billion people, a fifth of the world's population, had to survive on about 60 pence ($1 U.S.) a day.[18] Leonardo Boff commented:

> With the collapse of the East-West confrontation, which was largely ideological (liberalism-socialism), the prevailing opposition today is between North and South, which is economic and political in character. The contrast is one between the rich North where only 17 percent of humanity live, and the poor South, where 83 percent of humankind suffer. Who listens to their cries?[19]

In previous decades, serious alternatives to the market still existed. In the 1990s, even when free-market systems showed serious flaws—as they always had in Latin America, especially when viewed from the perspective of the poor— it would be hard to see what alternatives might be better.[20]

Many prominent liberation theologians met at Escorial (Spain) in 1992 (twenty-years after their influential first meeting there in 1972).[21] It was clear that there were no easy answers.[22] The need for liberation theology was as

---

[14] Comblin, *Called for Freedom*, p. 60.

[15] On a possible way forward on economic issues, see Comblin, *Called for Freedom*, p. 98.

[16] On some of the theological challenges raised by the free-market economies, see E. Dussel, "The Market from an Ethical Viewpoint of Liberation Theology," *Concilium* 1997/2 (1997), pp. 85–100.

[17] Data from UN Economic Commission for Latin America and Caribbean, cited in Green, *Silent Revolutions*, p. 68.

[18] United Nations, *United Nations Development Report* (New York: United Nations, 1998).

[19] L. Boff, *Ecology and Liberation: A New Paradigm* (trans. J. Cumming; Maryknoll, N.Y.: Orbis Books, 1995 [Portuguese orig. 1993]), pp. 68–69.

[20] Compare, for example, F. J. Hinkelammert, *The Ideological Weapons of Death: A Theological Critique of Capitalism* (Maryknoll, N.Y.: Orbis Books, 1986 [Spanish orig. 1977]) and Hinkelammert, "Liberation Theology in the Economic and Social Context of Latin America" in D. Batstone et al. (eds.), *Liberation Theologies, Postmodernity, and the Americas* (New York and London: Routledge, 1997).

[21] See J. Comblin, J. Ignacio González-Faus, and Jon Sobrino (eds.), *Cambio social y pensamiento cristiano en América Latina* (Madrid: Trotta, 1993).

[22] Comblin's book suggests that it may be far too early to even look for answers. He

pressing as ever, but the language of liberation no longer seemed appropriate. Gutiérrez warned:

A series of economic, political, and ecclesial events around the world, in Latin America, and in individual countries, lead one to think that the period when recent Latin American theological reflection was born is now coming to an end. Given the emerging new situation ... many earlier discussions do not respond to current challenges. All indications are that a different period is beginning. It is ever more necessary that all be involved in dealing with the enormous questions with which the reality of Latin America confronts us.[23]

Responding to the challenge was not easy. In earlier years, liberation theologians kept in close touch with each other and often responded to new challenges as a cohesive group. However, in the 1990s—with many of the early members quite advanced in years—their meetings declined. Individual theologians continued to engage with the issues, but the movement no longer had the profile or confidence of previous decades.[24] José Vigil summed up the sense that the era of liberation theology was coming to an end:

Theologians are writing very little, meeting very little and with fewer people. When they do meet they say nothing in public. All that is heard is their silence. Neoliberalism and 'globalisation,' which are enemies of the poor and are in full upswing, are not being discussed today in the same way they discussed the enemies of the poor in the past (military dictatorship, and capitalism at that time).[25]

At one level, the issues raised by postmodernism made any theological attempt to offer a clear response to the present and a vision of the future a much more fraught activity.[26] There were now many more questions and much more suspicion of anything claiming to be an answer than when liberation theology began in the late 1960s. The intellectual climate was no longer favourable to the meta-narrative of liberation. Recognising the challenges posed by the new situation—and the special difficulties in continuing to proclaim liberation—Pablo Richard argued that in the new situation the simple recovery and preser-

---

concludes *Called to Freedom* with the observation: "The social movements that led to social reform and to the welfare state started around 1870. Vatican II came ninety years later. A new social movement to respond to the new wave of economic revolution has barely begun. Now is the time to begin to work out new responses to the new challenges" (p. 217).

[23] Gutiérrez in Comblin, J. Ignacio González-Faus, and Jon Sobrino (eds.), *Cambio social y pensamiento cristiano en América Latina*, cited in J. Comblin, *Called for Freedom*, p. xiii.

[24] For a good overview, see J. L. Kater, "Whatever Happened to Liberation Theology?" *Anglican Theological Review* 83.4 (Fall 2001), pp. 735–773.

[25] J. M. Vigil, "Is there a Change of Paradigm in Liberation Theology?" *SEDOS* 29.12 (1997), pp. 315–321 (315).

[26] For a good collection on the postmodern challenge to liberation theology, see D. Batstone et al. (eds.), *Liberation Theologies, Postmodernity and the Americas* (New York and London: Routledge, 1997).

vation of hope was one of liberation theology's most important tasks.[27] Surveying the apparent global triumph of capitalism Richard noted: "For the poor, this so-called new international order represents a situation of death and the destruction of all hope."[28] He went on to declare:

> We are living through a deep crisis of hope. Today hope is presented as something belonging to the past. Reconstructing hope, with a solid base in economic and political alternatives to the current system of the free market economy, is seen as an irrational, and even subversive, act.[29]

For Richard the new phase of uncertainty and chaos suggested a shift from prophetic theology to apocalyptic theology.[30] He contrasted the time of prophecy (an organized world, where political and civil institutions—such as the monarchy, the law, and the temple—regulate life in long-established ways) with the time of apocalypse (a time of chaos and confusion when normal institutions have broken down). He argued that for this reason, in the ancient kingdoms of Israel and Judah, it was the prophets who denounced injustice and pronounced the message of God. However, after the fall of Jerusalem and the exile in 586 B.C.E., the apocalyptic literature started to appear. According to Richard: "In this new situation of chaos, oppression and persecution, the apocalyptic does not function as a prophet who denounces and acts, but rather takes on new task—reconstructing consciousness and spirituality in the midst of chaos and confusion."[31]

Elsa Tamez echoed Richard's views on the need to maintain hope. In *When the Horizons Close* Tamez argued:

> The Book of Qoheleth or Ecclesiastes has become timely again today, when horizons are closing in and the present becomes a hard master, demanding sacrifices and suppressing dreams. Today, at the beginning of the millennium, we are experiencing at the global level a lack of hope that there will be good times for all in the near future.[32]

---

[27] P. Richard, "Liberation Theology: Theology of the South," *Envio* 12 (June 1993), pp. 28–40.

[28] Richard, "Liberation Theology: Theology of the South," p. 28.

[29] Richard, "Liberation Theology: Theology of the South," p. 30.

[30] Richard, "Liberation Theology: Theology of the South," esp. pp. 39–40.

[31] Richard, "Liberation Theology: Theology of the South," p. 40. In his book *Apocalypse: A People's Commentary on the Book of Revelation* (Maryknoll, N.Y.: Orbis Books, 1995 [Spanish orig. 1994]), Richard develops this argument at greater length and draws on it in his reading of Revelation. A similar turn to apocalyptic can be seen in Richard's colleagues at the Department of Ecumenical Investigations in San José, Hugo Assmann and Franz Hinkelammert. See, for example, F. Hinkelammert, "Liberation Theology in the Economic and Social Context of Latin America" in D. Batstone et al. (eds), *Liberation Theologies, Postmodernity, and the Americas.*

[32] E. Tamez, *When the Horizons Close: Rereading Ecclesiastes* (Maryknoll, N.Y.: Orbis Books, 2000 [Spanish orig. 1998]), p. v.

She draws from the book the message that when there are few signs that social conditions will improve in the future, one must abandon false hopes but not despair completely. In turning from the future to the present and recognising that there is a season for everything, the everyday joys of life can be embraced and the dignity of human life upheld despite the closed horizons for liberation.

Pedro Trigo (a Spanish Jesuit working in Venezuela) suggested that liberation theology's politically orientated writings of the 1960s and 1970s were something of a false start. He suggested that it was only with Gutiérrez's *We Drink from Our Own Wells* (1986) that the everyday lives of ordinary people were made the starting point for theological reflection.[33] For Trigo, it was more important than ever that liberation theologians explore the spiritual resources for resistance and hope in the lives of the poor.

Gutiérrez himself provided further resources for this task with a magisterial work on his hero and forerunner Bartolomé de Las Casas. His book *Las Casas: In Search of the Poor of Jesus Christ* was published in 1992, to mark the Five Hundred year anniversary of Christianity in Latin America.[34] The work, which runs to nearly seven hundred pages in English translation, is a fitting tribute from one great theologian to another. At the end of the decade, Gutiérrez again indicated the importance of Las Casas and the other early Dominicans by seeking entry to the Dominican order.

In El Salvador, Jon Sobrino responded to critics who proclaimed the end of liberation theology. Sobrino pointed to the fact that in the 1990s there were many more people living in poverty in Latin America than there had been when liberation theology first began, and those in poverty were more impoverished than ever. Therefore, far from being irrelevant, the need for a theology that will strengthen the poor—regardless of what it is called—is greater as ever.[35]

Against this background, Sobrino continued to develop his christological understanding of contemporary history in the new context of civil peace after 1992. His two books *Jesus the Liberator* (1991) and *Christ the Liberator* (1999) offered a magisterial statement of his mature reflection.[36] Much of his work in the 1990s developed around the theme of martyrdom and the need to take the crucified people down from the cross.[37] In his book *The Principle of Mercy*,

---

[33] See P. Berryman, *Religion in the Megacity*, p. 118.

[34] Gutiérrez, *Las Casas: In Search of the Poor of Jesus Christ* (trans. R. R. Barr; Maryknoll, N.Y.: Orbis Books, 1993 [Spanish orig. 1992]).

[35] For example, Ellacuría and Sobrino (eds.), *Mysterium liberationis*, pp. ix–xiv.

[36] *Jesus the Liberator: A Historical-Theological View* (trans. P. Burns and F. McDonagh; Maryknoll, N.Y.: Orbis Books; Tunbridge Wells, Kent: Burns and Oates; 1994 [Spanish orig. 1991]); *Christ the Liberator: A View from the Victims* (trans. P. Burns; Maryknoll, N.Y.: Orbis Books, 2001 [Spanish orig. 1999]).

[37] Sobrino, *The Principle of Mercy*, p. viii. An important stimulus for these topics was the massacre of Ignacio Ellacuría, five other Jesuits, their cook, and her daughter on 16 November 1989. On the tragedy, its background, and the slow investigation that followed, see esp. T. Whitfield, *Paying the Price: Ignacio Ellacuría and the Murdered Jesuits of El Salvador* (Philadelphia: Temple University Press, 1994).

he argued for a new ethic of radical Christian action as the basis for a new solidarity between the First World and the Third World. Developing his previous reflections on the crucified people he presented the taking of the crucified people from the cross as the central demand of contemporary faith.[38] As he struggled to come to terms with the murder by the military of his entire community in El Salvador, Jon Sobrino reflected:

> I hope that when peace and justice comes to the country, succeeding generations remember that the Jesuits were among those who made it possible. I hope that future Christian generations . . . are grateful for their witness to the fact that faith and life in El Salvador are not contradictory but empower each other . . . that they recognise that in this way these martyrs guaranteed that faith in Jesus was handed on in El Salvador.

> The price to be paid for all this has been very high, but inevitable. Today when we hear so much about evangelising cultures, we should remember a deeper form of evangelisation, so that society itself becomes good news. And for this to happen it is necessary to become incarnate in that reality, as Archbishop Romero said in words that make us shiver to this day: 'I am glad, brothers and sisters, that they have murdered priests in this country, because it would be very sad if in a country where they are murdering the people so horrifically there were no priests among the victims. It is a sign that the Church has become truly incarnate in the problems of the people."[39]

Responses to Sobrino's challenge that the church incarnates itself in the problems of people and strives to take the crucified down from the cross, might take different forms. One initiative launched in 1996 was the campaign on debt-relief known as the Jubilee 2000. Inspired by the biblical ideals in Leviticus of release from debt-slavery, the movement lobbied Western leaders to mark the millennium by granting substantial debt relief on the unpayable debts of the poorest and most indebted countries. Many of those at the forefront of the movement in the Western churches and aid agencies were inspired by liberation theology and its ideas.[40]

Global economic initiatives like Jubilee 2000 were more important than ever as the consequences of economic and technological globalisation became clearer in the 1990s. On 1 January 1994 one of the most dramatic expressions of the neo-liberal economic order came into effect. The free-trade provisions that previously existed between the U.S. and Canada were extended to Mexico as the North American Free Trade Agreement (NAFTA). NAFTA provided for

---

[38] The inclusion of this phrase in the title of the book (*The Principle of Mercy: Taking the Crucified People from the Cross*) reflects the importance that this has for him.

[39] Sobrino, *Companions of Jesus: The Murder and Martyrdom of the Salvadoran Jesuits* (London: Catholic Institute for International Relations, 1990), pp. 56, 57.

[40] See Christian Aid, *Proclaim Liberty: Reflections on Theology and Debt* (London: Christian Aid, 1998); S. Taylor, "Forgiveness, the Jubilee and World Debt" in S. E. Porter, M. A. Hayes, and D. Tombs (eds.), *Faith in the Millennium* (RILP 7; Sheffield: Sheffield Academic Press, 2001), pp. 153–173.

the free flow of commodities across the vast North American region. Under NAFTA, it was easier than ever before for U.S. and Canadian firms to get access to Mexican markets.

Yet on the same day that NAFTA was redefining the free-trade framework for North America, the New Year celebrations in San Cristóbal de Las Casas (Chiapas, Mexico) were interrupted by masked men of the Zapatista Army of National Liberation (EZLN).[41] The Zapatista leader—who quickly become internationally known as Subcomandante Marcos—announced that "To us, the free trade treaty is the death certificate for the ethnic peoples of Mexico."[42] The Zapatista uprising in Mexico's predominantly Mayan highland state of Chipas ensured that concern over indigenous issues received more attention in the 1990s than ever before.

Between February 1995 and February 1998, Samuel Ruiz (who had been bishop of San Cristóbal since 1960) played a prominent role as mediator in Chiapas.[43] In August 1993, he raised the problems facing the indigenous peoples in Chiapas in a letter presented to the Pope during the third papal visit to Mexico.[44] His efforts to negotiate between the Zapatistas and the government met with early success, but were undermined by the government and the highly conservative apostolic nuncio Jerónimo Prigione. When the Mexican army broke previous agreements and occupied the whole area in 1998, Ruiz resigned as mediator leaving the conflict unresolved.

The five-hundred-year anniversaries of the first voyages of Columbus (1992) and Portuguese arrival in Brazil (2000) also helped to focus attention on the past failures of the church and address the injustices against indigenous peoples and Afro-Americans as a priority for the 1990s. In 1991, the General Assembly of the Latin American Relgious Conference addressed a special message "To the Native and Afro-American Sisters and Brothers of Latin America and the Caribbean."[45] It recognised the mixed record of the church's five hundred years in Latin America and expressed the wish:

> To make common cause with your legitimate right to a land where you can live fittingly, after having suffered plunder, being as natives the natural owners, or having endured centuries of slavery with all its inhuman consequences. Above all we wish to make common cause with your right to your own way

---

[41] On the history and political concerns of the movement, see J. Ross, *Rebellion from the Roots: Indian Uprising in Chiapas* (Monroe, Maine: Common Courage Press, 1995).

[42] Ross, *Rebellion from the Roots*, p. 21.

[43] Ruiz was an influential figure in the progressive church and advocate of liberation theology. He had been one of the bishops expelled from Ecuador in 1976 (see p. 162 above).

[44] See Klaiber, *The Church, Dictatorships and Democracy in Latin America*, p. 256.

[45] "Message of the XI General Assembly of the Latin American Religious Conference," pp. 16–17.

of life and organization, to be respected in the culture and language inherited from your elders.[46]

During the 1990s, various initiatives tried to make this commitment a reality. The Indigenous Missionary Council in Brazil was active in defence of the Yanomami and other indigenous peoples in the Amazon area. The Yanomami of the Orinoco river basin (in the state of Roraima on the border with Venezuela) suffered a 15% decline in population between 1987 and 1990, because of incursions into the area by miners and prospectors. The Indigenous Missionary Council helped to pressure the government to set up a homeland area (36,000 square miles) in 1991 to preserve the Yanomami way of life.[47]

The exploitation of the Amazon exemplified in the destruction of the Yanomami people also prompted a new ecological interest amongst some liberation theologians, led especially by the Brazilian Leonardo Boff and a number of feminist writers.[48]

During the 1980s, the Amazon became a centre of worldwide ecological concern.[49] In *Ecology and Liberation*, Boff outlined a number of environmental problems that liberation theology must start to address.[50] For example, he noted that Latin America makes up just 12% of the earth's surface, but possesses roughly two-thirds of the world's plant species. However, the scale of deforestation at the end of the twentieth century was remarkable. Up to 1970, five million hectares of the Amazon were deforested. After 1970, this accelerated rapidly so that from 1970 to 1988 it rose to twenty million.

Although deforestation was taking place in Brazil and other southern hemisphere countries, the main threat to the global environment came from the rich countries. In Europe and North America, the problems of acid rain, ozone depletion, and atmospheric pollution all contribute to global warming. Global warming in turn contributes to floods, desertification, and other natural disasters around the world. As world population continued to climb (from two and half billion in 1950, to four billion in 1975, to over five billion in 1990, and

---

[46] "Message of the XI General Assembly of the Latin American Religious Conference," p. 16.

[47] On the background to this initiative, see E. Kräutler, *Indians and Ecology in Brazil* (London: Catholic Institute of International Relations, 1990).

[48] In the 1980s, Enrique Dussel already raised some of these issues in his chapter on the ethics of culture and ecology in Dussel, *Ethics and Community*, pp. 194–204. In addition, many of the feminist pioneers of the 1980s were also leaders in addressing both ecological and indigenous concerns. For example, Tamez combined liberation theology with a feminist outlook, a sensitivity to environmental issues, and an openness to native Amerindian traditions in E. Tamez, "The Power of the Naked" in idem, *Through her Eyes*, pp. 1–14. For a good collection of later Latin American feminist writing on ecology, see R. R. Ruether (ed.), *Women Healing Earth: Third World Women on Ecology, Feminism, and Religion* (Maryknoll, N.Y.: Orbis Books; London: SCM Press, 1996), pp. 13–60.

[49] It was appropriate that the UN Earth Summit of 1992 took place in Rio de Janeiro.

[50] Boff, *Ecology and Liberation*, pp. 15–19.

over six billion in 2000) it placed an enormous strain on the world's ecological system. In typical style, he provided a telling image to encapsulate the issues.

Astronauts who have travelled into space and recorded their impressions of the earth described it as a ship on a voyage. In fact, in this ship which is the earth a fifth of the population are travelling in first class and in luxury class: they enjoy all the benefits. They consume 80 percent of the resources available for the voyage. The remaining 80 percent of the passengers are travelling steerage. They suffer cold, hunger, and all kinds of privations. Many ask why they are travelling steerage. Need forces others to rebel. It is not difficult to see what is at stake. Either everyone can be saved in a system of communal solidarity and participation on the ship—and in that case fundamental changes are necessary—or as a result of outrage and revolt, the ship will explode and throw everyone in to the sea.[51]

In 1964, the new (and more cautious) leadership of the CNBB created thirteen regional divisions to enhance Episcopal collaboration at a more local level. This had a particular impact on the Amazon bishops, and the Amazon soon became one of the most socially active church regions in the country.[52] The creation of the Amazonian region of bishops coincided with the decision of the military government to start the economic exploitation of the area after 1965, a policy that became known as Operation Amazon.[53]

SUDAM (Superintendency for the Development of the Amazon) was created in October 1966 to oversee this process.[54] Central to its operation were offers of tax relief on approved projects of up to 50% of their taxes from operations anywhere in Brazil provided that they invest in the Amazon area.[55] The majority of projects approved for this purpose were cattle ranches.[56]

The economic exploitation of the Amazon prompted increasing friction between the military government of the time and the Amazonian bishops. Large-scale agribusiness expelled Indians and peasants from the land, usually replacing subsistence farming with cattle-ranching and frequently leading to violent confrontations from the late 1960s onward.

---

[51] Boff, *Ecology and Liberation*, p. 18.

[52] They achieved a reputation for social concern that was second only to the bishops of the Northeast. However, whereas the bishops of the Northeast had this reputation since the 1950s, the Amazonian bishops had previously been seen as much more traditional.

[53] On the development of social teaching of Amazonian bishops (1964–1973), see Mainwaring, *The Catholic Church and Politics in Brazil*, pp. 84–94.

[54] For an overview of government policies after 1964, see M. Adriance, *Promised Land: Base Christian Communities and the Struggle for the Amazon* (Albany: State University of New York Press, 1995) pp. 13–24.

[55] A legal area, "Legal Amazônia" to include the area of tropical rainforest and surrounding states.

[56] In practice, SUDAM was flawed by very high levels of corruption and offered negligible supervision of the projects it authorised. In particular, it ignored environmentalist advice on the potential damage of large-scale forest burning and the poverty of the Amazon soil where the forest had once been. As a result, fewer than one-third of the ranches it authorised ever produced anything. See, Adriance, *Promised Land*, p. 16.

The bishops' criticism of this policy started in a series of statements dating from 1970. In 1971, Dom Pedro Casaldáliga was appointed bishop of São Félix do Araguaia (in Mato Grosso) where social conflicts over land were particularly intense. Once in post, Casaldáliga threw himself into the energetic criticism of how the poor were being treated. When he was harassed by intimidation and death threats, many other bishops—including those of a much more conservative inclination—felt compelled to defend the right of the church to speak on social issues.[57]

Along with other prominent Amazonian bishops, Casaldáliga published statements that were harshly critical of the capitalist development of the region and its effects on the people already living there. However, their main concern in the 1970s was the effects they saw on the peasant workers and Indian communities, rather than the ecological environment itself. Although the issue of land was highlighted, the focus was on economic (re)distribution rather than ecological conservation.

The *abertura* (the political opening which led to the restoration of democracy) ensured an improvement in civil rights in the cities, but the Amazon remained highly conflictual throughout the 1980s and into the 1990s.[58] In response to development policies, great areas of the Amazon were cleared with chainsaws or fires in the hope that the lush vegetation might be replaced with profitable pasture. In fact, the Amazon's soil structure has proved very delicate. It has been able to support a rich plant life when undisturbed, but as soon as the fragile balance is broken, its soil has quickly degraded and proved too poor to produce anything worthwhile. The topsoil has little depth and when the trees are cut down the rains quickly carry it away, leaving barren land in its place. At the same time as it has been devastating the natural environment, this deforestation has also spelled misery and death for indigenous people living in the Amazon. Mining operations have driven indigenous peoples from their traditional lands and polluted their rivers with mercury and other contaminants.[59]

In view of this relentless assault on the Amazon, Boff argued that ecological factors are a necessary addition to class analysis, but there is no suggestion that they should ever replace it.[60] In 1995, Boff asserted that: "The Amazon is the place where Gaia displays the lush riches of her body; it is also where

---

[57] In January 1972, Casaldáliga flew to Brasília with the CNBB general secretary Dom Aloiso Lorscheider to be interrogated by the minister of justice. In June, police searched his house and confiscated his papers, and in July he was placed under house arrest. See Mainwaring, *The Catholic Church and Politics in Brazil*, pp. 88–90.

[58] For example, Adriance reports that "More than 300 people, mostly peasant farmers, died in land conflicts in that region between 1980 and 1994" (*Promised Land*, p. 23).

[59] Boff, *Cry of the Earth, Cry of the Poor*, p. 99.

[60] ". . . the class category is essential for understanding social structure and conflicts of interest. To abandon it would mean impoverishing our understanding to the detriment of the interests of the weakest. The class struggle, therefore, by becoming sensitive to ecological and holistic interests, acquires a new style. Now, not only the interests of a class, or even of society as a whole were taken into account, but also the welfare of nature." Boff, *Ecology and Liberation*, p. 117.

she suffers the greatest violence. If we want to see the brutal face of the capitalist and industrial system, we need only visit the Brazilian Amazon."[61]

Boff argued that ecology was not an alternative to liberation theology's concern for the poor, but rather a necessary feature in concern for the poor. The
degradation of the earth called for a new ecological outlook.[62] He noted that
the arrogant urge to conquer, subdue, and dominate that drove the conquistadors in the sixteenth century continued to drive humanity's attitude to the
environment.[63] Liberation theology and ecology could work as partners in a
response to the cry of the poor for life and the cry of the earth groaning under
oppression.[64] The sons and daughters of Earth people had to take the mystery
of creation seriously and recognise human responsibility within it.[65] Recovering
the dignity of mother earth included recovering the dignity of the many poor,
whose very lives are threatened by the way the earth is pillaged. At a theological level, Boff suggested that this required a new "pantheism," in which God
is recognised in all and all is seen to exist in God.[66]

In retrospect, Boff's work on ecology and the other theological initiatives of
liberation theologians in the 1990s outlined above can be seen as positive
attempts to extend the work of liberation theology in different directions. This
was a necessary task if liberation theology was to continue its efforts to strengthen
and deepen its understanding of global oppression. However, liberation theology was already severely weakened as a theological and ecclesial movement in
the 1980s and its theological impact weakened as it struggled to take on new
issues. The new directions that individual theologians took in the 1990s exacerbated this problem even further. Works of liberation theology in the 1990s
lacked the cohesive focus and common agenda of early decades. Nor could it
rely on anything like the same support from progressive bishops or the base
community movement.

---

[61] Boff, *Cry of the Earth, Cry of the Poor*, p. 86.

[62] He discusses this in terms of ecotechnology (technologies and procedures designed
to preserve the environment), ecopolitics (strategies for sustainable development), social
ecology (human relations with the environment to regulate production and reproduction), mental ecology (human understanding of the environment and humanity's place
in it), and cosmic mysticism. Boff, *Ecology and Liberation*, pp. 19–43; compare L. Boff,
Cry of the Earth, Cry of the Poor, pp. 5–7.

[63] Boff, *Cry of the Earth, Cry of the Poor*, pp. 69–71.

[64] See *Cry of the Earth, Cry of the Poor*, pp. 104–114.

[65] He acknowledges that often the so-called new popular religious traditions have been
more successful than Christianity on this and suggests that this accounts for some of
their recent popularity in Brazil (Boff, *Ecology and Liberation*, p. 66).

[66] Boff is careful to distinguish this from a pantheism which sees God *as* everything
and everything *as* God. He notes: "All is not God. But God is in all and all is in God
by reason of the creation" (Boff, *Cry of the Earth, Cry of the Poor*, p. 153).

PROBLEMS FACING THE PROGRESSIVE CHURCH

When the Brazialian bishops made their *ad limina* visits to Rome in 1990, they were reminded to stay out of politics. In May of the same year, the Pope told the crowd at Chalco on the outskirts of Mexico City, "The option for the poor continues to be in the heart of the Church."[67] His encyclical *Redemptoris Missio* praised the role of base communities in evangelization, but the Vatican was determined to make sure that they were under institutional control.

In northeast Brazil, Hélder Câmara's successor as archbishop of Olinda and Recife, José Cardoso, continued his high-profile sanctions against liberation theology. In March 1990, he sent a letter to all clergy stressing the need for obedience. The following month, he disciplined two priests who worked with the poor in parishes on the outskirts of Recife by relieving them of their posts.[68]

In El Salvador, Fernando Saenz Lacalle, a conservative opponent of liberation theology and friend of *Opus Dei* was appointed as archbishop of San Salvador in 1995. He reversed the support that the base community movement had enjoyed under Rivera y Damas (1980–1995) and insisted on a conservative curriculum at the National Seminary.

The policy of acting through local bishops helped the Vatican reduce the high-profile conflicts that had attracted unwanted media attention in the 1980s. However, it remained ready to intervene directly against individual theologians when it felt the need. Despite the hopes raised in 1986, relations with the Vatican continued to be difficult for both Boff and Gutiérrez. Eventually, Boff left his religious order, the Franciscans, and resigned his priesthood in June 1992.[69] In 1995, the Vatican imposed a two-year period of silence on the Brazilian feminist theologian Ivone Gebara. Not only was this longer than Boff's period in the 1980s, but its conditions were also more humiliating. Gebara—who was a professor of theology and philosophy—was called to Europe to study traditional theology.[70] Regrettably, whereas Boff had received high-profile public solidarity

---

[67] See M. Walsh, *John Paul II: A Biography* (London: HarperCollins, 1994), p. 224. During this visit, the Pope beatified Juan Diego (the Indian peasant to whom the Virgin appeared in the sixteenth century).

[68] Nagle, *Claiming the Virgin*, p. 168.

[69] Boff's letter explaining his decision was printed in *The Tablet* (11 July 1992), pp. 882–883.

[70] In reporting the news, *The Tablet* (249 [1 July 1995], p. 851) notes: "It is thought that the points of theological dispute may include the image of God and patriarchy in the Church. In an interview with the Brazilian magazine *Veja*, she made controversial comments on abortion, speaking out of her experience of living in one of Recife's poorest slums. In a letter to cancel engagements as a result of her silencing, Ivone Gebara wrote: 'This honeybee, your friend, is to be sent far away from her hive and her country, accused of producing honey that has a different flavour from that of other bees.'" See also the interview with Mev Puleo in M. Puleo, *The Struggle is One* (Albany: State University of New York Press, 1994), pp. 205–216, and Gebara, "The Abortion Debate in Brazil: A Report from an Eco-Feminist Philosopher and Theologian under Siege," *Journal of Feminist Studies in Religion* 11.2 (1995), pp. 129–136.

in his relations with the Vatican, Gebara received much less support from her male liberationist colleagues.

CELAM IV in Santo Domingo—on the theme "New Evangelization, Human Development and Christian Culture"—marked another stage in conservative opposition to liberation theology.[71] The meeting took place in 1992 in the Dominican Republic to mark the five hundredth anniversary of Christian presence in the Caribbean and Latin America.[72] Preparations to exclude the involvement of liberation theologians were even more careful than at Puebla. It was made clear that only official advisers were welcome, and there should not be an unofficial camp outside the conference walls.[73] A consultative document was issued in February 1990 that was so conservative that it was even criticised by the Argentineans, the most traditionally conservative of Latin American national episcopates. As at Puebla, the Brazilian bishops, and especially the CELAM secretary, Bishop Raymundo Damasceno Assis, managed to influence a more acceptable revision—the *Second Report* or *Secunda Relatio* (February 1992)—which became the basis of the formal working document (April 1992).[74]

An important change to the methodology used at Medellín and Puebla can be seen in the way the conclusions began with doctrine rather than the contemporary social situation. This return to a more traditional methodology set the tone for what was to come.[75] The framework for the early topics was Christology, but there was no mention of how this might be related to experiences of contemporary martyrdom in Latin America.[76] The document emphasised Christ's work as reconciling humanity to God and presented Christ as entrusting this ministry to the church.[77] There was little reference to liberation, apart from the Pope's endorsement of the genuine praxis of liberation set out in *Libertatis*

---

[71] The final document is translated and published with accompanying analysis in A. T. Hennelly (ed.), *Santo Domingo and Beyond* (Maryknoll, N.Y.: Orbis Books, 1993).

[72] As with more secular celebrations of the anniversary, there was controversy on whether it was an appropriate to celebrate or lament the last five centuries. Five-hundred-year anniversaries scheduled for Brazil in the year 2000 were similarly contested.

[73] Even though they could not be in the country, advances in technology allowed some liberation theologians to contribute nonetheless. At Puebla, progressive bishops carried conference documents to them in person. At Santo Domingo, communication over much longer distances was possible by e-mail.

[74] See E. Cleary, "The Journey to Santo Domingo" in Hennelly (ed.), *Santo Domingo and Beyond*, pp. 2–23.

[75] See A. T. Hennelly, "A Report from the Conference" in Hennelly (ed.), *Santo Domingo and Beyond*, pp. 24–36. Hennelly observes (p. 34) that the bishops find a more prophetic voice when they speak for themselves in their "Message of the Fourth General Conference to the Peoples of Latin America and the Caribbean" than in the formal conclusions that were edited in Rome.

[76] Hennelly draws attention to this as "perhaps the most gaping lacuna" and notes that the Second Report had included a moving tribute to all those who had shed their blood in Latin America (Hennelly, "A Report from the Conference," p. 34).

[77] CELAM, *Santo Domingo*, § 6.

Nuntius (1984) and *Libertatis Conscientia* (1986), which he warned "must be kept in mind when the topic of liberation theologies comes up for discussion."[78]

The conference did not decisively reject the previous commitment to the poor, but it gave it far less emphasis than in the previous meetings. The prophetic thrust was clearest when the bishops said: "We make ours the cry of the poor. In continuity with Medellín and Puebla, we assume with renewed ardour the gospel preferential option for the poor."[79] However, such passages went against the generally cautious tone of the texts.

One area that might be seen as small step forward from Puebla was in the treatment of women, but the bishops remained highly conservative on gender issues. In her response to Santo Domingo, María Pilar Aquino noted that a preparatory meeting on "Women in the Latin American Church and Culture" in Bogotá (April 1992) was only partially effective in influencing the use of sexist language. She pointed out that English translations might remove this difficulty in their wish to be inclusive, but that this did not resolve the problem for Latin American women.[80] A little later, she noted that the same was true for the works of male liberation theologians published in English translation and questioned the long-term value of this policy: "While the translation makes these authors more attractive to North American readers, it does nothing to help Latin American women, because it does not change the patriarchal mentality of these authors. I would rather see the works translated as they appear in the original language, so as not to inflate false balloons."[81]

The bishops focussed some of their strongest criticism on the Protestant sects.[82] In his opening address, the Pope likened the bishops of the Catholic church to the good shepherd and the sects to rapacious wolves.[83] During the conference, the bishops used more moderate language, but had nothing positive to say in their treatment of them or their appeal.

The concern of the bishops was understandable. The declaration in the *New York Times* by a Brazilian Presbyterian that "The Catholic church opted for the poor, but the poor opted for the evangelicals" summarised a widely shared perception that Pentecostal churches had the upper hand in their competition

---

[78] "Opening Address of the Holy Father" in Hennelly (ed.), *Santo Domingo and Beyond*, pp. 41–60 (50–51).

[79] CELAM, *Santo Domingo*, § 296. See also §§ 178–181.

[80] M. P. Aquino, "Santo Domingo through the Eyes of a Woman" in Hennelly (ed.), *Santo Domingo and Beyond*, pp. 212–225 (21–22).

[81] Aquino, "Santo Domingo through the Eyes of a Woman," p. 225 n. 15.

[82] See CELAM, *Santo Domingo*, §§ 139–152. The term sects is highly pejorative in church circles. The Protestant theologian Guillermo Cook makes some brief but telling observations on the church's attitudes to the sects in G. Cook, "Santo Domingo through Protestant Eyes" in Hennelly (ed.), *Santo Domingo and Beyond*, pp. 184–201 (195–197).

[83] "Opening Address of the Holy Father" in Hennelly (ed.), *Santo Domingo and Beyond*, p. 47.

with the CEBs.[84] During the 1990s, there were many attempts to confront the growth of Pentecostalism as an urgent issue of concern.[85] Philip Berryman's investigations in Brazil and Venezuela published as *Religion in the Megacity* suggested how much ground the Catholic church had already lost to the Penteocstal churches.[86] Manuel Vásquez's study *The Brazilian Church and the Crisis of Modernity* (1998) set these problems in the framework of a wider crisis of modernity and humanistic discourses in Brazil.[87] Although Vásquez concentrates almost exclusively on Brazil, his argument is relevant for the problems facing liberation theology across the continent.

Early responses to Pentecostal churches often criticised them as cultural imperialism by North American groups, whose well funded mission ventures offered the poor material benefits but were disruptive of long-standing traditions and cultural ties in local communities. This was true in some areas, but there was far more to the success of Pentecostalism than this one-dimensional conspiracy theory suggested. Reasons for conversion could not be reduced to the simple hope of material gains. Most Pentecostal converts financially supported their church from their own limited resources—rather than benefited from foreign largesse. The critics of Pentecostalism generally ignored this challenging reality and avoided probing more deeply into why Pentecostalism found favour. Neither the traditionalist nor the liberationist Catholic church engaged in searching self-criticism to understand what Pentecostalism offered its converts and why they turned their backs on Catholicism.[88]

A more positive assessment of Pentecostal Protestantism—advanced by the British sociologist David Martin—was that the Protestant worldview helped believers to adapt to the new economic and social environment of Latin America. Martin argued that Protestantism's emphasis on personal participation in worship was well suited to Latin America's newly individualist and urban culture. Furthermore, Martin believed that the spread of Protestantism encouraged modernisation and democratisation in the wider society.[89]

---

[84] See J. Brooke, "Pragmatic Protestants Win Catholic Converts in Brazil," *The New York Times*, (4 July 1993), cited in P. Berryman, *Religion in the Megacity: Catholic and Protestant Portraits from Latin America* (Maryknoll, N.Y.: Orbis Books, 1996), p. 3.

[85] Two particularly influential studies in English have been D. Stoll, *Is Latin America Turning Protestant? The Politics of Evangelical Growth* (Berkeley: University of California Press, 1990), and *Tongues of Fire: The Explosion of Protestantism in Latin America* (Oxford: Basil Blackwell, 1990). See also the edited collection, Virginia Garrard-Burnett and David Stoll (eds.), *Rethinking Protestantism in Latin America* (Philadelphia: Temple University Press, 1993).

[86] Berryman, *Religion in the Megacity*, pp. 147–167.

[87] Manuel A. Vásquez, *The Brazilian Popular Church and the Crisis of Modernity* (Cambridge Studies in Ideology and Religion; Cambridge: University of Cambridge Press, 1998). See esp. pp. 74–98 for his treatment of the debate on competition from Pentecostal churches.

[88] See below on the discussion at CELAM IV.

[89] Martin, *Tongues of Fire*, pp. 271–295. For an earlier argument to a broadly simi-

At a more pragmatic level, Martin observed that the networks of mutual support in Protestant churches offered economic advantages to a variety of different social groups.[90] Cecília Mariz also stressed the mutual support that characterised how Pentecostal communities coped with poverty at a microsocial level and suggested that the poor might be attracted to Pentecostalism for very different reasons to those that were important for middle classes.[91] For example, the middle classes might like the emotionalism of its services and the supernatural element of healing miracles. By contrast, the poor—who were more familiar with the popular religious culture of Afro-Brazilian spirit religions such as Umbanda or Candomblé—might be attracted by Pentecostalism's relative rationalization.[92]

Most importantly, however, the rise of the Pentecostal churches raised questions on how adequately liberation theology satisfied the religious demands of the poor. The promise of sure salvation that Pentecostals preached in simple terms had an obvious appeal in times of heightened uncertainty. Pentecostalism seemed to put the believer in firm charge of his or her own individual destiny. No matter what difficulties one might encounter in one's work-life or family-life, there could be a comforting security in one's spiritual life. For many people people, this was a much more attractive vision than the stress on social involvement and struggle for the kingdom of God offered by the base communities.

---

lar conclusion see B. Roberts, "Protestant Groups and Coping with Urban Life in Guatemala" in *American Journal of Sociology* 73 (1968), pp. 753–767. It might also be noted that in areas of extreme conflict such as Gautemala and El Salvador, membership of a Pentecostal church afforded at least some protection against the widespread persecution of those suspected of sympathising with the progressive church.

[90] Martin writes: "Protestantism may in one context gain attention and adherence among those who are at the margins of subsistence and are threatened by the advance of a market economy and the depredations of local caciques [leaders]. In another context, Protestantism may acquire a base among small independent producers who need to band together and who are determined to assert themselves, in particular by by-passing the Ladino middle-man. Everywhere it offers a network of mutual support which may include a variety of services...." Martin, *Tongues of Fire*, p. 283.

[91] C. L. Mariz, *Coping with Poverty: Pentecostals and Christian Base Communities in Brazil* (Philadelphia: Temple University Press, 1994).

[92] Mariz, *Coping with Poverty*, p. 8. A Gallup poll in 1990 found only 0.4% of Brazilians were willing to admit their involvement, but the strength of Afro-Brazilian religions in Brazil is generally acknowledged to be much greater than the very low number of people that declare their personal affiliation. This is due to the greater respectability usually associated with Catholicism as opposed to Afro-Brazilian religions (which were officially discriminated against until 1945). In addition, personal loyalties may be less clear-cut than polls suggest. For example, initiates into Afro-Brazilian religions must have been baptised into Catholicism and may revert to Catholicism when polled. Furthermore, popular Catholicism in Brazil often shows a fusion of Catholic and African traditions which might also be hidden in statistical surveys (see Mariz, *Coping with Poverty*, p. 18).

CONCLUSION

During the 1990s, liberation theology lost its momentum as an organised theological movement and faced a crisis of relevance in the terminology of liberation. However, its commitment to the poor and oppressed and its methodological approach to theology remained highly relevant, and this is very likely to continue.

The collapse of socialism and fall of the Berlin Wall had very little direct impact on liberation theology, but it nonetheless exposed the changing political and economic dynamics that transformed Latin America in the 1980s and raised questions on the relevance of liberation. In the late 1960s and early 1970s, liberation theology had sought to offer a relevant economic analysis of oppression by engaging with political theorists, social scientists, and Marxists. After the mid-1970s, many of the leading liberation theologians moved away from this work to focus more directly on the lives of the poor. During the 1980s, liberation theologians made little attempt to address the macroeconomic changes and silent revolutions at an analytic level or identify alternatives to them; they were concerned more with how these impacted the lives of the poor. They therefore did not directly address the problems of continuing to speak of liberation in a rapidly changing economic context. When liberation theologians were forced to confront this in the 1990s, their responses were cautious and varied.

The terminology that drove the movement so powerfully in the late 1960s and 1970s no longer provided a topical message or a clear direction for theological reflection. The urgency of the theological task and importance of theological writings was as pressing as before, but a clear response was more difficult.

The Vatican's continuing opposition to liberation theology did not help. Conservatives were in the ascendancy in the national episcopates and liberation theologians had to be careful with what they said and wrote. Meanwhile, the CEBs were in decline as a social movement and facing strong competition from Pentecostal churches. There was much less international interest or support for liberation theology than there was in previous decades, and meetings between theologians became much less common.

In this context, most liberation theologians identified the problem, but nobody claimed to have the answers. In the future, this could be a strength. A greater pluralism in terminology and outlook could make the ideas of liberation theology more resistant to sudden setbacks. Some theologians, such as Leonardo Boff, pioneered new work on theology and the environment, and the church took a stronger stand on indigenous issues than ever before. However, as a cohesive movement liberation theology seemed to be reaching the end of its era. At the turn of the millennium, with many of the most prominent liberation theologians very advanced in years, it was hard to see how it might be reenergised. The death of Hélder Câmara in August 1999 seemed to symbolise the fact that it belonged to the last third of the twentieth century, but not to the twenty-first. Nonetheless, when its overall record since 1968 is evaluated, there is every reason to think that it should leave a permanent and potent legacy in many areas of theology.

CHAPTER FOURTEEN

Conclusion

> I was a Christian long before liberation theology and I
> will be a Christian long after liberation theology.
>
> Gustavo Gutiérrez[1]

Discussions of liberation theology have rarely treated it with sufficient attention to its theological development during the years that it was prominent as a theological movement. One of the consequences of the argument presented here is that it is rarely appropriate to talk of Latin American liberation theology without reference to its date. In particular, it is necessary to separate the distinctive strands that marked the evolution of liberation theology from the late-1960s to the 1990s.

In the option for the poor, liberation theology tried to break the church's traditional alliance with the rich and powerful. With a few notable exceptions, the Latin American church had always allied itself to the exploiters, and its theology only offered other-worldly comfort to the exploited.

However, it is vital to see that the option for the poor covered two related, but different dimensions of liberation theology: a political option and a later epistemological option. Both were important to the best works of the movement. Any historical understanding of liberation theology's history or assessment of its significance must recognise both sides of the option.

The political option is clearly recognisable from the late 1960s onward (though not necessarily named as such) and expanded in scope in subsequent decades. It called for the church to stand in solidarity with the exploited and join in their struggles for social justice. In these early years, Gutiérrez and others first formulated the principles of theology after the fact and the concern for orthopraxis. Their publications during this period reflected the radical politics of their contemporaries in other academic disciplines, including a Marxist analysis

---

[1] R. M. Brown, *Gustavo Gutiérrez: An Introduction to Liberation Theology* (Maryknoll, N.Y.: Orbis Books, 1990), p. 22.

293

of the social conflict implicit in Latin American life. Theological language of liberation was a new way to speak of integral salvation that was perfectly suited to the currents of the time and especially the critiques of dependency that were prominent in intellectual circles.

During these early years, liberation theology was at its most confident, but also its most controversial. The revolutionary language, the adoption of Marxist analysis and advocacy of socialism provoked strong reactions and allowed the movement to be misleadingly stereotyped. These features of early works were not the most important features of liberation theology, but it was hardly surprising that they proved the most provocative and got the most attention. Despite the dramatic changes that liberation theology underwent in the 1970s, this misleading stereotype stuck fast to it and remained the target of later criticism.

As the progressive church put into practice its political option to be a church of the poor, the grass-roots base communities began to reorientate liberation theology. This transformation in liberation theology came as an unexpected gift. In the face of bitter persecution across the continent, liberation theologians sought to engage the people in a genuine theological dialogue on the presence of God in their suffering. This gave liberation theologians new respect for the insights of the people and deepened their understanding of solidarity and service to the people of God. Above all, they started to see the hopes, struggles, and experiences of the poor as offering a special revelation of God's presence in the world. This epistemological option for the poor—which recognised the experiences of the poor as a privileged *locus* of revelation and insight—started to become explicit as a clear set of further principles after the mid-1970s.

The 1980s involved less dramatic, but still significant further methodological developments. The new focus on the daily lives of the poor encouraged reflection on spirituality. The contemplative side of theology received greater attention and there was stress on silence as well as action as the preconditions for theological reflection. Many of the most moving and inspirational works of liberation theology were written during this decade, including a number by women theologians who first came to prominence during the 1980s and integrated concern for poverty with their awareness of gender.

However, the crisis of the 1990s was created in the 1980s. The changing economic foundations resulting from the silent revolutions received little attention at a structural level. At the time, the increasing irrelevance of liberationist economic analysis did not seem fatal. First, liberation theology's concern for oppression broadened beyond economics to include race, ethnicity, and other cultural factors, as well as patriarchy and sexism. Second, the triumph of capitalism was not yet clear at a global level. Third, because of the methodological shifts of the 1970s, there was much less emphasis on macroeconomic analysis and the underlying economic structures. As a result, the crisis did not break until the 1990s.

The fall of the Berlin Wall in 1989 and the defeat of the Sandinistas in the 1990s were widely seen as the definitive triumph of the market over Marxism, and critics were quick to pronounce the death of liberation theology. Many of the obituaries were misguided, because they based their view on a distortion of what liberation theology had been, and a blindness to what it had become. Nonetheless, they helped expose the problems that liberation was facing. In the 1990s, there was no escaping that liberation theology now faced a serious crisis as a theological movement.

First, Latin American liberation theologians embraced important new issues, but met with less success than in their engagement with poverty. While liberation theology certainly needed to extend its awareness of oppression beyond economic poverty, few theologians were equipped to explore the new areas with the same insight and creativity, and male theologians were particularly weak when addressing gender issues. Second, even liberation theology's traditional strength in addressing poverty and economic issues was now in crisis. At the heart of this was a problem with what had once been its greatest strength—the terminology of liberation. In the 1990s, the language of liberation seemed to have little relevance to the political and economic realities of the global free market, but it was unclear what might replace it. Third, with the passing of time, the cumulative effect of steady opposition from the Vatican and local church hierarchies took a heavy toll. Whereas opposition and widespread persecution by military governments in the 1970s initially tended to inspire the movement, the ongoing conflict with the Vatican steadily sapped its energy and gradually discouraged creativity. Eventually, the papacy of John Paul II succeeded in blunting the impact of liberation theology in parishes across the continent.

It is impossible to tell the future, but it seems that liberation theology has had its time as a theological movement. John Paul's successor may be more sympathetic, but the generation of theologians who brought so much to the movement in its early days have grown old and not been replaced.

Despite this, liberation theology leaves a potent legacy within theology. It highlighted the political significance of all theological work, questioned the value of intellectual study divorced from action, stressed the value of dialogue with those beyond the academy, and identified the struggles of the poor and oppressed as a privileged epistemological *locus* for an engaged theology. To take the legacy of liberation theology seriously will mean continuing to work with these principles to reflect more deeply on the God of life and the lives of the people of God. The language of liberation may cease to be relevant, at least for a while; but liberation theology's methodological insights, especially the political and epistemological options for the poor, are likely to be enduring legacies for any future theological engagement between church and society or theology and social issues.

Successive Developments in Liberation Theology's Focus and Methodology

1968–1969   *Economic and Political Context.* Reforms and atmosphere of liberation.
Theological Focus and Challenges. Political commitment to solidarity with the poor.
Development of Methodology. Gutiérrez's early work highlights liberation as a political/historical/theological theme; argues for theology as critical reflection on commitment and action; and points to political and social analysis as helpful dialogue partners for theology.

1970s   *Economic and Political Context.* Polarisation and dictatorships.
Theological Focus and Challenges. Work with base communities reorientates liberation theology as theology that is not just for the poor but also *of* the poor and *by* the poor.
Development of Methodology. Work with the poor encourages dialogue with the poor as partners for theology, and the epistemological principle that the poor are a privileged *locus* of theology.

1980s   *Economic and Political Context.* Silent revolutions and restoration of limited democracy.
Theological Focus and Challenges. Expanding the concern for oppression beyond class to gender and race (with variable success) while defending itself against Vatican opposition and responding to the challenge of feminist theology.
Development of Methodology. Greater emphasis on spirituality and the importance of silence and contemplation in the theological process.

1990s   *Economic and Political Context.* Post-Cold War new economic order.
Theological Focus and Challenges. Responding to the triumph of capitalism, and preserving hope and engagement with indigenous issues and ecology. Search for alternatives to the language of liberation.

Bibliography

AACC, *The Drumbeats from Kampala* (London: Lutterworth Press, 1963).

AACC, *The Struggle Continues* (Nairobi: AACC, 1975).

Abesamis, Carlos, "Faith and Life Reflection from the Grassroots in the Philippines" in Virginia Fabella (ed.), *Asia's Struggle for Full Humanity*.

Abraham, K. C. (ed.), *Third World Theologies: Commonalities and Divergences* (Second General Assembly of EATWOT, Oaxtepec, Mexico, 7–14 December 1986; Maryknoll, N.Y.: Orbis Books, 1990).

Adriance, Marilyn, *Opting for the Poor: Brazilian Catholicism in Transition* (Kansas City: Sheed and Ward, 1986).

—— "Base Communites and Rural Mobilization in Northern Brazil," *Sociology of Religion* 55, 2 (1994).

—— *Promised Land: Base Christian Communities and the Struggle for the Amazon* (Albany: State University of New York Press, 1995).

—— "Agents of Change: Priests, Sisters, and Lay Workers in the Grassroots Catholic Church in Brazil," *Journal for Scientific Study of Religion* 30 (1991).

Albert, B., *South America and the World Economy from Independence to 1930* (London: Macmillan, 1983).

Alfaro, Juan, "Foreword" in Jon Sobrino, *Jesus in Latin America*.

Allende, Salvador, *Chile's Road to Socialism* (Harmondsworth: Penguin Books, 1973).

Althaus-Reid, Marcella, *Indecent Theology: Theological Perversions in Sex, Gender and Politics* (London and New York: Routledge, 2000).

Alvarez, Sonia E., "Women's Participation in the Brazilian 'People's Church': A Critical Appraisal," *Feminist Studies* 16.2 (1990).

Alves, Rubem, *A Theology of Human Hope* (Washington: Corpus Books, 1969). Spanish orig. *Religión: ¿opio o instrumento de liberación?* (Montevideo: Tierra Nueva, 1970).

—— "Theology and the Liberation of Man" in SODEPAX, *In Search of a Theology of Development*.

—— *Tomorrow's Child: Imagination, Creativity and the Rebirth of Culture* (London: SCM Press, 1972).

—— *Protestantism and Repression: A Brazilian Case Study* (trans. J. Drury; Maryknoll, N.Y.: Orbis Books, 1985). Portuguese orig. *Protestanismo e reprassão* (São Paulo: Editora Ática 1979).

Anderson, Thomas P., *Matanza: El Salvador's Communist Revolt* (Lincoln: University of Nebraska Press, 1971).

Anna, T. E., *The Fall of Royal Government in Mexico City* (Lincoln: University of Nebraska Press, 1978).

—— *The Fall of Royal Government in Peru* (Lincoln: University of Nebraska Press, 1979).

Appiah-Kubi, Kofi, and Sergio Torres (eds.), *African Theology En Route* (EATWOT Pan-African Conference of Third World Theologians held in Accra, Ghana, 17–23 December 1977; Maryknoll, N.Y.: Orbis Books, 1979).

Aquino, María Pilar, *Our Cry for Life: Feminist Theology from Latin America* (trans. D. Livingstone; Maryknoll, N.Y.: Orbis Books, 1993). Spanish orig. *Nuestro clamor por la vida: teología latinoamericana desde la mujer* (San José: Departmento Ecuménico de Investigaciones, 1992).

297

Aquino, Maria Pilar, "Latin American Feminist Theology," *Journal of Feminist Studies in Religion* 14.1 (1998).
—— "Santo Domingo Through the Eyes of a Woman" in Hennelly (ed.), *Santo Domingo and Beyond*.
Armony, Ariel C., *Argentina, the United States and the Anti-Communist Crusade in Central America 1977–1984* (Athens, Ohio: Ohio University Press, 1997).
Arnson, Cynthia (ed.), *Comparative Peace Processes in Latin America* (Washington, D.C.: Woodrow Wilson Centre Press; Stanford, Calif.: Stanford University Press, 1999).
Arrupe, Pedro, "Marxist Analysis by Christians," *Origins* 10 (16 April 1981); reprinted in Hennelly (ed.), *Liberation Theology*.
Assmann, H. *Teología de la liberación* (Montevideo: MIEC-JECI, 1970). Revised and reprinted as *Opresion–Liberación: Desafío a los Cristianos* (Montevideo: Tierra Nueva, 1971). Revised again and reprinted as *Teología desde de la praxis de la liberación* (Salamanca: Sígueme, 1973). English translation of *Teología desde de la praxis de la liberación* available as *Practical Theology of Liberation* (trans. P. Burns; London: Search Press, 1975); retitled in the U.S. as *Theology for a Nomad Church* (Maryknoll, N.Y.: Orbis Books, 1976).
Avalos, Hector, "Columbus as Biblical Exegete: A Study of the *Libro de las profecías*" in B. F. Le Beau and M. Mor (eds.), *Religion in the Age of Exploration: The Case of Spain and New Spain* (Omaha, Neb.: Creighton University Press, 1996).
Barbé, Dominique, *Grace and Power: Base Communities and Non-violence in Brazil* (trans. J. P. Brown; Maryknoll, N.Y.: Orbis Books, 1987). French orig. *La grâce et le pouvoir* (Paris: Éditions du Cerf, 1982). Portuguese trans. *A graça e o poder* (São Paulo: Edições Paulinas, 1983).
Barthel, M., *The History and Legends of the Society of Jesus* (New York: William Morrow, 1984).
Bastide, Roger, *The African Religions of Brazil* (Baltimore, Md.: Johns Hopkins University Press, 1978).
Bath, R. C., and D. Jones, "Dependency Analysis of Latin America," *LARR* 11.3 (1976).
Batista, Mauro, "Black and Christian in Brazil" in Torres and Eagleson (eds.), *The Challenge of Basic Christian Communities*.
Batstone, David, et al. (eds.), *Liberation Theologies, Postmodernity and the Americas* (New York and London: Routledge, 1997).
Bauer, G. (ed.), *Towards a Theology of Development* (Geneva, WCC, 1970).
Baum, Gregory, "German Theologians and Liberation Theology," *The Ecumenist* 16 (1978); reprinted in Hennelly (ed.), *Liberation Theology*.
Berger, Peter, *Pyramids of Sacrifice: Political Ethics and Social Change* (Garden City, N.Y.: Doubleday Anchor, 1974).
Berryman, Phillip, *The Religious Roots of Rebellion* (Maryknoll, N.Y.: Orbis Books; London: SCM Press, 1984).
—— *Liberation Theology: The Essential Facts about Revolutionary Movements in Latin America and Beyond* (New York: Pantheon; London: Taurus, 1987).
—— *Religion in the Megacity: Catholic and Protestant Portraits from Latin America* (Maryknoll, N.Y.: Orbis Books, 1996).
Bethell, Leslie, *The Abolition of the Brazilian Slave Trade: Britain, Brazil and the Slave Trade Question, 1807–1869* (Cambridge: Cambridge University Press, 1970).
—— (ed.), *The Independence of Latin America* (Cambridge History of Latin America 3; Cambridge: Cambridge University Press, 1987 [1985]).
Betto, F. *Fidel and Religion* (trans. from Spanish ed., Cuban Centre for Translation and Interpretation; New York: Simon and Schuster, 1987). Portuguese orig. *Fidel e a religião* (1987).
Bidegain, Ana Maria, "Women and the Theology of Liberation" in Marc H. Ellis and Otto Maduro (eds.), *The Future of Liberation Theology: Essays in Honour of Gustavo Gutiérrez* (Maryknoll, N.Y.: Orbis Books, 1989).

Bingemer, Maria Clara, "Preface" in K. C. Abraham (ed.), *Third World Theologies: Commonalities and Differences.*

—— "Woman: Time and Eternity: The Eternal Woman and the Feminine Face of God," *Concilium* 6 (1991).

Bishops of Nicaragua, "Christian Commitment for a New Nicaragua, 17 November 1979", *LADOC* 10 (March–April 1979); reprinted in Hennelly (ed.), *Liberation Theology.*

—— "Call to Dialogue," *Origins* 14 (26 July 1984); reprinted in Hennelly (ed.), *Liberation Theology.*

Boff, Clodovis, *Theology and Praxis: Epistemological Foundations* (trans. R. R. Barr; Maryknoll, N.Y.: Orbis Books, 1987). Portuguese orig. *Teología e practica* (Petrópolis, RJ: Editora Vozes, 1978).

Boff, Leonardo, *Jesus Christ Liberator: A Critical Christology of Our Time* (trans. P. Hughes; Maryknoll, N.Y.: Orbis Books, 1978; London: SPCK, 1980). Portuguese orig. *Jesus Cristo Libertador: Ensaio de cristologia critica para o nosso tempo* (Petrópolis: Editora Vozes, 1972). Spanish trans. *Jesucristo el liberador* (Buenos Aires: 1974).

—— *Teología do cativerio e da libertação* (Lisbon: Multinova, 1976).

—— *Ecclesiogenesis: The Base Communities Reinvent the Church* (trans. R. R. Barr; Maryknoll, N.Y.: Orbis Books, London: Collins, 1986). Portuguese orig. *Eclesiogênese: As comunidades eclesiais de base reinventam a Igreja* (Petrópolis, RJ: Editora Vozes, 1977).

—— *The Maternal Face of God: The Feminine and its Religious Expressions* (trans. R. R. Barr & J. W. Diercksmeier; San Francisco: Harper and Row; London: Harper Collins, 1987). Portuguese orig. *O rostro materno de Deus: Ensaio interdisciplinar sobre o feminino e suas formas religiosas* (Petrópolis, RJ: Editora Vozes, 1979).

—— *Church: Charism and Power: Liberation Theology and the Institutional Church* (trans. J. Diercksmeier; New York: Crossroad; London: SCM Press, 1985). Portuguese orig. *Igreja: Carisma e poder* (Petrópolis: Editora Vozes, 1981).

—— *Vida segundo o espiritu* (Petrópolis, RJ: Editora Vozes, 1982).

—— "Martyrdom: An Attempt at Systematic Reflection," *Concilium* 163 (1983).

—— "A Theological Examination of the terms 'People of God' and 'Popular Church,'" *Concilium* 176 (1984).

—— *Trinity and Society* (trans. P. Burns; TLS 2; Maryknoll, N.Y.: Orbis Books; Tunbridge Wells, Kent: Burns and Oates, 1988). Portuguese orig. *A Trinidade, a Sociedade e a Libertação* (São Paulo: CESEP, 1986).

—— "The Poor Judge: The Magisterium and the Liberation Theologians," *Concilium* 192 (1987).

—— "What are Third World Theologies?" *Concilium* 199 (1988).

—— "Anti-Communism: End of an Industry," *Concilium* 205 (1989).

—— *Good News to the Poor: A New Evangelization* (trans. R. R. Barr; Maryknoll, N.Y.: Orbis Books; Tunbridge Wells, Kent: Burns & Oates, 1992). Portuguese orig. *Nova Evangelicão: Perspective dos Oprimidos* (Petrópolis, RJ: Editora Vozes, 1990).

—— *Ecology and Liberation: A New Paradigm* (trans. J. Cumming; Maryknoll, N.Y.: Orbis Books, 1995). ET from Italian ed. *Ecologia, Mondialità, Mistica* (Assissi: Citadella Editrice, 1993). Portuguese orig. *Ecologia, Mundialização, Espiritualidade* (São Paulo: Editora Ática, 1993).

—— *Cry of the Earth, Cry of the Poor* (trans. Phillip Berryman; Maryknoll, N.Y.: Orbis Books, 1997). Portuguese orig. *Ecologia: Grito da Terra, Grito dos Pobres* (São Paulo: Editora Ática, 1995).

Boff, Leonardo, and Clodovis Boff, *Liberation and Salvation: In Search of a Balance Between Faith and Politics* (trans. R. R. Barr, Maryknoll, N.Y.: Orbis Books, 1984). Portuguese orig. *Da libertação: O sentido teológico das libertações sóciohistoricas* (Petrópolis, RJ: Editora Vozes, 1979).

—— *Introducing Liberation Theology* (trans. P. Burns; Maryknoll, N.Y.: Orbis Books;

Tunbridge Wells, Kent: Burns and Oates; 1987). Portuguese orig. *Como fazer Teología da Libertação* (Petrópolis, RJ: Editora Vozes, 1986).

Boff, Leonardo, and J. Elizondo (eds.), *La Iglesia Popular: Between Fear and Hope* (*Concilium*, 176; New York: Seabury; Edinburgh: T & T Clark, 1984).

—— *Option for the Poor: Challenge for the Rich Countries* (*Concilium*, 187; Edinburgh: T & T Clark, 1986).

—— *Theologies of the Third World: Convergences and Differences* (*Concilium*, 199, Edinburgh: T & T Clark, 1988).

Borda, O. F., *Subversion and Social Change in Colombia* (New York: Columbia University Press, 1969).

Bourne, R., *Getúlio Vargas: Sphinx of the Pampas* (London: Charles Knight, 1974).

Boyd, S., "Rape Laws Offer Women Scant Protection," *Latinamerica Press*, 29.28 (1997).

Boxer, Charles Ralph, *The Portuguese Seaborne Empire* (Harmondsworth: Penguin Books, 1973).

—— *The Dutch in Brazil (1624–54)* (Oxford: Clarendon Press, 1957).

—— *Mary and Misogyny: Women in Iberian Expansion Overseas, 1414–1815: Some Facts, Fancies and Personalities* (London: Duckworth, 1975).

Brackley, Dean, *Divine Revolution: Salvation and Liberation in Catholic Thought* (Maryknoll, N.Y.: Orbis Books, 1996).

Bradstock, Andrew, *Saints and Sandinistas: The Catholic Church in Nicaragua and its Response to the Revolution* (London: Epworth Press, 1987).

Bravo, Francisco, *The Parish of San Miguelito in Panama* (Cuernavaca: Centro Intercultural de Documentación, 1966).

Brooke, J. "Pragmatic Protestants Win Catholic Converts in Brazil," *The New York Times*, 4 July 1993.

Brown, Robert McAfee, *Religion and Violence* (Philadelphia: Westminster Press, 2nd ed., 1987 [1973]).

—— *Gustavo Gutiérrez: An Introduction to Liberation Theology* (Maryknoll, N.Y.: Orbis Books, 1990).

Bruneau, Thomas, *The Political Transformation of the Brazilian Catholic Church* (New York: Cambridge University Press, 1974).

Brusco, Elizabeth E., *The Reformation of Machismo: Evangelical Conversion and Gender in Colombia* (Austin: University of Texas Press, 1995).

Burdick, John, *Looking for God in Brazil: The Progressive Catholic Church in Urban Brazil's Religious Arena* (Berkeley: University of California Press, 1993).

—— *For God and Fatherland: Religion and Politics in Argentina* (Albany: State University of New York Press, 1996).

Burns, E. B., *A History of Brazil* (New York: Columbia University Press, 1970).

Bussmann, Claus, *Who Do You Say? Jesus Christ in Latin American Theology* (Maryknoll, N.Y.: Orbis Books, 1985). German orig. *Befreiung durch Jesus? Die Christologie der lateinamerikanischen* (Munich: Kösel-Verlag GmbH & Co, 1980]).

Cabestrero, Teófilo, *Revolutionaries for the Gospel: Testimonies of Fifteen Christians in the Nicaraguan Government* (Maryknoll, N.Y.: Orbis Books, 1986).

Cadorette, Curt, *From the Heart of the People: The Theology of Gustavo Gutiérrez* (Oak Park, Ill.: Meyer-Stone, 1988).

Caipora Women's Group, *Women in Brazil* (London: Latin America Bureau, 1983).

Câmara, Helder, "Violence and Misery," *New Blackfriars* 50, 589 (1969).

—— *Through the Gospel with Dom Hélder Câmara* (trans. A. Neame; Maryknoll, N.Y.: Orbis Books; London: Darton, Longman & Todd, 1986).

Caramuru, R. B., *Comunidade eclesial de base: uma opçã pastoral decisiva* (Petrópolis, RJ: Editora Vozes, 1967).

Cardenal, Ernesto, *The Gospel in Solentiname* (trans. D. D. Walsh; 4 vols.; Maryknoll,

N.Y.: Orbis Books, 1976–1982). Spanish orig. *El evangelio en Solentiname* (2 vols.; Salamanca: Ediciones Sígueme 1975–1977).

Cardenal, Fernando, "A Letter to My Friends," *The National Catholic Reporter* (11 January 1985); reprinted in Hennelly (ed.), *Liberation Theology.*

Cardoso, Fernando H., and Enzo Faletto, *Dependency and Development in Latin America* (trans. M. Uruqudi; Berkeley: University of California Press, rev. ed. 1979). Spanish orig. *Dependencia y dearrollo en América Latina* (Santiago: Siglo Veintiuno Editores, rev. ed. 1971 [1969]).

Carrasco, David, *City of Sacrifice: The Aztec Empire and the Role of Violence in Civilization* (Boston: Beacon Press, 1999).

Casaldáliga, Pedro, *Prophets in Combat: The Nicaraguan Journal of Bishop Pedro Casaldáliga* (Oak Park, Ill.: Meyer-Stone Books; London: Catholic Institute for International Relations, 1987). Spanish orig. *Nicaragua: Combate y profécia* (Madrid: Ayuso & Misíon Abierta, 1986).

Casaldáliga, Pedro, and José-María Vigil, *Political Holiness: Spirituality of Liberation* (trans. P. Burns and F. McDonagh; TLS 12; Maryknoll, N.Y.: Orbis Books; Tunbridge Wells, Kent: Burns and Oates, 1994). Portuguese orig. (São Paulo: CESEP, 1993).

Castañeda, Jorge G., *Compañero: The Life and Death of Che Guevara* (trans. Marina Castañeda; London: Bloomsbury, 1997).

Catholic Institute for International Relations (ed.), *Reflections on Puebla* (London: Catholic Institute for International Relations, 1980).

Cavanaugh, William T., *Torture and Eucharist: Theology, Politics and the Body of Christ* (Oxford: Basil Blackwell, 1998).

CDF, "Ten Observations on the Theology of Gustavo Gutiérrez" (March 1983); reprinted in *Dial* 22, March 1984; ET, Hennelly (ed.), *Liberation Theology.*

CDF, *Instruction on Certain Aspects of 'The Theology of Liberation,* (Vatican City: 1984). ET "Instruction on Certain Aspects of 'The Theology of Liberation,'" *Origins* 14 (13 September 1984); reprinted in Hennelly (ed.), *Liberation Theology.*

CDF, "Notification sent to Fr. Leonardo Boff regarding Errors in his Book, *Church: Charism and Power*," *Origins* 14 (4 April 1985); reprinted in Hennelly (ed.), *Liberation Theology.*

CDF, *Instruction on Christian Freedom and Liberation* (Vatican City: Libreria Editrice Vaticana, 1986); ET, *Origins* 15 (17 April 1986); reprinted in Hennelly (ed.), *Liberation Theology.*

CELAM, *The Church in the Present-Day Transformation of Latin America in the Light of the Council* (2nd ed.; Washington, D.C.: Bishop's Conference, 1973 [ET 1970]). Spanish orig. Consejo Episcopal Latinoamericano. *La iglesia en la actual transformacion de america latina a laluz del concilio* (Bogotá: CELAM, 1969).

CELAM, "Documento de Consulta" (Bogotá: CELAM, 1977).

CELAM, "Documento de Trabajo" (Bogotá: CELAM, 1978).

CELAM, *Puebla: Evangelization at Present and in the Future of Latin America: Conclusions* (Official English Edition of the Third General Conference of Latin American Bishops, Puebla, Mexico, 1979; Slough: St. Paul Publications; London: Catholic Institute for International Relations, 1980). Spanish orig. Consejo Episcopal Latinoamericano. *La Evangelización en el Presente y en el Futuro de America Latina* (Bogotá: CELAM, 1979). Portuguese orig. Conselho Episcopal Latinoamericano. *A Evangelização no presente e no Futuro da América Latina à Luz do Concílio* (Petrópolis, RJ: Editora Vozes, 1980).

CELAM, *Santo Domingo: Final Document* (Washington, D.C.: Bishop's Conference, 1993). Reprinted in Hennelly (ed.), *Santo Domingo and Beyond.*

Chilcote, R. H., and J. C. Edelstein (eds.), *Latin America: The Struggle with Dependency and Beyond* (New York: Halstead Press, 1974).

Chopp, Rebecca, *The Praxis of Suffering: An Interpretation of Liberation and Political Theologies* (Maryknoll, N.Y.: Orbis Books, 1986).

Christ, Carol P., "The New Feminist Theology: A Review of the Literature," *Religious Studies Review* 3.4 (1977).

Christ, C. P., and J. Plaskow, *Womanspirit Rising: A Feminist Reader in Religion* (San Francisco: Harper & Row, 1979).

Christo, Carlos A., *Against Principalities and Powers* (trans. J. Drury; Maryknoll, N.Y.: Orbis Books, 1977). UK ed. *Letters from a Prisoner of Conscience* (London: Lutterworth, 1978). Italian orig. *Dai Sotteranei dell Storia* (Rome: Arnoldo Mondadori Editore, 1971).

Cleary, Edward L., *Crisis and Change: The Church in Latin America Today* (Maryknoll, N.Y.: Orbis Books, 1985).

—— "The Journey to Santo Domingo" in Hennelly (ed.), *Santo Domingo and Beyond*.

—— *The Struggle for Human Rights in Latin America* (Westport, Conn. and London: Praeger, 1997).

—— (ed.), *Born of the Poor: The Latin American Church since Medellin* (Notre Dame, Ind.: Notre Dame University Press, 1990).

Cleary, Edward L., and Hannah Stewart-Gambino (eds.), *Conflict and Competition: The Latin American Church in a Changing Environment* (Boulder, Colo.: Lynne Rienner, 1992).

Cleary, Edward L., and Hannah W. Stewart-Gambino (eds.), *Power, Politics and Pentecostals in Latin America* (Boulder, Colo.: Westview Press, 1997).

Clendinnen, I., *Aztecs: An Interpretation* (Cambridge: Cambridge University Press, 1991).

CNBB, *Plano de Emergência para a Igreja do Brasil* (Rio de Janeiro: Livraria Dom Bosco Editôra, 1963).

CNBB, *Plano de Pastoral Conjunto 1966–70* (Rio de Janeiro: Livraria Dom Bosco Editôra, 1966).

CNBB, *Comunidades: Igreja na Base* (CNBB Studies, 3; São Paulo: Edições Paulinas, 1974).

CNBB, *Comunidades eclesiais de base no Brasil: Experiéncias e perspectivas* (CNBB 23; São Paulo: Edições Paulinas, 1979).

CNBB, *Comunidades eclesiais de base na base na Igreja do Brasil* (CNBB 25; São Paulo: Edições Paulinas, 1982).

Coleman, John A. (ed.), *One Hundred Years of Catholic Social Thought: Celebration and Challenge* (Maryknoll, N.Y.: Orbis Books, 1991).

Collier, Simon, and William F. Sater, *A History of Chile: 1808–1994* (Cambridge: Cambridge University Press, 1996).

Comblin, José, *Teología do desenvolvimento* (Belo Horizonte, 1968).

—— *Cristianismos y desarollo* (Quito: 1970).

—— *The Holy Spirit and Liberation* (trans. P. Burns; TLS 4; Maryknoll, N.Y.: Orbis Books; Tunbridge Wells, Kent: Burns and Oates, 1989). Portuguese orig. *O Espírito Santo e a Libertação* (Petrópolis, RJ: Editora Vozes, 1987).

—— *Called for Freedom: The Changing Context of Liberation Theology* (trans. P. Berryman; Maryknoll, N.Y.: Orbis Books, 1998). Portuguese orig. *Cristãos Rumo ao Século XXI: Nova Caminhada de Libertação* (São Paulo: Paulus, 1996).

Comblin, José, José González Faus, and Jon Sobrino (eds.), *Cambio social y pensamiento cristiano en América Latina* (Madrid: Trotta, 1993).

Concilium Editorial Board, "Statement of Solidarity with Liberation Theologians, 24 June 1984," *Origins* 14 (26 July 1984); reprinted in Hennelly (ed.), *Liberation Theology*.

Cone, James H., *Black Theology and Black Power* (New York: Seabury, 1969).

—— *A Black Theology of Liberation* (Philadelphia: Lipincott, 1970).

—— "A Black American Perspective on the Future of African Theology" in Appiah-Kubi and S. Torres (eds.), *African Theology En Route*.

—— "A Black American Perspective on the Asian Search for Full Humanity" in Virginia Fabella (ed.), *Asia's Struggle for Full Humanity: Towards a Relevant Theology*.

—— *My Soul Looks Back* (Nashville, Tenn.: Abingdon, 1982).

—— *For My People: Black Theology and the Black Church* (Bishop Henry McNeal Turner Studies in North American Black Religion, 1; Maryknoll, N.Y.: Orbis Books, 1984).

—— *Speaking the Truth* (Grand Rapids, Mich.: Eerdmans, 1986).

Conrad, G. W., and A. M. Demarest, *Religion and Empire: The Dynamics of Aztec and Inca Expansion* (Cambridge: Cambridge University Press, 1984).

Conrad, R., *The Destruction of Brazilian Slavery, 1850–1888* (Berkeley: University of California Press, 1973).

Constable, Pamela, and Arturo Valenzuela, *A Nation of Enemies: Chile Under Pinochet* (New York: Norton, 1991).

Cook, Guillermo, *The Expectation of the Poor: Latin American Basic Ecclesial Communities in Protestant Perspective* (Maryknoll, N.Y.: Orbis Books, 1985).

—— "Santo Domingo through Protestant Eyes" in Hennelly (ed.), *Santo Domingo and Beyond*.

Cooper, D. *To Free a Generation: The Dialectics of Liberation* (London and New York: Collier Books, 1968).

—— (ed.), *Liberation Theologies on Shifting Grounds: A Clash of Socio-economic and Cultural Paradigms* (Leuven: Leuven University Press, 1998). (*insert below "DeSchrijver, Georges"*)

Cortés, Hernan, *Letters from Mexico* (trans. and ed. A. Pagden; New Haven, Conn.: Yale University Press, 2nd ed., 1987 [ET 1972, Spanish orig. 1519–1526]).

Couch, Beatriz M., "Sor Juana Inés de la Cruz: The First Woman Theologian in the Americas" in J. C. B. and E. L. Webster (eds.), *The Church and Women in the Third World*.

Cox, Harvey, *The Silencing of Leonardo Boff* (Oak Park: Meyer Stone, 1988).

Cox, "Introduction" in Betto, *Fidel and Religion*.

Crawley, E., *Dictators Never Die: A Portrait of Nicaragua and the Somozas* (London: C. Hurst, 1979).

Croatto, José Severino, *Exodus: A Hermeneutics of Freedom* (trans. S. Attanasio; Maryknoll N.Y.: Orbis Books, 1981). Spanish orig. *Liberación y libertad: Pautas hermenéuticas* (Buenos Aires: Mundo Nuevo, 1973).

CTC and CCA, *Minjung Theology: People as the Subjects of History* (Singapore: CCA; Maryknoll, N.Y.: Orbis Books; London: Zed Books, 1981).

Curtin, P., *The Atlantic Slave Trade: A Census* (Madison: University of Wisconsin Press, 1969).

Daly, Mary, *The Church and the Second Sex* (New York: Harper & Row, 1968).

—— *Beyond God the Father: Towards a Philosophy of Women's Liberation* (Boston: Beacon Press, 1973).

Davies, N., *The Ancient Kingdoms of Mexico* (London: Allen Lane, 1982).

Dawson, Andrew, "The Origins and Character of the Base Ecclesial Community: A Brazilian Perspective" in C. Rowland (ed.), *Cambridge Companion to Liberation Theology*.

"Declaration of Los Andes," *CELAM* 24 (October–November 1985); reprinted in Hennelly (ed.), *Liberation Theology*.

Della Cava, Ralph, "Vatican Policy, 1978–90: An Updated Review," *Social Research* 59.1 (Spring 1992).

De La Bedoyere, Michael, *The Cardijn Story: A Study of the Life of Mgr. Joseph Cardijn and the Young Christian Workers' Movement* (London: Longman's, Green and Co., 1958).

De Schrijver, Georges, "Paradigm Shift in Third World Theologies of Liberation: From Socio-Economic Analysis to Cultural Analysis" in idem (ed.), *Liberation Theologies on Shifting Grounds*.

De Zárate, Agustín, *The Discovery and Conquest of Peru* (trans. J. M. Cohen; Harmondsworth: Penguin Books, 1968).

Díaz del Castillo, Bernal, *The Conquest of New Spain* (trans. J. M. Cohen; Harmondsworth: Penguin Books, 1963).

Dickson, Kwesi, and Paul Ellingworth (eds.), *Biblical Revelation and African Beliefs* (London: Lutterworth Press, 1969; Maryknoll, N.Y.: Orbis Books, 1971).

Dodson, Michael, and Laura Nuzzi O'Shaughnessy, *Nicaragua's Other Revolution: Religious Faith and Political Survival* (Chapel Hill: University of North Carolina Press, 1990).

Doering, B. E., *Jacques Maritain and the French Catholic Intellectuals* (Notre Dame, Ind.: University of Notre Dame Press, 1983).

Domínguez, J. I., *Insurrection or Loyalty: The Breakdown of the Spanish American Empire* (Cambridge, Mass.: Harvard University Press, 1980).

Dore, Elizabeth (ed.), *Gender Politics in Latin America* (New York: Monthly Review Press, 1997).

Dorr, Donald, *Option for the Poor* (rev. ed.; Dublin: Gill & Macmillan, 1992).

Douglas Meeks, M., *Origins of the Theology of Hope* (Philadelphia: Fortress Press, 1974).

Drogus, Carol A., *Women, Religion and Social Change in Brazil's Popular Church* (Notre Dame, Ind.: University of Notre Dame Press, 1997).

Dunkerley, James, *Power in the Isthmus: A Political History of Modern Central America* (London: Verso, 1988).

Dussel, Enrique, *A History of the Church in Latin America: Colonialism to Liberation (1492–1979)* (trans. and rev. A. Neely; Grand Rapids, Mich.: Eerdmans, 1981). Spanish orig. *Historia de la iglesia en América Latina: Coloniaje y liberación* (Barcelona: Nova Terra, 3rd ed., 1974 [1964]).

—— *History and the Theology of Liberation* (trans. J. Drury; Maryknoll, N.Y.: Orbis Books, 1976) Spanish orig. *Caminos de liberación latinoamericana I Interpretacion histórica de nuestro continente latinoamericano* (Buenos Aires: Latinoamericano Libros, 1973).

—— "Sobre la historia de la teología en America Latina" in Ruiz Maldonado (ed.), *Liberación y cautivera*.

—— (ed.), *The Church in Latin America: 1492–1992* (Maryknoll, N.Y.: Orbis Books; Tunbridge Wells, Kent: Burns & Oates, 1987).

—— "From the Second Vatican Council to the Present Day" in idem (ed.), *The Church in Latin America: 1492–1992.*

—— *Ethics and Community* (trans. R. R. Barr; TLS 3; Maryknoll, N.Y.: Orbis Books; Tunbridge Wells, Kent: Burns and Oates, 1988). Spanish orig. *Etica comunitaria* (Madrid: Ediciones Paulinas, 1986). Portuguese ed. (Petrópolis, RJ: Editora Vozes, 1986).

Eagleson, John (ed.), *Christians for Socialism: Documentation of the Christians for Socialism Movement of Latin America* (Maryknoll, N.Y.: Orbis Books, 1975).

Eagleson, John, and Philip Scharper (eds.), *Puebla and Beyond: Documentation and Commentary* (trans. John Drury; Maryknoll, N.Y.: Orbis Books, 1980).

Elizondo, Virgilio, *Guadalupe: Mother of the New Creation* (Maryknoll, N.Y.: Orbis Books, 1997).

Ellacuría, Ignacio, "Pueblo crucificado: ensayo de soteriologia historica" in na, *Cruz y resurrección* (Mexico: Centro de Reflexión Teológica, 1978); reprinted in *Revista Latinoamericana de Teología* 18 (1989). ET "The Crucified People" in Ellacuría and Sobrino (eds.), *Mysterium Liberationis.*

Ellacuría, Ignacio, and Jon Sobrino (eds.), *Mysterium Liberationis: Fundamental Concepts of Liberation Theology* (Maryknoll, N.Y.: Orbis Books, 1993). Abridged from Spanish orig. *Mysterium liberationis: conceptos fundamentales de la teología de la liberación* (2 vols.; San Salvador: UCA Editores, 1990). Further abridged U.K. ed., *Systematic Theology: Perspectives from Liberation Theology* (London: SCM Press, 1996).

Elliott, J. H., *Imperial Spain: 1469–1716* (Harmondsworth: Penguin, 2nd ed., 1972 [1963]).

Ellis, Marc, *Toward A Jewish Theology of Liberation* (Maryknoll, N.Y.: Orbis Books, 1987).

Ellis, Marc, and Otto Maduro (eds.), *Expanding the View: Gustavo Gutiérrez and the Future of Liberation Theology* (Maryknoll, N.Y.: Orbis Books, 1990); abridged from idem (eds.), *The Future of Liberation Theology: Essays in Honor of Gustavo Gutiérrez* (Maryknoll, N.Y.: Orbis Books, 1989).

Elorrio, J. G., "Bases of the Camilo Torres Latin American Encounter" in Hodges, *The Legacy of Che Guevara.*

Fabella, Virginia (ed.), *Asia's Struggle for Full Humanity: Towards a Relevant Theology* (EATWOT Asian Theological Conference, Wennappuwa, Sri Lanka, 7–20 January 1979; Maryknoll, N.Y.: Orbis Books, 1979).

Fabella, Virginia, and Sergio Torres (eds.), *Irruption of the Third World* (Fifth International Conference and First General Assembly of EATWOT, New Delhi, India, 17–29 August 1981; Maryknoll, N.Y.: Orbis Books, 1983).

—— (eds.), *Doing Theology in a Divided World* (Sixth International Conference of EATWOT, Geneva, Switzerland, 5–13 January 1983; Maryknoll, N.Y.: Orbis Books, 1985).

Fabella, Virginia, and Mercy Amba Oduyoye (eds.), *With Passion and Compassion: Third World Women Doing Theology* (Reflections from the Women's Commission of EATWOT, 1985–86; Maryknoll, N.Y.: Orbis Books, 1988).

Fanon, Franz, *The Wretched of the Earth* (trans. C. Farrington; New York: Grove Press, 1963).

—— *Studies in a Dying Colonialism* (trans. H. Chevalier; New York: Monthly Review Press, 1965).

Feitlowitz, Marguerite, *A Lexicon of Terror: Argentina and the Legacies of Torture* (Oxford: Oxford University Press, 1998).

Fierro, Afredo, *The Militant Gospel: An Analysis of Contemporary Political Theologies* (trans. J. Drury; London: SCM Press, 1977 [Spanish orig. 1974]).

Filochowski, Julian, "Medellin to Puebla" in Catholic Institute for International Relations (ed.), *Reflections on Puebla*.

Fisher, L. E., *The Last Inca Revolt, 1780–83* (Norman: University of Oklahoma Press, 1966).

Flannery, Austin (ed.), *Vatican Council II: The Conciliar and Post Conciliar Documents* (Northport, N.Y.: Costello Publishing Company; Dublin: Dominican Publications, rev. ed., 1996 [1975]).

Fleet, Michael, *The Rise and Fall of Chilean Democracy* (Princeton, N.J.: Princeton University Press, 1985).

Foroorhar, Manzar, *The Catholic Church and Social Change in Nicaragua* (Albany: State University of New York Press, 1989).

Fragoso, Antônio B., *Face of a Church* (trans. R. R. Barr; Maryknoll, N.Y.: Orbis Books, 1987). Portuguese orig. *O rosto de uma igreja* (São Paulo: Edições Loyola, 1982).

Frank, Andre Gunder, *Capitalism and Underdevelopment in Latin America: Historical Studies of Chile and Brazil* (New York: Monthly Review Press, rev. ed., 1969 [1967]).

—— *Latin America: Underdevelopment or Revolution* (New York: Monthly Review Press, 1969).

Freire, Paulo, *Pedagogy of the Oppressed* (trans. M. Ramos; New York: Continuum, 1970; London: Sheed and Ward, 1972 [1968]).

Freyre, G., *The Masters and the Slaves: A Study in the Development of Brazilian Civilisation* (trans. S. Putnam; New York: Alfred Knopf, 1963).

—— *Brazil from Monarchy to Republic* (New York: Alfred Knopf, 1970).

Furtado, Celso, *The Economic Growth of Brazil* (Berkeley: University of California Press, 1963 [1959]).

—— *Development and Stagnation in Latin America: A Structural Approach* (New Haven, Conn.: Yale University Press, 1965).

Galeano, Eduardo, *Open Veins of Latin America: Five Centuries of the Pillage of a Continent* (trans. C. Belfrage; New York: Monthly Review Press, 1973 [1971]).

Galilea, Segundo, "The Spirituality of Liberation," *The Way* 25.3 (July 1985).

Garrard-Burnett, Virginia, and David Stoll (eds.), *Rethinking Protestantism in Latin America* (Philadelphia: Temple University, 1993).

Gebara, Ivone, and Zwinglio Dias, "Everyday Life in India" in Fabella and Torres (eds.), *Irruption of the Third World*.

Gebara, Ivone, and Maria Clara Bingemer, *Mary, Mother of God, Mother of the Poor* (trans. P. Berryman; TLS 7; Maryknoll, N.Y.: Orbis Books; Tunbridge Wells, Kent: Burns and Oates, 1989). Portuguese orig. *Maria, Mãe de Deus e Mãe de Pobres* (Petrópolis, RJ: Editora Vozes, 1987).

—— "Mary" in Ellacuria and Sobrino (eds.), *Mysterium Liberationis*.

—— "The Abortion Debate in Brazil: A Report from an Eco-Feminist Philosopher and Theologian under Siege," *Journal of Feminist Studies in Religion* 11.2 (1995).

Gelin, A., *The Poor of Yahweh* (trans. K. Sullivan; Collegeville, Minn.: The Liturgical Press, 1964).

Gheerbrant, Alain, *The Rebel Church in Latin America* (trans. R. Sheed; Harmondsworth: Penguin, 1974 [French orig. 1969]).

Gibellini, Rosino, *The Liberation Theology Debate* (trans. J. Bowden; London: SCM Press, 1987). Italian orig. *Il Dibattito sulla Teologia della Liberazione* (Brescia: Editrice Queriniana, 1986).

—— (ed.), *Frontiers of Theology in Latin America* (Maryknoll, N.Y.: Orbis, 1979). Italian orig. *La nuova frontiera della teologia in America Latina* (Brescia: Editrice Queriniana, 1975).

Gibson, C., *Spain in America* (New York: Harper & Row, 1966).

—— *The Aztecs under Spanish Rule: A History of the Indians of the Valley of Mexico, 1519–1810* (Stanford, Calif.: Stanford University Press, 1964).

Girardi, Giulio, *Faith and Revolution in Nicaragua: Convergence and Contradictions* (trans. P. Berryman; Maryknoll, N.Y.: Orbis Books, 1989). ET from first half of Spanish ed. *Sandinismo, Marxismo, Cristianismo: La Confluencia* (Managua: Centro Ecumenico Antonio Valdivieso, 1987). Italian orig. *Sandinismo, Marxismo, Cristianesimo: La Confluenza* (Roma: Edizoni Borla, 1986).

Goodpasture, McKennie H. (ed.), *Cross and Sword: An Eyewitness History of Christianity in Latin America* (Maryknoll, N.Y.: Orbis Books, 1989).

Graziano, Frank, *Divine Violence: Spectacle, Psychosexuality, and Radical Christianity in the Argentine 'Dirty War'* (Boulder, Colo. and Oxford: Westview Press, 1992).

Gutiérrez, Gustavo, *La pastoral de la Iglesia en America Latina* (Montevideo: Ediciones de Centro de Documentación MIEC–JECI, 1968). Reprint (Lima: Editorial Universitaria, 1970). Revised and republished as *Líneas pastorales de la Iglesia en América Latina, Análisis Teólogico* (Lima: Centro de Estudios y Publicaciones, 1976).

—— "Notes on a Theology of Liberation" in SODEPAX, *In Search of a Theology of Development*; reprinted in *Theological Studies* 31.2 (1970).

—— *Hacia una teología de la liberacion* (Montevideo: MIEC Documentation Service, 1969); translated by Hennelly as "Toward a Theology of Liberation" in Hennelly (ed.), *Liberation Theology*.

—— *A Theology of Liberation: History, Politics and Salvation* (trans. and ed. C. Inda and J. Eagleson; Maryknoll, N.Y.: Orbis Books, 1973; London: SCM Press, 1974). Spanish orig. *Teologiá de la liberación: Perspectivas* (Lima: Centro de Estudios y Publicaciones, 1971).

—— "Liberation Praxis and Christian Faith" in Rosino Gibellini (ed.), *Frontiers of Theology in Latin America*.

—— "Two Theological Perspectives: Liberation Theology and Progressivist Theology" in S. Torres and V. Fabella (eds.), *The Emergent Gospel*.

—— *Teológia desde el reverso de la historia* (Lima: Centro de Estudios y Publicaciones, 1977). ET "Theology from the Underside of History" in idem, *The Power of the Poor in History*.

—— *The Power of the Poor in History* (trans. R. R. Barr; Maryknoll, N.Y.: Orbis Books; London: SCM Press, 1983). Spanish orig. *La Fuerza historica de las pobres* (Lima: Centro de Estudios y Publicaciones, 1979).

—— "The Irruption of the Poor in Latin America and the Christian Communities of the Common People" in Torres and Eagleson (eds.), *The Challenge of Basic Christian Communities*.

—— "Drink from Your Own Well," *Concilium* 159 (1982).

—— *We Drink from Our Own Wells: The Spiritual Journey of a People* (trans. M. J. O'Connell; Maryknoll, N.Y.: Orbis Books; London: SCM Press, 1984). Spanish orig. *Beber en su proprio pozo: En el itinerario espiritual de un pueblo* (Lima: Centro de Estudios y Publicaciones, 1983).

—— On Job: God-Talk and the Suffering of the Innocent (trans. M. J. O'Connell; Maryknoll, N.Y.: Orbis Books; London: SCM Press, 1987). Spanish orig. *Hablar del Dios desde el sufrimiento del inocente* (Lima: Centro de Estudios y Publicaciones, 2nd ed., 1986 [1985]).

—— *The God of Life* (trans. M. J. O'Connell; Maryknoll, N.Y.: Orbis Books; London: SCM Press, 1991). Spanish orig. *El Dios de la vida* (Lima: Centro de Estudios y Publicaciones, rev. ed., 1989 [1982]).

—— *The Truth Shall Make You Free: Confrontations* (trans. M. J. O'Connell; Maryknoll, N.Y.: Orbis Books, 1990). Revised from Spanish orig. *La verdad las hará libres: confrontationes* (Lima: Centro de Estudios y Publicaciones, 1986).

—— *Las Casas: In Search of the Poor of Jesus Christ* (trans. R. R. Barr; Maryknoll N.Y.: Orbis Books, 1993). Spanish orig. *En busca de los pobres de Jesucristo* (Lima: Centro de Estudios y Publicaciones, 1992).

—— *Sharing the Word Through the Liturgical Year* (Maryknoll, N.Y.: Orbis Books; London: Geoffrey Chapman, 1997). Spanish orig. *Compartir la palabra: A lo largo del año litúrgico* (Lima: Centro de Estudios y Publicaciones, 1995).

Hammond, N., *Ancient Maya Civilization* (Cambridge: Cambridge University Press, 1982).

Haring, Clarence H., *The Spanish Empire in America* (Oxford: Oxford University Press, 1947).

—— *Empire in Brazil: A New World Experiment with Monarchy* (Cambridge, Mass.: Harvard University Press, 1958).

Hebblethwaite, Peter, *John XXIII: Pope of the Council* (London: Fount, 1984).

—— *In the Vatican* (Oxford: Oxford University Press, 1986).

—— *Paul VI: The First Modern Pope* (London: Harper Collins, 1993).

Hemming, John, *The Conquest of the Incas* (New York: Harcourt Brace Jovanovich; London: Macmillan, 1970).

—— *Red Gold: The Conquest of the Brazilian Indians* (Cambridge, Mass.: Harvard University Press; London: Macmillan, 1978).

Hennelly, Alfred. T., "The Red-Hot Issue of Liberation Theology," *America* (24 May 1986); reprinted in idem (ed.), *Liberation Theology*.

—— *Theology for a Liberating Church: The New Praxis of Freedom* (Washington, D.C.: Georgetown University Press, 1989).

—— "A Report from the Conference" in idem (ed.), *Santo Domingo and Beyond*.

—— (ed.), *Liberation Theology: A Documentary History* (Maryknoll, N.Y.: Orbis Books, 1990).

—— (ed.), *Santo Domingo and Beyond* (Maryknoll, N.Y.: Orbis Books, 1993).

Hewitt, William E., *Base Christian Communities and Social Change in Brazil* (Lincoln: University of Nebraska Press, 1991).

Hinkelammert, Franz J., *The Ideological Weapons of Death: A Theological Critique of Capitalism* (Maryknoll, N.Y.: Orbis Books, 1986). Spanish orig. *Las armas ideológicas de la muerte* (rev. ed.; San José: Departmento Ecuménico de Investigaciones, 1981 [1977]).

—— "Liberation Theology in the Economic and Social Context of Latin America" in Batstone et al. (eds.), *Liberation Theologies, Postmodernity, and the Americas*.

Hodges, D. C., *The Legacy of Che Guevara: A Documentary Study* (London: Thames and Hudson, 1977).

Humphreys, R. A., and J. Lynch (eds.), *The Origins of the Latin American Revolutions, 1808–1826* (New York: Alfred A. Knopf, 1965).

Hynds, Patricia, "Bishops Letter Deepens Church-State Estrangement," *Latinamerica Press* (24 May 1984); reprinted in Hennelly (ed.), *Liberation Theology*.

Idowu, Emanuel Bolaji, *Towards An Indigenous Church* (London: Oxford University Press, 1965).

Ines de la Cruz, Juana, *Sor Juana Anthology* (trans. A. S. Trueblood; Cambridge, Mass.: Harvard University Press, 1988).

Instituto Fe y Secularidad, *Fe cristiano y cambio social* (Encuentro de El Escorial, Spain, 1972; ed. J. Alvarez Bolardo; Salamanca: Sígueme, 1973).

International Theological Commission, "Human Development and Christian Salvation," *Origins* 7 (3 November 1977); reprinted in Hennelly (ed.), *Liberation Theology*.

Ivereigh, A., *Catholicism and Politics in Argentina* (New York: St Martin's Press; London: Macmillan, 1995).

James, Cyril Lionel Robert, *The Black Jacobins* (New York: Vintage Books, 2nd ed., 1963 [1938]).

Jerez, Cesar, *The Church and the Nicaraguan Revolution* (London: Catholic Institute for International Relations, 1984).

John Paul II, "Letter to the Brazilian Bishops," *L'Osservatore Romano* (English ed.; 28 April 1986); reprinted in Hennelly (ed.), *Liberation Theology*.

Kaplan, S., (ed.), *Indigenous Responses to Western Christianity* (New York: New York University Press, 1995.

Kee, Alistair, *Marx and the Failure of Liberation Theology* (London: SCM Press, 1990).

King, Ursula (ed.), *Feminist Theology from the Third World: A Reader* (London: SPCK, 1994).

Kirk, John M., *Politics and the Catholic Church in Nicaragua* (Gainesville: University of Florida Press, 1992).

Kirkpatrick, F. A., *The Spanish Conquistadores* (London: A & C Black, 3rd ed., 1963 [1934]).

Klaiber, Jeffrey, *The Catholic Church in Peru, 1821–1985: A Social History* (Washington, D.C.: Catholic University of America Press, 1988). Revised from Spanish orig. *La Iglesia en el Perú: su historia social desde la independencia* (Lima: Pontificia Universidad Católica del Perú, 1988).

—— *The Church, Dictatorships and Democracy in Latin America* (Maryknoll, N.Y.: Orbis Books, 1998).

Kloppenburg, Bonaventura, *The People's Church: A Defense of My Church* (trans. M. J. O'Connell; Chicago: Franciscan Herald Press, 1978). Spanish orig. *Iglesia Popular* (n.p.: Ediciones Paulinas, 1977).

Koning, H., *Columbus: His Enterprise* (London: Latin America Bureau, 2nd ed., 1991 [1976]).

Kräutler, Erwin, *Indians and Ecology in Brazil* (London: Catholic Institute of International Relations, 1990). Portuguese orig. *Destruir a Terra é Destruir os Filhos da Terra* (Brasilia: 1990).

Lancaster, Roger N., *Thanks to God and the Revolution: Popular Religion and Class Consciousness in the New Nicaragua* (New York: Columbia University Press, 1988).

—— *Life is Hard: Machismo, Danger and the Intimacy of Power in Nicaragua* (Berkeley and London: University of California Press, 1992).

Las Casas, Bartolome de, *A Short Account of the Destruction of the Indies* (trans. N. Griffin; Harmondsworth: Penguin Books, 1992 [Spanish orig. 1542]).

—— *In Defence of the Indians* (DeKalb, Ill.: Northern Illinois Press, 2nd ed., 1992 [ET 1974, Spanish orig. c. 1549]).

León-Portilla, M. (ed.), *The Broken Spears: The Aztec Account of the Conquest* (trans. L. Kemp; Boston: Beacon Press, rev. ed., 1992 [1961]).

Lernoux, Penny, *Cry of the People: The Struggle for Human Rights in Latin America—The Catholic Church in Conflict with U.S. Policy* (New York: Penguin Books, rev. ed., 1982 [1980]).

—— *People of God: The Struggle for World Catholicism* (New York: Viking, 1989).

Levine, Daniel H., "On Premature Reports of the Death of Liberation Theology," *The Review of Politics* 57.1 (1995).

Levine, R. M., *Vale of Tears: Revisiting the Canudos Massacre in Northeastern Brazil, 1893–1897* (Berkeley: University of California Press, 1992).

Lewis, Paul H., *Paraguay under Stroessner* (Chapel Hill: University of North Carolina Press, 1980).

Linden, Ian, "People before Profit: The Early Social Doctrine of John Paul II" in Vallely (ed.), *The New Politics*.

Liss, Sheldon B., *Marxist Thought in Latin America* (Berkeley: University of California Press, 1984).

Lockhart, J., and S. B. Schwartz, *Early Latin America: A History of Spanish America and Brazil* (Cambridge: Cambridge University Press, 1983).

Longley, Clifford, "Structures of Sin and the Free Market: John Paul II on Capitalism" in Vallely (ed.), *The New Politics*.

López Vigil, María, *Death and Life in Morazan: A Priest's Testimony from a War-Zone in El Salvador: Father Rogelio Ponseele Talks to María López Vigil* (trans. D. Livingstone; London: Catholic Institute for International Relations, 1989). Spanish orig. *Muerte y Vida en Morazán: testimonio de un sacerdote* (San Salvador: UCA Editores, 1987).

Löwy, Malcolm, *The War of the Gods: Religion and Politics in Latin America* (London: Verso, 1996).

Lynch, John, *Spanish Colonial Administration, 1782–1810: The Intendant System in the Vice-royalty of Río de la Plata* (London: Athlone, 1958).

—— *Spain under the Habsburgs* (2 vols.; London: Oxford University Press, 1964 and 1969).

—— *The Spanish American Revolutions 1808–1826* (New York and London: W. W. Norton, 2nd ed., 1986 [1973]).

Mainwaring, Scott, *The Catholic Church and Politics in Brazil, 1916–1985* (Stanford, Calif.: Stanford University Press, 1986).

Marcuse, Herbert, "Liberation from an Affluent Society" in Cooper, *To Free a Generation*.

—— *Eros and Civilization* (Boston: Beacon Press, 1955).

—— *One Dimensional Man* (Boston: Beacon Press; London: Routledge & Kegan Paul, 1964).

—— *An Essay on Liberation* (Boston: Beacon Press; London: Allen Lane, 1969).

Marins, José, *Comunidade eclesial da Base* (São Paulo: n.p., 1968).

Marins, José, Teolide Maria Trevisan, and Carolee Chanona, *The Church from the Roots: Basic Ecclesial Communities* (Quezon City, Philippines: Claretian, ET 1983; London: Catholic Fund for Overseas Development, 1989).

Maritain, Jacques, *Integral Humanism* (trans. J. E. Evans; New York: Scribner's Sons, 1968 [ET 1938, French orig. 1936]).

Mariz, Cecília L., *Coping with Poverty: Pentecostals and Christian Base Communities in Brazil* (Philadelphia: Temple University Press, 1994).

Martin, David, *Tongues of Fire: The Explosion of Protestantism in Latin America* (Oxford: Basil Blackwell, 1990).

Marty, Martin E., and D. Peerman (eds.), *Theology and Revolution* (New York: Macmillan, 1969).

Masur, G., *Simón Bolívar* (Albuquerque: University of New Mexico, 1969).

Mbiti, John, *African Religions and Philosophy* (London: Heinemann, 1969; New York: Doubleday, 1970).

McGovern, Arthur F., *Marxism: An American Christian Perspective* (Maryknoll, N.Y.: Orbis Books, 1980).

—— *Liberation Theology and Its Critics: Towards an Assessment* (Maryknoll, N.Y.: Orbis Books, 1989).

McSweeney, Bill, *Roman Catholicism: The Search for Relevance* (Oxford: Basil Blackwell, 1980).

Medcalf, John, *Letters from Nicaragua* (London: Catholic Institute for International Relations, 1988).

Melhuus, Marit, and Kristi Anne Stølen (eds.), *Machos, Mistresses, Madonnas: Contesting the Power of Latin American Gender Imagery* (London and New York: Verso, 1996).

Memoria del primer Congreso Nacional de teologia: Fe y desarrollo (2 vols; Mexico City: 1970).

Messori, Vitorio, *The Ratzinger Report: An Exclusive Interview on the State of the Church* (trans. Salvator Attansio and Graham Harrison; San Francisco: Ignatius Press, 1985). Italian orig. *Rapporto Sulla Fede* (Milan: Edizioni Paoline, 1985).

Mesters, Carlos, "The Use of the Bible in the Christian Communities of the Common People" in Torres and Eagleson (eds.), *The Challenge of Basic Christian Communities*.

—— *Defenseless Flower: A New Reading of the Bible* (Maryknoll, N.Y.: Orbis Books, 1989). Portuguese orig. *Flor sem defesa: Uma explicação da bíblia a partir do povo* (Petrópolis, RJ: Editora Vozes, 1983).

Metford, J. C., *San Martín the Liberator* (London: Longman, 1950).

Métraux, A., *The History of the Incas* (New York: Pantheon Books, 1969).

Metz, Johannes Baptist, *Theology of the World* (trans. W. Glen-Doepl; New York: Herder and Herder, 1969).

Míguez Bonino, José, "Teología de la liberación," *Actualidad Pastoral* 3 (1970).

—— *Doing Theology in a Revolutionary Situation* (Philadelphia: Fortress Press, 1975). U.K. ed. *Revolutionary Theology Comes of Age* (London: SPCK, 1975).

—— "Commonalities: A Latin American Perspective" in Abraham (ed.), *Third World Theologies*.

—— (ed.), *Faces of Jesus: Latin American Christologies* (trans. R. R. Barr; Maryknoll, N.Y.: Orbis Books, 1984). Spanish orig. *Jesús: Ni vencido ni monarca celestial* (Buenos Aires: Tierra Nueva, 1977).

Miranda, José Porfirio, *Marx and the Bible: A Critique of the Philosophy of Oppression* (trans. J. Eagleson; Maryknoll, N.Y.: Orbis Books, 1974; London: SCM Press, 1977). Spanish orig. *Marx y la biblia: Crítica a la filosofía de la opresión* (Salamanca: Ediciones Sígueme, 2nd ed., 1972 [1971]).

—— *Being and the Messiah: The Message of St. John* (Maryknoll, N.Y.: Orbis Books, 1977). Spanish orig. *El ser y el Mesías* (Salamanca: Ediciones Sígueme, 1973).

—— *Marx against the Marxists: The Christian Humanism of Karl Marx* (trans. J. Drury; Maryknoll, N.Y.: Orbis Books; London: SCM Press, 1980 [Spanish orig. 1980]).

—— *Communism in the Bible* (trans. R. R. Barr; Maryknoll, N.Y.: Orbis Books; London: SCM Press, 1982). Spanish orig. *Comunismo en la biblia* (México, DF: Siglo Veintiuno Editores, 1981).

Mitchell, David, *The Jesuits: A History* (New York: Franklin Watts, 1981).

Moltmann, Jürgen, *Theology of Hope* (trans. J. W. Leitch; London: SCM Press, 1967 [German orig. 1964]).

—— *Religion, Revolution, and the Future* (trans. M. Douglas Meeks; New York: Charles Scribner's Sons, 1969).

—— *The Crucified God* (trans. R. A. Wilson and J. Bowden; London: SCM Press, 1974 [German orig. 1973]).

—— "An Open Letter to José Míguez Bonino," *Christianity and Crisis* (29 March 1976); reprinted in Hennelly (ed.), *Liberation Theology*.

Morison, S. E., *Admiral of the Ocean Sea: A Life of the Admiral Christopher Columbus* (2 vols; Boston: Little Brown, 1942).

Mörner, M., *The Expulsion of the Jesuits from Latin America* (New York: Alfred Knopf, 1965).

Morse, Christopher, *The Logic of Promise in Moltmann's Theology* (Philadelphia: Fortress Press, 1975).

Moser, Antônio, and Bernardino Leers, *Moral Theology: Dead Ends and Ways Forward* (trans. P. Burns; TLS 9; Maryknoll, N.Y.: Orbis Books; Tunbridge Wells, Kent: Burns and Oates, 1990). Portuguese orig. *Teologia moral: impasses e alternativas* (Petrópolis, RJ: Editora Vozes, 1987).

—— "Sexualidad" in Ellacuría and Sobrino (eds.), *Mysterium liberationis*.

Mujeres para el Dialogo, "Women, Praxis and Liberation Theology: Tepeyac, Mexico, 1–5 October, 1979," *Voices from the Third World* 2, 2 (1979); reprinted in Cora Ferro, "The Latin American Woman: The Praxis and Theology of Liberation" in Torres and Eagleson (eds.), *The Challenge of Basic Christian Communities*.

Muñoz, Ronaldo, "An Open Reply to Cardinal López Trujillo," *LADOC* 16 (November–December, 1985); reprinted in Hennelly (ed.), *Liberation Theology*.

—— *The God of Christians* (trans. P. Burns; TLS 11; Maryknoll, N.Y.: Orbis Books; Tunbridge Wells, Kent: Burns and Oates, 1991). Translated from Spanish ed. *Dios de les cristianos* (Madrid: Ediciones Paulinas, 1988). Portugese orig. (São Paulo: CESEP, 1987).

Muzorewa, Gwinyai H., *The Origins and Development of African Theology* (Maryknoll, N.Y.: Orbis Books, 1985).

Mveng, Engelbert, "Third World Theology—What Theology? What Third World?: Evaluation by an African Delegate" in Fabella and Torres (eds.), *Irruption of the Third World*.

NA, *John Paul II in Mexico: His Collected Speeches* (London: Collins, 1979).

Nagle, Robin, *Claiming the Virgin: The Broken Promise of Liberation Theology in Brazil* (New York and London: Routledge, 1997).

National Commission on Disappeared People [CONADEP], *Nunca Más: A Report by Argentina's National Commission on Disappeared People* (trans. Writers and Scholars International; Boston and London: Faber & Faber, 1986). Spanish orig. Comisión Nacional sobre la Desaparición de Personas, *Nunca Mas: Informe de la Comisión Nacional sobre la Desaparación de Personas* (Buenos Aires: Editorial Universitaria, 1984).

Nazzari, Muriel, "Sex/Gender Arrangements and the Reproduction of Class in the Latin American Past," in Dore (ed.), *Gender Politics in Latin America*.

Nessan, Craig L., *Orthopraxis or Heresy: The North American Theological Response to Latin American Liberation Theology* (Atlanta, Ga.: Scholars Press, 1989).

Neuhaus, Richard John, *The Naked Public Square* (Grand Rapids, Mich.: Eerdmans, 1984).

Novak, Michael, *Will it Liberate?* (New York: Paulist Press, 1986).

O'Brien, David J., "A Century of Catholic Social Teaching" in Coleman (ed.), *One Hundred Years of Catholic Social Thought*.

O'Brien, David J., and Thomas A. Shannon (eds.), *Catholic Social Thought: The Documentary Heritage* (Maryknoll, N.Y.: Orbis Books, 1998).

O'Brien, Kate, "Feminists to Liberation Theologians: 'Challenge Church on Sexism,'" *Latinamerica Press* (23 January 1986).

Oliveros, Roberto, *Liberación y teología: Génesis y crecimiento de una reflexión, 1966–1976* (Lima: Centro de Estudios y Publicaciones, 1977).

O'Shaugnessy, Hugh, *Pinochet: The Politics of Torture* (London: Latin America Bureau, 2000).

Ott, Thomas O., *The Haitian Revolution* (Knoxville, Tenn.: University of Tennessee, 1973).

Parry, J. H., *The Age of Reconnaissance: The Age of Discovery, Exploration and Settlement, 1450–1650* (London: Weidenfeld and Nicolson, 1963).

Paz, Néstor, *My Life for My Friends* (Maryknoll, N.Y.: Orbis Books, 1975).

Pearce, Jenny, *Under the Eagle: U.S. Intervention in Central America and the Caribbean* (London: Latin America Bureau, 2nd ed., 1982 [1981]).

Pearson, Raymond, *The Rise and Fall of the Soviet Empire* (London: Macmillan Press, 1998).

Perkins, D., *A History of the Monroe Doctrine* (Boston: Little Brown, 1955).

Peruvian Bishops' Commission on Social Action, *Between Honesty and Hope: Documents from and about the Church in Latin America* (trans. J. Drury; Maryknoll, N.Y.: Orbis Books, 1970 [Spanish orig. 1969]).

Pescatello, A. (ed.) *Male and Female in Latin America* (London and Pittsburgh: University of Pittsburgh Press, 1973).

Peterson, Anna L., *Martyrdom and the Politics of Religion: Progressive Catholicism in El Salvador's Civil War* (Albany: State University of New York Press, 1997).

Pieris, Aloysius, "Towards an Asian Theology of Liberation: Some Religio-Cultural Guidelines" in Fabella (ed.), *Asia's Struggle for Full Humanity*.

—— "The Place of Non-Christian Religions and Cultures in the Evolution of Third World Theology" in Fabella and Torres, *Irruption of the Third World*.

Pironio, Eduardo, "Teología de la liberación," *Criterio* 1607–1608 (Nov 1970).

Pixley, George V., *On Exodus: A Liberation Perspective* (trans. R. R. Barr; Maryknoll, N.Y.: Orbis Books, 1987). Spanish orig. *Exodo: una lectura evangélica y popular* (Mexico, DF: Casa Unida de Publicaciones, 1983).

Pixley, Jorge, and Clodovis Boff, *The Bible, the Church and the Poor* (trans. P. Burns; TLS, 6; Maryknoll, N.Y.: Orbis Books; Tunbridge Wells, Kent: Burns and Oates, 1989). Portuguese orig. *Opção pelos pobres* (Petrópolis: Editora Vozes, 1987).

Pollack, B., and H. Rosenkranz, *Revolutionary Social Democracy: The Chilean Socialist Party* (London: Frances Pinter, 1986).

Poole, Deborah, and Gerardo Rénique, *Peru: Time of Fear* (London: Latin America Bureau, 1992).

Porter, Stanley E., Michael A. Hayes, and David Tombs (eds.), *Faith in the Millennium* (Sheffield: Sheffield Academic Press, 2001).

"Puebla: Moment of Decision for the Latin American Church," *Crosscurrents* 28.1 (1978).

Puleo, Mev, *The Struggle Is One: Voices and Visions of Liberation* (Albany: State University of New York Press, 1994).

Rahner, Karl, "Letter to Cardinal Juan Landázuri Ricketts of Lima," 16 March 1984; reprinted in N. Greinacher, *Konflikt um die Theologie der Befreiung: Diskussion und Dokumentation* (Cologne: Benziger Verlag, 1985); ET in Hennelly (ed.), *Liberation Theology*.

Ranke Heinemann, Uta, *Eunuchs for the Kingdom of Heaven: Women, Sexuality and the Catholic Church* (trans. P. Heinegg; New York: Doubleday, 1990).

Ratzinger, Joseph, "Liberation Theology," *30 Giorno* (March 1984); reprinted in Hennelly (ed.), *Liberation Theology*.

Regan, Donald, *Church for Liberation: A Pastoral Portrait of the Church in Brazil* (Dublin: Dominican Publications, 1987).

Ress, Mary Judith, "Feminist Theologians Challenge Churches," *Latinamerica Press* (31 May 1984); reprinted in Hennelly (ed.), *Liberation Theology*.

Rezende Figueria, Ricardo, *Rio Maria: Song of the Earth* (trans. and ed. M. Adriance; Maryknoll, N.Y.: Orbis Books; London: Catholic Institute for International Relations, 1994). Abridged from Portuguese orig. *Rio Maria: Canto da Terra* (Petrópolis, RJ: Editora Vozes, 1992).

Rhodes, A., *The Vatican in an Age of Dictatorship, 1922–1945* (London: Hodder & Stoughton, 1973).

—— *The Vatican in the Age of Liberal Democracies, 1870–1922* (London: Sidgwick & Jackson, 1983).

Richard, Pablo, *Death of Christendom, Birth of the Church* (Maryknoll, N.Y.: Orbis Books, 1987). French orig. *Mort de Chrétientés et Naissance de l'Église* (Paris: Centre lebret, 1978).

—— et al., *The Idols of Death and the God of Life: A Theology* (trans. B. E. Campbell and B. Shepard; Maryknoll, N.Y.: Orbis Books, 1983). Spanish orig. *La lucha de los dioses de la opresión y la búsqueda del Dios Liberador* (San José: Departmento Ecuménico de Investigaciones; Managua: Centro Ecumenico Antonio Valdivieso, 1980).

—— "A Latin American Evaluation of Oaxtepec" in Abraham (ed.), *Third World Theologies*.

—— "Liberation Theology: Theology of the South," *Envio* 12 (June 1993).

—— *Apocalypse: A People's Commentary on the Book of Revelation* (Maryknoll, N.Y.: Orbis Books, 1995). Spanish orig. *Apocalipsis: Reconstrucción de la esperanza* (San José: Departmento Ecuménico de Investigaciones, 1994).

Riding, Alan, "Pope Shifts Brazilian Church to the Right," *New York Times* (8 June 1988); reprinted in Hennelly (ed.), *Liberation Theology*.

Roberts, B., "Protestant Groups and Coping with Urban Life in Guatemala," *American Journal of Sociology* 73 (1968).

Rocha, Jan, *Brazil in Focus: A Guide to the People, Politics and Culture* (London: Latin America Bureau, 1997).

Rock, David, *Argentina: 1516–1987: From Spanish Colonisation to Alfonsín* (Berkeley and Los Angeles: University of California Press, rev. ed., 1987 [1985]).

Rodríguez León, M. A., "Invasion and Evangelization in the Sixteenth Century" in Dussel (ed.), *The Church in Latin America*.

Romero, Oscar, *Voice of the Voiceless: The Four Pastoral Letters and Other Statements* (trans. M. Walsh; Maryknoll N.Y.: Orbis Books, 1985). Abridged from Spanish orig. *La voz de los sin voz: la palabra viva de Monseñor Oscar Arnulfo Romero* (eds. R. Cardenal, I. Martín-Baro, and J. Sobrino; San Salvador: UCA Editores, 1980).

—— *The Violence of Love: The Words of Oscar Romero* (trans. J. Brockman; New York: Harper & Row, 1988; London: Collins, 1989).

—— *Archbishop Oscar Romero: A Shepherd's Diary* (trans. I. B. Hodgson; London: Catholic Agency for Overseas Development and Catholic Institute for International Relations, 1993).

Rostow, Walter W., *The Stages of Economic Growth: A Non-Communist Manifesto* (Cambridge: Cambridge University Press, 1960).

Rowland, Christopher (ed.), *Cambridge Companion to Liberation Theology* (Cambridge: Cambridge University Press, 1999).

Roxborough, Ian, *Theories of Development* (Critical Social Studies; London: Macmillan, 1979).

Ruether, *Liberation Theology* (New York: Paulist Press, 1972).

—— "Outlines for a Theology of Liberation," *Dialog* 11 (Autumn 1972).

—— "Sexism and the Theology of Liberation," *Christianity and Crisis* 90 (12 December 1973).

—— "A Feminist Perspective" in Fabella and Torres (eds.), *Doing Theology in a Divided World*.

Ruether, Rosemary Radford (ed.), *Women Healing Earth: Third World Women on Ecology, Feminism, and Religion* (Maryknoll, N.Y.: Orbis Books; London: SCM Press, 1996).

Ruiz Maldonado, Enrique (ed.), *Liberación y cautivero: debates en torno al método de la teología en América Latina* (Encuentro Latinoamericana de Teología, Ciudad México del 11 al 15 de agosto, 1975; Mexico, DF: Clavería, 1975).

Russell, Letty M., *Human Liberation in a Feminist Perspective: A Theology* (Philadelphia: Westminster Press, 1974).

—— "A First World Perspective" in Fabella and Torres (eds.), *Doing Theology in a Divided World*.

Russell-Wood, A. J. R., (ed.), *From Colony to Nation: Essays on the Independence of Brazil* (Baltimore, Md.: Johns Hopkins University Press, 1975).

Saiving, Valerie, "The Human Situation: A Feminine View," *The Journal of Religion* (April 1960); reprinted in Christ and Plaskow, *Womanspirit Rising*.

Sanderlin, G. (ed.), *Witness: Writings of Bartolomé de Las Casas* (Maryknoll, N.Y.: Orbis Books, 2nd ed., 1992 [1971]).

Santa Fe Committee, *A New Inter-American Policy for the 80s* (Washington, D.C.: 1980).

Schall, James V. (ed.), *Liberation Theology in Latin America* (San Francisco: Ignatius Press, 1982).

Scheper-Hughes, Nancy, *Death Without Weeping: The Violence of Everyday Life in Brazil* (Berkeley: University of California, 1992).

Schleiermacher, Friedrich D., *On Religion: Speeches to its Cultured Despisers* (trans. J. Oman; New York: Harper & Row, 1958.

Schüssler Fiorenza, Elisabeth (ed.), *Searching the Scriptures: A Feminist Introduction* (New York: Crossroad, 1993; London: SCM Press, 1994).

Segundo, Juan Luis, *Funcion de la Iglesia en la realidad rioplatense* (Montevideo: Barreiro y Ramos, 1962).

—— "The Future of Christianity in Latin America," *Cross Currents* 13 (Summer 1963); French orig. *Lettre* 54 (Paris, 1963); reprinted in Hennelly (ed.), *Liberation Theology*.

—— *The Community Called Church* (Theology for the Artisans of a New Humanity, vol. 1; trans. J. Drury; Maryknoll, N.Y.: Orbis Books, 1973). Spanish orig. *Esa comunidad llamada iglesia* (Buenos Aires: Ediciones Carlos Lohlé, 1968).

—— *Grace and the Human Condition* (Theology for the Artisans of a New Humanity, vol. 2; trans. J. Drury; Maryknoll, N.Y.: Orbis Books, 1973). Spanish orig. *Gracia y condicion humana* (Buenos Aires: Ediciones Carlos Lohlé, 1969).

—— *Our Idea of God* (Theology for the Artisans of a New Humanity, vol. 3; trans. J. Drury; Maryknoll, N.Y.: Orbis Books, 1974). Spanish orig. *Nuestra idea de Dios* (Buenos Aires: Ediciones Carlos Lohlé, 1970).

—— *The Sacraments Today* (Theology for the Artisans of a New Humanity, vol. 4; trans. J. Drury; Maryknoll, N.Y.: Orbis Books, 1974). Spanish orig. *Los sacramentos hoy* (Buenos Aires: Ediciones Carlos Lohlé, 1971).

—— *Evolution and Guilt* (Theology for the Artisans of a New Humanity, vol. 5; trans. J. Drury; Maryknoll, N.Y.: Orbis Books, 1974). Spanish orig. *Evolucion y culpa* (Buenos Aires: Ediciones Carlos Lohlé, 1972).

—— *The Liberation of Theology* (trans. J. Drury; Maryknoll, N.Y.: Orbis Books; 1976). Spanish orig. *Liberatión de la teología* (Buenos Aires: Ediciones Carlos Lohlé, 1975).

—— *Jesus of Nazareth, Yesterday and Today*, I. *Faith and Ideologies* (trans. J. Drury, Maryknoll, N.Y.: Orbis Books; London: Sheed and Ward; 1984). Spanish orig. *El hombre de hoy ante de Jesus de Nazaret*, I. *Fe e ideologia* (Madrid: Ediciones Cristianidad, 1982).

—— *Jesus of Nazareth, Yesterday and Today*, II. *The Historical Jesus of the Synoptics* (trans. J. Drury, Maryknoll, N.Y.: Orbis Books; London: Sheed and Ward, 1985). Spanish orig. *El hombre de hoy ante de Jesus de Nazaret*. II. *Historia y actualidad: Sinópticos y pablo*, 1 (Madrid: Ediciones Cristianidad, 1982).

—— *Jesus of Nazareth, Yesterday and Today*, III. *The Humanist Christology of Paul* (trans. and ed. J. Drury; Maryknoll, N.Y.: Orbis Books; London: Sheed and Ward, 1986). Spanish orig. *El hombre de hoy ante de Jesús de Nazaret*, II *Historia y actualidad: Sinópticos y pablo*, 2 (Madrid: Ediciones Cristianidad, 1982).

—— "Two Theologies of Liberation," *The Month* 17 (October 1984); reprinted in Hennelly (ed.), *Liberation Theology*.

—— *Jesus of Nazareth, Yesterday and Today*, IV. *The Christ of the Ignatian Exercises* (trans. and ed. J. Drury; Maryknoll, N.Y.: Orbis Books, 1987; London: Sheed and Ward, 1988). Spanish orig. *El hombre de hoy ante de Jesús de Nazaret*, III. *Cristo de los ejercicios espirituales*, 1 (Madrid: Ediciones Cristianidad, 1985)

—— *Jesus of Nazareth, Yesterday and Today*, V. *An Evolutionary Approach to Jesus of Nazareth* (trans. J. Drury; Maryknoll, N.Y.: Orbis Books, 1988; London: Sheed and Ward, 1989). Spanish orig. *Lineas actuales de interpretacion de Jesus de Nazaret*, III. *El hombre de hoy ante de Jesús de Nazaret*, 2 (Madrid: Ediciones Cristianidad, 1985).

—— *Theology and the Church: A Response to Cardinal Ratzinger and a Warning to the Whole Church* (trans. J. W. Diercksmeier; Minneapolis, Minn.: Winston Press; London: Geoffrey Chapman, 1985).

—— (ed.), *Iglesia Latinoamericana: ¿Profeta o Profecia?* (Avellanda, Argentina: Ediciones Busqueda, 1969).

Selvidge, Marla J., *Notorious Voices: Feminist Biblical Interpretation 1500–1920* (London: SCM Press, 1996).

Shaull, Richard, *Encounter with Revolution* (New York: Associated Press, 1955).

—— "La liberación humana desde una perspectiva teológica," *Mensaje* 168 (1968).

Shorter, Aylward, *African Culture and the Christian Church* (London: Geoffrey Chapman, 1973).

Sigmund, Paul, *The Overthrow of Allende and the Politics of Chile: 1964–1976* (Pittsburgh: University of Pittsburgh Press, 1977).

—— *Liberation Theology at the Crossroads: Democracy or Revolution?* (Oxford: Oxford University Press, 1990).

Siker, Jeffrey, "Uses of the Bible in the Theology of Gustavo Gutiérrez: Liberating Scriptures of the Poor," *Biblical Interpretation* 4 (1996).

Simpson, L. S., *The Encomienda in New Spain* (Berkeley: University of California Press, 1950).

Skidmore, Thomas E., *Politics in Brazil, 1930–1964: An Experiment in Democracy* (New York: Oxford University Press, 1967).

Skidmore, Thomas E., and Peter H. Smith, *Modern Latin America* (Oxford: Oxford University Press, 4th ed., 1997 [1984]).

Smith, Brian, *The Church and Politics in Chile: Challenges to Modern Catholicism* (Princeton, N.J.: Princeton University Press, 1982).

Smith, Christian, *The Emergence of Liberation Theology: Radical Religion and Social Movement Theory* (Chicago and London: University of Chicago Press, 1991).

Sobrino, Jon, "El conocimiento teológico en la teología europea y latinoamericana" in Ruiz Maldonado (ed.), *Liberación y cautivero.*

—— *Christology at the Crossroads: A Latin American View* (trans. John Drury; Maryknoll, N.Y.: Orbis Books; London: SCM, 1978). Spanish orig. *Cristología desde américa latina: esbozo a partir del seguimientio del Jesús histórico* (Mexico: Centro de Reflexión Teológica, 1976).

—— "The Witness of the Church in Latin America" in Torres and Eagleson (eds.), *The Challenge of Basic Christian Communities.*

—— *Jesus in Latin America* (trans. various; Maryknoll, N.Y.: Orbis Books, 1987). Spanish orig. *Jesús en América Latina: Su significado para la fe y la cristología* (Santander: Editorial Sal Terrae; San Salvador: UCA Editores, 1982).

—— *The True Church and the Poor* (trans. Matthew O'Connell; Maryknoll, N.Y.: Orbis Books; London: SCM, 1984). Spanish orig. *Resurrección de la Verdadera Iglesia: Los Pobres, lugar teológico de la eclesiología* (Santander: Editorial Sal Terrae, 1981; San Salvador: UCA Editores, 1986).

—— *Spirituality of Liberation: Towards a Political Holiness* (trans. R. R. Barr; Maryknoll, N.Y.: Orbis Books, 1988). Spanish orig. *Liberación con espíritu: Apuntes para una nueva espiritualidad* (Santander: Sal Terrae, 1985; San Salvador: UCA Editores, 1987).

—— *Companions of Jesus: The Murder and Martyrdom of the Salvadoran Jesuits* (London: Catholic Institute for International Relations, 1990).

—— *Jesus the Liberator: A Historical-Theological View* (trans. P. Burns and F. McDonagh; Maryknoll, N.Y.: Orbis Books; Tunbridge Wells, Kent: Burns and Oates; 1994). Spanish orig. *Jesucristo liberador: lectura histórica-teológica de Jesús de Nazaret: Su significado para la fe y la cristología* (Madrid: Editorial Totta; San Salvador: UCA Editores, 1991).

—— *The Principle of Mercy: Taking the Crucified People from the Cross* (trans. various; Maryknoll, N.Y.: Orbis Books, 1994). Spanish orig. *El Principio-Misericordia: Bajar de la cruz a los pueblos crucificados* (Santander: Editorial Sal Terrae, 1992; San Salvador: UCA Editores, 1993).

—— *Christ the Liberator: A View from the Victims* (trans. P. Burns; Maryknoll, NY: Orbis Books, 2001). Spanish orig. *La fe en Jesucristo: Ensayo desde las víctimas* (Madrid: Editorial Trotta; San Salvador: UCA Editores, 1999).

Sobrino, Jon, Ignacio Martín-Baró, y Rodolfo Cardenal (eds.), *La voz de los sin voz* (San Salvador: UCA Editores, 1980).

SODEPAX, *In Search of a Theology of Development: Papers from a Consultation on Theology and Development held by SODEPAX in Cartigny, Switzerland, November 1969* (Geneva: WCC, 1970).

Sölle, Dorothee, "Dialectics of Enlightenment: Reflections of a European Theologian" in Fabella and Torres (eds.), *Doing Theology in a Divided World.*

—— *Celebrating Resistance: The Way of the Cross in Latin America* (trans. J. Irwin; Minneapolis, Minn.: Augsburg Fortress Press; London: Mowbray, 1993).

Spooner, Mary H., *Soldiers in a Narrow Land: The Pinochet Regime in Chile* (Berkeley: University of California Press, 1994).

Stevens, Evelyn P., "Machismo and Marianismo," *Society* 10.6 (1973).

—— "Marianismo: The Other Face of Machismo in Latin America" in Pescatello (ed.), *Female and Male in Latin America.*

Stoll, David, *Is Latin America Turning Protestant? The Politics of Evangelical Growth* (Berkeley: University of California Press, 1990).

Suh, David Kwang-Suh, "Korean Theological Development in the 1970s" in CTC and CCA, *Minjung Theology: People as the Subjects of History.*

Szeminski, J., "From Inca Gods to Spanish Saints and Demons" in Kaplan (ed.), *Indigenous Responses to Western Christianity.*

Tamez, Elsa, *Bible of the Oppressed* (trans. M. O'Connell; Maryknoll, N.Y.: Orbis Books, 1982). Chs. 1–5 are the Spanish orig. *La Biblia de los oprimidos: La opresión en la teología bíblica* (San José: Departmento Ecuménico Investigaciones, 1979); Chs. 6–7 are *La hora de la vida* (San José: Departmento Ecuménico Investigaciones, 1978).

—— "Reflections by Elsa Tamez" in Fabella and Torres, *Irruption of the Third World*.

—— (ed.), *Through Her Eyes: Women's Theology from Latin America* (Maryknoll, N.Y.: Orbis Books, 1989). Spanish orig. *El rostro femenino de la Teología* (San José: Departmento Ecuménico de Investigaciones, 1986).

—— "The Power of the Naked" in idem (ed.), *Through Her Eyes*.

—— "A Latin American Perspective" in Abraham (ed.), *Third World Theologies*.

—— *The Amnesty of Grace: Justification by Faith from a Latin American Perspective* (trans. Sharon Ringe; Nashville: Abingdon Press, 1993). Spanish orig. *Contra toda condena: La justificacion por la fe desde los excluidos* (San José: Departmento Ecuménico de Investigaciones, 1991).

—— *When the Horizons Close: Rereading Ecclesiastes* (Maryknoll, N.Y.: Orbis Books, 2000). Spanish orig. *Cuando los horizontes se cierran: Relectura del libro de Eclesiastés o Qohélet* (San José: Departmento Ecuménico de Investigaciones, 1998).

Tamez, Elsa, S. A. Park, and others, "Worship Service: This Hour of History" in Fabella and Torres, *Irruption of the Third World*.

Taylor, Simon, "Forgiveness, the Jubilee and World Debt" in Porter, Hayes, and Tombs (eds.), *Faith in the Millennium*.

Third World Bishops, "A Letter to the Peoples of the Third World" (15 August 1967); reprinted in Hennelly (ed.), *Liberation Theology*.

Thomas, Hugh, *The Conquest of Mexico* (London: Pimlico, 1994 [1973]).

—— *Cuba or The Pursuit of Freedom* (London: Eyre and Spottiswoode, 1971).

Tombs, David, "Crucifixion, State Terror and Sexual Abuse," *Union Seminary Quarterly Review* 53 (Autumn 1999).

—— "Liberating Christology: Images of Christ in the Work of Aloysius Pieris," in S. E. Porter, M. A. Hayes, and D. Tombs (eds.), *Images of Christ: Ancient and Modern* (RILP 2; Sheffield: Sheffield Academic Press, 1997).

—— "Machismo and Marianismo: Sexuality and Liberation Theology," in Michael Hayes, Wendy Porter, and David Tombs (eds.), *Religion and Sexuality* (Roehampton Institute London Papers, 4; Sheffield: Sheffield Academic Press, 1998).

—— "The Legacy of Ignacio Ellacuría for Liberation Theology in a 'Post-Marxist' Age," *Journal of Hispanic/Latino Theology* 8.1 (2000).

Torres, Camilo, *Revolutionary Priest: The Complete Writings and Messages of Camilo Torres* (ed. J. Gerassi; trans. J. de Cipriano et al.; London: Cape, 1971).

—— *Father Camilo Torres: Revolutionary Writings* (ed. M. Zeitlin; trans R. Olsen and L. Day; New York: Harper & Row, rev. ed., 1972 [Spanish orig. 1967]).

Torres, Sergio, "A Latin American View of the Asian Theological Conference" in Fabella, (ed.), *Asia's Struggle for Full Humanity*.

—— "Introduction" in Torres and Eagleson (eds.), *The Challenge of Basic Christian Communities*.

—— "Divergences: A Latin American Perspective" in Abraham (ed.), *Third World Theologies*.

Torres, Sergio, and John Eagleson (eds.), *Theology in the Americas* (Papers from the Theology in the Americas Conference, Detroit, August 1975; trans. J. Drury; Maryknoll, NY: Orbis Books, 1976).

—— (eds.), *The Challenge of Basic Christian Communities* (EATWOT International Ecumenical Congress of Theology, São Paulo, Brazil, 20 February–2 March 1980; Maryknoll, N.Y.: Orbis Books, 1981).

Torres, Sergio, and Virginia Fabella (eds.), *The Emergent Gospel: Theology from the*

Underside of History (EATWOT Dialogue held in Dar-es-Salaam, Tanzania, 5–12 August, 1976; Maryknoll, N.Y.: Orbis Books, 1978).

Trexler, Richard C., *Sex and Conquest: Gendered Violence, Political Order, and the European Conquest of the Americas* (Cambridge: Polity Press, 1995).

Trigo, Pedro, *Creation and History* (trans. R. R. Barr; *TLS* 10; Maryknoll, N.Y.: Orbis Books; Tunbridge Wells, Kent: Burns and Oates, 1992). Trans. from Spanish ed. *Creación e historia en el proceso de liberación* (Madrid: Ediciones Paulinas, 1988). Portugese ed. *Criação e história* (Petrópolis, RJ: Editora Vozes, 1988).

United Nations, *United Nations Development Report* (New York: United Nations, 1998).

Vallely, Paul, *The New Politics: Catholic Social Teaching for the Twenty-First Century* (London: SCM Press, 1998).

Vásquez, Manuel A., *The Brazilian Popular Church and the Crisis of Modernity* (Cambridge Studies in Ideology and Religion; Cambridge: University of Cambridge Press, 1998).

Vekemans, Roger, *Teología de la liberación y Cristianos por el Socialismo* (Bogotá: CE-DIAL, 1976).

Vigil, José M., "Is there a Change of Paradigm in Liberation Theology?" *SEDOS* 29.12 (1997).

Walker, William, *The War in Nicaragua* (Phoenix: University of Arizona Press, 1985 [1860]).

Walsh, Michael, *John Paul II: A Biography* (London: Fount, 1994).

Watts, P. M., "Prophecy and Discovery: On the Spiritual Origins of Christopher Columbus' 'Enterprise of the Indies,'" *American Historical Review* 90 (1985).

Webster, J. C. B. and E. L. (eds.), *The Church and Women in the Third World* (Philadelphia: Westminster Press, 1985).

Weschler, Lawrence, *A Miracle, A Universe: Settling Accounts with Torturers* (Chicago and London: University of Chicago Press, rev. ed. 1998 [1990]).

Whitaker, A. P. (ed.), *Latin America and the Enlightenment* (Ithaca, N.Y.: Cornell University Press, 1961).

Whitfield, Teresa, *Paying the Price: Ignacio Ellacuría and the Murdered Jesuits of El Salvador* (Philadelphia: Temple University Press, 1994).

Williams, E., *From Columbus to Castro: The History of the Caribbean, 1492–1969* (London: Andre Deutsch, 1970).

Williams, Phillip J., *The Catholic Church and Politics in Nicaragua and Costa Rica* (London: Macmillan, 1989).

Williamson, Edwin, *The Penguin History of Latin America* (Harmondsworth: Penguin Books, 1992).

Wilmore, "The Role of Afro-America in the Rise of Two-Third World Theology: A Historical Reappraisal" in Appiah-Kubi and Torres (eds.), *African Theology En Route*.

Womack, J., "Priest of Revolution?," *New York Review of Books* (23 October 1969).

Wright, R. *The Colour Curtain: Report on the Bandung Conference* (New York: The World, 1956).

Zoé-Obianga, Rose, "From Accra to Wennappuwa: What is New? What is More?" in Fabella (ed.), *Asia's Struggle for Full Humanity*.

Index